The Shuttle-Craft Book of
American Hand-Weaving

THE MACMILLAN COMPANY
NEW YORK · BOSTON · CHICAGO
DALLAS · ATLANTA · SAN FRANCISCO

MACMILLAN AND CO., LIMITED
LONDON · BOMBAY · CALCUTTA
MADRAS · MELBOURNE

**THE MACMILLAN COMPANY
OF CANADA, LIMITED**
TORONTO

Revised edition of a book on weaving which first appeared over twenty years ago (Book Review Digest 1929). "An account of the rise, development, eclipse, and modern revival of a national popular art, together with information of interest and value to collectors, technical notes for the use of weavers & a large collection of historical patterns." (Subtitle) Index

Booklist 47:330 My 15 '51

"For schools and organized, teacher-led groups. It is not for the beginner to use at home, as it assumes a certain fundamental knowledge of weaving impossible for a beginner to have."

Kirkus 18:585 S 15 '50 90w

"The completely revised edition of a very useful handbook on American weaving."

+ **Wis Lib Bul** 47:85 Ap '51

"Our American textiles are beautiful in themselves."

(1) Double-woven coverlet in three colors, from the Boston Museum of Fine Arts. Pattern, Double Snow-Ball with Pine-Tree border. See draft number 235.

THE SHUTTLE-CRAFT BOOK of American Hand-Weaving

BEING an Account of the Rise, Development, Eclipse, and Modern Revival of a National Popular Art Together with Information of Interest and Value to Collectors, Technical Notes for the Use of Weavers, & a Large Collection of Historic Patterns

BY **Mary Meigs Atwater**
With ILLUSTRATIONS : Revised Edition

NEW YORK
The Macmillan Company
1951

Copyright, 1928, 1951, By The Macmillan Company.

All rights reserved—no part of this book may be reproduced in any form without permission in writing from the publisher, except by a reviewer who wishes to quote brief passages in connection with a review written for inclusion in magazine or newspaper.

First Printing

PRINTED IN THE UNITED STATES OF AMERICA

Foreword

A TRUE national popular art—shaped by the necessities and colored by the dreams of a whole people—is a deeply touching and a very precious thing.

We in America are a young nation, but there have been years enough for a true national popular art to grow up among us, to develop characteristic forms of beauty, to flourish greatly, to languish, and finally to be revived. There is now no danger that it will ever become a lost art.

The following pages are dedicated in loving gratitude to the unnamed artists of America's early day, and are offered to the new craftsmen of America's great present in the hope of adding a little to the general appreciation of a fine and a beautiful thing.

MARY M. ATWATER.

Index of Chapters

Chapter One	Origins and Development	1
I	The Old Time	1
II	The Decline of Hand-Weaving, and Weaver Rose	14
III	The Revival—Modern Hand-Weaving	17
Chapter Two	Weaving Horizons—the Scope of This Book	21
I	What Weaving Is	21
II	A Few Definitions	22
Chapter Three	Beginner's Problems	26
I	Instruction	26
II	Equipment	30
III	Materials	42
Chapter Four	Design of the Fabric	43
I	Over-all Proportions	43
II	Choice of Weave	45
III	Choice of Material—Cottons	47
IV	Wool and Worsted	54
V	Linens	61
VI	Synthetic Yarns	67
VII	Warp-Setting	69
Chapter Five	Choice of Pattern and Color	72
I	Choice of Pattern	72
II	Choice of Color	79

[*ix*]

Chapter Six		Setting up the Loom	82
	I	Warping	82
	II	Drawing-in or Threading	87
	III	Sleying	89
	IV	Tying-In	89
Chapter Seven		Adjustments, Knots, the Tie-Up	91
	I	Knots Used in Weaving	91
	II	Adjustments, Four-Harness Tie-Up	95
	III	Treadle Tie-Up	97
Chapter Eight		Weaving	101
	I	First Shots—Corrections	102
	II	Weaving	103
	III	Loose Ends	107
Chapter Nine		The Plain Weave	109
	I	Tabby	110
	II	Warp-Faced Rep in Plain Weave	111
	III	Weft-Faced Rep	113
	IV	A "Fifty-Fifty" Weave	113
Chapter Ten		The Twill Weave	115
	I	Plain Three-Harness and Four-Harness Twills	115
	II	"Corkscrew" and Eight-Harness Twills	117
	III	Return Twills—Modified Twills	122
Chapter Eleven		The Four-Harness Overshot Weave	123
	I	Structure of the Overshot Weave	125
	II	Overshot Weaving—Draft Writing	128
	III	Arranging a Pattern for the Loom—Borders	135
	IV	Treadling	141
	V	Notes on the Overshot Drafts	149

Chapter Twelve		Additional Four-Harness Weaves	198
	I	Counterpanes	198
	II	Two Weaves for Linens	204
	III	The Crackle Weave	205
Chapter Thirteen		The Summer-and-Winter Weave	211
	I	Structure	212
	II	Tie-Ups and Treadling	218
	III	Patterns	239
Chapter Fourteen		The "Spot" or "Bronson" Weave	240
	I	Structure	240
	II	Warp-Setting and Treadling	243
	III	Variations	245
Chapter Fifteen		Double-Faced Twill and Damask	247
	I	Structure	247
	II	Patterns, Tie-ups, and Treadling	251
Chapter Sixteen		The Double Weave	252
	I	Structure	255
	II	Patterns in Double Weave	257
	III	Quilted Weaving	263
Chapter Seventeen		Leno	266
	I	The Set-Up	268
	II	Leno Patterns	275
Chapter Eighteen		Rug-Making	277
	I	Rag Rugs in Plain Weave	278
	II	The Pattern Weaves as Used for Rug-Making	279
	III	The Special Weaves for Rug-Making	282

Chapter Nineteen	Pick-Up Weaving	293
I	Pick-Up Forms of the Standard Weaves	295
II	Nine Native American Pick-Up Weaves	301
Chapter Twenty	Finishes	329
I	Woven Finishes	330
II	Knotted and Braided Fringes	331
	Index	337

List of Diagrams

Diagram No.	Illus. No.	Page	Subject
1	(13)	33	Weaving Equipment
2	(18)	41	Warping board, raddle, warp-chain
3	(43)	93	Knots used by weavers
4	(44)	96	Loom balance
5	(45)	98	Simple tie-ups
6	(49)	114	Two-harness rep
7	(50)	116	Twill
8	(51)	118	Corkscrew twills, eight-harness twills
9	(52)	120	Return twills
10	(53)	121	Modified twills
11	(56)	129	Notation
12	(59)	132	Weaving on paper
13	(61)	138	Borders
14	(65)	150	Drafts, four-harness overshot weave
15	(66)	152	Drafts, four-harness overshot weave
16	(68)	154	Drafts, four-harness overshot weave
17	(69)	156	Drafts, four-harness overshot weave
18	(70)	157	Drafts, four-harness overshot weave
19	(71)	158	Drafts, four-harness overshot weave
20	(72)	160	Drafts, four-harness overshot weave
21	(73)	162	Drafts, four-harness overshot weave
22	(74)	163	Drafts, four-harness overshot weave
23	(76)	167	Drafts, four-harness overshot weave

Diagram No.	Illus. No.	Page	Subject
24	(78)	169	Drafts, four-harness overshot weave
25	(79)	170	Drafts, four-harness overshot weave
26	(80)	172	Drafts, four-harness overshot weave
27	(81)	173	Drafts, four-harness overshot weave
28	(82)	174	Drafts, four-harness overshot weave
29	(83)	178	Drafts, four-harness overshot weave
30	(84)	180	Drafts, four-harness overshot weave
31	(85)	182	Drafts, four-harness overshot weave
32	(86)	183	Drafts, four-harness overshot weave
33	(87)	186	Drafts, four-harness overshot weave
34	(88)	188	Drafts, four-harness overshot weave
35	(89)	189	Drafts, four-harness overshot weave
36	(90)	190	Drafts, four-harness overshot weave
37	(91)	191	Drafts, four-harness overshot weave
38	(95)	196	Eight-harness overshot
39	(97)	200	Counterpane patterns
40	(98)	202	Four-harness weaves for linen
41	(99)	206	Crackle weave drafts
42	(102)	213	Summer-and-winter weave,
43	(104)	215	Summer-and-winter weave, two-block patterns
44	(106)	217	Summer-and-winter weave, three-block patterns
45	(109)	222	Summer-and-winter weave, four-block patterns
46	(112)	225	Summer-and-winter weave, four-block patterns
47	(114)	227	Summer-and-winter weave, four-block patterns
48	(115)	228	Summer-and-winter weave, four-block patterns

Diagram No.	Illus. No.	Page	Subject
49	(117)	230	Summer-and-winter weave, four-block patterns
50	(118)	231	Summer-and-winter weave, five-block patterns
51	(119)	232	Summer-and-winter weave, six-block patterns
52	(121)	234	Summer-and-winter weave, six-block patterns
53	(122)	235	Summer-and-winter weave, six-block patterns
54	(123)	236	Summer-and-winter weave, "Step" pattern
55	(124)	241	Bronson weave, four-harness
56	(125)	244	Bronson weave, eight-harness
57	(126)	249	Double-faced twill and Damask
58	(128)	253	Double plain weave
59	(136)	267	Leno
60	(144)	284	Saddle-blanket weave
61	(145)	286	Two-warp rugs
62	(148)	296	Tie-ups for pick-up weaving
63	(151)	303	Tabby pick-up
64	(152)	306	Double weave pick-up
65	(153)	308	Patterns for pick-up
66	(154)	310	"Earth and Sky" motif
67	(155)	312	One-skip and Two-skip pick-up
68	(156)	316	Motifs in twill pick-up
69	(157)	318	Mexican warp-pattern weave
70	(160)	324	Mexican two-warp pick-up
71	(161)	326	Picked up Leno and Lace-weaves
72	(162)	332	Finishes

Chapter One: Origins and Development

I *The Old Time*

The art of weaving is a very old art indeed. It had its beginnings in the twilight time before history began, for man has been a weaver ever since he has been man—and perhaps longer. It may well be that the weaving instinct in the hands and brain of some less than human ancestor of the human race has had much to do with the fact that man is man and not some different creature.

Weaving is so old that in fundamentals it is the same in all parts of the world, so old that nothing really new has come to it for hundreds of years. The gossamer linens of ancient Egypt, fine enough to be drawn through a finger-ring, are finer than anything we make to-day; nothing more gorgeous than the old brocades of the East will probably ever be woven; our great machines of to-day produce nothing that could not be made long, long ago without their help. And still it is a living, growing art, always ready to meet man's new needs in new ways.

Though everywhere the same in principle, during the long ages of its existence weaving has developed minor differences and special excellencies here and there, conditioned by the way of life of national groups,—each type with a logic and a charm of its own. For Americans there is, naturally enough, a quite special interest in the native American forms of the art—not only because of association and sentiment, though these are precious, but because our American textiles are beautiful in themselves and because, too, they fit us and express us as no other can; they look well in our houses, match our temper and our minds, and are somehow "right" for us.

American weaving derives from much more ancient forms, brought to the

New World by the early colonists,—by the Dutch of New Amsterdam, by the Mennonites who settled in Pennsylvania, by the Scotch who took up land in the South, by the Irish who came to New Hampshire, and by the English Puritans of New England. Our art like our people comes of mixed ancestry.

In rural England, at the time when the Mayflower set sail upon her amazing adventure, weaving was a household function, as it had been from very early days. Every homestead was a textile factory, and as one historian puts it "cloth was a by-product of agriculture."

In the cities, to be sure, the thing was more complex. Here specialized groups devoted themselves each to one particular branch of cloth-making, and were banded together into craft guilds. And very powerful and very despotic these ancient societies became so that finally they encroached too much on public liberties and were suppressed. Some of them have, however, actually lived on into our day, though in a very pallid and enfeebled form.

The guild of the weavers is believed to be the most ancient of all the English guilds. Its exact age is unknown, but mention of its activities is made in a document of the year 1100. Very little is definitely known concerning the practice of the art in those highly antique times, but shuttles and looms as shown in ancient pictures were much like the looms and shuttles of to-day.

The first textile factory in England was the one established at Winchester by the Romans for the weaving of cloth to clothe the Roman army of occupation. The ancient Britons appear to have relied for clothing chiefly on the skins of animals, and on the blue dye of woad with which they smeared their bodies. No doubt they took kindly to the greater comfort of woolen cloth.

The making of woolen cloth was England's first great industry. It was a certain Jack of Newbury who invented the stout fabric known as broadcloth, and made it on the hundred looms he is said to have had in his house, in the year 1327. These great looms were so wide that a weaver must stand on either side of the broad web in order to pass the shuttle back and forth.

A little later there was the famous Thomas Cole of Reading who "made great quantities of the most excellent cloth which he sent up to London on waggons, so many that they crowded the road." What sort of cloth it was, the old account fails to mention. It may have been "fustian" such as was worn by the gentle knight of Chaucer's Canterbury Tales, or perhaps a "double worsted"

1. Belgian
2. Dutch
3. Weavers Guild of London
4. Belgian
5. French
6. Flemish

(2) Insignia of Weavers' Guilds

like that of the good Friar's gown as he traveled along in company with the knight. And these fabrics were probably not very different from the fustian and double-genoa made centuries later in the first American textile factory at Rowley.

The name of Thomas Blanket will live on down the ages as long, certainly, as that of the immortal Shakespeare. And why should it not? Which after all has made the greater gift to humanity? On cold winter nights the answer would be easy.

Fine silks and flowered and figured textiles as intricate as the most elaborate modern webs were made in very early times on the wonderful loom called the draw-loom. This loom, invented in China so long ago that its origin has become myth, was introduced into southern Europe very early in the Christian era, but did not reach England till some centuries later. It is written, however, that in the year 1573 John Tice of London, a weaver of note, "had attained to the perfection of making all sorts of tufted taffeties, cloth of tissues, wrought velvets, branched satins, and other kinds of curious silk stuffs." This sentence from an old book is like a bright little window opened on the life of a time long gone by. No doubt the worthy John was a personage of renown and a man of substance in his day, and no doubt many fine ladies and magnificent cavaliers came to him to leave orders for the gorgeous stuffs of their court-costumes. His loom, for such elaborate weaving, was certainly a great draw-loom,—a maze of thousands of linen cords, with its complicated "simple," and its hard-working draw-boy. See John himself enthroned on the high bench, shuttle in hand,—a wizard practicing his wizardry!

The old day, like our present, was a time of enterprise and progress. In the year 1575 stout Morgan Habblethorne, a master-weaver, was sent by his guild on a journey to distant Persia to learn at first hand the Eastern art of carpet-making. A great adventure that must have been. We do not know what knowledge he brought back to his fellow craftsmen, nor indeed whether or no he ever returned at all.

But though weaving, as we see, was a highly developed art in England long before the Puritan exodus to America, the first American weaver was no John Tice, no skilled master weaver. The Puritan settlers were from rural communities, and the first weaver in America was probably some "Dame Marjory" or "Mistress Priscilla," stepping ashore on Plymouth Rock in the year

(3) Sunrise coverlet in two shades of brown. Boston Museum. See draft number 102. This is one of the most ancient of American patterns.

1620—a country housewife whose weaving was of the rude cottage variety. Fortunately so. An art to be a true national and popular art cannot be the art of experts; it must be a simple art produced by simple means and by artists who lack the specialized training for mastery.

It was in 1638 that a certain Master Ezekiel Rogers established at Rowley, not far from Ipswich, Massachusetts, the first textile factory on American soil. Twenty families of cloth-makers were brought from Yorkshire and settled in the place. They were, an old account declares, "very zealous and thrifty, and caused their little ones to be diligent in the spinning of cotton-woole." At Rowley, too, a few years later, John Pierson built a fulling mill for the finishing of woolen cloth—a mill that is known to have been in active operation as late as 1809.

The output of the Rowley industry was in the main cloth for clothing—"fustian," sometimes also called "thick-sett," which appears to have been the fabric we call corduroy, together with twilled cloth or "tweeling," "jean," "doornock," "linsey-woolsey" and the like.

The second textile factory in America was probably the one established in Philadelphia by William Penn himself—"in a house rented at forty pounds a year, at the southwest corner of Ninth and Market Streets." Somewhat later a linen factory was set up in New York, in a loft overlooking the harbor, and still later a company of linen weavers came from Ireland and settled in New Hampshire. There were also settlements of weavers in Rhode Island and elsewhere. But till after the Revolution the chief output of textile fabrics was from the household looms of the homesteads.

One of the chief problems encountered by the first American weavers was the difficulty of obtaining a supply of raw materials. Cotton could not be grown in New England, and though it was planted in the South in very early days it was not grown in commercial quantities till after the Revolution. The early supplies of "cotton-woole" were imported from the Indies.

Wool came from Balboa or Malaga. Sheep were being raised in the colonies, but not in sufficient numbers at first to supply the need, and England had put a strict embargo on the exportation of raw wool—preferring extension of the market for her finished product to development of the infant industry of the colonies. This selfish and shortsighted policy on the part of the mother-country

(4) Early Jacquard weaving. Boston Museum of Fine Arts.

no doubt contributed heavily to the resentments that finally resulted in the War of Independence.

In fact the spinning-wheel deserves a place among the honored emblems of our freedom. The colonies fostered and encouraged in every way the planting of flax. Free seed was distributed, subsidies were offered, and free schools were opened for the instruction of the younger generation in the art of spinning. It became an act of patriotism to spin, and in Rhode Island and probably in other colonies women held all-day sessions of spinning. Doubtless other youngsters than those of Rowley were "caused to be diligent" at the work.

Patriotic brides were married in native fabrics; the class of 1768 at Harvard College earned praise by electing to receive its degrees while clothed in cloth of domestic manufacture. Independence was in the air.

There were at the time of the Revolution a number of textile factories in America. These were, of course, not like modern textile mills—places of clanking machinery and of quantity production. They were lofts or houses filled with looms that were much like the hand-looms of to-day and of the Middle Ages, each loom manned by an operative who opened the sheds, threw the shuttle, and banged with the batten for each "pick" or "lay" of the new cloth.

Every homestead was a textile factory, and all members of the household worked at times at the textile trade. The youngest children wound cops and bobbins for the warping creel and the busy shuttles; older children carded and spun; the housewife leaned for long hours over her steaming dye-pots, and even the goodman himself often worked at the loom—especially during the long winter months when his heavy labor on the land was at a standstill. It was among these "domestic manufacturers" that our American art of weaving developed its typical forms and its amazing variety of patterns.

The Revolution marks the end of an epoch in American weaving—not so much because of the war and of the political changes that followed it as because about this time power machinery for spinning and weaving began to displace the ancient hand-looms and spinning-wheels.

As early as 1730 a young man named Kay—in England—took out the first patent on a machine for "twining and dressing thread." His invention was not hailed with delight by the industry he expected to benefit. In fact he found himself treated as an enemy of society and was driven from place to place by

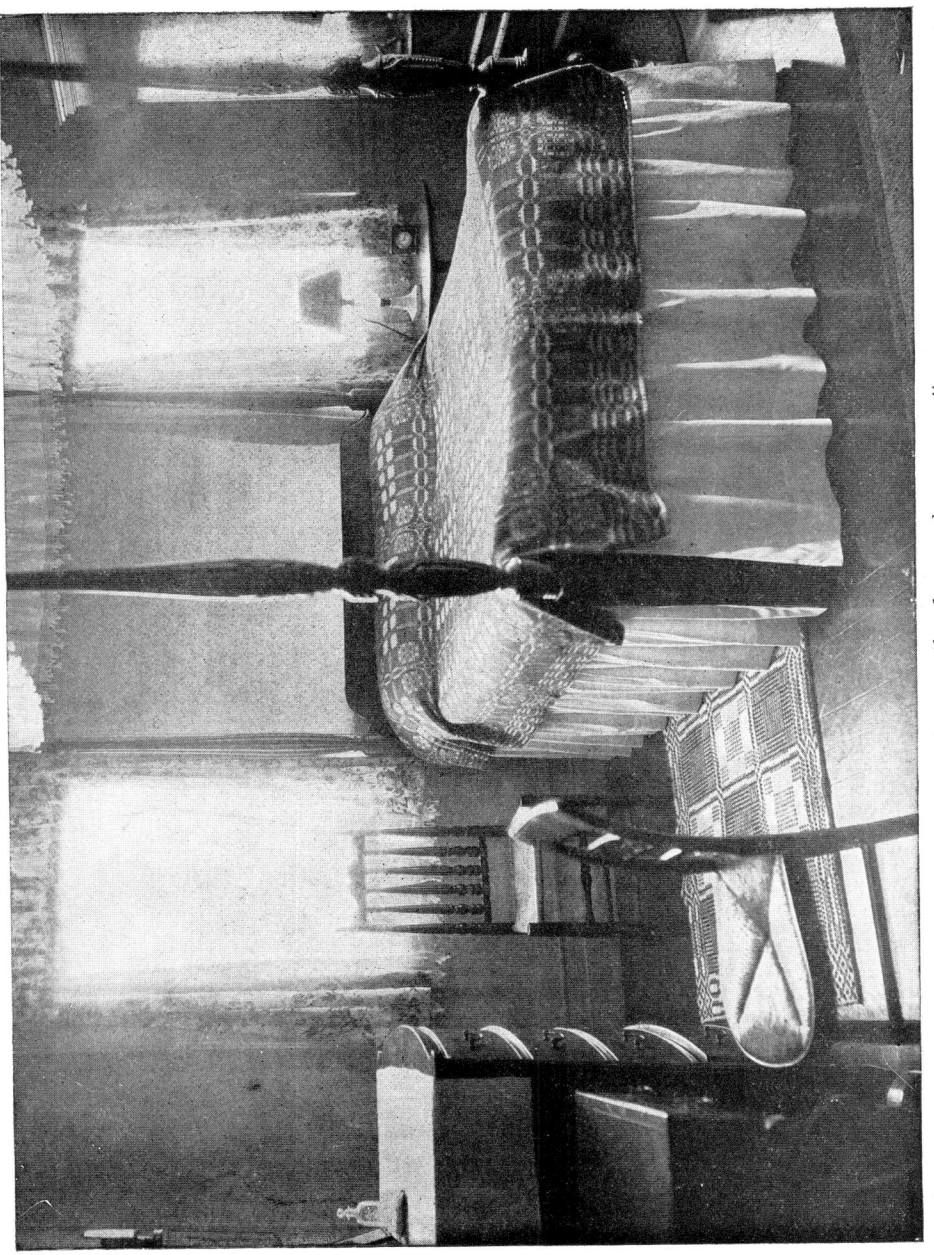

"Our American textiles fit us and express us."

(5) The coverlet on this old four-post bed is a modern piece of hand-weaving in the Twenty-five Snow-Balls pattern. The rug is in the Sunflower pattern.

the persecutions of outraged workmen. He finally turned over his machinery to the poorhouse, where it was operated by the inmates, and he himself died in poverty in France.

But of course nothing could prevent the great industrial changes that were about to take place. The age of machinery was at hand.

The first really practical spinning-machine—the "spinning-jenny"—was invented by a poor and ignorant workman named Hargreaves. He patented his invention in 1770, superseding patents taken out many years earlier by Arkwright.

It is natural that spinning by machine came some years before machine weaving, for spinning was by far the most laborious part of cloth manufacture, and the processes involved were much simpler than the processes of weaving. A hand-weaver can produce from one to eight yards of fabric a day, the yardage depending on the fineness of the cloth as well as upon the skill of the weaver. About eight spinners were required to keep one weaver supplied with yarns.

The first spinning-machines made an inferior thread that could be used for weft or woof but was too soft for warp. Even so, the saving in labor was very great.

It was long years, however, before spinning-machinery found its way to the United States. The patents were jealously guarded, and although a number of efforts were made to smuggle models out of England these attempts were always discovered and frustrated. A set of models cast in brass was to have been shipped to France and from there to America, but was seized and destroyed. Finally, however, a model of wood was constructed and this, after being cut into small pieces that were shipped separately to France, did finally escape the vigilant guards and safely reached Philadelphia. Soon after that spinning-machinery was in general operation in the new republic.

Of course it was a question merely of time when power would be harnessed to the business of weaving cloth as well as to the spinning of yarn. The actual impulse and invention came about in an amusing way.

There lived in England in the year 1784 a certain Dr. Cartwright who was a scholarly man and a minister of the gospel. He was a friend of the poet Crabbe and had published a legendary poem of his own—"The Armine and Elvira." Besides being a poet he appears to have been a person of great per-

(6) Indian War. Draft number 22. (A favorite pattern with Weaver Rose.)

sistence, and it is quite probable that his friends and neighbors sometimes dubbed him stubborn. This personage chanced one afternoon to be taking tea in a public-house where he became interested in the talk of two Manchester merchants seated at an adjoining table. It appeared from their discussion that the textile industry was in a distressingly disturbed condition owing to the introduction of spinning-machinery; the machines, they said, were producing yarns at such a prodigious rate of speed that the weavers were swamped, large stocks of spun yarn were accumulating with an unsettling effect upon prices.

The learned doctor remarked, casually enough, that the obvious remedy would be to harness looms as well as spindles, and to weave by machinery.

To the Manchester gentlemen who were familiar with all the intricacies of the weaving craft this appeared the absurd and impractical notion of a poet. Weave by machinery, indeed! Preposterous! They were at some pains to explain to Cartwright just how foolish an idea this was.

If they had shown less heat or more tolerance the invention of weaving machinery might have been delayed for years, and certainly some other than Cartwright would have had the honor; but as it was, the more the Manchester men derided and ridiculed the notion the more hotly the good clergyman defended it. He had the advantage in this, that his imagination was untrammeled —he had never seen a loom in operation and knew nothing whatever either of weaving or of mechanics.

Cartwright went home from this encounter thoroughly convinced by his own arguments that weaving by machinery was practicable, and determined to demonstrate the soundness of his ideas. He caused a loom to be built by the local carpenter and blacksmith, and when it was finished the thing actually made cloth after a fashion—which was a sort of miracle. In 1785 Cartwright took out a patent on his invention, and then—but not till then—gave himself the trouble to examine a loom, and to observe a weaver at work. What he saw caused him to modify some of his ideas. He went home again and spent some time experimenting with his loom, improving it in many ways, and in 1787 he took out his final patent.

Cartwright's first loom was not, strictly speaking, a power loom at all, but was what we know as an automatic loom. The shed was changed and the shuttle thrown by the action of the batten or "laith" in the hands of the weaver. Looms of this type are manufactured to this day for use in the rug-weaving trade.

Later, power was harnessed to the loom. It is said that the power plant in Cartwright's first factory consisted of a bull!

A handbook of weaving published in Utica, New York, in 1818 makes derogatory mention of automatic looms, which are called "new-fangled," and said to be "too complicated for ordinary use." The old-style hand-looms, according to this work, "are demonstrated as more satisfactory, both for factory and domestic weaving." Amusing shortsightedness in the light of what was so soon to happen!

In 1826 the first Jacquard loom to be brought to the United States was set up in Philadelphia. Power weaving was still in its infancy, and the first Jacquard looms—such as the one on which the famous La Tourettes wove their elaborate coverlets—were probably of the automatic, fly-shuttle type, and may even have been operated by hand. However, power was soon added and the day of modern weaving had begun.

Not that there is anything very modern about the Jacquard coverlets of the middle of the nineteenth century—they are no more modern than antimacassars, Mansard roofs, and iron stags on the front lawn. And with their screaming eagles, scrolls of patriotic sentiments, portraits of Washington, all surrounded by the quaint roofs and towers of the "Boston Town Border," they are American enough in all conscience! But the art of them is not the old simple and austerely geometric household art. Somehow the old poetry is lost.

The housewives of the period, however, no doubt considered the product of the Jacquard loom a much more elegant thing than their own handiwork. They took down their old looms and stored them away in haylofts or garrets to lie forgotten for the next hundred years, and carried their beautifully dyed homespun yarns to the weave shop to be turned into an "E Pluribus Unum" coverlet with name and date woven into the corner.

In color and texture many of the ancient pieces of Jacquard weaving are charming, thanks to the madder and indigo of the home dye-pot and to the fineness and softness of the hand-spun yarns. Sometimes, too, as in the example from the Boston Museum, the patterns are graceful and lovely, but more often, alas, they are hideous, grotesque, and altogether regrettable.

The Jacquard loom, though it killed for a time our American art of weaving, is a very wonderful machine. Any one who is interested in weaving will find it well worth while to visit the nearest textile mill and watch such a loom in operation. By means of the Jacquard machine it is possible to govern separately each of the thousands of threads in a wide warp, and the pattern possibilities are practically limitless. It can do nothing, however, that could not be done in much the same manner on the ancient draw-loom such as the one used by John Tice in the weaving of his famous "branched satins." In fact the Jacquard machine is simply an efficient mechanical substitute for the draw-boy, whose arduous task it was to draw down the cords of the simple. The inventor, Jacquard, was a mechanic in the silk-weaving city of Lyons, France, and his invention followed an earlier but impractical effort made by another Frenchman. As appears to be usually the case, the inventor reaped little profit from his invention, and Jacquard, like Kay, might have suffered want if Napoleon Bonaparte had not awarded him a state allowance—on condition that his patents revert to the city of Lyons. It is said that before Jacquard's death more than thirty thousand looms of his pattern were in operation in Lyons.

Jacquard weaving, it is safe to say, was always professional weaving. Coverlets of the Jacquard type that show a seam up the middle were woven by hand. These are rare. Most are woven full width, which indicates fly-shuttle or mechanical weaving.

II *The Decline of Hand-Weaving, and Weaver Rose*

For many years after the introduction of machinery the old art of hand-weaving persisted, side by side with the new industrial developments in the cloth-making industry. As late as the time of the Civil War much weaving was still being done on household looms, especially in the country districts. Many excellent pieces in the simple overshot pattern weave date from this time—as witness such names for coverlet patterns as "Missouri Trouble," and "Lee's Surrender." Double weaving, however, and the summer and winter weave had almost entirely disappeared. The movement that set in was a recessive movement and the newer and more elaborate ways of weaving were forgotten first.

Between the Civil War and our own day very little hand-weaving of any sort was done. A few old women, it is true, continued to weave rag rugs on their ancient looms, but there was hardly any home weaving of the better sorts. Fortunately in some isolated communities of the South—particularly in the Kentucky and Tennessee mountain districts—the old tradition lived on and has persisted to our day. It is chiefly to the mountain women of the South that modern weavers are indebted for the old patterns that are again current among us.

In New England the craft died out much more completely than in the South. In fact it survived in only a few scattered individuals and in a single outstanding figure—"Weaver Rose" of Kingston, Rhode Island.

Weaver Rose—this last of the old-time weavers—was something of a character and a good deal of a local celebrity. Here is a word portrait taken from an article in the Providence *Sunday Journal* of some sixteen years ago:

"He is anything but conventional, as Narragansett Pier and neighboring resorts measure conventionality. His bare feet, his two-piece costume—with none too much care taken in the piecing—his long white hair, his shrewd eyes that supplement his infrequent and somewhat gruff speech, his constant recourse to the contents of the serviceable snuff-box which is his invariable companion, all contribute to the visitor's pleasure in the meeting."

This venerable and eccentric personage lived alone with an equally aged and eccentric sister—he never had a wife or children—in a quaint little old cottage beside the road. It was marked by large white-washed bowlders set on the low wall, probably as a sign-post for those seeking the place. The huge, clumsy old-fashioned looms on which he wove were housed in a loft over an ell behind the cottage—a place where only a few trusted friends ever penetrated.

His neatly printed card announced:

W. H. H. Rose
weaver of
RAG CARPETS, PORTIERES
Chenille mats
HAP-HARLOTS AND COVERLETS

"Hap-harlot," the great new Oxford dictionary tells us, is a very ancient word meaning "wrap-rascal," and was used for a sort of coarse blanket or coverlet.

No doubt it was the fame of his quaint personality as much as the fame of his work that drew people in flocks to his isolated homestead to buy of his wares. At any rate they came. Weaver Rose made his simple living exactly as many old-time weavers had done before him, by throwing a hand-shuttle and treading out patterns on his ancient looms.

His weaving was all of the simple "overshot" type, and many handsome examples of his art are of course still in existence. He was a famous writer of drafts and his patterns—clearly and carefully noted down on bits of coarse wrapping paper—are still being passed from weaver to weaver, as drafts were exchanged in the old day. He had the old tradition, kept it pure and handed it on. Weavers of to-day owe him much.

In fact Weaver Rose may be said to have done more than any other one person toward the modern revival of hand-weaving in New England. In 1912, not many years before his death, he invited a number of people who were interested in weaving to meet at his house on Labor Day. Some seven or eight enthusiasts gathered and it was decided to form an organization. Whether or not this had been Weaver Rose's intention in sending out his invitations does not appear to be clear. The proceedings, though informal, resulted in the formation of the "Colonial Weavers' Association."

The organization did not have many meetings nor did it function very actively, but an impulse was given that was of lasting value to the weaver's art. Many of the members of that early association are still weaving, and many of them have gone out from that meeting to teach others and to carry on the great tradition.

I have before me a letter addressed to one of these people by the old master himself, enclosing a draft. There is no salutation:

> I was much pleased to Receive your Picture at the Loom weaving Church Windoes a different pattern From the one i use as Near as i can see i inclose a little draft i have not used it.
>
> 'Whh Rose Kingston R I'

The draft was "Guess Me." (Pattern No. 66.)

There is no picture of Weaver Rose—he was camera-shy and no picture of him was ever taken. Toward the end of his life he became seclusive and no longer welcomed visitors. After his death his old sister lived on for a few years in complete isolation, guarding very jealously the old looms and the great store of patterns hidden away in the old house. Now she is dead, too.

But Weaver Rose's work lives on in many a fine coverlet of pleasant pattern and honest workmanship,—and many modern weavers are using patterns that came from him. A number of the patterns in this book are drafts given by him to members of his circle—carefully written and well-considered drafts they are, for he was a master-craftsman.

III The Revival—Modern Hand-Weaving

Weaving by hand is again being practised all over the world—which is after all not nearly as surprising as that the art should have been so nearly lost here in America. In the countries of Europe the introduction of power machinery caused violent social disturbances, far more serious than the sporadic rioting that marked the same readjustments in America, but machinery never conquered the entire field there as it did here. In Europe hand-weaving continued in the country districts and has come down to our day not greatly changed. In England brocades and velvets were and still are woven by hand by professional hand weavers, and the Scotch hand-woven tweeds and the Irish linens of cottage manufacture are well known.

The Swedish government encourages hand-weaving by setting up standards, sponsoring schools, and employing skilled weavers and spinners to go out through the country districts to teach the women on the farms. Much the same thing is being done in Canada by the Province of Quebec where hand-weaving is a multi-million dollar business. Italy is encouraging the native Perugian types of hand-weaving and much fine Italian work finds its way to this country. In Spain a great deal of gorgeous hand-weaving is done. Russian weaving, Hungarian weaving—we know many kinds of hand-weaving better than we know our own. To many people it may be a new idea that we have an American art of the loom.

In the Spanish Americas there has always been much very fine weaving. In

Guatemala all weaving is still being done by hand, and textile "factories" are equipped with hand-looms only. Some of the most beautiful textiles of all time were made in ancient Peru and the Peruvian government is doing a great deal to preserve the ancient art. In Mexico there is still much fine hand-weaving, though there has been great deterioration due to the undiscriminating demands of the tourist trade and the consequent production of quantities of trash. Much fine weaving is still being done by the Navajos and other Indian tribes of our own Southwest, but here again there has been severe deterioration.

In the United States the revival of hand-weaving has shown a steady, unhurried development since the day of Weaver Rose and his little group of enthusiasts. It has never become a "fad"—one of those things that everyone is doing today and nobody tomorrow. It can hardly be called a "hobby," either, as hobby usually carries the implication of a more or less impractical diversion. Weaving is instead an interesting and useful part-time or full-time occupation that bids fair to be again a national popular art. There are actually more hand-looms in operation at the present time than there were at the time of the Revolution when all textiles were woven by hand.

Innumerable studios and small industries all over the country are turning out hand-woven tweeds and decorative fabrics for sale. Hand-woven linens, scarves, neckties, and many other things are shown in the shops.

In the South, where hand-weaving lingered on, through the eclipse, among the people in isolated mountain communities, the craft has in recent years been greatly stimulated through various charitable and educational agencies—chiefly as a means of relieving the poverty of the people. The teachers are often young women from the North who devote themselves to the work, riding long distances on horseback through the hills to carry help, and the instruction that means self-help, to the mountain women whose lives are almost unbelievably starved and limited.

The development of hand-weaving in the Northern states has taken a rather different course. As the aim in the South has been chiefly economic, the aim in the North has been chiefly cultural and artistic, fostered by arts-and-crafts associations, museums, schools and colleges. Of course there are those in the South who weave for pleasure and for artistic expression, as there are many in the North who weave chiefly or altogether for profit, but in general this difference of interest exists.

One of the most interesting ways in which hand-weaving is being used for the benefit of society is in the occupational therapy treatment of the sick and disabled. Beauty and the creation of beauty are comforting to the depressed and soothing to the nervous and irritable. Color and texture and rhythmic movements have great curative value when intelligently used. Most modern hospitals that treat chronic diseases—hospitals for the insane, for instance, and sanatoriums for the treatment of tuberculosis—have craft shops in which hand-looms are an important part of the equipment. Occupational therapy offers an interesting and rewarding profession to both men and women.

In my opinion, the cultural values of the craft are far more important than the economic values. Weaving as a business is a "job of work" like anything else, and the profits are not outstanding. In making articles for sale the weaver must produce something that the customer with money in his pocket can be induced to accept in exchange for his precious dollars. It is his taste and not one's own that rules. Moreover the thing must be made in quantity or the sales-costs will be prohibitive, and it must be made at the lowest possible expense for time and materials. Those who weave chiefly for their own satisfaction need not count the cost of time. They may experiment with design, with odd color combinations and unusual textures. Of course there are solid economic values here, too. A hand-woven tweed for a suit, hand-woven draperies exactly right for those queer-shaped windows in the living room, a rug just the right size and shape for a difficult corner or doorway, a gay scarf for daughter's pretty throat, a sturdy wool shirt for the hunting season—all these things have practical dollars-and-cents values as well as giving the satisfaction of exactly what one wants for some special use, simply by warping and weaving it.

The people to whom hand-weaving means the most are those who need creative work as a rest from monotonous labors in some other field. Women, for instance, whose household duties are not exigent and who find it hard to cheat boredom with bridge and the movies, may open for themselves this door into the world of art—where there is much refreshment for the spirit. Professional people, too, whose work is all with abstractions, find great comfort in coordinating mind and body for the making of a bit of fine linen or a lap-robe for the car. People suffering from anxieties about which they can do nothing, people trying to live again after some shattering loss, people whose lives are unsatisfactory or incomplete, all find in weaving a great resource. It is so impersonal, so very old, so practical, with such boundless variety, such opportunities for beauty! And there is for most people a curiously instinctive pleasure in the handling of threads—something that has come down to us through the ages. For weaving is an ancient "mystery" as well as a bit of earnest work with a handsome reward.

It is, I think, to these who weave for personal satisfaction rather than to those who weave for money-profit that we owe the interesting modern developments in hand-weaving, and it is to this group that we may look for further developments in the future.

Chapter Two: Weaving Horizons – the Scope of This Book

I What Weaving Is

Weaving is essentially a simple matter, requiring no special talents, no lofty intellect or high degree of manual skill for its accomplishment. It is made up of a number of separate processes, each easy in itself but each requiring care and accuracy in its performance. If it seems complicated at first this is only because there are so many ways to weave.

Each age and each country has its own weaves and patterns, and nobody could possibly know and follow them all. The hand-weaver has a "horizon unlimited." This is one of the charms of our beautiful craft. For those who crave adventure there is always something new and untried ahead, with no danger that one will ever come to the end.

This book lays no claim to giving a complete account of hand-weaving in all its phases. A whole library of books would be required for that. The purpose is to pass along the results of a long and intimate experience with the craft, to provide beginners with detailed and practical directions for the fundamental processes, to give an account of the weaves and patterns current in Colonial America, and to supply information—not available elsewhere—on some of the "native" American weaves from Mexico, Guatemala, Peru, and our own Southwest.

No directions will be given for tapestry weaving as this is a whole world in itself and is amply documented. Many Scandinavian weaves are common practise among American weavers, but these are excellently set forth in the many Scandinavian books on weaving that are readily obtainable, so they will not be explained here—except in the case of one or two weaves of Scandinavian origin that have taken new forms here in America. There will be no notes on plaiting, "card" weaving, "inkle" weaving, braiding and knotting—except for the fringe-ties explained in the chapter on "finishes." There will be no information on draw-loom or fly-shuttle weaving.

II A Few Definitions

It seems desirable at the start to have a few definitions. Weaving is a technical craft and the words used in it have exact meanings. If these terms are used loosely—as too often happens—confusion ensues.

A TEXTILE FABRIC we will take to be a fabric composed of two sets of yarns or fibres that cross—usually at right angles—and interlace according to some regular plan. Felt, and the "tapa cloth" of the South Sea Islands cannot properly be rated as textile fabrics.

The yarns running lengthwise of the fabric compose the WARP, and the yarns running crosswise, the WOOF or WEFT.

The WEAVE of a fabric we shall take to be the plan of interlacement of warp and weft—as "tabby," "twill" and so on. PATTERN, we shall take to mean the decorative figure, if any. The same pattern may be carried out in several different weaves. There is sometimes confusion here as people occasionally refer to the weaving DRAFT as the pattern. The DRAFT is the threading plan and includes both weave and pattern. It seems useful to make the distinction. The DESIGN of a weaving project includes weave and pattern, color arrangement, dimensions, borders if any, and complete directions.

The TEXTURE of a fabric is its structure, its "feel" or "handle"—stiffness, pliability, thickness, smoothness, roughness and so on. Texture depends on the materials used, the warp-setting, the weave and the beat.

A rather meaningless term that has recently appeared in weaving literature is TEXTURE WEAVING. This appears to mean the making of fabrics without decorative design or pattern, deriving their interest solely from the material and the colors used, the weaves being for the most part simple interlacements like tabby or twill. The term is vague because, of course, every fabric has a "texture," so that strictly speaking all weaving is "texture weaving." The implication of the term, however, seems to be definitely "lack of pattern."

(7) Whig Rose. Draft number 91. (One of the most ancient patterns, known also in Europe.)

By HAND-WOVEN we mean a fabric made by a hand-thrown shuttle. Of recent years a term HAND-LOOMED has appeared. This seems to mean a fabric not woven by hand but produced on a fly-shuttle loom. It is a misleading term, probably intentionally so—to avoid the objections raised to the marketing of fly-shuttle textiles as "hand-woven," which, of course, they are not. But if understood and accepted, the term serves well enough, perhaps. Fly-shuttle weaving, though it is mechanical weaving, is still in a different class from power-loom weaving and needs a definite name of its own. It is somewhat the

(8) Coverlet (modern) in summer and winter weave. Pattern: Twenty-five Snow-Balls. Similar to draft number 229.

same relationship as exists between hand-sewing, machine-sewing, and power-machine-sewing.

Other technical terms used in weaving will be explained as they occur. The definitions given will follow the American usage, which occasionally differs from the British.

I should like to urge weavers to use the "cant" of our craft carefully and accurately. To use technical terms hit-and-miss causes confusion and misunderstanding.

Chapter Three: Beginner's Problems

The would-be weaver is confronted by three main problems: where to get information and instruction; what equipment to purchase; what stock of materials to assemble.

I Instruction

This book has been designed to answer as many weaving questions as possible, so that anyone who wishes may teach himself to weave through a study of its pages—but to have the man-to-man help of a skilled weaver will make the first steps easier and progress more rapid.

It is important, however, to make certain that the proposed teacher *knows how to weave* and is *willing to teach.* It might seem unnecessary to make this suggestion, but unfortunately it is not. People sometimes set themselves up as teachers without having taken the trouble to master even the rudiments of the craft. There are also some highly skilled weavers who are so jealous of their art that they give a pupil as little as possible, with the result that at the end of his course he may find himself almost as helpless as at the beginning. Primary instruction should include loom adjustments and tie-up, warping, reading a draft, drawing-in, sleying, tying-in, correct handling of the shuttles and batten, weaving a pattern "as drawn in," simple draft-writing. Anyone unable or unwilling to supply this minimum of instruction cannot, in my opinion, be considered an adequate teacher.

I am told that there are so-called schools of weaving where the pupil is supplied with a loom and a lot of indiscriminate material and is invited to invent

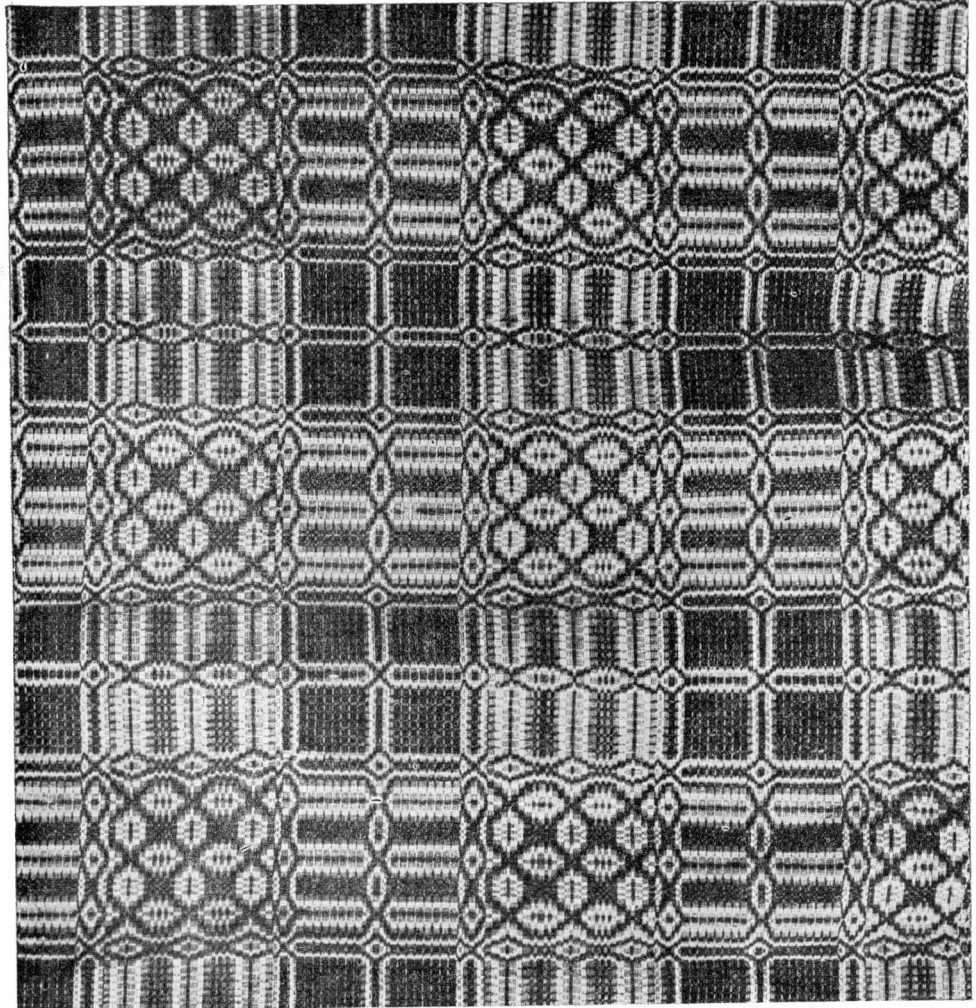

(9) Tennessee Trouble. Draft number 54. Missouri Trouble is a similar pattern.

weaving for himself. This is supposed to be in the interest of "originality." If left entirely to this system the new weaver might in a year or two progress as far as the Stone Age along the line of weaving history. It is quite unlikely that he would produce anything either very handsome or very useful, and he

(10) Elaborate double-woven coverlet from Pennsylvania, Double and Single Snow-Ball pattern with Pine-Tree border. Similar to draft number 233.
(Possibly woven by John Landes.)

(11) Simple Jacquard or draw-loom weaving.

would certainly waste a great deal of time. It would be a little like inviting a student of literature to begin by inventing a language and an alphabet.

A good deal of nonsense is talked and unfortunately taken seriously by many people on the subject of originality. The traditional weaves and designs that have come down to us through the ages are apt to have a fundamental rightness that is unlikely to appear in something you or I dream up overnight. It is not servile copying to reproduce an old coverlet pattern in all its traditional charm, any more than it is for a musician to play a classic composition instead of some improvisation of his own. The craftsman who follows the precepts of William Morris, producing only "what he knows to be useful or believes to be beautiful," will not go far wrong. One cannot be original to order. The craftsman who happens to have what the psychologists call a "source mind" will find new and unusual uses for the traditional material, which will show originality and which may or may not be interesting and beautiful. But to strive for originality simply by doing something queer is unlikely to have any very valuable result. It would no doubt be original to interweave sand-burs in the fabric of a pillow-top, or to make a window-curtain of old love-letters cut in strips, but what of it? Originality may safely be permitted to take care of itself.

The beginner, at any rate, should learn to *weave*—to make an honest fabric without streaks and with good edges, pleasing to the eye and to the touch, useful for something. To do this with the least effort and loss of time it is just as well to follow the methods that have been found most convenient down the ages.

II Equipment

A loom is a piece of equipment designed to facilitate the textile process. There is little pleasure and no profit in trying to weave on a loom that will not do its share of the work willingly, accurately and easily.

People sometimes point out that very beautiful weaving is done in various parts of the world on primitive looms composed of a few sticks. And this is true. The Maori weaver drives two stout stakes into the ground at a distance apart to suit her purpose, stretches a stout thread between the stakes and her loom is complete. I once watched a Bovilian Indian woman at her weaving. She had driven four stakes into the ground at the corners of her proposed fabric and had stretched her warp between them. In weaving she crawled about on the web on hands and knees. A Guatemalan weaver attaches one end of her warp to a tree or the side of the cabin and the other end to her body. She squats on the ground on her heels to weave, producing sheds by lifting sticks that carry loops of thread, by way of heddles, and regulates the tension of the warp by

(12) Bolivian bag in warp-faced rep and pick-up weaving. Note finishing braid around top and edges.

leaning forward and back. Any of us may weave so if we choose—provided we have the time and skill and the age-old patience. But for most modern weavers a proper loom is more satisfactory.

The loom has three main functions: (1) it holds the warp in order and at a tension; (2) it holds the warp apart to make "sheds" for the passage of the shuttles; (3) it drives the weft threads together for the production of a solid web. A loom that will not do these three things correctly should be rebuilt or discarded.

The frame of a loom—even a small one—should be of hard wood and sturdy construction to withstand the pull of a stretched warp and the constant pounding of the batten. A flimsily constructed loom is good for nothing but fire-wood. The frame carries four main beams as shown on diagram No. 1: (e) the "warp-beam" on which the unwoven warp is wound; (f) the "slab-stock" or back-beam over which the warp is carried from the warp-beam; (b) the "breast-beam"; (c) the "cloth-beam" on which the woven web is wound up as made. Sometimes there is also an idler between the breast-beam and the cloth-beam to give the weaver more knee-space under the web. These beams must be absolutely parallel and square with the sides of the frame. If there is a deviation of so much as a fraction of an inch the web will weave crooked—longer on one edge than the other.

The frame should ordinarily be longer from front to back than from side to side, to provide ample weaving space. If the frame is very shallow it is impossible to weave more than an inch or two without releasing the tension and winding up the web, which is a nuisance. Also undue strain is put on the warp when the sheds are opened.

On old looms, Swedish looms, very small looms, and some others the warp-beam consists of a solid roller, but for convenience and time-saving in warping, a "sectional" warp-beam is desirable. It is an advantage to have the loom equipped with two warp-beams.

Warp-beam and cloth-beam should carry good ratchets to control the tension. Some ancient looms and foreign looms are provided instead with pegs to be inserted in the end of the beam, or with weights on cords attached to the beam. Ratchets are far more practical. **They should be of metal.**

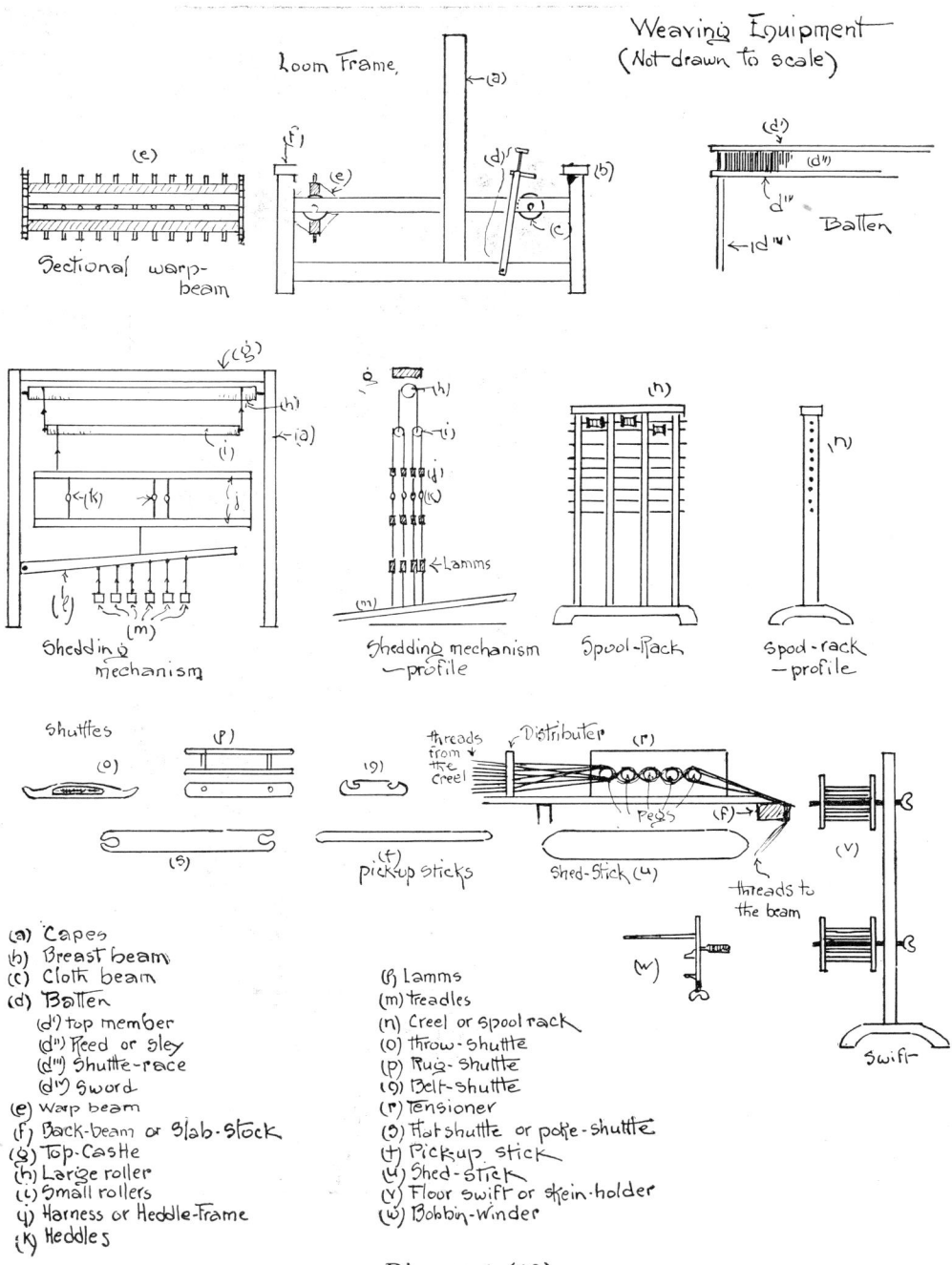

(14) Coverlet after a pattern from the John Landes book.

A demand has developed recently for looms constructed with folding frames for convenience in handling. In my opinion this is not good practise. A folding frame never has the rigidity of a solid frame, and this rigidity is necessary to keep the beams properly alined. Small looms go readily through doors without folding and large looms usually stay where set up and can be taken down when necessary.

The shedding mechanism of the conventional modern hand-loom consists of two or more "harnesses" or "heddle-frames" carrying "heddles," operated to rise and sink by means of foot-treadles or hand-levers. Two side-pieces or uprights, known as the "capes" of the loom, support the "top-castle" from which the harnesses are suspended over rollers or pulleys, or from "jacks." In some modern patented looms the top-castle is omitted and the jacks are placed below the harnesses.

A two-harness loom will make only two sheds and is limited to the plain weave.

The four-harness counterbalanced loom, illustrated on Diagram 1, was the type most popular among the old time "domestic manufacturers" and is still the loom used by more hand-weavers than any other. However, the recent tendency is toward looms of the "jack" type—which permit operating each harness independently of the others—often carrying eight, ten, or twelve harnesses instead of four. On such a loom many weaves and patterns may be produced that are difficult or impossible on a loom of the counterbalanced type.

In modern looms the heddles are usually either wire or flat steel. String heddles are to be found on ancient looms and on some looms of the Swedish type. String heddles make a picturesque looking loom, but metal heddles are far more convenient. The harness frames should be so hung and so constructed that they may be taken out of the loom without difficulty when one wishes to shift the heddles, and the catches holding the flat metal strips on which the heddles run should be easy to open. This last may seem a minor detail but has its importance in the matter of broken fingernails and ruffled tempers.

In table-looms and some other very small looms the harnesses are operated by hand-levers, but in floor-looms the sheds are opened by means of foot-

(15) A coverlet in the Double Chariot-Wheel pattern lends charm to this New England bedroom.

treadles. These may be attached either at the front or back of the loom. A large loom is somewhat lighter to operate if the treadles are attached at the back. The treadles hang from a set of "lamms" or levers attached to one or the other of the capes of the loom and extending across the bank of treadles. These levers are attached to the harness frames at the center and insure drawing down the harnesses levelly, as would be impossible if the treadles were attached directly to the harnesses.

It is possible to operate a four-harness loom by means of four treadles, but it is far more convenient to use six treadles, and most modern four-harness looms are so equipped. An eight-harness loom should carry a minimum of fourteen treadles and as many more as the space under the loom will permit.

The beater or "batten" is a swinging frame set crosswise of the loom—shown at (d), (d^I), (d^{II}), (d^{III}) and (d^{IV}) on the diagram—that carries a slotted metal strip known as the "reed" or "sley," which serves to space the warp drawn through the slots or "dents." It swings either from the floor, as in the diagram, or from above on an extension of the top-castle. The batten should be heavy and entirely rigid. It should have a broad bottom member—a sort of narrow shelf—called the "shuttle-race" on which the shuttle travels, and it should have a removable top-member to hold the reed firmly in place and to permit a change of reeds when desired. Most modern looms are built with the batten swung from below. The batten, falling forward against the edge of the web, delivers most of the beat by its own weight, which is not true of a batten swung from above. Moreover, in the latter construction it is necessary to hold the batten back out of the way with one hand while throwing the shuttle with the other. This is awkward. Battens are sometimes built without an adequate shuttle-race, but this is a defect because when deprived of this little shelf to run upon, the shuttle sometimes takes a nose-dive through the warp, damaging to the shuttle and also to the temper of the weaver.

The desirable size of loom depends on the kinds of weaving one has in mind, and also on available space. Small pieces may be made on a wide loom but it is impossible to weave such things as coverlets, rugs, and tweeds on a very small loom. A very wide loom is, however, heavier to operate than a narrow loom, and to most weavers it is difficult to throw the shuttle for a greater

"*An old loom is experienced, responsive.*"
(16) A modern weaver at an ancient loom.

width than 42 inches. People usually find a weaving width of 32 inches or 36 inches ample for most purposes. In Canada, to be sure, many double-width looms are used for the making of coverlets and blankets without a seam, and for large tablecloths. These looms are equipped with two sets of treadles and are operated by two weavers. Very wide looms operated by two weavers are also used in some places in the United States for the making of double-width suitings and the like. As a rule, however, when one comes upon a seamless coverlet or a double-width tweed it is likely to be hand-loomed rather than hand-woven—a fly-shuttle product.

There are many small looms on the market. Some are treadle looms designed to occupy as small a space as possible, for use in small apartments and restricted quarters. But most of the very small looms are table-looms operated by hand-levers. Looms only a few inches wide are simply toys and have little or no practical use, but on those that weave 20 inches wide many small articles may be woven with success. Small looms are convenient for experimental work and for the making of samples, and they have the advantage of portability. However, it takes much more time and effort to weave on a hand-lift, table-loom than on a floor-loom with foot treadles.

In addition to the loom some other equipment is required. For sectional warping it is necessary to have a "creel" or "spool-rack" with a capacity of at least sixty spools. A "tensioner" to use in sectional warping, while not an absolute necessity, is a great convenience. One should also have a supply of shuttles of three kinds—at least two of each sort—boat-shaped "throw-shuttles" carrying bobbins, flat "poke-shuttles," and large "rug-shuttles." Also a "swift" or skein holder and a winder for winding shuttle-bobbins and warp-spools for the creel. For some kinds of weaving flat "pick-up sticks" and wider, flat "shed-sticks" are required. And to weave comfortably a suitable loom-bench is necessary. Moreover, though one may do most of the warping by the sectional method, a warping board of five- to ten-yard capacity is convenient for the making of short warps and special warps. An illustration of a warping board will be found on Diagram 2. For the beaming of a warp made on the board a "raddle" is a convenience. And though many popular kinds of warp are now supplied on spools for the creel, some warps—wool and worsted for instance—must be spooled by the weaver, and a stock of large wooden spools is necessary.

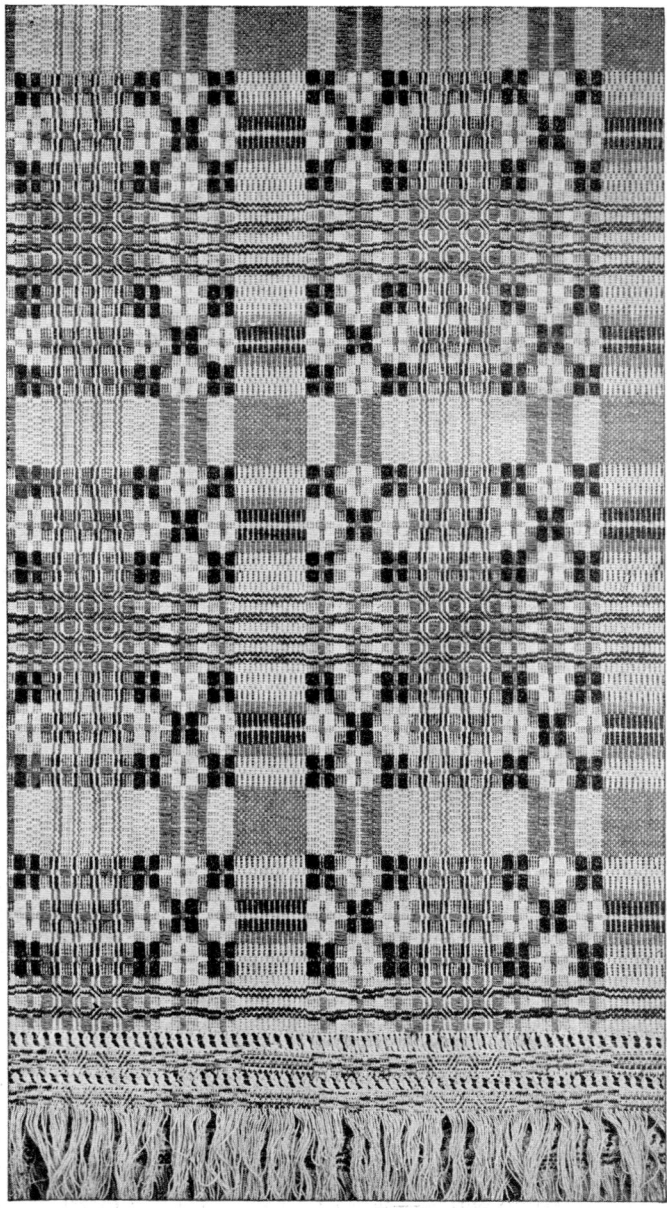

(17) Ancient coverlet in rose and green. Pattern similar to Rose of Sharon. Draft number 22.

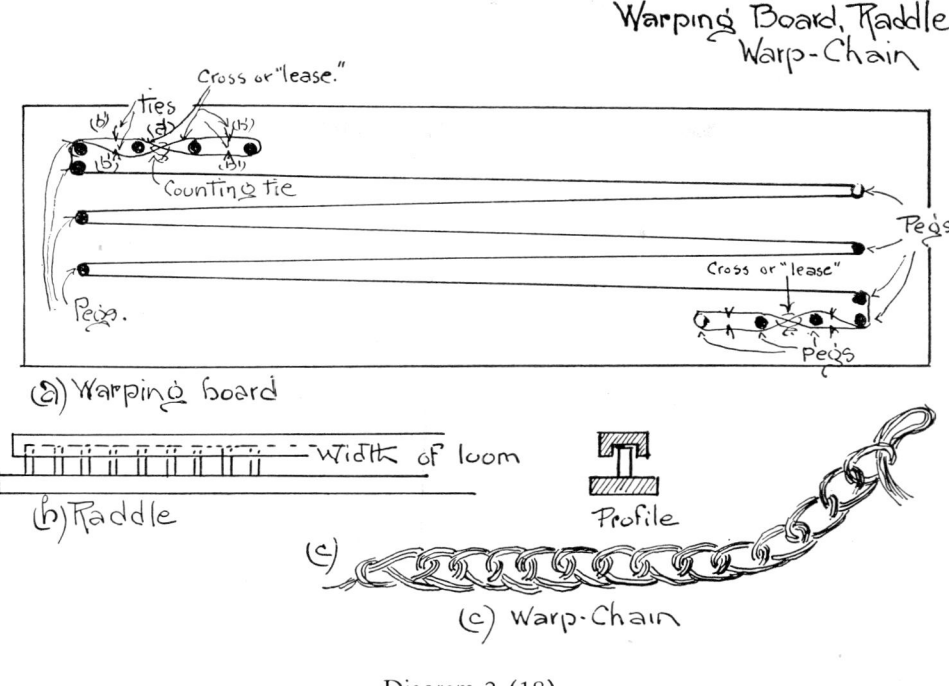

Diagram 2 (18)

Summary List of Equipment

(1) A *good* loom equipped with a sectional warp-beam (optional)
(2) An adjustable loom bench
(3) A spool-rack or creel
(4) A small warping board
(5) A tensioner (required for sectional warping)
(6) 100 or more large warp-spools (for sectional warping)
(7) A raddle
(8) A swift or skein-holder
(9) A bobbin winder
(10) Shuttles and bobbins
(11) Pick-up sticks
(12) Scissors, tape-measure, pins.

It is also desirable to have several reeds in addition to the one supplied with the loom. The correct setting of the warp is extremely important, and a single reed will suit only a few warps. A fifteen-dent reed is usually supplied with the loom, as this is the reed in most common use, but one should also have a twelve-dent and an eighteen-dent, and for some settings, a twenty-dent and a ten-dent; for close-set warps used in warp-face weaving an eight-dent and a six-dent. These are given in the order of usefulness. For some special warp or special purpose other reeds may be required.

III Materials

It is not necessary for the beginner to lay in a large stock of materials. Simple overshot pattern weaving is the easiest way into the craft, and for this a good cotton warp of medium weight is required. Very coarse warps and very fine warps should be avoided at the beginning. The warp suggested is a 24/3 cotton of good quality, to be set at thirty ends to the inch. This material may be purchased on small spools for the warping creel and for sectional warping sixty small spools will be required. This quantity of warp is, of course, much more than required for a first effort, but it is standard material that should be kept in stock.

For pattern weft—the warp material may be used for the tabby weft—a variety of materials are suitable. The best pattern weft for first weaving is a good wool or worsted yarn of medium weight. Strand cottons may also be used. The mercerized "perle" cottons are sometimes used but are not altogether satisfactory in the overshot weave. Linens are undesirable in this weave and over a cotton warp, and so are most rayons, "fancy" yarns, and any very hard-twisted and wiry material.

The materials to use depend on the type of fabric to be woven, and more detailed notes on the choice of material will be found in the following chapter.

Chapter Four: Design of the Fabric

Before proceeding to the business of weaving, the weaver must have a plan in mind. He must know what type of fabric he wishes to produce, for what purpose, in what weave, pattern and colors. No matter how perfectly it may be woven, a poorly designed piece will be a failure.

The choices of weave, material, warp-setting, pattern and colors that must be made are interrelated, and all depend fundamentally on the purpose for which the piece is intended. The weaves in general use among modern American hand-weavers are described in detail in succeeding chapters, but the following notes may prove helpful in making the initial choices.

I   Over-all Proportions

A matter sometimes overlooked by inexperienced weavers is the importance of the over-all shape of the piece they plan to make. Of course if the plan is for a tweed yardage this need not be considered, but for a rug, for instance, the relation of length to breadth is important. In a general way—unless planned for a particular spot—the length should be not less than one and a half times the width and not more than one and three quarters times the width. If shorter the appearance is of not-quite-square, which is annoying to the eye, and if the length is twice the width or over you have a runner rather than a "throw-rug."

Again, for linen towels, consider how they look when folded and hung on the rail. The hem should be either extremely narrow, or wide enough to make a part of the design, and the border, if any, should not be a skimpy few lines of color, or so wide that it reaches over half way to the rail. The size of the piece, of course, controls the width of borders.

44 —

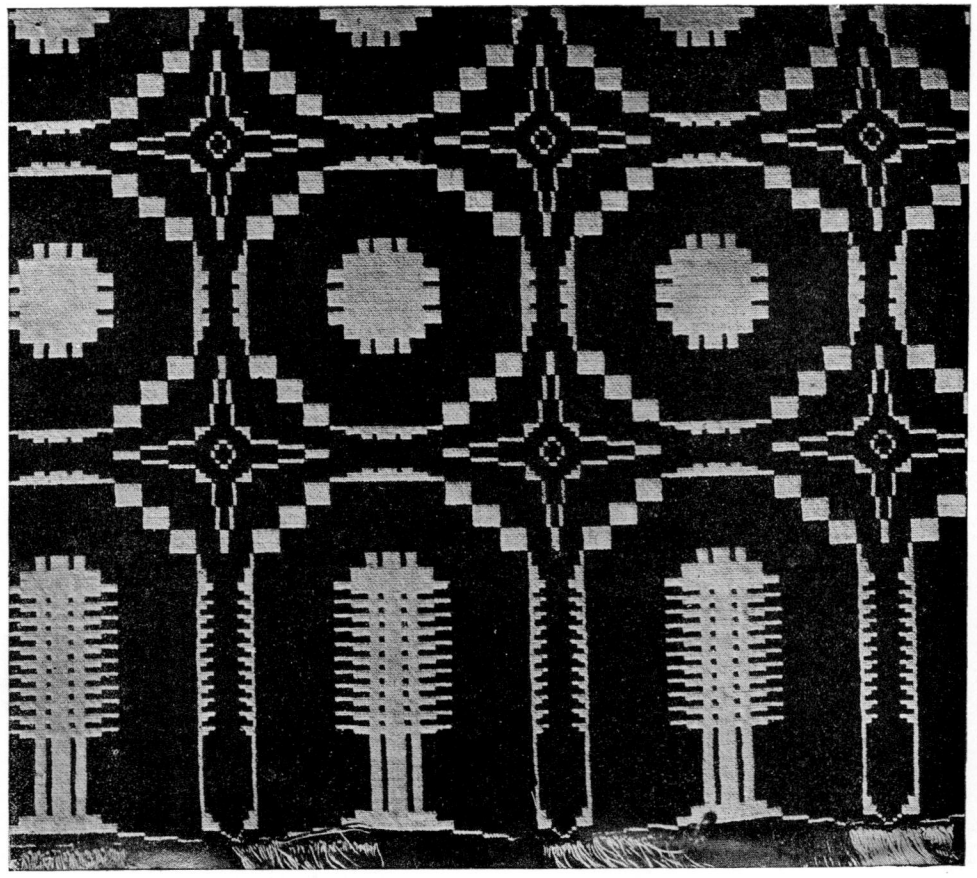

(19) Single Snow-Ball with Pine-Tree border, Boston Museum of Fine Arts. See draft number 234.

When arranging a border for a piece in plain weave, such as a towel, it is poor practise to begin at once with a wide border strip. If done in colors it is well to begin by weaving two tabby shots in color; four tabby shots in white; a tabby shot in color and a very narrow border—usually three pattern shots, on opposite sheds will be enough—then a tabby shot in color followed by four tabby shots in white and then the broad border, followed by the narrow borders as at the beginning. If a broad border in colored pattern weaving is woven across a plain weave piece without these introductory remarks it has the appearance of an appliqued strip of another fabric and does not seem a part of the piece.

II Choice of Weave

The choice of a suitable weave for a given project is fundamental. If the weave is wrong the piece will be a failure no matter how well planned otherwise and no matter how well woven. And on the choice of weave depend to a large extent the choices of material, pattern and color.

Weaves may be divided into three general groups: weaves in which the effect is in the warp, and the weft is subsidiary or entirely covered; weft-faced fabrics in which the effect is in the weft and the warp is largely or altogether covered by the weft; the fifty-fifty weaves in which warp and weft are the same or similar and the same number of weft shots are woven to the inch as there are threads to the inch in the setting of the warp in the reed. Most of the typical Colonial pattern weaves are of the weft-faced order, but for linens and all-wool fabrics the fifty-fifty weaves are best.

Among the popular pattern weaves of the weft-faced order, used for many purposes, are the "overshot" weave, the "summer-and-winter" weave, and "crackle" weave.

In the old day the overshot weave was used altogether for coverlets. It may also be used for window drapery and, with restrictions, for bags, pillow-tops, table-pieces and even for upholstery. It is an unsuitable weave for linens, dress-fabrics, all-wool fabrics or rugs. Summer-and-winter weave and crackle weave are suitable for coverlets and excellent also for upholstery and hangings and useable for rugs. These weaves are not suitable for linens or all-wool fabrics.

Rugs are most successful when woven in one or another of the special rug-weaves. None of the fifty-fifty weaves should be used for rugs.

For linens the best weaves are damask and double-faced twill, the "Bronson" or "spot" weave, "Ms and Os" and "Huck."

For tweeds the material must be a singles wool yarn usually known as "homespun," and the weave must be twill in one or another of its many variations.

(20) Summer-and-winter weave coverlet—"Snow-Ball" with "Pine Tree Border."

For scarves and light-weight fabrics for suits, shawls and the like, the weave may be any of the "fifty-fifty" weaves and the material worsted.

For patterns of the modern type the summer-and-winter weave is excellent—also the double weave and many of the pick-up weaves.

For upholstery one must have a closely combined, extremely firm fabric. The warp-faced and weft-faced reps are widely used. These are ribbed fabrics in which the warp is set close enough to cover the weft completely, making a warp-faced rep with the ribs running crosswise; or with the warp set far enough apart so that it is completely covered by the weft, to make a weft-faced rep with the ribs running lengthwise. The summer-and-winter weave is excellent for upholstery fabrics, as are double-faced twill and damask. The overshot weave is unsuitable except in patterns made up entirely of very short skips.

For belts and girdles and other small decorative pieces one or another of the pick-up weaves will give the most sprightly effects.

III *Choice of Material—Cottons*

The choice of weave often conditions the choice of material, though of course most materials may be used in a number of different weaves.

The following notes will not supply information on the composition and manufacture of yarns, as this information is contained in many technical books that may be consulted in the nearest public library, but will instead supply practical suggestions—taken from experience—to assist in the selection of materials for hand-weaving.

In a general way, the yarns used by hand-weavers should be of high quality. The chief cost of a hand-woven fabric is time, and it is a waste of time to weave poor material by hand. A hand-woven fabric can never be cheap, in competition with machine-made textiles of the same type. The hand-woven piece must be handsomer and more durable than the commercial product, more satisfactory for the purpose in mind, or it is not worth making. The quality of being "hand-made" has not in itself any particular virtue, and a handsome machine product is more desirable than a poor hand-woven one—except perhaps to the weaver.

As cottons make the foundation of so much of our work it seems suitable to consider them first.

Cotton has been a much misunderstood and underrated material among us, and has only of late begun to come into its own. To be sure, in very early Colonial days cotton was unobtainable and linen was used as a makeshift as flax could be grown by any homesteader, retted and broken and hackled and spun by the "domestic manufacturer," and in consequence many of the earliest coverlets have a tabby foundation in linen rather than in cotton. But cotton is much better for the purpose as linen is heavy and cold and combines very

(21) A simple arrangement of stars with a table. Similar to draft number 42.

ill with wool. After the British embargo on the shipment of yarns to the colonies was raised, and after the South began raising cotton, the material became relatively plentiful and linen went back to its proper uses.

Because it was plentiful among us and because it was less costly than other yarns, we seem to have felt that cotton was an inferior material. As a result we did not use it as cleverly as we might, or as it was used in other countries:

(22) Blazing Star (top) and Double Bow-Knot (bottom). Draft number 115.

and the manufacturers made little effort to give us the kinds of cotton we wanted for hand-weaving. Now, however, things are different. We have come to appreciate the endearing nature of cotton, and cotton manufacturers are supplying a variety of beautiful and useable yarns.

Cotton makes the most easily managed warp of any material—provided it is a good long-stapled cotton with sufficient twist. Egyptian cottons are the handsomest and strongest, but the "sea-island" cottons are also excellent. As warp, cotton has elasticity and does not require dressing. A beginner is well advised to choose cotton for his first warp.

For the traditional overshot weave Colonial coverlets, and also for window draperies and small articles such as bags, pillow-tops and the like, the most satisfactory warp is Egyptian cotton 24/3 at a setting of thirty ends to the inch. This material, when used for warp and tabby with pattern weft in homespun wool yarn, gives very much the texture and effect of the old coverlets.

Mercerized cottons are strong and handsome and may also be used for warp—though not for a period coverlet as the mercerizing process is a modern invention and the shine detracts from the traditional effect.

The soft, fairly heavy, pliable cotton fabrics of Guatemala are made by using very fine unmercerized cotton warp, threaded double and set so close that the weft is covered.

The soft-twist, unmercerized cottons are intended chiefly for weft, but make a beautiful warp when handled with discretion.

Cotton carpet warp is a harsh, rather unhandsome material and is used chiefly for very coarse fabrics and for fabrics in which the warp is covered by the weft—as, for instance, in weft-faced reps.

A plain tabby fabric in cotton is not very handsome or interesting and is used by American hand-weavers chiefly as the foundation weave for such pattern weaves as overshot and the summer-and-winter weave. But when done in stripes, checks or plaids in color the cotton tabby makes an excellent dress-fabric. Many fabrics of this sort come from Mexico and from Sweden, and the cotton tabby fabrics of Guatemala enlivened by patterns in tied-dying or "jaspé" are coming into popularity. American hand-weavers may some day find this field interesting, but with the many attractive machine-woven ginghams and printed cotton fabrics available at much lower cost this seems doubtful.

Cotton warps are sometimes woven with linen weft to produce a "union" fabric for towelling, table pieces and the like. This is a practise I do not recommend. Both materials lose their characteristic good qualities in the combination. And cotton does not combine well with silks or rayons.

When used as pattern weft in the overshot weave, mercerized cottons give fairly good results if the pattern chosen is one in which there are no long skips. Mercerized cotton is hard and slippery and the threads do not cling together, so that when woven in long skips the result is apt to be stringy. The softer unmercerized cottons are better for the purpose. Mercerized cottons may be used in the summer-and-winter weave, in which there are no long skips, though even here the dull-finished materials are, I think, better.

The "fancy" cottons may be used with great freedom, not to say abandon, in the weaving of drapery fabrics of all kinds.

Cotton chenille is an excellent material for rugs, and so are the heavy cottons with a fairly close twist. The soft and loosely twisted cotton "roving" some-

(23) The White Mountain coverlet. Draft number 19.

times sold under the name of "rug-filler," has been much used for rugs but is a poor material for the purpose as after a few washings it is apt to have a very bedraggled appearance.

To calculate the quantities of material required for a particular project it is necessary to know the yardage per pound of the material in question. For many materials these yardages are given by the manufacturers, but for cotton yarns the yardages are given in the "count" of the yarn, as 10/2, 24/3 and so on. Cotton counts are based on the ancient English—and entirely unmetric—base of 840. That is to say that a #1 singles cotton yarn runs 840 yards to the pound. A 20/2 yarn, composed of two threads of #20, runs 840 × 20 ÷ 2, or 8,400 yards to the pound, and a 24/3 runs 840 × 24 ÷ 3 or 6720 yards to the pound.

To determine the total yardage of a proposed warp use the following formula:
No. of warp-ends per inch × no. of inches in width × no. of yards in length.

For instance, suppose that the warp is to be of 24/3 cotton, at thirty ends to the inch, 20 inches wide and 20 yards long: 30 × 20 = 600 × 20 = 12000, which will be the total linear yardage in the warp. Dividing by the yardage per pound—in this case 6720—we get a result of 1.785 or about 1⅘ lbs.

If the material to be woven is a tabby fabric, the same quantity of material will be required for weft, except that there is a certain length of warp at the ends that goes unwoven and of course no weft material is required for this.

However, for any but a "fifty-fifty" fabric it is necessary to calculate the weft-yardages from a sample of the fabric to be woven. Use the following formula:
No. of weft-shots per inch × no. of inches in width × no. of yards in length.

For instance if the 20-inch warp figured above is to be woven in an overshot pattern and the sample shows twenty-four tabby shots to the inch, the calculation will be:
24 × 20 × 20 = 9,600 ÷ 6720. 1.428 or a little less than 1½ lbs.

In this instance there will also be 9,600 yards of pattern weft, probably in a wool or worsted yarn, and as these yarns are irregular it is necessary to have the manufacturer's figure of yardage per pound.

It is impractical, however, to calculate material too closely. If the material

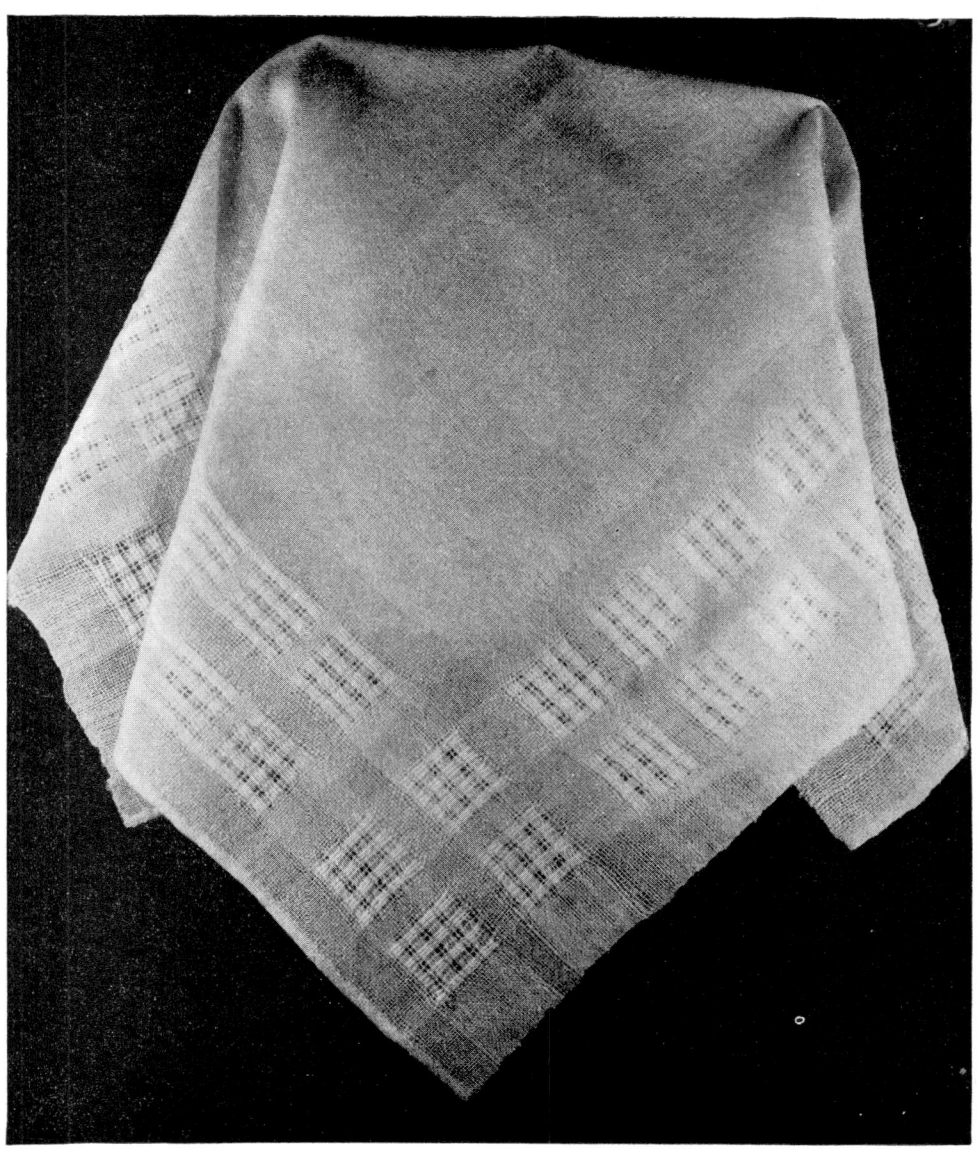

(24) Shawl with border in lace-Bronson weave.

is supplied on spools, the weights are "net" and there is no yardage in the weight of the spool. Also one may beat a little more closely than the sample and weave, perhaps twenty-five weft shots to the inch instead of twenty-four. There is also the possibility of wastage. It is cheaper to have a little material left over than to run a little short and have the loom tied up, perhaps for weeks, waiting for additional material. Left-overs may always be used in one way or another—for small pieces or for samples.

In calculating a warp it is always necessary to allow for shrinkage, take-up, and wastage, and it is also a good idea to warp an extra yard for samples and experiments. The wastage on a large loom need not be more than one yard and can hardly be less. Shrinkage differs with the material used and also with the beat—a solidly woven fabric shrinks less than an open fabric. An allowance of one additional yard to every ten will usually be enough, though not for springy wool and worsted yarns. Here again it is wise to figure generously rather than to take the risk of running a little short.

IV *Wool and Worsted*

Wool and worsted yarns are used extensively in hand-weaving—in combination with cotton for coverlets, rugs, and many small articles, and by itself for tweeds and other suitings, for scarves, hoods and the like.

The differences between wool and worsted yarns are in the manufacture and in the resulting textures. Wool yarns are made much in the same way that hand-spun yarns are made—simply by carding and twisting the wool fibres as they come from the sheep. Worsted yarns are made from long-stapled fibres, specially treated and loosely twisted to make them light and fluffy. Some worsted yarns are mercerized to give them a high lustre.

Whether to use a wool or a worsted yarn for a particular project depends, of course, on the type of fabric one wishes to produce. In Colonial times there were no worsted yarns, and mercerizing was unknown; for a strictly "Colonial" coverlet, therefore, one should use a wool yarn for the pattern weft. Tweeds, also, are made of wool yarns—the wool singles known as homespun. If a worsted yarn is used the resulting fabric is not tweed. Wool yarns are also best for rugs, for automobile blankets and fabrics for upholstery, due to their superior wearing qualities. Worsted yarns are best for scarves, baby-blankets and smooth-finished dress-fabrics. Worsted yarns are available in great profusion, in many kinds and in every imaginable color, but for good wool yarns in any variety we may have to send to Canada. The "Harris" yarn from which the famous Harris tweeds are woven may be obtained from Scotland. This is a wool yarn with a peculiarly hard and wiry quality, due to the admixture of wool from Highland sheep. American and Canadian wool yarns are softer than Harris, and though excellent, do not produce the same texture or amazing durability.

There are also innumerable mixed yarns on the market—combinations of wool and cotton, wool and rayon and so on. To make certain of a 100 per cent wool yarn it is easy to make the following test: prepare a strong alkaline solu-

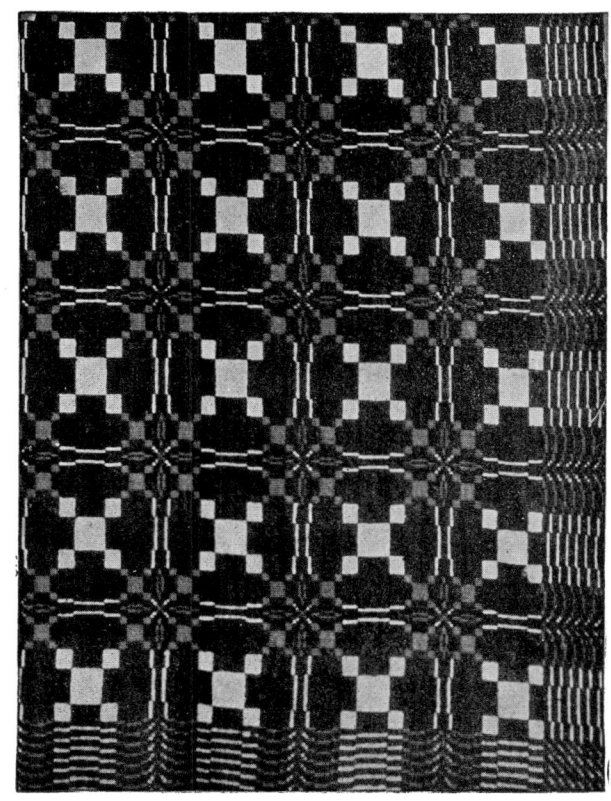

(25) Wheel and Star, ancient double weaving, Newark Museum. Draft number 195.

tion with lye and water, and put into it a strand of the questioned material. If the yarn dissolves completely it is all wool; if there is a residue it is not.

In the old day wool was sometimes used in combination with linen—in coverlets and for the heavy, stiff fabric called "linsey-woolsey" used for workclothes. This was not from choice but chiefly due to the fact that in very early times in the Colonies cottons were unobtainable and flax could be produced on the homestead acres. A linen warp is sometimes used for upholstery fabrics woven in wool, but in a general way wool and linen are antagonistic and should rarely if ever be used in combination.

The chief uses for wool and worsted warns are for all-wool fabrics such as tweeds, serge suitings, fabric for sports shirts, for scarves, shawls, blankets and so on.

People sometimes hesitate to attempt a wool warp because of the supposed difficulties, but when proper warp-yarns are used and correctly handled a wool warp need give no more trouble than one of cotton.

Extremely soft, loosely twisted and fuzzy yarns should not be used for warp, even when treated with warp-dressing as explained below, because they fuzz in the reed and break. There are few things more tiresome than mending broken warp-ends at each shoot of the shuttle, and no doubt an unhappy experience with a poorly chosen and badly handled warp is the reason for the wariness some weavers feel toward warping in wool. A hard-twisted yarn, such as "Fabri" makes an ideal warp for light worsted fabrics. Homespun yarns are supplied in both warp and weft qualities. The warp homespun may be used to advantage for both warp and weft in tweeds as it is harder and stronger than the weft homespun; but the weft homespun should never be used for warp.

Wool and worsted yarns are supplied in skeins rather than on spools or cops, for the reason that if left spooled for any length of time the yarn loses its life and elasticity. The same applies to a warp wound on the warp-beam. These yarns should be spooled and warped only when ready to use, and should be woven off as rapidly as possible.

A warp such as the Fabri yarn referred to above need not be treated with warp-dressing but should be kept damp during weaving. A homespun warp should always be dressed. There are a number of commercial warp-dressings on the market but as a rule these can be bought only in wholesale lots, and

(26) The Rebecca Garrison coverlet from North Carolina. Draft number 69.

most hand-weavers prepare their own dressing by boiling flaxseed in water. Exact proportions do not matter. The resulting solution should be strained to remove the seeds and should be diluted with water if necessary to give it the consistency of thin starch. The skeins of warp-yarn may be soaked in this solution and permitted to dry before the warp is spooled and beamed, or the warp-chain—if this method of warping is used—may be soaked and dried before beaming, or the warp may be beamed and the dressing applied to the stretched warp with a sponge or cloth as weaving progresses. And even if dressed the warp should be kept damp during weaving.

My practise is to dampen thoroughly the part of the stretched warp between the heddles and the back beam, just before releasing the tension and winding up the woven web. When the web has been wound back the dampened part of the warp will be in the heddles. Then I again dampen the back part of the warp and lay a wet bath-towel over the back-beam and forward for a few inches.

It is highly important to release the tension when the loom is not in use—even when one leaves the loom for a short time only. And in weaving wool or worsted the beat should be kept light.

The overshot weave, the summer-and-winter weave, crackle weave and so on—in general the pattern weaves ordinarily woven on a cotton foundation—are unsuited to all-wool fabrics. The best weaves for all-wool textiles will be found in what we call the "fifty-fifty" group—weaves in which warp and weft are the same, or at any rate the same in grist, woven with the same number of weft shots to the inch as there are warp-ends to the inch in the setting.

People sometimes make the mistake of combining several kinds of yarn in a fabric for clothing—worsted, perhaps, with a worsted-and-rayon yarn. Sometimes this can be done successfully, but the resulting fabric is certain to present a difficult problem in finishing as various yarns have different rates of shrinkage. If the warp is all of one yarn and the weft all of another the difficulty is less than when the yarns are combined in both warp and weft. If a mixed fabric is contemplated it is wise to weave a large sample before making the set-up, see how it looks when off the loom, wash and press it and judge the result.

Another point is this: if a smooth fabric in plain tabby is to be woven the warp-yarn and weft-yarn used should be twisted in opposite directions, otherwise when finished the fabric will have a crepey effect. The right-hand or "Z" twist is usually the warp-twist and the left-hand or "S" twist the weft-twist, but this does not seem to be an invariable rule. In a yarn made up of several strands if the twist given in doubling is in the same direction as the twist of the separate strands a hard yarn results. If the doubling twist is opposite to the twist of the strands a softer yarn is produced. Some crepe

— 59

(27) Granite State. Draft number 56.

(28) The Walls of Jericho. Draft number 104.

fabrics are made by combining Z-twist and S-twist yarns in certain arrangements in both warp and weft. For a twilled or otherwise patterned fabric little attention need be paid to using yarns of opposite twist in warp and weft though the effect of observing this difference is somewhat better and more clear-cut. In a rough fabric like tweed this is unimportant but in a smooth fabric such as serge the rule should be observed.

All-wool fabrics should always be washed when taken from the loom. Wool yarns are usually quite greasy and require thorough scouring, but an all-worsted fabric should also be washed, to give it a finish and to permit it to shrink. Use mild soap and lukewarm water and wash by squeezing the soapy water through and through the cloth. In old days the cloth was put in a tub of soapy water and washed by trampling with the feet, and wool fabrics were also treated in a fulling mill which had the effect of felting the fabric. The nap was raised by brushing with teasles. For most fabrics we make, however, washing and a light pressing while the fabric is still damp gives all the finish required. Or the piece of yardage may be taken to a tailor shop and steam pressed after washing. The washing, however, should never be omitted; dry-cleaning does not give the same finish.

V Linens

New weavers are apt to approach the making of a linen warp with even more misgivings than a wool warp. But it is true for linens, as for wool, that if treated correctly the material need not be any more troublesome than cotton. Linen has always seemed to me like a very worthy but stubborn person—when handled "along the grain" all is well, but when treated in an adverse manner there are dire repercussions. It is perfectly true that one can get into more kinds of trouble with a linen warp than with any other muddle I know of—but this need not happen.

When there is trouble this is usually the result of using an unsuitable warp. A good warp-linen costs a great deal more than even the best weft-linens, and one is sometimes tempted. However, as warping with weft-linen usually ends in cutting the whole thing off the loom and throwing it away, to do this is hardly an economy.

There are three main types of linen in general use among hand-weavers: (1) "singles" or "line" linens; (2) plied or "round" linens; (3) "floss" linens —plied but not as hard twisted as round linens and somewhat flattened in finishing; sometimes mercerized.

Floss linens are used chiefly for weft, and round linens are more freely used for warp by weavers than other linens because of their strength and

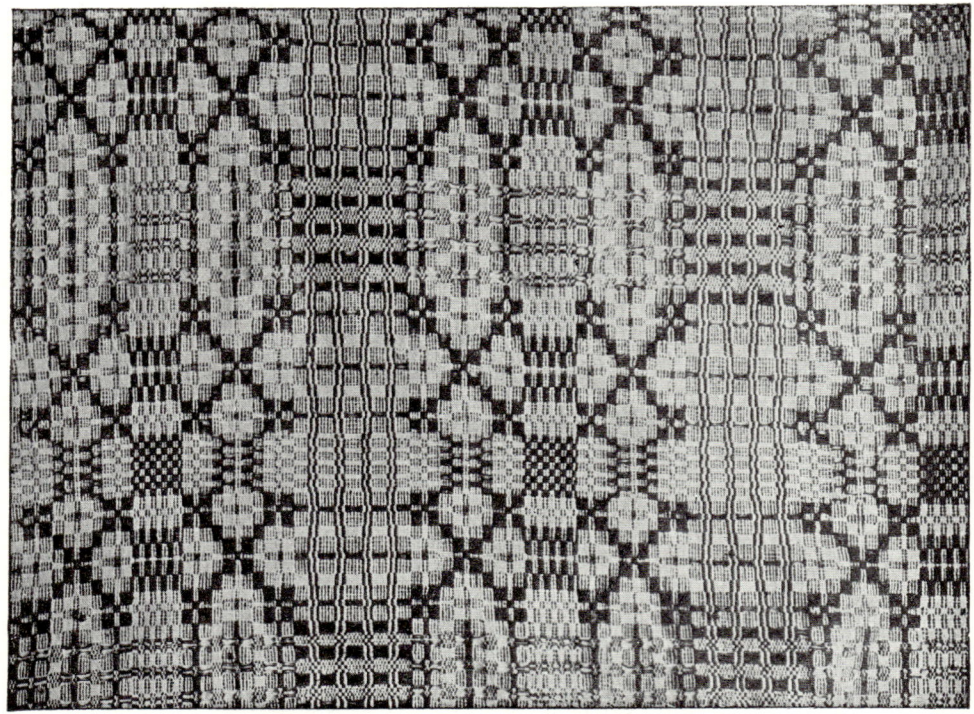

(29) Pattern similar to Rose of Sharon. An ancient coverlet in the Newark Museum.

smoothness and the relative ease in handling. However, a singles linen fabric has an interesting, slightly irregular texture that for many things is handsomer than the somewhat wiry texture of a piece in round linen.

Linen is extremely refractory to dyeing, and dyers have told me that to get a strong dark color on linen it is sometimes necessary to use equal weights of yarn and dye-stuff. For this reason colored linens are very expensive and run largely to pastel shades. But linen is so beautiful in itself, either in natural "grey" which seems to include the yellowish shade of some unbleached linens, or in bleached white, or in a combination of the two, that for many purposes it is perhaps as well to use the material only in these shades leaving color-effects to cotton, wool and other materials.

A warp of round linen does not require dressing, but must be kept thoroughly dampened during weaving. Singles linen warps, however, must be dressed as well as woven wet. Linen has a great affinity for water. When completely dry it becomes brittle and has no elasticity; a single incautious thump with the batten may snap a dozen warp-ends, which is extremely annoying. When wet it becomes slightly elastic and the danger of snapped threads is less. But it is never wise to hammer linen.

When damp it is possible to put a reasonable tension on a linen warp—enough to give a clear shed without sagging threads to catch the shuttle and spoil the weave. But if a stretched warp is permitted to dry out this elasticity disappears and one may return to the loom after an hour or two to find a large number of snapped threads. It is urgently necessary to release the tension when leaving the loom even for a short time.

The same flaxseed warp-dressing described in the previous chapter may be used for linen as well as for wool. As linens are usually supplied on spools or cops the dressing must be applied as one weaves, unless a chained warp is made and dressed before beaming.

The weaves best suited to linen are those in the "fifty-fifty" class, as for all-wool fabrics. This rules out the overshot weave, summer-and-winter, crackle weave and so on. It is true that these weaves are sometimes used with a measure of success for borders in tabby linen towels and mats, but should be avoided as a rule. If the overshot weave is used in this manner a pattern should be chosen in which there are no long skips. The summer-and-winter weave produces a closely combined fabric without long skips, but the effect when woven in linen is that of a poor damask and is not satisfactory.

The handsomest weave for linen is, perhaps, damask. But for even a simple two-block pattern in this weave eight or ten harnesses are required, and for a four-block pattern sixteen or twenty harnesses. Very few hand-looms carry as many harnesses as this, and damasks are usually woven on draw-looms. A "four-heddle damask" requires four harnesses for each pattern block and the richer, handsomer, "five-heddle damask," five harnesses to the block.

To be sure patterns as elaborate as one chooses may be woven in damask by the pick-up method, as will be explained in the chapter on pick-up weaving, but this is a rather slow process and though useful for small pieces and borders would be toilsome for a large tablecloth.

(30) Wheel and Diamond Square. An ancient coverlet from New Jersey.

Double-faced twill is an excellent weave for linen and when done in the 2-1 "jeans" twill takes fewer harnesses than damask—three harnesses to the pattern block instead of four or five. Such patterns as those on diagram 44 may be produced in this weave on nine harnesses, and the four-block patterns on twelve. The weave is richer, however, when woven in 3-1 twill with four harnesses to the block.

The "spot" weave or "Bronson" weave is an excellent weave for linens. It was much used in the old day and many old pieces are still to be found in museums and among family heirlooms. Interesting pattern effects may be produced in this weave on simple equipment. Though more interesting patterns may be woven on eight harnesses than on four, there are a number of good four-harness effects.

Other four-harness weaves for linen are the "Huck" weave in one or another of its many variations—such as the handsome "Rain-Drops" pattern—and the "Ms and Os" weave, also in a number of variations.

A plain tabby fabric is handsome in linen.

In all the above weaves, warp and weft should be the same or at any rate the same in grist. Some weavers use a round linen for warp, woven with a singles weft in the same grist,—a 40/2 warp, for instance, woven with a #20 singles weft. This is permissible but not, I think, the best practise. It is better to weave a round linen warp with round linen weft, and singles with singles.

Linen counts, for some unknown reason, are figured on a base of 300 instead of 840 like cottons. A #1 singles linen runs 300 yards to the pound, and a 40/2 linen runs 40 × 300 divided by 2, or 6,000 yards to the pound.

(31) Coverlet pattern Velvet Rose.
Draft number 147.

Calculations for quantities of material are made as described in the previous chapter, but as most of the weaves used are "fifty-fifty" weaves the same quantity of warp and weft are required, less the inevitable warp-wastage.

A matter of importance is the proper finishing of linens after they are taken off the loom. Linen must always be washed, and this washing should be much more severe than in the case of all-wool fabrics. It is well to soak a new piece of linen for several hours or overnight, rub it out vigorously in mild soapsuds, rinse, and iron while still quite damp, going over and over the piece on either side till it is perfectly dry. Linens grow handsomer with each washing for a long time, so the first washing cannot well be too severe. Linen when it comes from the loom has a rather harsh and open appearance as the threads do not beat as close as cotton or wool. Washing brings the threads together and gives the fabric firmness, and the heavy ironing brings out the

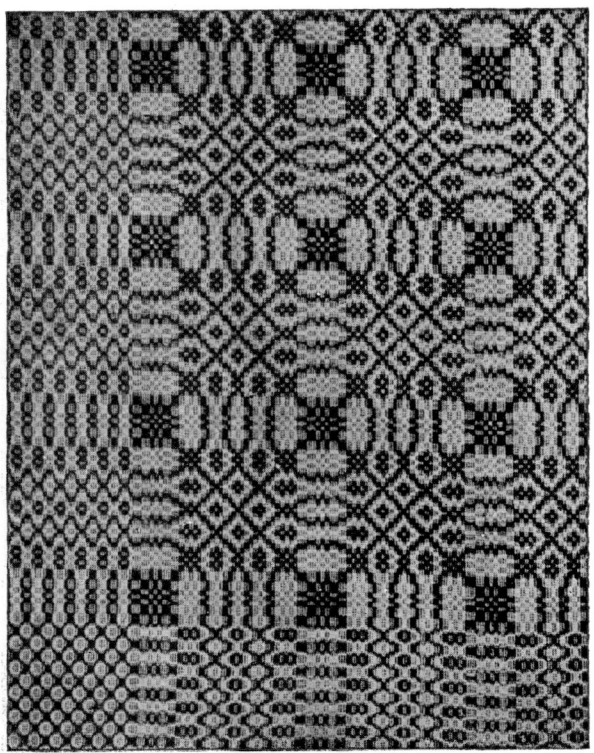

(32) Lover's Knot. Draft number 79.

silky sheen. This first washing should be considered part of the manufacturing process and should never be omitted.

Oddly enough, linen combines very pleasantly with silks, rayon and nylon yarns for draperies and similar fabrics. Very rough, coarse linens may be used as warp, woven with heavy rayon "art silk" to produce an unusual and distinctive fabric.

Ramie, a plant-fibre somewhat similar to linen, is a very pleasant material with many of the good qualities of linen without some of the disadvantages. Very beautiful hemp yarns are sometimes to be had. These should be woven in exactly the same way as linen. Most jute is too coarse and stiff for more than a limited use in hand-weaving, but the finer jute yarns make a good warp for some kinds of rug-weaving.

VI Synthetic Yarns

The synthetic yarns are becoming more and more interesting to hand-weavers. Rayon of several kinds, and other "artificial silks" we have had for a long time, of course, but every day brings new developments and a great deal of experimental work will have to be done before the new materials find their place in our art.

The heavy, shiny rayon art silk always seemed to me a disagreeable material until I saw it combined with a rough tow warp. The combination was unexpectedly handsome. "Wool-spun" rayon is an excellent material—exceedingly strong and durable and without the specious glitter of rayon art silk. The new wool-spun nylons are even finer. This will prove a marvellous material for dress fabrics when it becomes more available.

The plastic yarns are interesting for some purposes and not too difficult to weave. They may be used for bags, mats, and even—in a leno mesh—for window-screening. The difficulty in weaving with this material is, of course, the stiffness and the difficulty in beating it together firmly enough. I found that the best way to do this was to hold the reed, after the beat, hard against the edge of the web till the shed had been changed. This prevented the weft from springing back after the beat. The coarser plastic yarns I found excellent for knotting and braiding.

Yarns made of spun glass are occasionally offered. I have never woven with this material myself, but those who have done so complain of sore fingers as a result of getting microscopic splinters of glass under the skin. Perhaps this material will some day be improved and will offer some special advantages, but at present it appears to be still in the experimental stage.

Cellophane in strips was at one time used a good deal for table mats—a fashion I was glad to see die out as the fabric seemed to me meretricious, though if woven over a leno warp a similar fabric might have some attractions as window-drapery. Glitter is its outstanding quality. The chief use for cellophane at present seems to be in the non-tarnishing "metallic" threads. These are being woven into many fabrics to give them glitter. All well enough for a silk or rayon fabric for evening bags, perhaps, but I confess that when glitter is woven into linen table pieces I feel unhappy. Linen is such a beautiful material, and so long lasting; it seems a pity to give it a tinselly effect like something on a Christmas tree. However this is a highly personal opinion and there are many who differ with me.

(33) Lee's Surrender. Draft number 107.

We hear of yarns made from milk and of yarns made from this and that, more or less in the experimental stage. Some of these may prove to have lasting merit and some may not. In any case it is wise to do a good deal of experimental work with any unfamiliar material before embarking on a large project. Those who enjoy "trying things" may find this work interesting and profitable. Those, however, who are interested chiefly in producing useable and handsome fabrics may do well to confine their efforts to the materials that have proved their worth and usefulness. A time may come when it will not be necessary to raise sheep in order to have warm clothing and fluffy blankets, when there need be no blue-flowered flax in the fields or snowy bolls of cotton, and all our yarns will be poured out of a vat or spun from a ladle, but that time is probably still far away and in the meantime we have a wealth of yarns of every conceivable texture and color to use in our work.

VII Warp-Setting

Though the texture of a fabric may seem to depend primarily on the choice of weave and material, the setting of the warp in the reed—the number of warp-ends per inch—is perhaps the most important factor in the problem of texture. To beginners it is a difficult problem because no rules can be laid down, and it is impossible to make a schedule of settings for particular materials, because the same material may be set in many different ways with entirely different results. As we have seen, if the warp is set far apart so that it is completely covered by the weft we have a weft-faced rep, which is a heavy, firm fabric suitable for upholstery but entirely unsuitable for most other purposes. If the warp is set so close that the weft is completely covered we have a warp-faced rep— also a firm, heavy fabric. If we set the warp at such a distance apart that it can be woven in the "fifty-fifty" manner we have a tabby fabric. But we may make a firm tabby with the warp set close and a very firm beat or we may make a light, open tabby with the warp set farther apart and a light beat. All that is possible is to give rule-of-thumb settings—settings for certain warp materials in certain weaves that usually give satisfactory results. Directions of this type are given in the chapters dealing with the various weaves.

Most new looms when received are supplied with only one reed—usually a

(34) Single Chariot-Wheel woven as drawn in. Note the diagonal. Draft number 80A.

reed with fifteen dents to the inch which may be used for settings of fifteen ends to the inch, or double-sleyed for settings of thirty ends to the inch. People sometimes sley a warp double-and-single, that is to say two threads in the first dent, one in the second, two in the third, one in the fourth, and so on. For some kinds of pattern weaving this is allowable, but for the plain weave it is impractical as the resulting fabric is in streaks that do not readily wash out.

Weavers who have only one reed must confine themselves to weaves and materials that may be correctly sleyed through that reed. But those who like to use a variety of materials and a variety of weaves should provide themselves with additional reeds as previously noted.

The reed any individual weaver finds most useful depends, of course, on the material habitually used and the type of fabric woven.

If it should happen that a piece on the loom seems not quite right in texture—too open, for instance, or too dense, too "warpy" or with too little warp showing—try a different reed and a more open or a closer setting.

We once had an interesting object lesson on setting at one of my classes; we had two looms set up to patterns in crackle weave, on one the setting was far too close and on the other not nearly close enough. We made samples of each and then reset the warps correctly and wove samples. This made a very valuable demonstration of what not to do, and why not—one that anybody might repeat for himself to advantage.

Chapter Five: Choice of Pattern and Color

Though, as we have seen, the most important choices in the design of a new fabric are weave and material, and though satisfactory fabrics may be made without a definite pattern figure, and in all-black or all-white—which are not, properly speaking, colors at all—most fabrics depend on pattern and color for interest and charm.

I Choice of Pattern

Many people appear to be afraid of pattern, as others are afraid of color, and it is entirely true that when badly used both pattern and color may be acutely distressing, so there are grounds for fear. But if people approach the subject with confidence in their instinctive pleasure-pain reactions, as children and savages do, without attempting to follow rules or to rationalize, they rarely go wrong.

Some people are pattern-blind as others are color-blind, but these conditions are infrequent. Most normal people have an inborn need of both pattern and color.

Nature rarely makes anything without pattern. Pattern is simply the flowering of orderly arrangement and is part of the fundamental geometry of the universe. An unpatterned world is inconceivable.

This is not the place for a discussion of decorative design, but I should like to make the practical suggestion that those who are without training in this field of art and who feel the lack may acquire an awareness of pattern and a cultivated taste quite easily, simply by spending a little time in turning over the pages of books on historic and modern ornament such as may be found in any public library. It is even more helpful to make tracings of figures and decorative details that strike the fancy.

Pattern has the function of adding interest to life and comfort to the eye by breaking up plain surfaces and by adding spots of excitement to an otherwise dull effect. But too violent or too complete a breaking up of plain surfaces may be very unpleasant. Too much pattern—especially too much of the *same* pattern—may create an effect that is hard to bear.

I once saw a long corridor carpeted in a very vigorous modern design of angles and slanted lines. I was told that—though the piece was machine woven—the pattern had been taken from a rug woven by a distinguished hand-weaver. In a small rug, planned to enliven a dull corner, this would have been very handsome, but yards and yards of it, in a remorseless procession of triangulations were enough to give a sensitive person indigestion.

Another outstanding example of the misuse of pattern has always seemed to me the "hand-woven" bedroom at the White House, once pictured in a double-page, colored spread in *Ladies' Home Journal*. The pattern used was the honest but rather stodgy figure known as "Sun, Moon and Stars" (draft number 74), done in Colonial blue. There are blue wheels on the coverlet, which is all very well, but the same blue wheels are all over the floor, and blue wheels—standing on their rims—all up and down the window-casings, blue wheels on the dresser, blue wheels everywhere the tortured eye comes to rest. That room must be hard to live in.

So economy and variation should be watchwords in the use of pattern.

Patterns should be functional as far as that is possible and should conform to the shape and style of the surroundings and the article to be decorated. It has always seemed to me that the choice of the handsome old "Wheel of Fortune" pattern as a dress for the old wing chair in illustration (35) was a mistake. The pattern is too insistent and does not set off the architectural lines of the chair. The pattern of the piece used on the settle, illustration (36), is more agreeable.

In the early days of our revival of hand-weaving the old Colonial patterns were used in many unsuitable ways—for portières, for instance, where they gave the somewhat painful effect of an old blanket hung in a door to keep out the cold; and for coat-fabrics which suggested having cut up grandmother's

(35) The wing chair is upholstered in "Wheel of Fortune." See draft number 193.

old bedspread to walk about in. Fortunately these things are no longer being done.

Patterns of the Colonial type are, with few exceptions, symmetrical between two centers and completely static. The modern taste finds this balance somewhat stiff and a bit prim. Modern design has a far more subtle balance and usually has a motion either to the left or to the right. It is more exciting, less self-satisfied, far more intricate—even when it appears simpler—than the more ancient art. Also it is a great deal more difficult—which may be one of the reasons for the escape from pattern by the so-called "texture" weavers.

There is great charm in the patterns of the old coverlets. These things were practically the only art expression of that austere time and in them flowered the

(36) "What materials to use for a given piece of work depends on taste."
A piece of coverlet weaving in a chariot-wheel pattern used for cover of settle.

love of beauty that is in all hearts. In their amazing variety they seem to have grown as naturally as flowers, or frost crystals—these old patterns—and thanks to the limitations of the simple four-harness looms on which they were made, and the overshot weave with its four square blocks in which they were woven, none of the old patterns are ugly. Take four squares that may be of different sizes—within strict limits—and arrange them symmetrically in any order you please, and a plesant pattern will result. It is impossible to go wrong, though of course some arrangements will be more pleasing than others.

The old patterns are curiously like music; like little melodies of four notes, full of runs, trills and returns. When noted down on paper they *look* like music, so that one feels it should be possible to play them on a violin or to sing them. There is a story of a new weaver who had a loom but no pattern draft, so threaded her loom to Mendelssohn's "Spring Song." And perhaps some day an American composer will write a "Weavers' Symphony" with "Whig Rose" or "Pine Bloom" for motif over the whirr of the shuttle and the dull thump of the batten for accompaniment—embroidered all over and in and out with the weaver's thoughts, gay or sad or contemplative.

Many of us—most of us, perhaps—still feel happier and more comfortable with the simple old patterns than with the exciting new ones that, though sometimes very beautiful, are often extremely hideous, and almost always slightly insane. It is a matter of taste.

Oddly enough—or perhaps not oddly at all—the patterns we find among the textiles of ancient Peru, of Mexico and Guatemala suit modern interiors very well. They have the off-center rhythms, the bold stylizations of natural forms, the spirit and humor that fit delightfully into modern ways. And these old, old patterns—so much more ancient than the stars and roses of the Colonial coverlets—were a part of America long before the days of the Pilgrims or, for that matter, before the days of Columbus. Tradition means a great deal in design. A figure that was in the beginning probably a symbol with deep meanings and that has come down to us through hundreds of years, satisfying the love of order and beauty in many, many hearts, is something that can be counted upon to give pleasure again. To have survived through the centuries it must answer to something fundamental in us. It is a part of our rich inheritance.

(37) The Tuning-Fork coverlet (double weaving).
Draft number 184.

A few practical suggestions: for the main piece in a large room it is wise to select a small, rather formal pattern, depending on small pieces of a different type to provide accents. For a small room a large pattern is best. To give added height to a room that seems oppressively low, window draperies in perpendicular lines of color or pattern are desirable. For the ugly, tall, narrow windows in some of the old houses we still live in, draperies in horizontal bands are

(38) Two-warp runner rug in blue, green, orange, brown and tan. Pick-up weaving, Peruvian motifs.

better. If the room is dull, the pattern used should be sprightly or perhaps even shocking; if the room is unrestful bring it peace with something bland and mild. And avoid like the plague the impulse to make everything match. We know these things instinctively, but we do not always have the courage to follow our instincts.

II Choice of Color

No matter what anybody says, there can be no hard-and-fast rules about the use of color—except the rule to "try it and see." Our pleasure-pain reactions to color are conditioned by time and place, by tradition, by the fashion of the moment. Color combinations that give us keen pleasure today would have pained our Victorian forbears, while their liver colored or oatmeal colored plain walls seem to us extremely depressing. Not long ago the soft greys of Japanese art were the height of fashion; today we prefer the more robust color schemes of China and old Peru. It is impossible to take a color chart and a slide rule and arrive at an always pleasing result by mixing so much of this with so much of that. This is especially true in weaving because as a rule the colors used do not stand sharply apart but interweave and produce quite unpredictable secondary shades that may either help or ruin the effect.

Unfortunately we are not all equipped with a reliable color-sense. I believe, however, that most of us can safely trust our eyes if we free them from inhibitions. Somebody has told us that this color does not "go" with that, so when we see them together, instead of looking at them with an open mind, we shudder. If there is any rule about color it is this: any color or colors may be combined with any other color or colors provided the proportions are so adjusted that the effect is pleasing.

It is also true that colors may be combined practically at will provided all are strong, clear shades. The introduction of a single dull shade into such a combination, however, may spell disaster, and it is for that reason that the interweaving of colors in the web is so important.

Dull colors are far more difficult to combine agreeably than are brilliant colors, but the raw primary shades are rarely attractive. The Chinese color scale that—instead of the primary colors—uses for each two shades, is far more

(39) Two-warp rug, green, orange and tan, 10-harness "Step" pattern. Two repeats, draft (d¹) Diagram 61.

pleasing. Not a primary red, for instance, but an orangy red and a purplish red; not a primary green but a yellow-green and a blue-green—and so on.

It is usually a mistake to combine a color with equal quantities of its exact opposite. The result is not, as might be expected, a sharp contrast but results instead in a muddy greyish tone that is usually far from interesting. Therefore it is wise to avoid combinations of greens with their directly opposite reds—an unhappy combination which for some unaccountable reason appears to be first choice with people unused to dealing with color. The blues with their directly opposite yellows should also be avoided.

In Colonial times the color problem was extremely simple: what was not blue, dyed in the family indigo-vat, was red or rose, dyed with madder. Occasionally some hardy soul seeking novelty might dye her yarn brown with walnut shells. With this restricted palette the Colonial weaver would have found it difficult to commit color atrocities. With us today the thing is far more complicated as we are provided with materials in thousands of shades. But even so we are unlikely to go far wrong—unless we suffer from definite color-blindness—if we overcome our fear of color and trust our reactions.

A practical suggestion: a weaver who has had the misfortune to produce a color-monstrosity—things sometimes look very different on the loom than off—may save the day by treating the offending piece to a light dye-bath in a shade selected to bring warring colors into harmony, or a shade to strengthen one color and subdue another. Some very pleasant effects may be obtained in this fashion. I knew a weaver who made a practise of buying remnants of yarn at reduced rates, often in atrocious colors, and weaving them together indiscriminately, depending on an after-weaving dying to produce harmony. I do not recommend this as a regular practise as it is not always successful, but in an emergency it may serve.

Chapter Six: Setting up the Loom

Having discussed hand-weaving in some of its phases and having, it is hoped, a good loom standing ready; having chosen a pattern and materials, we seem to be ready for the major adventure of "dressing the loom."

In dressing the loom four processes are involved: I, warping; II, drawing-in through the heddles; III, sleying through the reed; IV, tying in to the cloth-beam.

I *Warping*

There are several methods of warping: some good; some poor but useable; some vicious. Warping is to most weavers the least interesting and the most troublesome step in the textile process, so it would appear that the quickest and easiest method—other things being equal—ought to be the method to use. This is undoubtedly the "sectional" method by which the warp is measured and beamed in one simple operation. Some weavers who cling to the old ways insist —sometimes with a good deal of heat—that a good warp cannot be made by the sectional process, but they are mistaken. As a matter of fact, a better warp, with less wear on the warp-material, may be made sectionally than in any other way, and the saving in time and effort is worth considering. To measure off a long, wide warp as for a pair of coverlets, using the warping board, would take over a day, and to beam the warp, with three helpers, would take most of another day. With the help of the sectional-beam the same thing can be done, by one person, in about two hours.

To be sure, for short warps and special warps of one kind and another, it is convenient to use the warping board, but for a real job of warping the sectional method is best.

For sectional warping the loom must be equipped with a sectional beam, described in Chapter Three, and also a spool-rack or creel. A tensioner is useful but not absolutely necessary.

To warp, set the creel about four feet behind the loom and parallel with the back-beam. As most beams are divided into sections that correspond to two inches in the reed, arrange in the creel a number of spools of warp equal to the warp-ends in two inches of the proposed fabric. For instance, if the warp is a fine cotton to be set thirty ends to the inch, allow sixty spools. In arranging the spools on the wires of the creel make certain that they all turn in the same direction. Next thread the ends from the spools through the holes in the guide, taking them in order and arranging them so that they will not cross. If a tensioner is not used the guide—usually a metal plate punched with holes—should be set upright in the groove along the top of the back-beam. If a tensioner is used, the guide is part of the tensioner, and after going through the guide the threads should be taken over and under the tension pegs—not as a group but alternately, the first thread under and over, the second thread over and under, and so on.

The tensioner or guide should be set up opposite the center of the loom, and a middle section should be warped first. Some warp-beams are equipped with a tape or cord in each section, and some with a bar attached to the beam. In either case bring the "bout" of threads down over the back-beam and attach to the tapes or bar.

If a tensioner is used the warp may simply be wound on the beam by making as many revolutions of the beam as may be required for the desired yardage. Sectional beams are usually a yard in circumference—small beams are impractical—and each revolution of the beam makes a yard of warp. Watch the warp as it goes on to make sure that no threads catch on the pegs of the beam.

If no tensioner is used the bout of warp must be held in a holder or between the fingers to insure a sufficient tension, and the person doing the holding must be careful to keep each section at exactly the same tension or there will be trouble with the weaving.

(40) Irish Chain. Draft number 89.

When the desired yardage has been reached for the first section, loop the bout of threads around a peg with two half-hitches, cut the bout and attach it in the next section. Move the tensioner or guide to a position directly over the second section and proceed as before. Continue in this manner, working from the center toward the sides till the desired width of warp has been beamed.

In sectional warping it is unnecessary to take off a "lease," as the warp goes on in a smooth flat ribbon and may be threaded without danger of crosses. If one wishes, a strip of gummed paper tape may be pasted across the bout before it is looped over a peg and cut. This will keep the ends in regular order.

Chained warps are made on a warping board or drum. The drum is used for large warps, and is unnecessary equipment if the sectional method of warping is used. Every weaver should, however, have a warping board for small occasional warps. A sketch of such a board is shown on Diagram 2. Usually a capacity of five or six yards will serve. The group of extra pegs at each end of the warp are for the cross or lease which must always be put in to keep the threads in order. A chained warp would become hopelessly tangled without the lease. Sometimes the lease is made at one end only, but it is a convenience to have a lease at each end. (See Diagram No. 2.)

To make the warp, attach the thread to the peg at the lower end, and take it back and forth over the pegs as indicated on the sketch. After each ten, or twenty, or fifty ends have been warped—according to convenience—a counting tie should be made through the cross as shown on the sketch, at (a^1). When the desired number of ends has been reached, make additional ties as shown at

(41) Bonaparte's March. Draft number 20.

(b^1), (b^1), on the sketch. Now grasp the warp a foot or so from the end and release it from the end pegs. Loop it together with a sort of chain stitch as indicated at (c). It is then ready for beaming.

The best method of beaming a chained warp is by means of a "raddle," which is like a coarse comb or a half-reed with a removable top member. The raddle ordinarly has four spaces to the inch, and should be the width of the loom or at any rate as wide as the proposed warp. Attach it firmly to the back-beam of the loom and arrange the warp-ends in the spaces or dents of the raddle. Clamp down the top-member so that the warp cannot slide out of the dents, and attach the warp-ends to the bar of the warp-beam. Spread the warp and put two sticks—the lease-sticks—one on either side of the cross behind the raddle, and if a second lease has been made, two sticks through this cross also. If the warp is short and there is space, unchain the warp for its full length and have an assistant hold it at a tension over the sticks while another assistant turns the beam to roll up the warp and a third person draws the first set of lease sticks along the warp to take out any twists or tangles or loose threads.

In beaming a chained warp it is necessary to roll up with the warp a number of small sticks, or—which I consider better practise—to roll in a length of heavy paper all the way. Wrapping paper or two or three thicknesses of newspaper will serve, though for a very close-set warp it may be desirable to roll in a few turns of corrugated wrapping paper now and then. The paper, of course, must be wider than the warp. The reason for using the sticks or the paper is that on a plain beam the edge threads tend to run tighter than the rest of the warp and any weaving done on such a warp has a hammocky effect that is anything but satisfactory. If a chained warp is beamed to a sectional beam it is usually unnecessary to insert sticks—paper is, of course, impossible because of the pegs dividing the sections.

A method of beaming a chained warp, used by some weavers, is to work from the front of the loom, taking the warp first through the reed and then through the heddles. The reed acts then as a raddle. After threading, the warp is attached to the warp-beam, after passing over the back-beam, and is then wound on—together with sticks or a strip of paper as described. The objection to this method of warping is that it is extremely hard on the warp-material. A very strong, hard cotton will withstand it, but a fine wool may be so greatly damaged that the fabric woven of it will be rough and uneven, and weak in spots. During the beaming process one person must revolve the beam while one to three hold the warp at the front of the loom to give it a tension, combing out loose threads and twists with their fingers. The holders must hold the warp-strands at exactly the same tension or the warp will go on unevenly and the fabric will be uneven. This is perhaps the worst method of warping, but may result in a weaveable warp if enough care is taken and the warp-material is strong enough to stand it. A comb should not be used in combing out the chain, as it breaks the threads.

If through some misfortune the warp has been improperly beamed—if it is full of loose ends and twists—it will be impossible to weave a satisfactory fabric, no matter how skillfully the shuttle may be thrown. There is no cure for a bad warp except to chain it off at the front and rebeam it. Of course this means dragging the warp back and forth through the heddles and the reed, and is extremely hard on the warp material, so errors in beaming should be avoided. One or two loose warp-ends may, to be sure, be drawn down to the edge of the web and fastened around a pin, to be threaded into the fabric with a needle after the fabric is taken from the loom; but if the warp is really bad—with one side looser than the other, or a whole strand of loose or twisted threads—rebeaming is absolutely necessary.

II *Drawing-in or Threading*

If the warp has been beamed from the back the second step in dressing the loom is taking the warp through the heddles—a process known as "drawing-in."

For this a threading draft for the desired pattern is required. In a threading draft for overshot weaving—draft number 1, for instance, each thread of the repeat is indicated by a small black square, and the heddle through which it is to be threaded is shown by the horizontal row in which the square occurs. Drafts are read from right to left, and the bottom row of the draft is taken to indicate the front harness or harness 1. The first thread of this pattern, then, should be threaded through the eye of a heddle on harness 1; the second thread through a heddle on harness 2; the third on harness 1 again; the fourth on harness 2; the fifth on harness 3, and so through the draft. When the end of the draft is reached, repeat it from right to left as many times as may be required.

There are several methods of drawing in, and the weaver should use the method best suited to his personal convenience. If the loom is a large floor-loom the batten may be removed and the drawer-in, seated on the cloth-beam or on a chair set inside the frame of the loom, inserts a special instrument—the "drawing-in hook"—through the eye of the required heddle, engages a thread held by an assistant at the back of the loom and draws it through. The hook should be used slotted side down.

When drawing in alone on a large loom the best method is to stand facing the right-hand cape of the loom, with a strand of warp over the back-beam and over the tops of the harness frames. Hold the strand taut with the left hand and select a thread with the right hand, taking the threads carefully in order. Double the end of the thread over as in threading a darning needle and take it through the eye of a heddle selected by the left hand. No hook is used. Working alone, it is possible to draw in faster by this method than for two people working with a hook. However, if the warp is very wide it may, toward the end, become necessary to thread from the left side of the loom. This is somewhat unhandy but not really difficult.

To avoid troublesome mistakes in threading it is wise to check at the end of each repeat. The simplest way to do this is to count the threads on each harness as shown by the draft. Draft number 1 has a repeat of twenty-six ends: 7 threads on harness 1, 7 on harness 2, 6 on 3 and 6 on 4. If the threaded heddles of the repeat on the loom correspond to the count the threading may be taken to be correct. If not, an error has been made and the threading should be checked over, thread by thread. Before passing on to the next repeat the threads should be caught together with a loop-knot to keep them from falling out of the heddles.

It should be noted that some patterns require many more heddles on one harness than on another, and it is well before beginning to draw in to calculate the required heddles on each harness for the entire threading, and to make any readjustments that may be necessary. It is easier to shift heddles when the loom is empty than after part of the threading is in.

III Sleying

Sleying is a very simple process, but it is easy to make mistakes, and difficult to correct mistakes when made without doing at least a part of the work over. Too many threads in a dent, or a missed dent, will make an ugly streak for the full length of the web, and should never be permitted to pass.

Many people use a hook in sleying—the same hook that is sometimes used in threading. It should be held with the slotted side down, the threads being drawn through the reed with a downward cutting motion. However, an ordinary kitchen knife is a better tool than the hook as it does not catch in the warp. The knife should be used with the dull edge down, and with the same cutting motion described for the hook.

It is easier to sley from right to left than from left to right, so if the warp is designed to fill the reed, begin at the right-hand end of the reed. Take up a number of threads in the left hand. With the hook or the knife select the heddles carrying the threads to be sleyed through the first dent; push these heddles a little toward the right and hook the threads they carry over a finger of the left hand. Insert the knife through the desired dent and "cut" the threads through with a downward motion.

If the warp is a narrow strip at the center of the loom it may prove more convenient to begin at the center.

During sleying the batten should stand in an upright position between the heddles and the breast-beam. It may be fastened in place by cords before the sleying begins, or may be anchored by a loop-knot tied in the first group of threads sleyed, the batten being held meanwhile by the wrist of the left hand.

IV Tying-In

Tying-in, or attaching the warp to the cloth-beam, is a simple process, but like every other step in weaving, must be carried out correctly.

It will be found that attached to the cloth-beam is an "apron," or perhaps a bar held in place by cords or tapes. Unroll this and bring it up in front of the breast-beam and over the beam a few inches toward the reed. Take a strand of warp-ends at the center of the warp and carry the strand down over the bar or through an eyelet in the apron. Separate the strand and bring up half on one side and half on the other side of the original strand. Cross these strands above and then below. Bring them up and tie with a bow, omitting the "bend" usually tied before making a bow-knot. As illustrated at (f) in Diagram 3.

Tie a group of threads at each edge of the warp in the same manner. Take up a notch or two on the tension. Tie the rest of the warp in the same way, making every effort to keep an even tension and to draw out any loose threads.

If the tension is not the same in all parts of the warp it will be difficult to weave. Some knots may have to be retied, but this is easy if the bow-tie has been made correctly, as it opens with a jerk on one of the ends.

Chapter Seven: Adjustments, Knots, the Tie-Up

Most looms when received from the dealer are completely assembled and tied up, ready for weaving, but frequently the tie-up is faulty, and in any case before embarking on a new project it is advisable to go over the loom to make sure that it operates correctly. This can be done most conveniently after the loom has been dressed, so it is considered in this place.

It is amazing to find that many good weavers will struggle along on a loom that is out of adjustment when they could save themselves a great deal of time and trouble by going over the cords and ties by which the loom is operated.

Most table-looms are operated by metal "jacks" and metal connections and do not require adjustment except in case of breakage, and some floor-looms also have special metal connections, but most floor-looms are operated by cords and as these cords stretch at first and sometimes break, and as special tie-ups are required for certain weaves and patterns, it is important to know the knots.

I   Knots Used in Weaving

For convenience, all the knots ordinarily used in weaving are grouped together on Diagram 3. The "square knot" and the "granny knot" are familiar to most people. The illustration will make the difference between these two knots perfectly clear. The square knot is used chiefly for tying together ends of weft, and is used because it can be taken out without untying. The square knot should never be used in tying warp ends, as it works loose in passing through the reed. To take it out without untying pull apart the two ends that lie close together, the knot will then become a double hitch that can be slid off. The

(42) An old coverlet in the Boston Museum. (A simple pattern on opposites.)

granny knot cannot be undone in this fashion as it binds. It is used in tying string heddles, and has—as far as known—no other legitimate use.

The weaver's knot is used chiefly in tying warp-ends, as for this a knot is required that will not come undone. The weaver's knot is properly a "bowline" knot tying two ends instead of making a loop. It may be tied in several ways—the method illustrated in detail on the diagram is both quick and easy. Cross the two ends with the left-hand end in front of the other, and hold this cross between the thumb and finger of the left hand. With the right-hand "bight" of cord make a loop around the crossed ends, and then a smaller loop around the free end on the right. Take this free end and turn it back under the

Knots used by Weavers

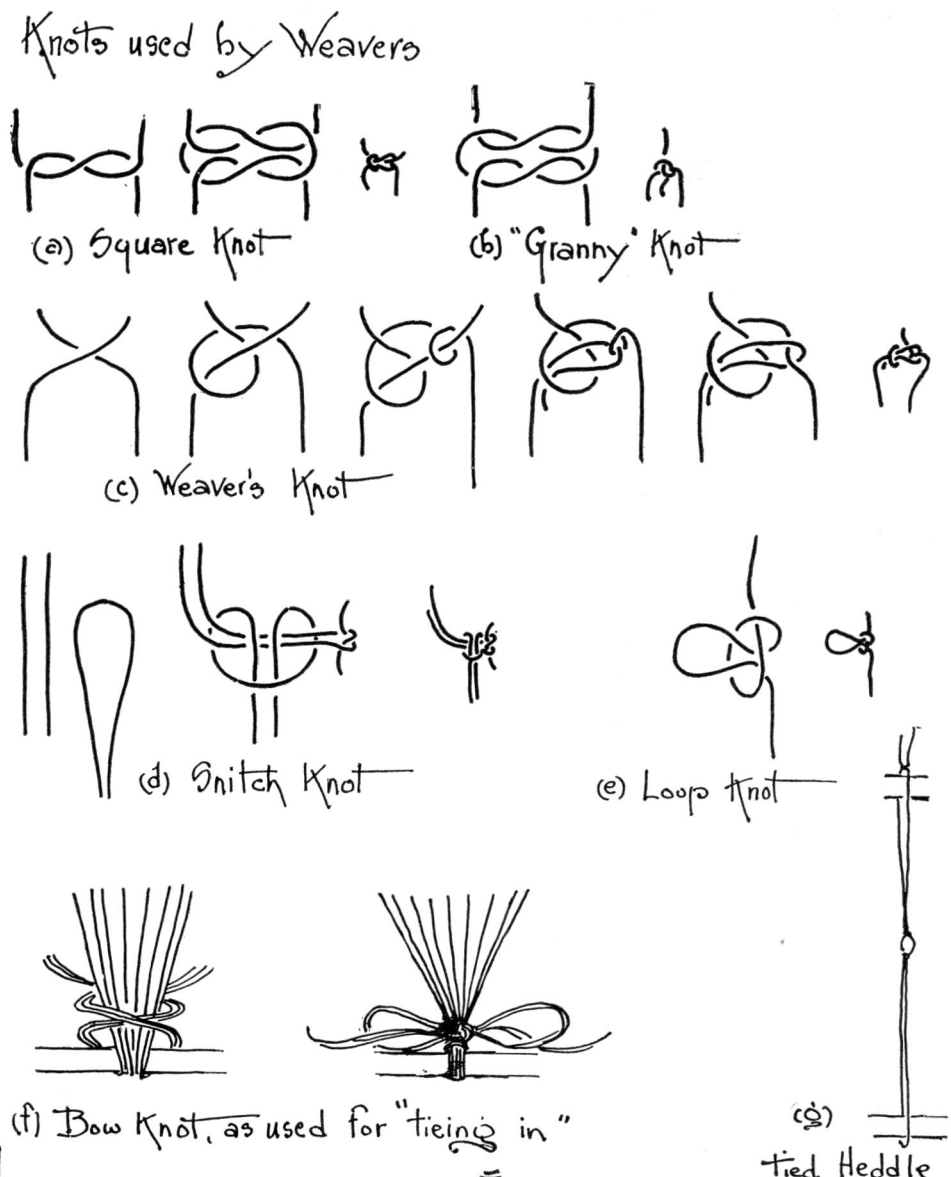

Diagram 3 (43)

left-hand loop, holding it firmly between the thumb and finger, along with the original cross. Draw the knot tight by pulling on the right-hand bight of the cord. This appears in description more complicated than it is in practice. It is well worth the time and bit of effort required to master it.

The snitch-knot is, however, the most important of the weaver's knots. Without this knot it is entirely impossible to tie up a loom correctly or to keep it in adjustment. It should be used for all ties on the loom.

The knot consists of two parts—a loop and a double end. To make the knot turn over the top of the loop till it forms a double loop which sailors call "two half-hitches." Through this double loop pass both free ends and tie them together with a simple "bend"—like the first half of a square knot. Draw the loops tight, and the thing is done. This knot will never bind no matter what strain is put on it and no matter how long it remains on the loom. It may be adjusted at any height by sliding the hitch along the double ends and letting out or drawing up the bend at the end, as the case may require. Care must be taken, however, to tie the bend straight across, as otherwise one of the ends will pull through the knot and the adjustment will be lost. The sketch on the diagram makes all this clear.

The loop-knot shown at (e) of the diagram is used chiefly to tie groups of warp-ends after they have been drawn in through the heddles in order that they may not slip back. It is simply half a bow-knot and pulls out instantly.

The two sketches at (f) of the diagram illustrate the knot used in tying warp-ends to the apron or lease-stick attached to the cloth beam. A strand of threads is brought over the stick (or down through the eyelet in the apron), is divided into two strands that are brought up, one on either side of the original strand, crossed above and then below, drawn tight and finally tied in a double bow-knot. No hard knot is tied at all and by drawing out the bow-knot the strand may be released instantly.

Untying a knot is just as important as tying, and the general rule is never to tie a knot on the loom that cannot be taken out without difficulty. Disregard of this rule results in wasted cords that may have to be cut away, or in broken finger nails and loss of time.

The only place where a hard knot is allowable is in the tying of heddles—sketched at (f) of the diagram. All the heddles for a loom are sometimes made of cord and are then tied over pegs set in a board, but most modern weavers now use wire or flat steel heddles and use a tied heddle only on occasion, when it is necessary to correct a mistake in threading.

II   Adjustments, Four-Harness Tie-Up

The cord used in loom tie-ups should be a woven cord—of linen if possible—and not too heavy. A cord used in upholstery, and a heavy varnished cord used in deep-sea fishing are suitable. So are the heavy grades of Jacquard cord, though this material is costly.

The usual four-harness loom has a large roller at the top from which are suspended two small rollers, as shown in Diagram 1. Two long double cords should be attached to one of the two small rollers—the one at the back—with two loops attached to the other roller. The double cords should pass once around the large roller and be tied into the loops on the second small roller by means of the snitch-knot. The cords should not be nailed to the large roller. The small rollers should hang about half way between the tops of the harness frames and the large roller.

When these first ties have been made and the small rollers leveled, they should be tied together to keep them in place.

In the same manner, and with the same knot, the four harness frames should be hung in pairs from the small rollers. The harnesses should hang at the exact level permitting the warp to pass in a straight line from the back-beam to the breast-beam. If the warp is deflected downward by the heddles the harnesses hang too low. If the warp is deflected upward the harnesses hang too high. And the threads should come through the center of the reed.

In a jack-type loom of the Swedish variety, with a double set of lamms, this adjustment is the same. But in a modern "rising shed" jack-loom, such as most table-looms and most of the modern floor-looms of the jack type—which do not make a shed by raising some harnesses and sinking others but by raising certain harnesses, only—the adjustment is different. In looms of this type the warp should make a downward angle at the heddles and should lie flat on the shuttle-race when the loom is at rest.

This is an important matter, as it is impossible to weave properly if this adjustment is incorrect. It will be apparent from a study of Diagram 4.

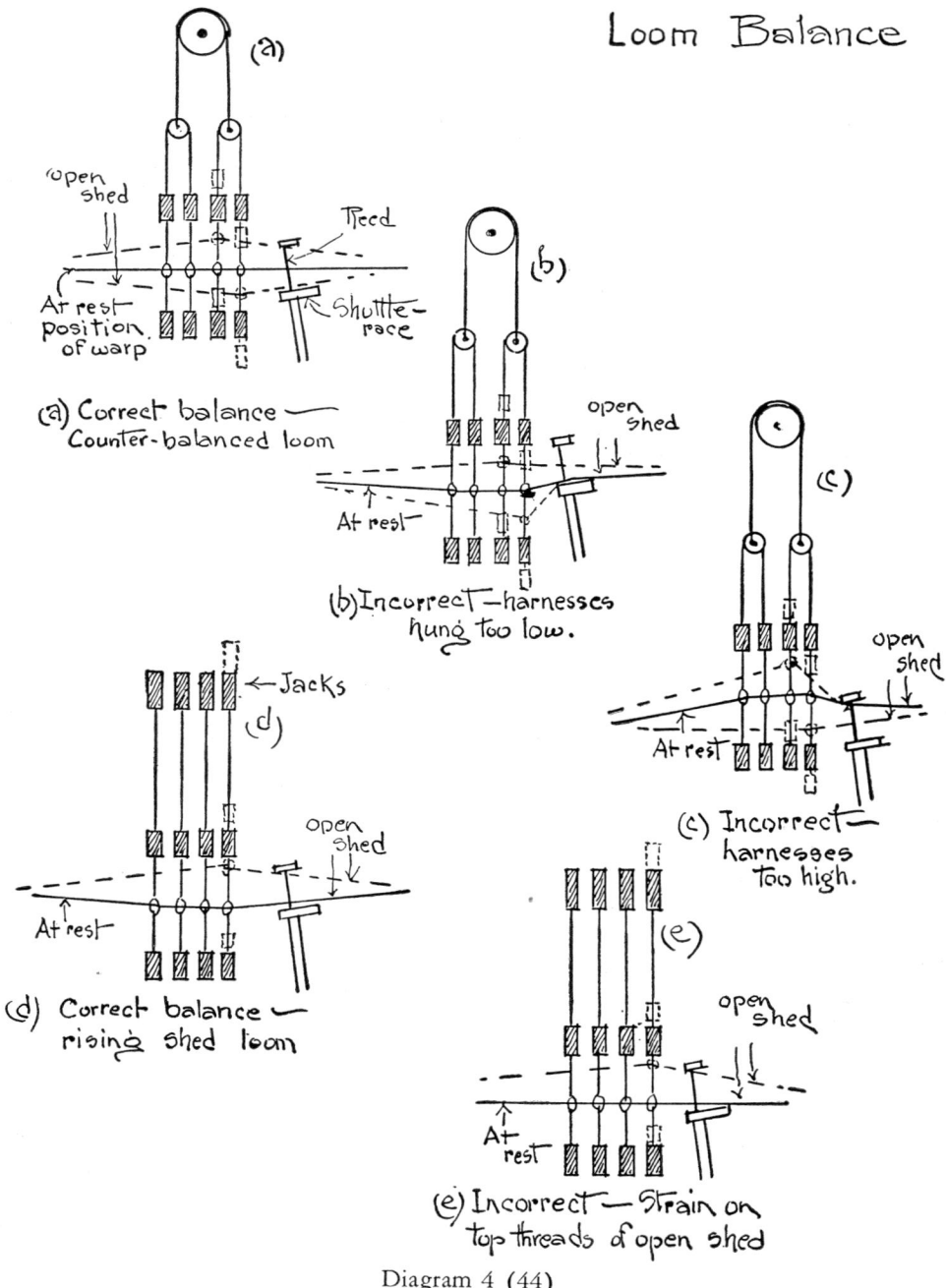

Diagram 4 (44)

Unfortunately a good many loom builders appear to be unaware of this matter of balance. Many table-looms have been made in which the warp is brought straight through the loom, and when the shed is opened by raising certain harnesses the raised part of the warp is stretched tight and the bottom of the shed is slack. This produces ridges and "creeping" in the web, and will not do at all. However it may be corrected quite easily by raising the back-beam and the breast-beam sufficiently to give the warp the correct downward angle.

In looms of the rising shed type it is the weight of the harnesses that holds the warp down at the heddles, and sometimes—when using a very heavy warp at a strong tension—additional weight is required. In this case the harness frames may be weighted, or a weighted treadle may be used, with a tie to each harness.

When the harnesses have been hung at the correct level, they should be tied to keep them in place while the tie-up is made to the lamms and treadles.

The lamms are a set of levers attached to one or the other of the capes of the loom, a foot or more below the harnesses and extending across the bank of treadles. The purpose of the lamms is to insure bringing down the harnesses evenly. It is obvious that if the treadles were attached directly to the harnesses all treadles except one at the center would pull down the harnesses at a slant.

A cord from the center of each harness frame should be attached to the corresponding lamm, usually by a cord, and again the tie should be made with the snitch-knot. The lamms should be given a slight upward slant to keep them from striking against the outer treadles when the sheds are opened. When they have been adjusted correctly they should be tied together to keep them in position while the tie-up to the treadles is being made.

III Treadle Tie-Up

The correct tie-up to the treadles differs with the weave and with the type of loom used. Only the tie-ups for two-harness and four-harness weaving will be considered in this chapter, the tie-ups for other weaves being given in the chapters devoted to these weaves. All ties to the treadles should be made with the snitch-knot.

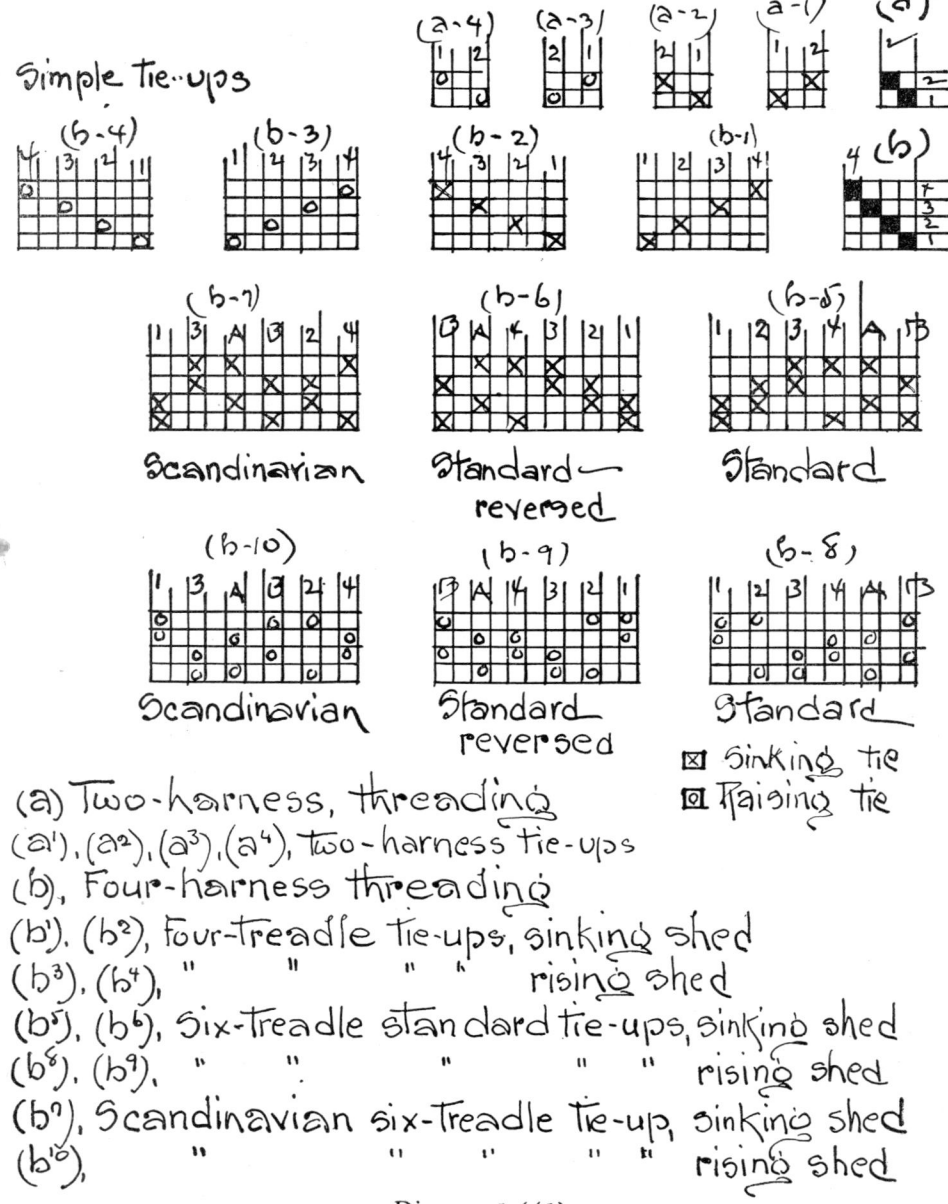

(a) Two-harness, threading
(a¹), (a²), (a³), (a⁴), two-harness tie-ups
(b), Four-harness threading
(b¹), (b²), Four-treadle tie-ups, sinking shed
(b³), (b⁴),   "   "   "   rising shed
(b⁵), (b⁶), Six-treadle standard tie-ups, sinking shed
(b⁷), (b⁸),   "   "   "   "   rising shed
(b⁹), Scandinavian six-treadle tie-up, sinking shed
(b¹⁰),   "   "   "   " rising shed

Diagram 5 (45)

As we have seen, some looms operate with a "sinking shed" and others—even four-harness looms of the modern type—operate with a "rising shed." A tie-up draft indicates the ties to be made to each treadle, sinking ties by convention being written in "X's" and the raising ties in "O's." The raising tie-up is the direct opposite of the sinking tie-up, of course.

There are only two sheds in two-harness weaving and it makes little or no difference how the tie-up is made, though it may be made in four different ways as shown on Diagram 5.

Four-harness tie-ups are more complex. If the loom is equipped with only four treadles, each treadle operates a single harness and the various sheds are produced by holding down from one to three treadles at a time. The four treadles may be arranged in any order desired but the arrangement shown at (b–1) is that generally used. The raising levers of a hand-lift table-loom are arranged as at (b–3).

In most four-harness weaves the harnesses are operated in pairs—two down and two up on each shed. On tie-up (b–1) to produce these sheds it is necessary to use both feet. It is far more convenient to tie a shed to each treadle so that one foot will make the desired opening for the passage of the shuttle. As there are six pairs in four—1–2, 2–3, 3–4, 1–4, 2–4 and 1–3—most looms are equipped with six treadles, tied in the order given above and shown at (b–5) on the diagram. This, and the corresponding "rising shed" tie-up at (b–8), we call the "standard" four-harness tie-up, and the treadlings given in this book are based on this arrangement. For looms tied up as at (b–1) these treadlings should be transposed: "treadle 1" on the standard tie-up means 1 and 2 together on tie-up (b–1); "treadle 2" is read as treadles 2 and 3 together, and so on. On a hand-lift loom the treadlings should be read as for tie-up (b–8), "treadle 1" being read as levers 3 and 4, and so on.

Some weavers use the Scandinavian tie-up given at (b–7) and (b–10), but the treadlings are the same if it is borne in mind that the treadles are not numbered in regular order.

In making the adjustments, both tie-ups to the same treadle should be made at the same tension so that the shed will open evenly, and the treadles should be given an upward slant. If the space between treadles and lamms is wide, make a set of loops, tied with the weaver's knot, and attach these to the treadles.

Attach double cords to correspond to the lamms. The cords should work straight up and down and not at a slant. If the space is narrow it is more convenient to make the tie with a single cord: double the cord at the center and take the "bight" from front to back through the screw-eye on the under side of the lamm, then from back to front through the screw-eye on the treadle, and make the tie in the usual way. Some looms have holes for the cords instead of screw-eyes, in which case loops and double cords must be used.

Some four-harness weaves require special tie-ups, which will be given when these weaves are described, but for most four-harness weaving the standard tie-up meets all requirements.

Chapter Eight: Weaving

We come now to the actual weaving—the easiest and most interesting part of the textile process—throwing the shuttle, thumping with the batten, and watching a beautiful new fabric build up thread by thread.

Before Colonial Mistress Priscilla reached this point she had not only dressed the big loom that stood in a corner of the kitchen, she had perhaps helped to shear the sheep; she had certainly sorted, carded, spun and scoured the yarn. And when the nights were warm in summer she had set a smelly indigo vat down by the barn and had stirred it faithfully, getting up three or four times every night to go out in her nightdress under the stars to work it over. After that she had dyed the yarn that dark blue with the overtone bloom of madder that made it so handsome. As she put a foot on a treadle to open the first shed she may have wondered whether the new pattern sent her by Aunt Sarah would turn out as well as Aunt Sarah said it would, thinking that perhaps it would have been better to make another "Governor's Garden" or "Ladies' Delight." Those were always good. At any rate, no doubt she felt a thrill as the shuttle slid through the shed, trailing the first shot of weft behind it, and the batten came down with a vigorous thump.

Weavers of today have not, as a rule, gone through the hard work of preparing the yarn before they sit down to weave, but even for us there is a thrill in the first shot of a new fabric. A new weaver does well to begin at this point, on a loom already set up to a simple pattern in overshot weaving. It is not logical, perhaps, to begin with weaving, but the actual practise of the craft answers many questions, and gives meaning to the preliminary steps.

(46) A Sunrise pattern. Draft number 105.

I *First Shots—Corrections*

To begin, weave a few shots in coarse material to bring the warp together above the knots of the tie-in. If the first two shots are put in close to the reed and then pushed down firmly with the batten, fewer shots will be required than otherwise. The material used may be strips of rag, coarse cotton roving or rug-wool. Above these preliminary shots a tabby "heading" in weft like the warp should be woven.

At this point it is advisable to examine the set-up for possible errors. Any crosses produced in sleying must be corrected. Also, it may be found that too many threads have been drawn through a single dent of the reed, or a dent may have been missed. Also one may find that there are double or triple warp-threads in the tabby. These indicate errors in threading.

There is no cure for errors in sleying except taking out and doing over, but minor errors in threading may sometimes be corrected without such drastic treatment.

Suppose the tabby shows a double thread; this is due either to an omitted thread or to two threads being drawn through the same heddle or through adjoining heddles on the same harness. An extra thread may merely be suppressed by taking it out of the heddle and allowing it to dangle at the back of the loom—messy but not troublesome. If a thread has been omitted, an extra thread—wound on a spool—may be introduced. Take the end around the warp-beam, up over the back-beam and through the heddle and reed. It will usually weave off well enough, though it sometimes gives trouble, and if there is more than one such error, or if a very long warp is on the loom, it is better to rethread. Of course in either case resleying will be necessary.

If three threads lie together in the tabby the middle thread has probably been threaded on the wrong harness. In this case tie a string heddle on the correct harness and take the thread through this new heddle.

To tie a string heddle take a length of linen or of a good mercerized cotton, longer than twice the height of the harness frame. Take it under the bottom heddle-bar of the frame and, bringing up the two ends, tie them together in a granny knot at the level of the bottom of the heddle eyes. Bring the faulty thread through above this knot and tie a second granny knot at the level of the top of the heddle eyes. Finally tie to the upper heddle bar of the harness and clip off the ends.

Of course if a serious mistake in threading has been made, such as the omission of a pattern block or part of a repeat, rethreading to the nearer edge is necessary. But if drawing-in has been done with care this is rarely required.

II *Weaving*

Weaving consists of three simple movements: treadling to open the shed; throwing the shuttle; beating.

The order in which the treadles are used depends upon the pattern. The treadles are tied in a logical order and the feet should learn to find them. The weaver should be careful not to fall into the habit of bending down to watch the feet. This is a waste of time and also produces a crick in the neck. In case of uncertainty observe the harnesses and see whether the right ones rise.

It is desirable to weave in light shoes or moccasins. Scandinavian weavers wear no shoes at the loom. On one occasion I had a loom set up at an arts-and-crafts exhibition and was performing upon it when a woman—a Swedish woman, to judge by her flaxen hair and general appearance—stopped to watch. Finally she said: "Weaving!" And in a tone of intense scorn: *"With shoes on!"* Clearly she thought very little of such ways. But it is true that the foot is far more intelligent when lightly shod than over a heavy sole.

In the overshot weave, and a number of other weaves, two shuttles are used, one carrying material like the warp for making the tabby foundation fabric and the other carrying the pattern weft. The tabby shuttles may be alternated either way—tabby A from the right, tabby B from the left; or tabby B from the right, tabby A from the left. But one should make a habit of one system or the other as this helps to avoid throwing the same tabby twice. A wrong tabby makes an ugly streak through the work and sometimes involves inches of "unweaving."

If boat-shaped shuttles are used, they should be thrown with the flat edge toward the reed and the curved edge outward. The curve is designed to keep

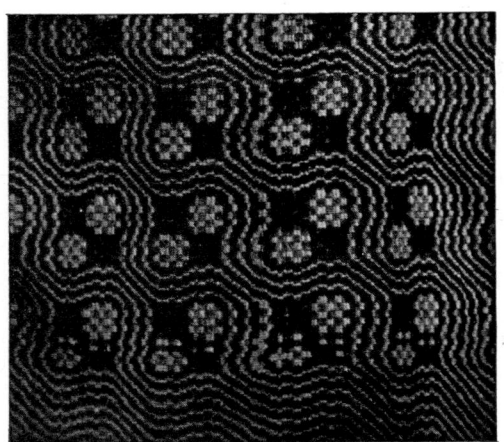

(47) Snail Trail. Draft number 38.

the shuttle against the reed and on the shuttle-race, to avoid nose dives. When two shuttles are being used the tabby shuttle should run ahead of the pattern shuttle, as: B tabby, right to left; pattern shuttle from right to left; A tabby, left to right; pattern, left to right, and so on.

The weft should not be drawn tight, but should be permitted to lie loosely in the shed, at a slant toward the heddles, to allow for take-up. Otherwise the edges will narrow in and presently it will become impossible to beat closely, the edge threads will saw off and a very ragged edge will result. However, the weft should not lie so loose that it makes loops, and forms picots along the edges. A slight narrowing in is permissible, especially when weaving with coarse materials as in rug-making, but the web should be kept out almost to the width of the warp as it comes through the reed. Some weavers use a "template" to keep the web stretched to the correct width, but this makes little holes along the selvages and is clumsy to work over—and is unnecessary if a little care is taken at first, till good weaving habits have been established.

A word about the winding of bobbins: a poorly wound bobbin will waste a great deal of time and material, so it is worth while to wind them correctly. Shuttle bobbins are ordinarily little metal tubes or tubes made of paper. Wooden spools with heads may be used in large shuttles, but take up a good deal of space so that they do not carry much material. They, of course, may be wound any way one likes, but the tubes without heads are more difficult as the material tends to run off the ends into a wretched tangle.

A winding device of some kind should be used for filling bobbins. An electric winder fitted to take shuttle bobbins and also warp-spools is the most convenient, but a hand winder serves very well. Bobbins may also be wound on the sewing machine. Begin by winding a lump at each end a little distance in from the end, making the effect of a little dumb-bell. Then wind between these two lumps, never going past them, till the bobbin is as full as it will hold and still fit easily into the shuttle.

The beat necessarily varies with the fabric being woven. A light worsted fabric, for instance, requires an extremely gentle beat, while rugs must be given a heavy pounding. The beat also varies to some extent with the hand on the batten, so that it is very difficult for two people to work on the same piece without producing changes of texture.

(48) Wheel of Fortune. Draft number 100.

For fabrics such as a piece in overshot weaving, which should be firm without being stiff, the best method of beating is as follows: open the shed and beat—two short, sharp blows with the batten are better than one heavy thump. Throw the shuttle, and with the shed still open, beat again. Repeat.

In beating grasp the batten at the center so that the beat will be equal on both sides, and do not beat always with the same hand; throw the shuttle from right to left with the right hand; catch it with the left; beat with the right hand. Throw the shuttle from left to right with the left hand; catch it with the right hand; beat with the left.

These may seem small details, but they are part of the rhythm of weaving and it is well to cultivate correct habits as this means a saving in time and effort.

The beat should be as even as possible, to avoid streakiness in the fabric, and to that end the warp should be kept at the same tension throughout the weaving. After the tension is released in order to roll up the web on the cloth-beam, there may often be a streak where weaving is resumed unless special care is taken.

For some weaves the warp should be stretched tighter than for others, but it should rarely be stretched as tight as possible. This is particularly true of rising shed looms. If the warp is stretched very tight the harnesses will tend to rise and the warp will no longer lie on the shuttle-race. When this happens the tension should be released sufficiently to retsore the correct balance of the loom. Sometimes, however, with a very heavy warp additional weight on the harnesses is required to keep the warp in correct position. The easiest way to weight the harnesses is to use an extra treadle at the center of the loom, hung directly to the bottom member of each harness frame. The weight of the treadle is usually sufficient, but if not, an extra weight may be attached to the treadle. This treadle is not used in weaving, of course, except on occasion to return the harnesses to correct position. The harness frames may be weighted individually if one prefers, by adding extra heddles or by attaching weights of some kind.

III   Loose Ends

When starting a new thread at the edge of the warp, do not permit the end to hang loose out of the selvage. With the shed still open, after throwing the shuttle, turn the end around the edge thread and back into the shed under a few warp-ends and bring it up out of the warp. When it has been woven in it may be clipped off.

When joining two ends of weft, lap them under a few warp-ends and bring the loose ends up out of the warp. It is desirable to make these joinings close to one edge or the other, especially in a piece of plain weaving, as they tend to show a little. A weft-knot should never be woven in.

Warp-knots should not be woven in, either. If a warp-thread breaks attach a new end at the back of the loom, bring the new end forward through the heddle and the reed, being careful to thread it correctly without making a cross or putting too many threads in a dent of the reed. Set a pin in the edge of the web opposite the correct dent and wind the thread around the pin. After the work is taken off the loom, thread one of the ends into the web with a needle.

After the weaving over the new thread has progressed far enough, bring the original thread back into the web and attach it to a pin as before.

Knots occur occasionally in warp-material, and when one of these comes up in the weaving it should be eliminated in the same manner, by using a supplementary thread till the original thread can be brought back into the web.

Chapter Nine: The Plain Weave

The plain weave is the simple over and under interlacement of warp and weft and only two harnesses are required, though the weave may be produced on any set-up that includes the two plain sheds.

It is far more difficult to weave a satisfactory plain-weave fabric than it is to make a piece in simple pattern weaving. For the sake of logical sequence the plain weave is considered here, but the beginner is advised to pass on to the chapter on the four-harness overshot weave. In plain weaving slight variations in beat show as very obvious streaks, especially if warp and weft differ in color, and an even beat comes only with practise.

Three different types of fabric may be woven on the plain-weave set-up: the fifty-fifty "tabby" weave; "warp-faced rep" with the warp set so close that the weft is largely or entirely hidden; "weft-faced rep" with the warp set so far apart that it is covered by the weft.

It is a mistake to think that a two-harness loom and the plain weave can be used only for the making of "hit and miss" rag rugs. Some of the finest and most intricate weaves are produced on the two plain sheds—tapestry, for instance, requires only two harnesses. Knotted pile, too, as in Oriental rugs and Swedish "flossa," rugs in picked-up tufting, tabby fabrics in plaids and checks for blankets and clothing, the Spanish openwork weave for linens, plain rep fabrics for upholstery, the tabby pick-up weaves of Mexico and Peru, and many others. One might weave for a lifetime on two harnesses with profit and pleasure. But it is true that most two-harness weaving requires a good deal more skill than simple forms of four-harness and eight-harness weaving.

I Tabby

The "fifty-fifty" type of plain weaving is commonly called "tabby." In this weave warp and weft are the same or similar in grist and there are exactly the same number of weft-shots to the inch as there are warp-ends to the inch in the setting. A tabby fabric may be fine or coarse, closely woven or open, all in one color or in stripes, checks, plaids and a variety of color effects.

Cotton tabby is woven in Mexico, Sweden and Guatemala for dress-fabrics, those from Guatemala frequently done in patterns by the tie-dying process. Many of these fabrics are very handsome, but modern weavers in the United States seem to be content to let machinery produce these things.

A tabby fabric in homespun yarns is often woven for suitings and light sports-coats. This is sometimes called "tweed" though this is an error—the name "tweed" applies to a twilled fabric. The correct name for the tabby fabric is "hop-sacking" but as this name appears displeasing to some people it is often called "homespun," which is perhaps allowable.

Color-patterns in great variety may be produced in the tabby weave; checks and plaids, for instance, and the little figure known as "shepherd's plaid," the "log-cabin" pattern, and so on. For shepherd's plaid, warp two threads dark and two threads light, and weave in the same order. For log-cabin, thread alternately dark and light for ten threads—or a greater number if desired. Then ten threads alternately light and dark. Repeat. Weave in the same order. The result is alternating squares in perpendicular and horizontal lines of color.

A tabby fabric in linen may be very handsome. If it is desired to ornament the piece later with hemstitching or drawnwork, a space for the needlework may be left by weaving in a flat stick or strip of cardboard of the desired width.

A plain-weave tabby fabric in linen—not a true tabby as the warp should be finer and more widely spaced than the weft—is used as a foundation for the beautiful Spanish openwork weave. As this is described elsewhere the directions will not be given here.

The chief use for the tabby weave, however, is as the foundation fabric in such pattern weaves as overshot, crackle, summer-and-winter, etc.

II Warp-Faced Rep in Plain Weave

There are some interesting uses for warp-faced rep fabrics. Patterned reps cannot be made in plain weave, but by the use of color it is possible to produce some very handsome and lively effects. Many of the "mantas" from Guatemala are made of fine warp in stripes of many colors, set so close that the weft—heavier than the warp—is completely covered. In pieces from Sololá these striped fabrics are given interest by the introduction of a few tie-dyed strands at the center of some of the stripes. These fabrics might be used with excellent effect for upholstery.

The color-arrangement of a very handsome girdle from Guatemala—quoted from my "Guatemala Visited"—is given below. The weave is plain weave, with the warp set close as for warp-faced rep, but a very lively effect of pattern is produced.

Threaded as for plain weave. Arrangement of colors as follows:
20 ends, dark blue
 6 ends, red, purple alternately
 6 ends, purple, red alternately
 8 ends dark blue
 8 ends red, mauve, alternately
 8 ends mauve, red
 8 ends dark blue
10 ends, red, white alternately
10 ends, white, red alternately
12 ends dark blue
 8 ends green, purple, alternately
 8 ends purple, green alternately
10 ends dark blue
 8 ends gold, grey, alternately
 8 ends grey, gold, alternately
14 ends dark blue
 8 ends red and purple, alternately
 8 ends purple, red, alternately
14 ends dark blue
 8 ends white, purple, alternately
 8 ends purple, white, alternately
14 ends dark blue

(*Continued*)

```
 8 ends red, mauve, alternately
 8 ends mauve, red, alternately
14 ends dark blue
 8 ends red, gold, alternately
 8 ends gold, red, alternately
14 ends dark blue
 8 ends white, purple, alternately
 8 ends purple, white, alternately
14 ends dark blue
 8 ends gold, grey, alternately
 8 ends grey, gold, alternately
14 ends dark blue
10 ends green, rose, alternately
10 ends rose, green, alternately
14 ends dark blue
 8 ends red, purple, alternately
 8 ends purple, red, alternately
14 ends dark blue
 8 ends white, grey, alternately
 8 ends grey, white, alternately
14 ends dark blue
 8 ends red, gold, alternately
 8 ends gold, red, alternately
14 ends dark blue
10 ends gold, grey, alternately
10 ends grey, gold, alternately
14 ends dark blue
 8 ends red, white, alternately
 8 ends white, red, alternately
14 ends dark blue
 8 ends gold, mauve, alternately
 8 ends mauve, gold, alternately
20 ends dark blue
```

Weft: a strand of two ends and a strand of four ends, woven as follows: coarse, fine, coarse, fine, coarse, coarse, fine, coarse, fine, coarse. Repeat. Finished with a short braided fringe.

The same technique is to be seen in Navajo and Mexican belts and girdles, and somewhat similar pieces come from Europe—bags from Italy, belts from Sweden.

For an old Colonial rug, and the Swedish "matta" technique, see the chapter on rug-making.

III Weft-Faced Rep

Pattern effects in weft-faced rep, similar to those in warp-faced rep, may also be woven. The warp for this weave should be coarse and set far apart and the weft fine enough to beat close and cover the warp completely. The fabric produced is thick and firm and may be used for mats and for upholstery; also for heavy blankets. A typical pattern is shown on Diagram 6. Two wefts are required, one dark and one light; weave treadle 1 dark, treadle 2 light for one pattern block; and treadle 1 light; treadle 2 dark for the other. The lines in plain color are, of course, with all shots light or all shots dark. A number of colors may be introduced if one wishes, and the effects are interesting.

IV A "Fifty-Fifty" Weave

A two-harness "fifty-fifty" weave with two-block pattern effects is sometimes woven for afghans and similar pieces. It consists in threading such a pattern as draft 121 as follows: two threads on harness 1; two threads on harness 2; two threads, 1; two threads, 2; eight threads on 1; eight threads on 2; two threads on 1; eight threads on 2; eight threads on 1; two threads on 2. Repeat. A heavy wool for warp, woven in the order of the threading with a similar yarn in a different color, produces the effect of a pattern. This is, however, a poorly combined fabric, likely to pull apart over the larger blocks, and is not recommended.

For the pattern illustrated—in weft-faced rep—thread as indicated: 1, 1, 1, 2, 2, 2, and repeat as desired.

Weave as follows, in material fine enough to cover the warp completely.

Edge:
  8 shots, dark; 12 shots light

Border:
  1 dark; 1 light; four times ⎫
  1 light; 1 dark; four times ⎬ (a)
  1 dark; 1 light; four times ⎭
  8 light
  8 dark
  1 dark; 1 light; four times ⎱ (b)
  8 dark
  8 light
  1 dark; 1 light; four times ⎫
  8 dark ⎪
  1 light; 1 dark; sixteen times ⎬ (c)
  8 dark ⎪
  1 dark; 1 light; four times ⎭
  8 light
  Repeat (b)
  8 light
  Repeat (a)
* 12 light

Middle section:
  1 light; 1 dark; twice ⎱ 6 times (d)
  1 dark; 1 light; twice ⎰
  1 light; 1 dark; four times ⎫
  1 dark; 1 light; four times ⎬ (e)
  1 light; 1 dark; four times ⎭
  1 dark; 1 light; twice ⎱ 6 times (f)
  1 light; 1 dark; twice ⎰
  Repeat (a)
  Repeat (e)
  Repeat (d)
  Repeat (f)
***12 light
  Repeat border, *–**
  12 light
  8 dark

For a warp-faced rep in the same pattern follow the weaving directions from * to *** as a repeat for the warp, which should be set close enough to cover a three-strand weft.

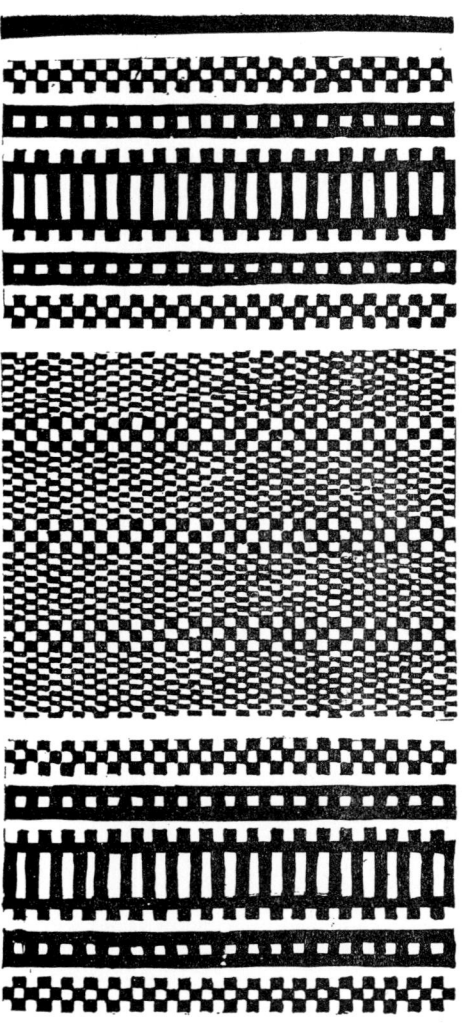

Diagram 6 (49)

Chapter Ten: The Twill Weave

If anybody were to ask, "Which of all the weaves is the most useful?" the answer would unhesitatingly be "Twill." The twill weave is a basic weave common to all ages and to all peoples and it is used in so many ways and for so many different purposes that to give an adequate account of it would take several large books. There are, in fact, a number of technical books concerned entirely or almost entirely with twill. What can be said here is merely an introduction to the subject.

I Plain Three-Harness and Four-Harness Twills

The three-harness 2–1 twill, known as the "jeans" twill is shown at (a), Diagram 7. It was used in the old days for the weaving of stout work-clothes and we still find it in machine-woven fabrics of a similar kind such as denim. It is little used by modern hand-weavers except for patterns in double twill on six, nine or twelve harnesses. I found it once in an interesting linen weave from Finland—not described here.

Twill may be written on any number of harnesses, but the four-harness form shown at (b) on the diagram is no doubt the one most in use. Woven in 2–2 form—treadles 1, 2, 3, 4 or the reverse—is the commonest weave for tweeds and other dress fabrics such as tartans, also for blankets, scarves and much other all-wool weaving. The twill threading is also used for many other weaves such as tubing, double width fabrics, double twill, damask, and a dozen forms of pick-up weaving. Selvages for many pattern weaves are threaded to twill.

For most of the twill weaves, warp and weft should be the same or similar material, woven with the same number of weft-shots to the inch as there are

Three-Harness "Jeans" Twill
Four-Harness Twills

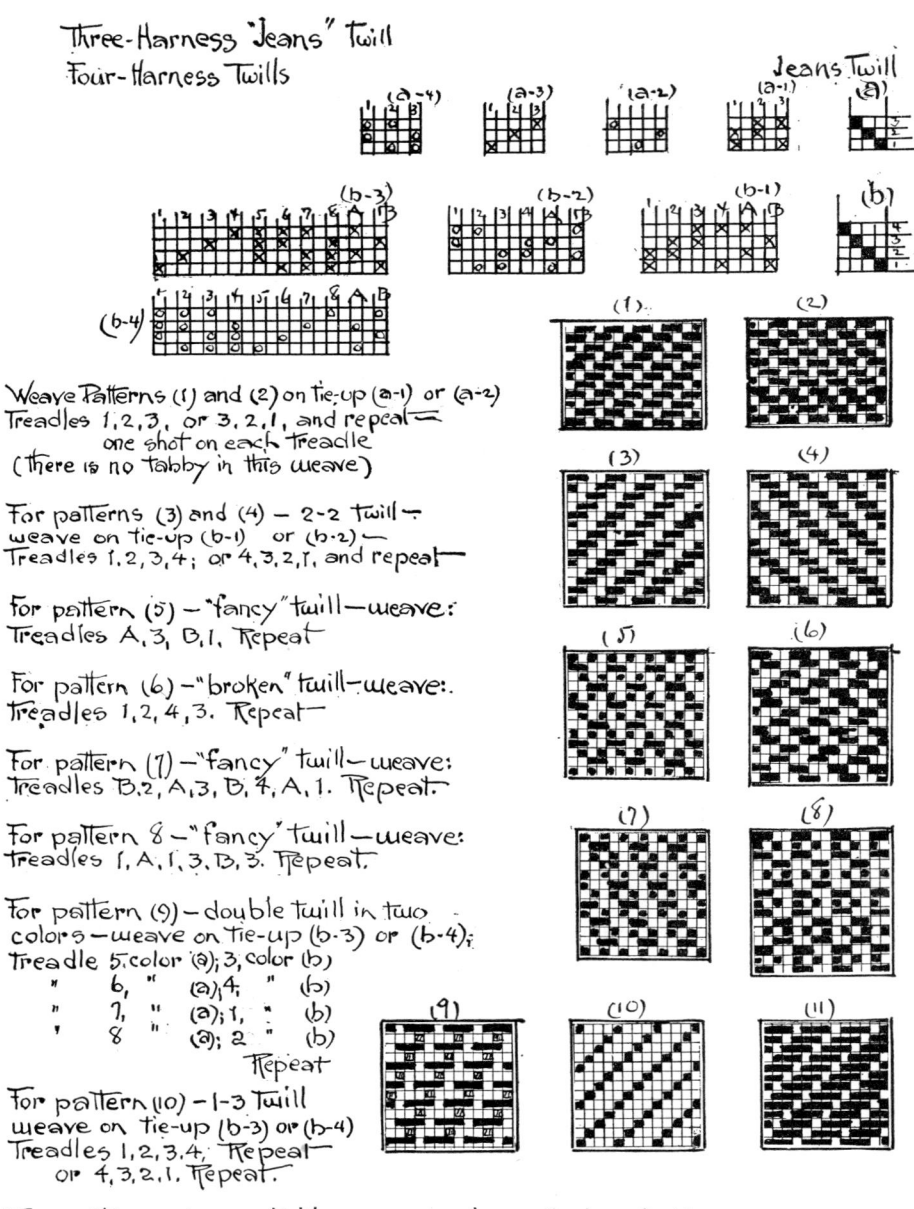

Weave Patterns (1) and (2) on Tie-up (a-1) or (a-2)
Treadles 1, 2, 3, or 3, 2, 1, and repeat —
one shot on each treadle
(There is no tabby in this weave)

For patterns (3) and (4) — 2-2 twill —
weave on tie-up (b-1) or (b-2) —
Treadles 1, 2, 3, 4; or 4, 3, 2, 1, and repeat

For pattern (5) — "fancy" twill — weave:
Treadles A, 3, B, 1. Repeat

For pattern (6) — "broken" twill — weave:
Treadles 1, 2, 4, 3. Repeat

For pattern (7) — "fancy" twill — weave:
Treadles B, 2, A, 3, B, 4, A, 1. Repeat

For pattern 8 — "fancy" twill — weave:
Treadles 1, A, 1, 3, B, 3. Repeat.

For pattern (9) — double twill in two
colors — weave on tie-up (b-3) or (b-4);
Treadle 5, color (a); 3, color (b)
" 6, " (a); 4, " (b)
" 7, " (a); 1, " (b)
" 8, " (a); 2 " (b)
Repeat

For pattern (10) — 1-3 twill
weave on tie-up (b-3) or (b-4)
Treadles 1, 2, 3, 4. Repeat
or 4, 3, 2, 1. Repeat

For pattern (11), — 3-1 twill — weave on tie-up (b-3) or (b-4)
Treadles 5, 6, 7, 8 or 8, 7, 6, 5. Repeat

(For patterns (10) and (11), only four Treadles need be tied for either.)

Diagram 7 (50)

warp-ends to the inch in the setting, so it belongs to the "fifty-fifty" group of weaves.

When woven as shown at (b) 1 and 2 on the diagram it makes a pattern of 45 per cent diagonals, either right or left. If the diagonals are in the direction of the twist of the yarn a smoother fabric will result than if woven in reverse. The twill fabric is heavier and more pliable than a tabby fabric of the same material, and these qualities make it the most desirable weave for suit-fabrics and coat-fabrics.

A few of the many variations of four-harness twill are given on diagram No. 7. Those who do not wish a diagonal rib, for instance, use treadling No. (5) or No. (6) which give an all-over effect. If a heavy rib is desired one may weave a 3–1 twill as at (11). No. (10) shows the reverse of (11) with the heavy rib in warp rather than in weft.

By treadling as at (9)—both warp-face and weft-face over and under the same warp—a very heavy fabric for blankets or heavy coats may be woven. If desired it may have the two sides in different colors. Both sides, of course, will be in weft-faced weaving.

The tie-ups at (b-3) and (d-4) require more treadles than usually found on a four-harness loom. The two-faced effect may be woven on a six-treadle tie-up, though not as conveniently as on the tie-up shown. Tie each harness to a single treadle and add the two tabby treadles, as: 1, 2, 3, 4, A, B, tie-up (b-3) and treadles 5, 6, 7, 8, A, B, tie-up (b-2). The three-harness sheds must then be made by depressing one or the other of the tabby treadles with the required additional treadle.

Anyone planning a twill project is well advised to set up a narrow warp of two yards or so for samples and experiment before putting a large warp on the loom.

II "Corkscrew" and Eight-Harness Twills

The five-harness and seven-harness twills given at (a) and (b), Diagram 8, are particularly good for tweeds and similar fabrics. These weaves produce a very firm fabric with the effect of a steep diagonal going one way and a flat diagonal in the opposite direction.

118 —

Corkscrew Twills—
  (a) and (b)
Eight-Harness Twills
  (c)

(All Tie-ups are for the rising shed.)

Weave (a): 1, 2, 3, 4, 5.
  (b): 1, 2, 3, 4, 5, 6, 7

Weave (C-1), (C-2),
(C-3), (C-4), (C-5), (C-6):
Treadles
  1, 2, 3, 4, 5, 6, 7, 8.
Weave (C-7)
Treadles 1, 2, 3, 4, 5, 6, 7, 8, 9, 10, 11, 12, 13, 14.

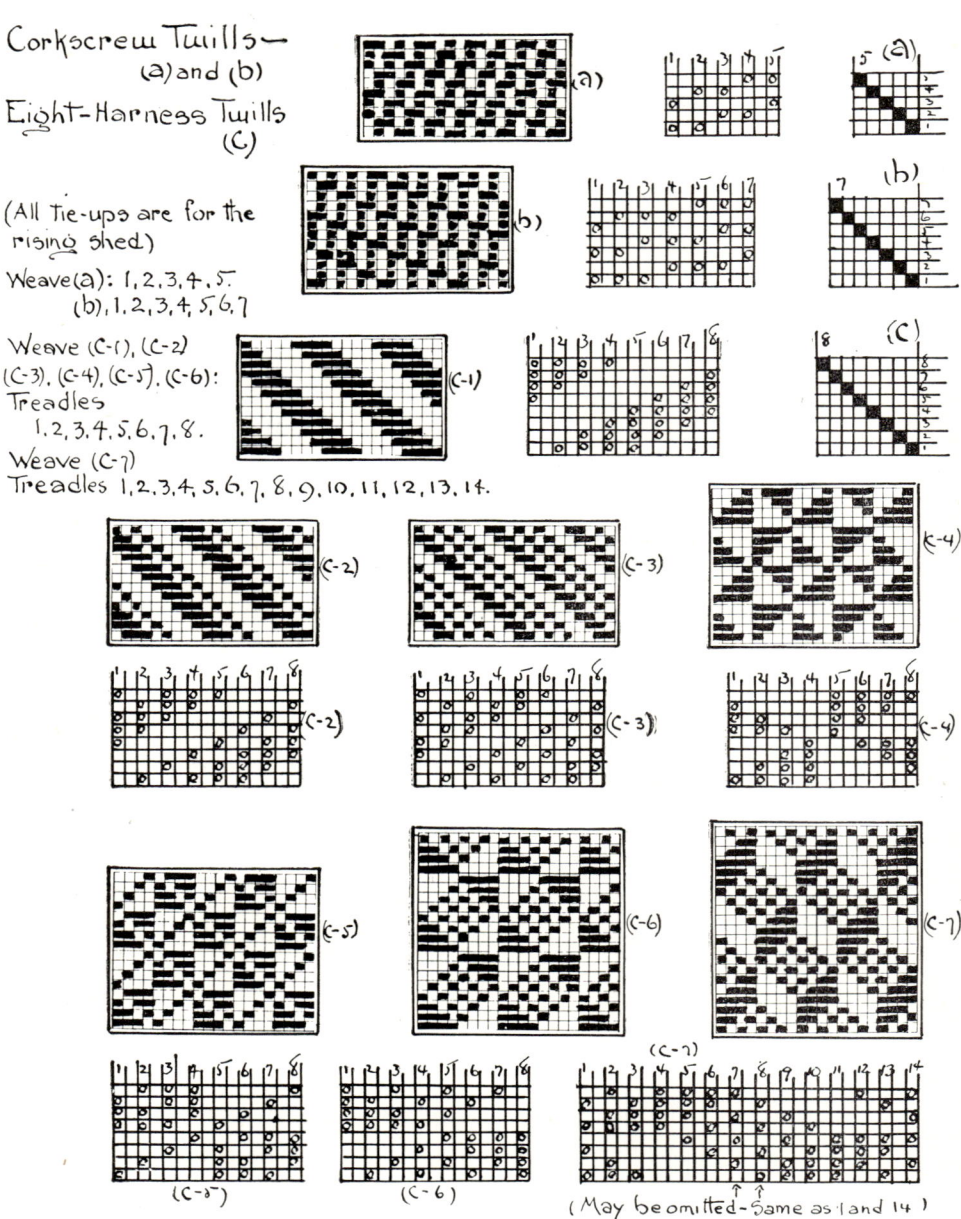

(May be omitted—Same as 1 and 14)

Diagram 8 (51)

The eight-harness twill threading may be woven in a great many ways, a few of which are shown on the diagram. A special tie-up is required for each of these patterns as indicated on the diagram, the treadling being always the same, weaving the treadles in turn, one shot on each treadle, either from left to right and repeat or from right to left and repeat. The very open weaves such as (c–6) and (c–7) are excellent for couch blankets and baby blankets. The closer weaves such as (c–3) are excellent for coat-fabrics. The pattern at (c–4) is one often seen in colored cotton tablecloths from Sweden. It has the effect of little windmills.

Tweeds and other fabrics in plain twill are usually woven with warp in one color and weft in another. If the colors are in sharp contrast the figure becomes prominent. If the colors differ only a little in value an interesting blend results. Many twill patterns depend on a special arrangement of two colors in both warp and weft. The favorite "shepherd's check" or "hound's-tooth" for instance, is produced by warping two threads dark and two light and weaving in the same order, two shots dark, two shots light. The "Glengarry" effects that are so popular are designed: two threads dark, two light, for a certain number of repeats, and then four dark and four light for a narrower space. Woven in the same arrangement of colors. There are numberless variations.

Something should be said about the edges. If a four-harness twill is set up on an even number of ends, with the first thread on harness 1 and the last thread on harness 4, it will be found that a single thread along one edge or the other will fail to weave in. On which side this skip will occur depends on whether the shuttle for the first shot is thrown from right to left or from left to right. To avoid this minor difficulty, begin the threading on 2 or end on 3.

The edges for some of the more open eight-harness twills are sometimes quite a nuisance. If the loom carries ten harnesses, a narrow selvage on each side may be set in plain weave on the two extra harnesses. If extra harnesses are not available the most practical way to overcome the difficulty is to weave with two shuttles, both carrying the same material. Weave the shuttles alternately. If the shuttles are laid down in correct order so that the two weft threads catch each other at the edges a good selvage will result.

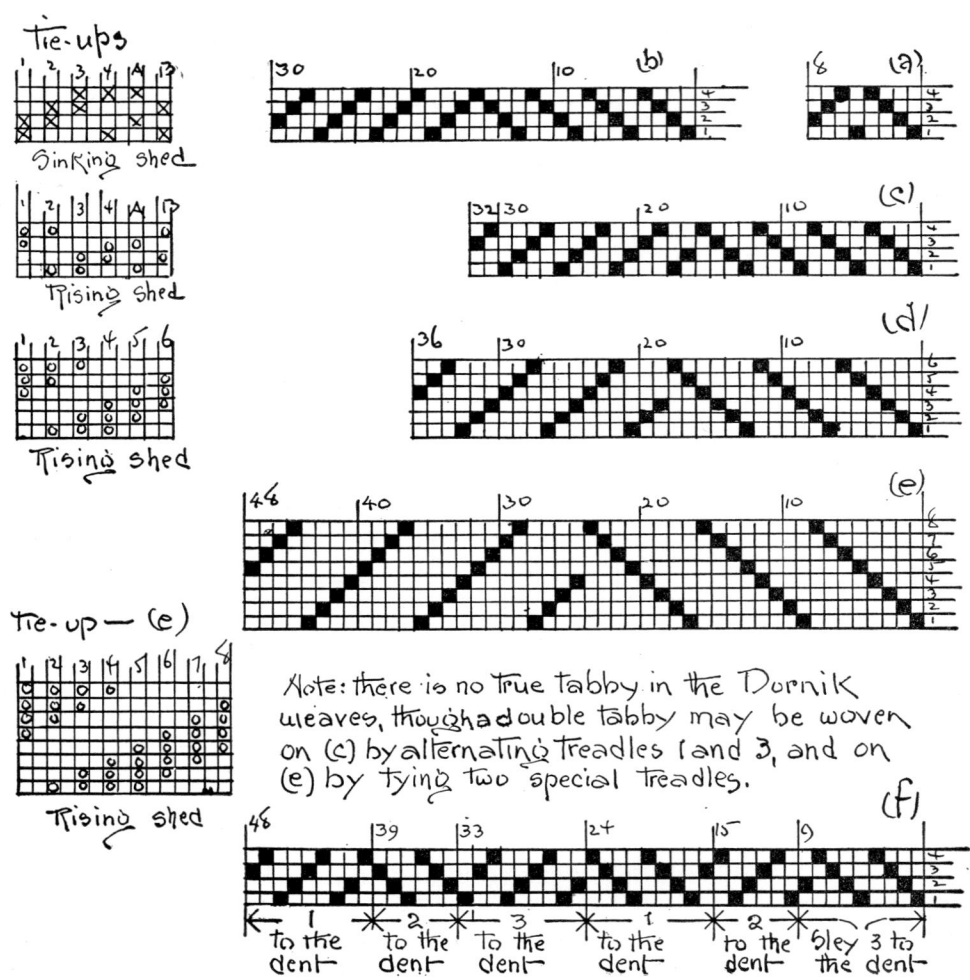

Diagram 9 (52)

Modified Twills

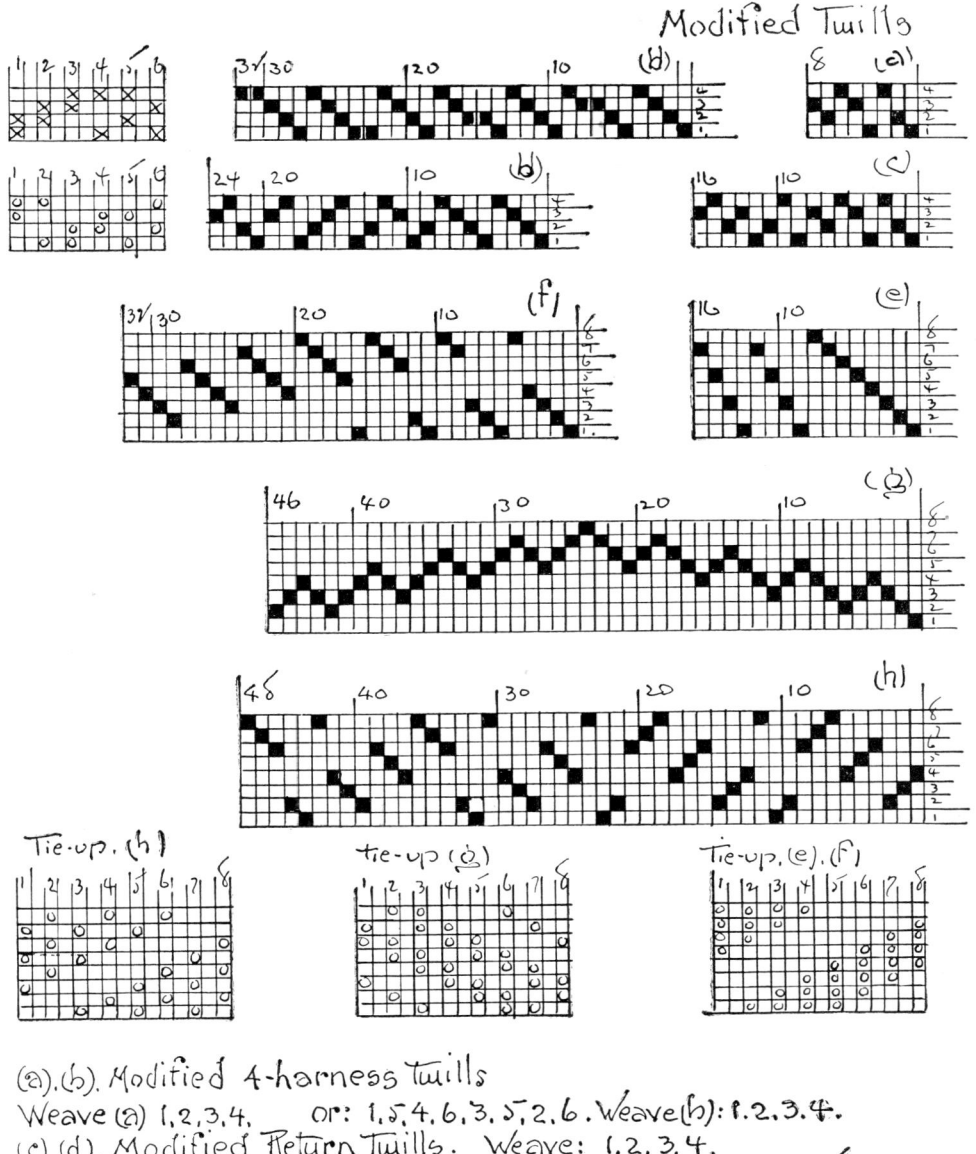

(a),(b). Modified 4-harness Twills
Weave (a) 1,2,3,4, or: 1,5,4,6,3,5,2,6. Weave (b): 1,2,3,4.
(c),(d). Modified Return Twills. Weave: 1,2,3,4.
(e),(f). Modified 8-harness Twills. Weave: 1,2,3,4,5,6,7,8
 (f) may also be woven: 1,2,3,4,8, 1,2,3,7,8, 1,2,6,7,8,
  · 5,6,7,8, 4,5,6,7, 3,4,5,6, 2,3,4,5
(g),(h). Return Twills. Weave: 1,2,3,4,5,6,7,8,7,6,5,4,3,2.

Diagram 10 (53)

III Return Twills—Modified Twills

What may be called "return" twills are of much interest. The little pattern at (a), Diagram 9, is composed of two runs of twill, the second one reversed. This pattern is called "Rosengang" in the Swedish books and is the foundation of much Swedish weaving. In Colonial days it was called "Bird-Eye" and was used chiefly as a small diamond-shaped, all-over figure in linen towelling and also in blankets—the latter usually set in a large plaid pattern in two colors, woven: treadles 1, 2, 3, 4, 3, 2 and repeat, one shot on each treadle and no tabby.

The pattern at (b) is called "Goose-Eye" when woven to make diamond figures, and "Herringbone" when woven to make chevrons. For the first, weave: treadles 1, 2, 3, 4, repeated three times; 1, 2, 3, 2, 1; then, 4, 3, 2, 1, repeated twice; end 4, 3, 2, and repeat. For herringbone weave: treadles 1, 2, 3, 4 and repeat. This weave may also be used for linens and other materials, but when woven in wool for tweeds a variation of the threading known as "Dornik" is usually used instead. This consists, as a study of draft (c) on the diagram will show, of omitting one thread each time at the point of "return" of the pattern. The purpose of this is to eliminate the three-thread skips that otherwise occur at these points. They break the structure of the weave and have the effect of recurring small mistakes in weaving.

The name "dornik," I have read, is derived from the name of a town in Belgium where this innovation was first introduced.

The draft at (f) shows an interesting use of a conventional dornik threading that depends for its unusual effect on the manner in which it is sleyed. The piece from which the draft was written was a necktie sent from England, done in a fine wool yarn. The weave is also excellent for scarves, and is best when warp and weft are of the same material and in the same color.

There are innumerable modified twills, of which only a few can be given here, Diagram 10. Those who enjoy experiment will find this a wonderful field.

Chapter Eleven: The Four-Harness Overshot Weave

When the revival of hand-weaving began, soon after the turn of the century, the four-harness overshot weave appears to have been the only form of pattern weaving still known and practised in this country by hand-weavers. Weaver Rose in Rhode Island made his coverlets and "hap-harlots" in this weave, and so did the few ancients still weaving in the backwoods of Kentucky and Tennessee. There were old pieces in museums and private collections done in other forms of weaving, but in several books on the subject these were solemnly proclaimed as a "lost art." There can, of course, be no "lost art" in weaving as long as a sample survives.

There are still a good many weavers who work only in overshot, but their number is declining, and most of the weavers of today use a variety of techniques. Overshot, to be sure, still holds a charm for many—not only because it is a part of our American tradition but also because it is handsome and effective, with extremely varied pattern possibilities—and is very simple and easy.

The weave is ancient and is common to many countries. It probably came to us with the Puritan settlers of New England, as some of the old pattern names seem to indicate. Curiously enough, however, though many old coverlets have come down to our time in good useable condition, my English correspondents tell me that they have been unable to discover so much as a single example in England.

The Scandinavian books on weaving show this weave, but in a few patterns, only. The amazing proliferation of patterns appears to have been a purely American Colonial development, so they constitute an authentic American popular art. Weavers exchanged "draughts," written on the backs of old docu-

124 —

(54) Lace and Compass, from North Carolina, woven in brown and gold. Draft number 76.

ments or scraps of paper—for paper was precious in those days—carefully sewed together in strips and usually annoted with a quaint old name and the directions "Wove as drawn." While some exchanged, others kept their patterns as a secret, as women exchange or hoard recipes for cooking. One comes upon them in old trunks or laid away between the yellowed pages of old diaries. Some are in unfamiliar notation, and most contain at least one mistake.

As previously noted, overshot is not a suitable weave for some things, such as rugs and dress-fabrics, or for linens, but it remains a delightful weave with many uses.

A beginner's first weaving should, I think, be in four-harness overshot. The thing is surprisingly simple and effective, and a first piece will be an exciting adventure, like seeing a little flower garden spring into blossom under one's fingers. I can remember the thrill of my first piece—the pattern was "Double Chariot-Wheels," sometimes called "Church Windows," made up of groups of four little wheels with star-figured centers, separated by nice square "tables." I could scarcely believe it was happening—and so easily and quickly with a few passes of the shuttles back and forth.

I Structure of the Overshot Weave

In overshot weaving the pattern is produced in an arrangement of "skips" or "floats," usually in a fairly heavy colored material—wool or worsted by preference—over a foundation tabby fabric in material finer than the pattern weft.

In this weave, as in most four-harness weaves, the harnesses are operated in pairs—two up and two down on each shed. In four harnesses there are six pairs: 1–2; 2–3, 3–4, 1–4, 2–4 and 3–1. There are three sets of "opposite" pairs: when harnesses 1 and 2 are down, harnesses 3 and 4 are raised; when 3 and 4 are down, 1 and 2 are raised, so these are opposite pairs. In the same way the 2–3 and 1–4 pairs are opposites and also the 2–4 and 1–3 pairs. One pair of opposites must be reserved for the two tabby sheds on which the foundation fabric is woven, leaving four sheds for the pattern. Any one of the three pairs of opposites may be used for tabby, but the general practise among modern weavers is to write the tabby on 2–4 and 1–3—odds against evens. This is merely a matter of convenience and many old drafts, especially those from the South, are written on a 1–2, 3–4 tabby, and even a few on the 2–3, 1–4 tabby. All overshot drafts in this book are written on the 2–4, 1–3 tabby.

The skips are produced by threading sections of the warp on one or the other of the shed combinations. It is obvious that if a group of threads is threaded: 1, 2, 1, 2, 1, 2, when harnesses 1 and 2 are brought down together these threads will all be down and the shuttle will pass over them, making a skip. In the same manner three other skips may be produced. These are known as the four "blocks" of the pattern, and the figure depends on the arrangement and different widths of these four blocks.

In most of the Colonial patterns in this weave the blocks follow one another in "twill" succession. That is to say that the last thread of the first block is the first thread of the second block, and so on. The blocks overlap by one thread. A block threaded on the 1–2 shed may end on either a 1 or a 2. If it ends on 2 the following block will be a 2–3 block, and if it ends on 1 the succeeding block will be on the 1–4 shed.

It makes no difference in the result which shed is used for the first block of a pattern, and four different drafts may be written that, when woven, will produce exactly the same result. For the sake of uniform appearance on the page, the drafts in this book have been written with the first block on the 1–2 shed.

Most of the old patterns are written with the blocks arranged symmetrically between two centers, which may or may not be on the same shed. For convenience in arranging patterns for the loom, most of the drafts in this book have been written from center to center of the smaller of the two figures of which a pattern is usually composed. However, when patterns include a square "table" figure this has usually been written first, simply because when written so the pattern is clearer to the eye.

It will be noted by a study of the drafts that blocks that follow in regular sequence are always of an even number of threads, but that the centers—the blocks on which a pattern "returns"—must be of an uneven number of threads to keep the correct alternation of odd and even and so to preserve the tabby. A thread on harness 1 should never be preceded or followed by a thread on harness 3, as the result would be a double thread in the tabby; and the same is true of threads on 2 and 4.

Again, a study of the drafts will show that when a pattern shed is woven the weft will pass over all groups of threads threaded on that shed, to make a skip, and will pass under all groups threaded on the opposite shed, to make a skip under the tabby foundation, and will weave over alternate threads of the other two blocks, which occur on either side of the skip. Where the pattern weft tabbies in this fashion it produces a "half-tone." As a result we have a pattern in skips, a secondary pattern in plain blocks of tabby foundation, and a shadowy half-tone filling the spaces between.

The half-tone areas soften the effect of the figure in skips, and a much more brilliant effect results if the half-tone is eliminated. This may be accomplished by writing a pattern on opposite sheds, so that the pattern weft skips over and under the tabby foundation without interweaving with the warp. Patterns of this type are drafts 121–125 in this book.

It will be obvious that these patterns are limited to two blocks. In pattern 121, for instance, written on the 1–2 and 3–4 pattern sheds, if a 2–3 shed were to be woven it would tabby across both pattern blocks and would weave a little two-thread skip where the shift is from 1–2 to 3–4. A 1–4 shot would also tabby across both blocks and would weave a two-thread skip where the shift is from 3–4 to 1–2.

Many four-block patterns are written with one figure on one pair of opposites and the other figure on the other pair. The result of this is a figure in skips against a plain tabby foundation, with half-tone over the second figure, the small two-thread skips producing an odd effect of perpendicular lines in the background. We call these lines "accidentals." They cannot be eliminated except by writing the draft on eight harnesses, as in drafts 148 and 149.

(55) Star in the Wilderness from North Carolina, woven rose-fashion, in blue, rose and tan. Draft number 76.

Sometimes part of a pattern is written on opposites while the rest is written in the conventional manner. Sometimes a pair of opposites is put at the center of a figure to give it a high-light.

Illustration (42) shows a four-block pattern on opposites in which the accidentals are prominent. On illustration (92), No. 1 is a two-block pattern on opposites; 2, 4 and 6 are four-block patterns on opposites; 3 and 7 are patterns partly on opposites. Illustration (93) is a four-block pattern on opposites. Other examples will be noted.

The Scandinavian custom is to write patterns on opposites right through in the same direction, as in draft 132 which gives a different accidental on either side of the blocks. For instance, in the table figure in this draft there is a 2–3 accidental between the first two blocks and a 1–4 accidental between the second and third blocks. Our New England weavers, however, with their passion for symmetry, often balanced the accidentals from a center, as in the old coverlet shown in illustration (42). The draft-writer has a choice in the matter, and by shifting the accidentals may improve or mar a pattern.

II Overshot Weaving—Draft Writing

To weave intelligently the weaver should have a thorough understanding of the drafts—should be able to "prove" drafts on paper, and to write drafts with ease and accuracy from samples or photographs. The ability to do these things is the chief difference between a weaver and a "shuttle-pusher."

The form of notation in general use among modern hand-weavers, for patterns in overshot weaving and for most four-harness weaves, is the one used in this book. The harnesses are represented by the spaces between the ruled lines, the bottom horizonal space, numbered 1, being taken to represent harness 1, the front harness of the loom; and the top space, numbered 4, the fourth harness. A black square in the lowest row represents a warp-thread drawn through the eye of a heddle on harness 1, and so on. This form of draft is shown at (a), Diagram 11.

Several other forms of notation are sometimes encountered and should be noted to avoid confusion. The form at (b), Diagram 11, is an English form of notation and is to be found among old drafts from New England. In this draft

Systems of Notation for threading Drafts
The Four-Harness Weaves.

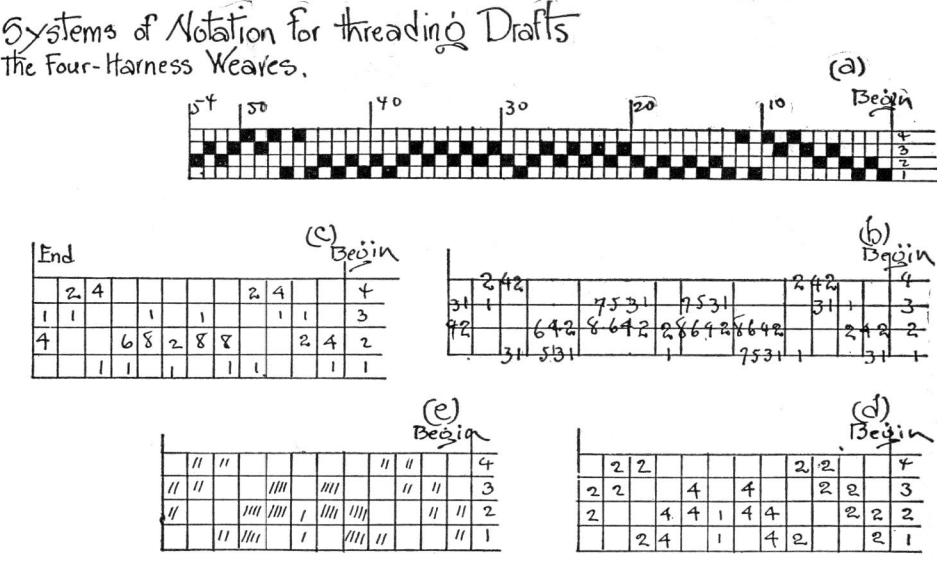

Diagram 11 (56)

the ruled lines represent the harnesses and the figures indicate the threads. The perpendicular lines divide the draft into blocks. At (c) is a short form of the same draft, each perpendicular space representing a block of the pattern and the figures the first and last threads in each block. These are entirely clear and workmanlike forms of draft, which cannot be said for the drafts at (d) and (e). These forms, still in use among the mountain weavers of the South, do not indicate the first and last threads of the blocks and result in inconsistencies. Suppose block one, draft (d), is threaded as shown, with four threads: 1, 2, 1, 2; and the following block with four threads: 3, 2, 3, 2, followed by 3, 4, 3, 4. It is plain that the second block—as it overlaps the first and third blocks each by one thread—will be a six-thread block instead of a four-thread block. In pieces threaded from drafts written in this manner the corresponding blocks on either side of a center are always two threads different in size. This peculiarity may be seen very plainly in the piece illustrated on (34). The New England weavers did not tolerate such lopsidedness, and it does not appear to be a thing worth preserving. Old drafts from the South should be rewritten in the better form of notation and corrected before used on the loom.

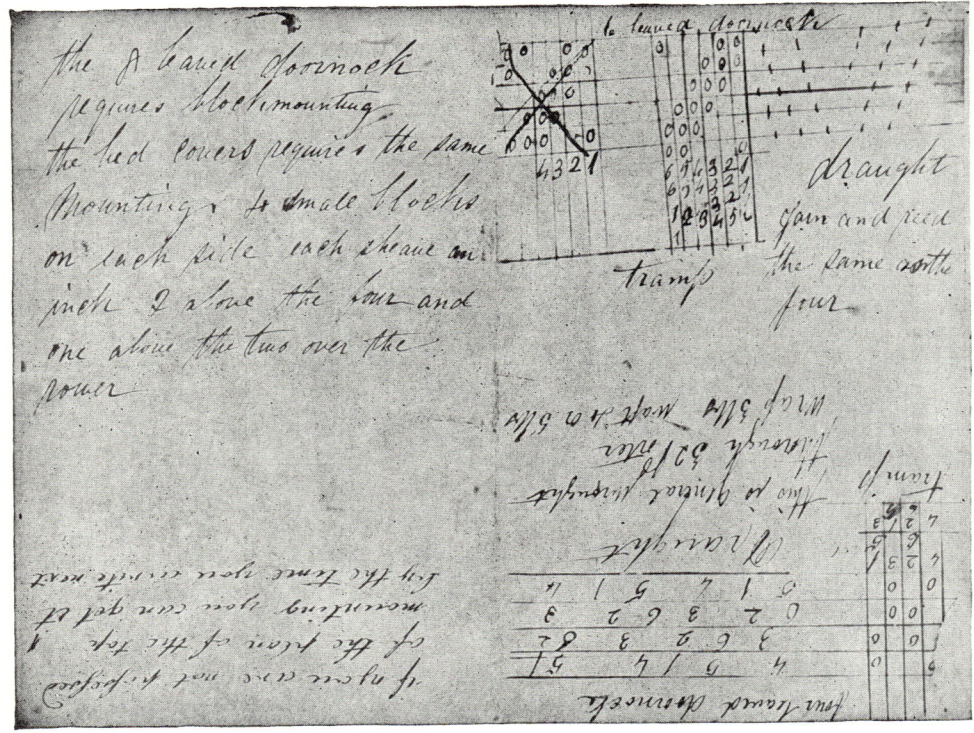

(57) An old letter from one weaver to another. Front page.

The only advantage of this form of notation is that it takes little space and can be written rapidly. For taking notes in museums or at exhibitions it may be used if one wishes, though such notes should be rewritten as suggested for use or for filing away permanently.

Recently some teachers have advocated writing drafts for overshot weaving in what they call the "profile" form of notation. This is a convenient and accepted form for drafts in some other weaves, but for the overshot weave it leaves too much to the imagination and threadings made from such drafts are apt to show errors.

Before putting a pattern on the loom it is wise to "weave" it first on paper in order to make sure the draft is correct and also to judge the effect of the pattern. For this work use cross-section paper and a heavy lettering pen. The

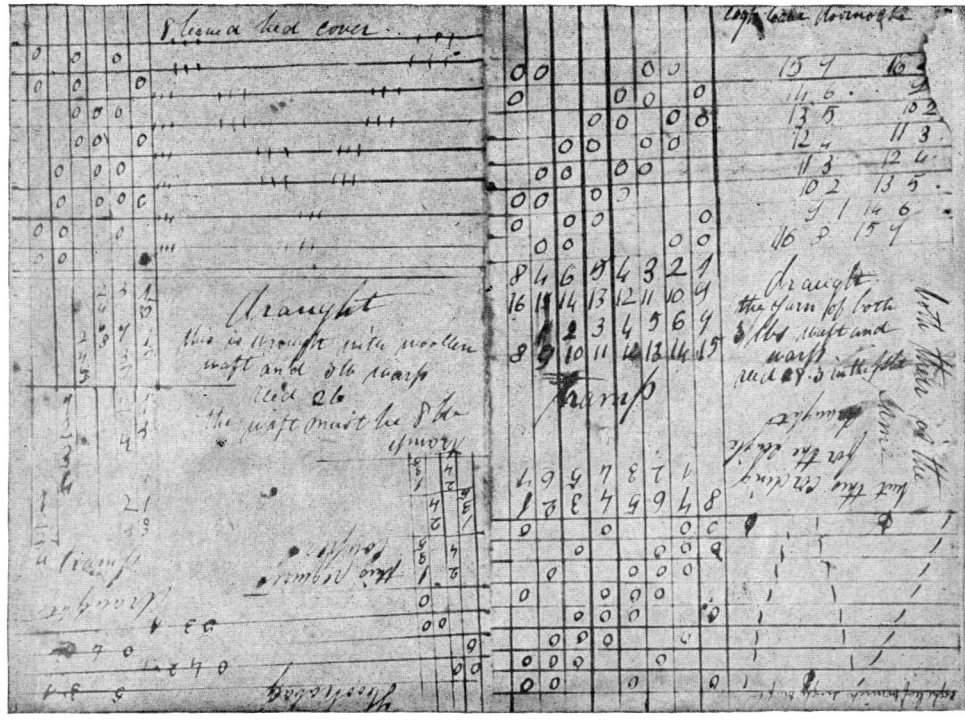

(58) Back page of the same letter.

best paper to use is that with a ruling of 16 x 16 to the inch, which makes the pattern when drawn upon it exactly the size it would be if woven on a warp set at sixteen ends to the inch. However, this is somewhat hard on the eyes and paper ruled 10 x 10 to the inch may be used instead. The resulting drawings are much larger, of course, but when pinned to the wall and seen from a distance they give the effect well enough.

No training in drawing is required for this work. Set down the draft across the top of the paper, putting in a little more than a single repeat. If there should be an error in the draft, in ninety-nine cases out of a hundred it will occur at the point of repeat, so this should be tested. Also as the point of repeat is usually one of the two centers of the pattern, the figure will not be shown satisfactorily unless the drawing is carried beyond the center.

Weaving on Paper

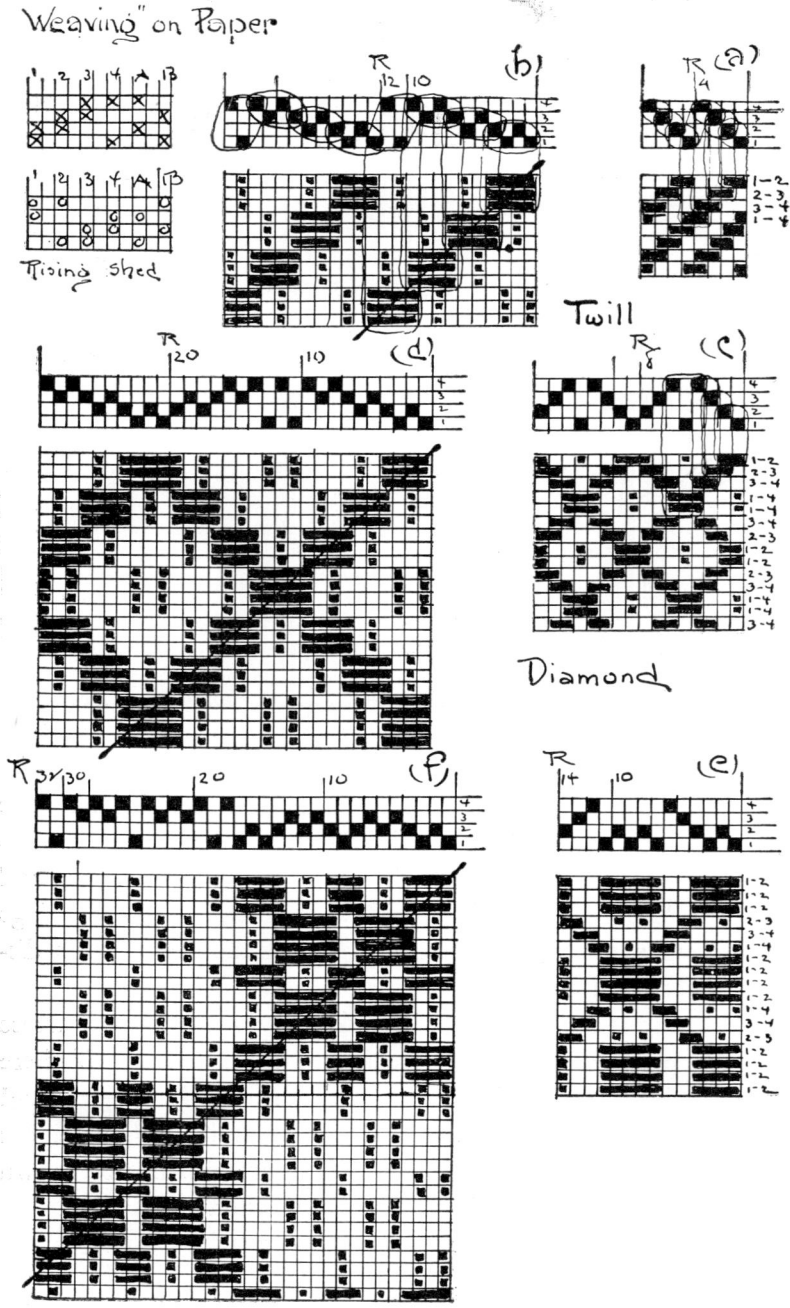

Diagram 12 (59)

The ruling of the paper is taken to represent the tabby foundation of the fabric, with a warp threaded as in the draft and the perpendicular spaces of the paper representing the warp. The horizontal spaces represent the weft.

Put in the pattern weft with the pen, exactly as it would be woven with a shuttle across the threaded warp, except that the pattern develops downward instead of upward as when one sits at the loom. At (a), Diagram 12, is shown a run of four-harness twill and at (b) a twill succession of four-thread blocks, and below each the development. Note that each shed should be "woven" with one weft shot less than the number of warp-ends under the block. This is to compensate for the overlapping of blocks by one thread. In the twill pattern all the blocks are two-thread blocks that require a single weft-shot. The four-thread blocks in draft (b) require three weft-shots each. Note that each pen-stroke should be carried all across the draft—in horizontal lines to indicate the skips and in dots over the threads of the adjoining blocks where the pattern weft tabbies to make the half-tone.

"Weave" the first block of the draft in this manner. Next weave the second block in the same manner, with the number of penstrokes required to square it—one stroke less than the number of warp-ends under the block. And so continue through the draft. It will be noted that the blocks follow one another along a diagonal line, and when this line runs from the upper right hand corner to the lower left hand corner, under the last block of the draft, the drawing will be complete and will show the figure exactly as it would appear when woven.

This diagonal line runs through all patterns in this weave, when woven according to the draft. But in many patterns the blocks on the same shed may differ considerably in size. For instance in the draft at (a), Diagram 11, the first block is a four-thread 1-2 block and should be woven with three pen-strokes, even across the fifth block which is an eight-thread block. When the fifth block is reached in the development it should be indicated by seven pen-strokes instead of three, though it is on the same shed as the first block.

A somewhat more rapid way to make these developments, and just as accurate as a representation of the pattern, is to block in the pattern squares in solid black and to represent the half-tone by perpendicular pen-lines, as shown in a number of the drawings in this book—in illustration (48) for instance. First drawings, however, should be made by the method first described as it shows each weft-shot exactly as laid by the shuttle.

Writing a threading draft from a woven sample or from a photograph is simple enough. Take, for instance, the old piece shown in illustration (60); ignoring the border for the moment, it will be observed that the pattern consists of a square "table" figure and a connecting cross. Theoretically the draft may be written from any block to the next corresponding block, but for convenience it is well to make the first block of the draft either the block at the upper right hand corner of the table, or the block at the center of the cross. Suppose we decide to begin with the table; the first block may be written on any one of the four pattern sheds, but it is convenient to begin with 1-2. This is not a

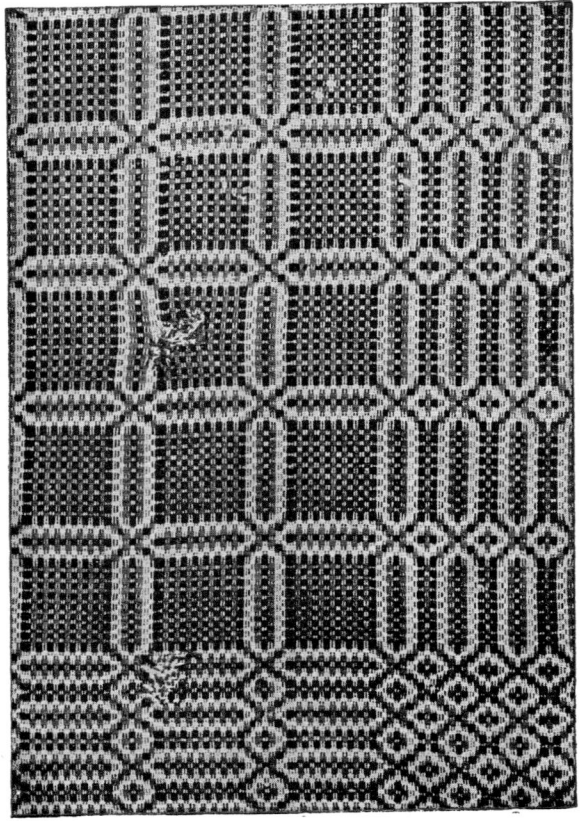

(60) A simple pattern similar to Butternut, but larger. From an ancient coverlet in blue and rose. Draft number 8.

return block, so it will be of an even number of threads, apparently six, written: 1, 2, 1, 2, 1, 2. The second block will be a 2–3 block, and as it is a return block will be of five threads—the 2 which is the last thread of the first block and four more: (2), 3, 2, 3, 2. Next is a return block on the first shed, also of five threads: (2), 1, 2, 1, 2. These two five-thread blocks alternate till the eighth 1–2 block is reached, which makes the lower left hand corner of the table if the blocks are followed through along the diagonal. This will be of an even number of threads, like the first block. In the illustration it is larger than the first block, probably due to a draft in the southern style of notation, but it would be better to make it the same as the first block. It should be written: (2), 1, 2, 1, 2, 1.

The first block of the cross figure will necessarily be on the 1–4 shed, as the first thread is a 1 and it is not a 1–2 block. In the illustration some of the blocks of the cross figure are of four threads and some of six. It is just as well to follow the New England custom and make them all of the same number of ends—either four or six, as preferred. Suppose we write them of six ends each with the center block, which must be of an uneven number of ends, on five threads. The threading for the cross figure then would be: (1), 4, 1, 4, 1, 4; next block: (4), 3, 4, 3, 4, 3; following block: (3), 2, 3, 2, 3, 2, and the center block: (2), 1, 2, 1, 2. The first block past the center would of course be: (2), 3, 2, 3, 2, 3; followed by: (3), 4, 3, 4, 3, 4; and (4), 1, 4, 1, 4, (1). The last "1" being the first thread of the next repeat.

In patterns like this one, and all those that show a diagonal, it is easier to write the blocks along the diagonal rather than straight across. The diagonal is like the magic clue in the old stories that leads one safely through a maze.

Anyone planning to be a weaver should write and prove many drafts till the process becomes as simple as writing one's name and address.

III Arranging a Pattern for the Loom—Borders

A good deal of simple arithmetic is involved in arranging a pattern for a specific project, as for a coverlet or table runner. In the case of a large pattern covering several hundred warp-ends it is sometimes quite difficult—especially if a predetermined number of warp-ends in the warp must be taken into account. Sometimes the arrangement may necessitate modifying the draft to some extent

—adding a pair of blocks to a "table" figure, for instance, to make the pattern a few threads larger, or decreasing the table in the same manner. Or a pair of threads may have to be added to the blocks of the main figure, and so on. In doing this one must be careful not to change the proportions of the figure so much as to spoil the effect. When a border is planned, the troublesome threads may usually be added to or subtracted from the border. In any event, it is well to prove the modified arrangement on paper before putting it on the loom.

If no side borders are required for the project in hand, the arrangement consists merely in centering the pattern so that it will come out symmetrically on the edges, and so that it will end at some logical point in the pattern. Suppose, for instance, that we have a warp of 600 ends—as on a 20-inch table-loom set up with a fine cotton warp at 30 ends to the inch—and that a small all-over pattern is desired and draft No. 8, "Butternut," has been selected. Our 600 warp-ends will give us sixteen repeats of the draft with a remainder of 24 threads. Three threads will be required to complete the last repeat, threaded: 1, 2, 1. This leaves 21 threads for selvages, to be threaded in twill. The complete arrangement then would be:

Selvage, 3, 4, 1, 2, 3, 4, 1, 2, 3, 4	10 threads
Sixteen repeats of the draft	576
End of last repeat, 1, 2, 1	3
Selvage, 4, 3, 2, 1, 4, 3, 2, 1, 4, 3, 2	11
	600

For a large pattern to be used for a pillow-top, on the same number of warp-ends, suppose we choose draft 109: This is a composite pattern consisting of three figures—a large "sunrise" figure, threads 1–157; two small "table" figures, threads 157–253 and threads 333 to the end of the draft; and a central "star" figure, threads 253–353. The pattern will be symmetrical if we use one complete repeat of the draft followed by the sunrise figure—565 threads, leaving a remainder of 35 threads. These threads might all be threaded to twill for selvages, but if we prefer we may add 2 threads to the first block, the center block and the last block of each of the sunrise figures, which would account for 12 threads, leaving 23 threads for selvages. Or we might add 2 threads to each of the 3-thread blocks in the small 1–2 and 3–4 tables—at threads 203, 213,

223, 343, 353 and 363. This also would account for 12 threads. If we use both devices we shall have 11 threads for selvages—5 on one side and 6 on the other.

Of course if a special warp is made for the project the exact number of ends should be warped.

Arranging a pattern for a coverlet is a little more difficult. Coverlets in the overshot weave are ordinarily made in two strips, each 42 inches wide, and should have borders all around.

A concrete example will best illustrate the method of making the arrangement. Suppose the warp of the proposed coverlet is to be cotton 24/3 set at 30 ends to the inch. As the warp is to be 42 inches wide, there will be 1,260 warp-ends in the threading. Suppose further, that we wish to use the well-liked "Queen's Delight" pattern, draft No. 61, and suppose we wish a border between 6 and 8 inches wide.

As the coverlet is to be in two strips, seamed through the center, where is the place for the seam? It might run through the center of the square table figure or through the center of the star-and-rose figure. It would show less in the latter place, the 1–4 block, threads 142–144 on the draft. Beginning the threading at thread 142 and threading to the end of the draft requires 73 warp-ends. A six-inch border would take 180 more. Subtracting 253 from 1,260 leaves us 1,007 threads for the pattern. This will give us four complete repeats of the pattern with 151 threads as a remainder. However, the draft ends with the star-and-rose figure, and a better effect would be to have the table figure in the corners, including the first star and the blocks that make the frame around the table. This would be the first 101 threads of the draft. If we add the remaining 50 threads to the border we should have a border a little less than 8 inches wide, which would be satisfactory.

How should the border be threaded? Theoretically, any pattern in the same weave might be used as a border for any other pattern, but some combinations would be very unfortunate. For most patterns a small, simple figure makes the best border, but if the main pattern is a small figure the border pattern may be large and elaborate. The threadings most often used for borders are a twill succession of four-thread blocks—the first 12 threads of draft No. 1 used as a repeat—or one of the "diamond" threadings, as draft No. 1 and draft No. 2.

Borders in Overshot Weave

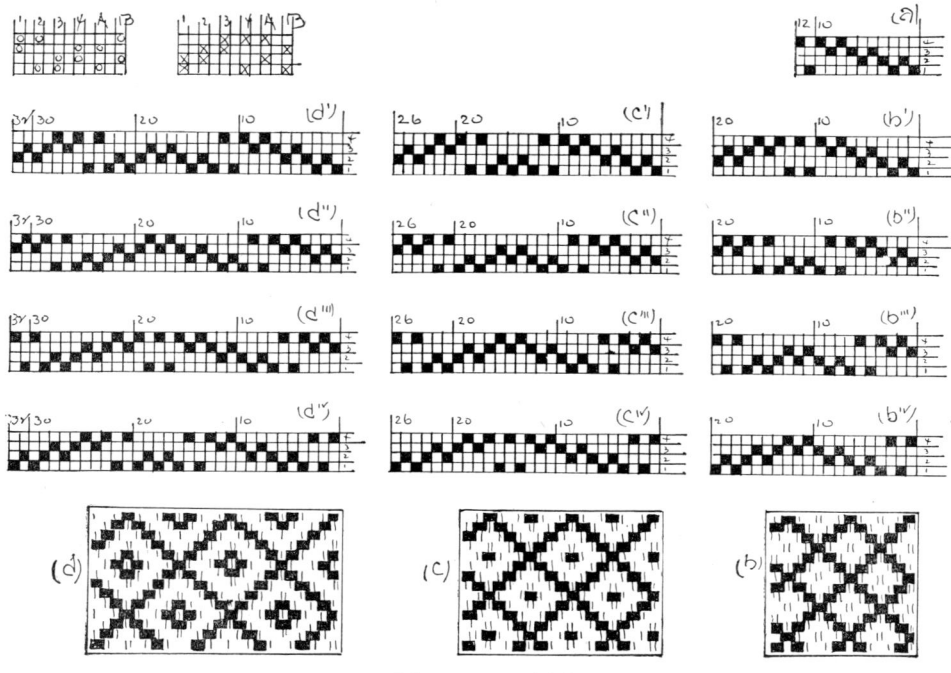

Diagram 13 (61)

(a) Twill succession of blocks
(b^I) Diamond pattern with the return on the fourth block—draft No. 2, Diagram No. 14. Returns on the 1–2 and 1–4 sheds
(b^II) The same pattern with the returns on 2–3 and 1–2
(b^III) The same pattern with the returns on 3–4 and 2–3
(b^IV) The same pattern with returns on 1–4 and 3–4
(c^I) The Diamond pattern with returns on the fifth block—draft No. 1, Diagram 14. Both returns on 1–2
(c^II) Returns on 2–3
(c^III) Returns on 3–4
(c^IV) Returns on 1–4
(d^I) Diamond pattern with returns on the sixth block. Returns on 1–2 and 2–3
(d^II) Returns on 2–3 and 3–4
(d^III) Returns on 3–4 and 1–4
(d^IV) Returns on 1–4 and 1–2

Note: These border threadings are for use with patterns written "to twill," with overlapping blocks. With patterns on opposites use draft No. 3, Diagram 14, or draft No. 5—re-written with four-thread blocks. For a pattern partly on opposites use draft No. 4.

For patterns on opposites, No. 3 or No. 5, written with smaller blocks, or for patterns partly on opposites, draft No. 4. Large patterns sometimes include a diamond figure, and when this is the case this figure may be used as a repeat for the border.

A border done in a twill run of blocks is rather lacking in interest, and though this threading makes a suitable frame for some patterns it should not be used for a wide border. Illustrations (76) and (69) show the effect. A diamond border is shown on illustration (29) and illustration (48). The latter is a very poorly arranged border as it does not join the main pattern correctly—the circle around the figure in the corner should, of course, be complete. The old-time weavers appear to have found the border problem difficult, even as you and I.

To return to our projected "Queen's Delight" coverlet: This pattern does not include a small diamond figure but the diamond pattern would make a suitable border. However, a border threading should center on the same block or blocks as the main pattern. The diamond pattern as given in draft No. 1 centers on the 1–2 block while the centers of the star-and-rose figure of our pattern are on the 1–4 and 3–4 blocks. Neither draft No. 1 nor draft No. 2 as given on Diagram 14 would fit this pattern. As has been explained previously, a draft may be written four different ways and will produce exactly the same figure when woven as drawn in. For convenience in arranging borders, three forms of the diamond figure are given, on Diagram 13, each written in four different ways, so that a border threading to fit any pattern may be selected without difficulty. For our problem draft (d^{III}) would give the best effect.

The final problem, of course, is joining the border to the main pattern. If the pattern and the border do not meet correctly the effect may be very bad. Illustration (48) has already been cited. Another poor joining is shown on illustration (108) where an incomplete rose-figure leads very awkwardly into the border.

We ended the threading for our proposed "Queen's Delight" coverlet on thread 101 of the draft. This thread should, of course, be the first thread of the border threading. Should this be the first thread of draft (d^{III}) or thread 13? Obviously the latter. We can now complete the arrangement as follows:

Arrangement for a coverlet in "Queen's Delight" pattern, Draft No. 61

Thread 142 to end of draft	73 threads
Complete draft, four times	856
First 101 threads of the draft	101
Border draft, thread 14 to end	19
Border threading, six times	192
Selvage, 1, 2, 3, 4 five times	20
	1261

The last thread of the selvage may be omitted.

This example was chosen because it illustrates several of the problems encountered in making an arrangement of this kind. Many patterns can be arranged much more easily. For instance draft No. 69, a "Lover's Knot" pattern: The point at which the draft begins is a good place for the seam. Repeat the pattern as written and add a border.

Draft 69, repeated eight times	1088 threads
Border, draft No. 1 eight times	160
Edge, 1, 2, 1	3
Selvage, 4, 3, 2, 1, 4, 3, 2, 1, 4	9
	1260

Note that no selvage is threaded on the seam edge of the coverlet. It would make an ugly streak through the piece. This edge must be watched carefully during weaving. If for reasons of lighting or personal idiosincracy the weaver ordinarily makes a better edge on one side than the other, the seam edge should be threaded on that side. The arrangements given have the seam edge on the right, but by reversing the order of the arrangement, beginning with the selvage and border, the seam edge may be threaded on the left.

As an example of an elaborate border and a simple main pattern, arrange draft No. 108 as follows: one complete repeat of the draft, for the border; repeat the last 44 threads of the draft as may be required for the center of the piece, ending the last repeat at the center of one or the other of the "Dog-Track" figures—at thread 432 or thread 454 of the draft. This will be the seam edge. For a narrow bed with a deep overhang this is an excellent pattern.

Another attractive border arrangement consists in threading a succession of plain twills—1, 2, 3, 4 and repeat—to the width desired, then one complete figure of the main pattern, followed by a series of reverse twills—4, 3, 2, 1— for the desired width.

IV Treadling

Any threading in the overshot weave may be treadled in a variety of ways, but for each pattern there is one method of treadling that is always correct and is the method of weaving for which the pattern was designed. This is to weave the pattern as threaded or "weaving as drawn in." For this no special treadling directions are required, and such directions if used are often misleading as the number of weft-shots to be woven over a given pattern block varies with the weight of the weft material, so that if written treadlings are followed implicitly the pattern may be squatty—if the weft is fine—or too long-drawn-out if the weft is coarse. The rule for correct treadling is to follow the diagonal, as explained in the chapter on weaving on paper, and to "square" each block as it comes up along the diagonal.

To weave in this manner it is not necessary to have the draft, or even to know what the pattern looks like. One may sit down at a loom threaded to an overshot pattern and weave it off correctly and easily like climbing up a flight of stairs. This may seem a little like magic, but it is very practical magic, and new weavers should practise this method of treadling from the beginning, as it saves time and makes for correct results.

I wish to make a point of this as so many weavers still refuse to believe it can be done. A woman once came to me with a sad story of having received a loom all threaded to a pattern but with no treadling directions and not even the name of the pattern. She said she spent two weeks trying to count the heddles and determine what the pattern might be and then gave up and re-threaded. When I told her she could have woven off the pattern and had a look at it before taking the threading out of the loom she refused to believe me. Fortunately I had a loom just threaded, standing ready, so I set her at it and as the pattern developed she was so pleased that I promised myself not to let anybody get away from me without this bit of useful knowledge.

Suppose, then, that you sit at a loom threaded to a pattern in overshot weaving, that you have woven a tabby heading and are ready to make the pattern. Open the shed that will weave a skip close to the right hand selvage. Usually it is the 1–2 shed on treadle 1, but it may not be. However, there are only four possible sheds so it takes very little time to find the correct treadle. Weave this first block square with the number of pattern shots that may be required—alternating tabby shots and pattern shots, of course. When this block is the right size find the shed for the second block. If the pattern is written in the conventional manner the second block will overlap the first block by one thread, and if the first block was on the 1–2 shed the second block will be either on the 2–3 shed or on the 1–4 shed. It is simple enough to try the treadles and find which is correct. Weave the second block square. The third block will be either a return to the first or will be the next block in regular succession. By this time the beginning of the diagonal will be apparent, and by following this line block by block the entire pattern will soon appear. If the diagonal is too flat, too few shots are being woven over the blocks; if it is too steep, too many shots are being used. If the line shows a break, the wrong shed has been woven. The diagonal should run straight at a 45-degree angle from the right hand lower corner right through the work. If the diagonal is correct the pattern will be correct, no matter how intricate it may be. Just why this is so I do not know. I have asked eminent mathematicians for an explanation, and one of them constructed an elaborate affair of wires that seemed to him to solve the mystery, but I confess it meant nothing to me.

The law of diagonals holds good for patterns written on opposites, though in such patterns some of the blocks do not overlap. If the pattern is on opposites the space to the left of the first block—under what will be the second block—is in tabby background instead of in half-tone. In that event, the second block should be woven on the shed opposite to that used for the first block. If the first block was on 1–2, for instance, the second block will be on 3–4. It is no more difficult to follow the diagonal through such a pattern than through a pattern written to twill.

Though all patterns may be woven correctly by the method described above, and though all patterns may be treadled and woven in a variety of fancy effects, there is one standard modification of treadling often used for patterns that include a star-figure, as so many do. The stars may be woven as roses, and no diagonal runs through the pattern. Some patterns, such as the "Queen's Delight" pattern and "Wheel of Fortune," include both the star and rose figures, and a study of the drafts will show how the effect is produced, the rose figure

— 143

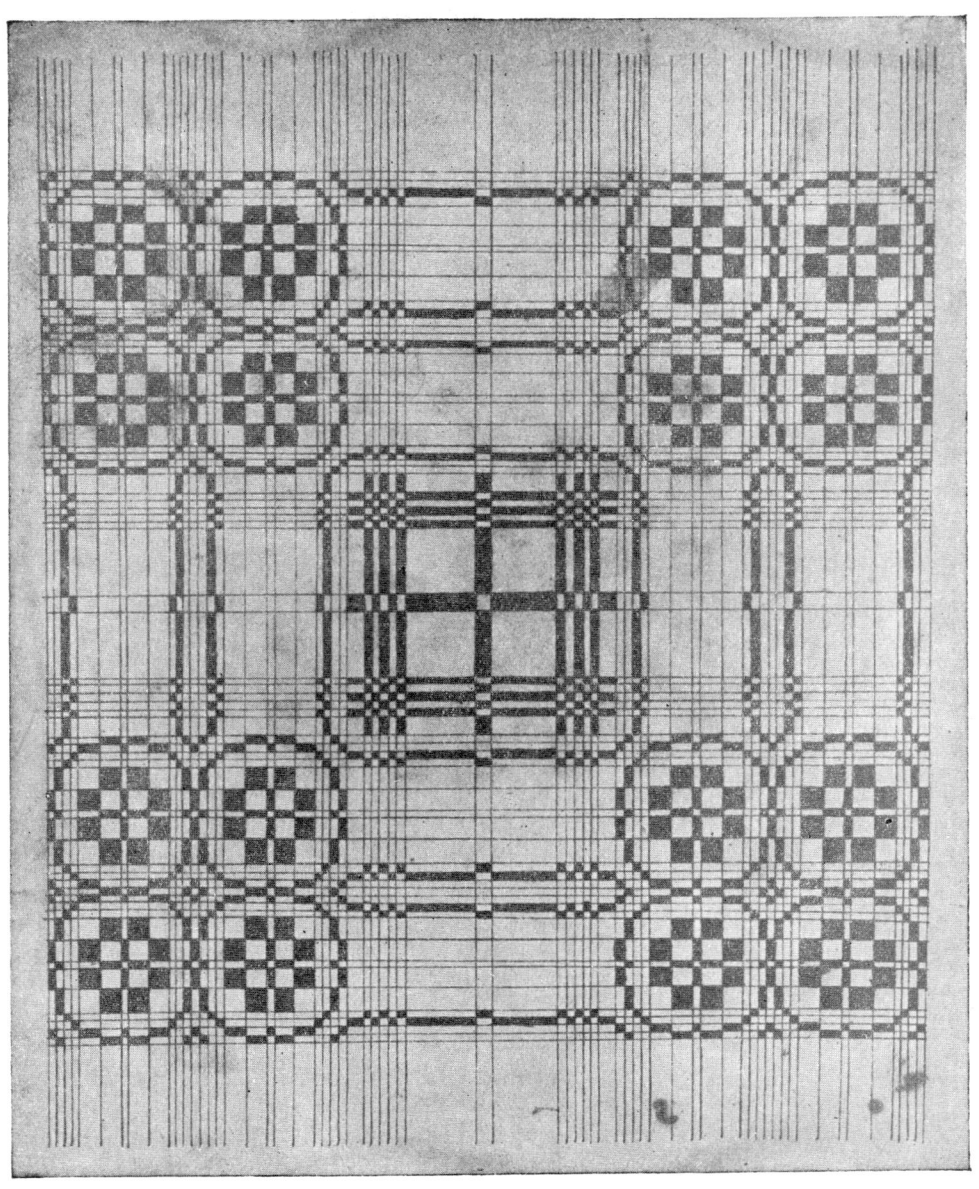

(62) A pattern from the John Landes book of drawings in the Pennsylvania Museum.

being written on the same two sheds as the star figure but with the order reversed. The rose effect is produced in treadling by reversing the order of the treadles for the star figure. Note illustrations (54) and (55). A friend from the South sent me the two old coverlets from which these illustrations were made with the request that I write the drafts. It developed that both were woven on the same draft—the pattern at (54) woven as drawn in, and the one at (56) woven rose-fashion. The favorite old pattern "Whig Rose" is simply a rose-fashion treadling of a simple "Lover's Knot" threading. The regular treadling and the rose-fashion modification of a simple little star-figure threading is shown with draft No. 30, Diagram 18. In this figure the star is on the 1–2 and 2–3 sheds, and when woven regularly the first block is treadle 1, seven shots—as on paper; as woven on the loom more or fewer according to the material used—treadle 2, six shots; treadle 1, two shots; treadle 2, six shots; treadle 1, seven shots. To turn this into a rose the treadling would be: treadle 2, seven shots; treadle 1, six shots; treadle 2, two shots; treadle 1, six shots; treadle 2, seven shots. To reverse the little three-block cross treadle 3, three shots; treadle 4, four shots; treadle 3, three shots. Note that the number of shots should be as for the block as written, though using the sheds in reverse order.

Some patterns are a little difficult to reverse correctly and it is wise to work them out on paper before attempting to weave them. Patterns such as the one shown in illustration (31) do not lend themselves to the rose-fashion modification, and patterns like "Wheel of Fortune," written with reversed figures, are the same when treadled rose-fashion as when treadled as drawn in.

Patterns written on opposites, when woven as drawn in, will produce the rose-fashion figure on the reverse side of the fabric. For this reason such patterns are useful for fabrics such as hangings that should be as handsome on one side as on the other.

Patterns in the overshot weave, whether or not *written* on opposites, may be *woven* on opposites in two contrasting colors. This method of weaving produces a thick, heavy fabric with the warp completely covered. Treadle the 1–2 block: treadle 1, pattern color; treadle 3, background color—repeat as required to square the block. In the same manner weave the 2–3 block on treadle 2 for pattern shots and treadle 4 for background shots; the 3–4 block with pattern on treadle 3 and background on treadle 1; the 1–4 block with pattern on treadle 4 and background on treadle 2. The fabric is firmer if a tabby shot is woven after each pair of opposites, and if the fabric is well beaten up and the warp set somewhat farther apart than for ordinary weaving, the tabby shots will not show.

An interesting manner of treadling an overshot pattern, adapted from Italian cotton towelling, consists in weaving the background in alternating pattern shots rather than in tabby. This produces a soft, fairly thick fabric, more pliable and not as heavy as that produced by weaving on opposites. It goes like this:

Weave a 1–2 block: treadle 1, pattern
                            2, background
                            1, pattern } Repeat as desired
                            4, background
             end: 1, pattern

Weave a 2–3 block: treadle 2, pattern
                            3, background
                            2, pattern } Repeat as desired
                            1, background
             end: 2, pattern

Weave a 3–4 block: treadle 3, pattern
                            4, background
                            3, pattern } Repeat as desired
                            2, background
             end: 3, pattern

Weave a 1–4 block: treadle 4, pattern
                            1, background
                            4, pattern } Repeat as desired
                            3, background
             end: 4, pattern

The Italian towelling in this weave is usually woven with all shots in soft white cotton, but the weave may also be carried out in colors—one color for the pattern shots and a contrasting color for the background shots, or in three colors with two different colors in the background. If the three-color effect is used, the color used for the pattern shots should be the strongest, and usually the darkest, color and the other two should be similar to each other in value though different in shade.

(63) Simple Rose pattern with table from North Carolina. Similar to draft number 57.

Another method of treadling a simple threading for overshot weaving, seen in Italian pieces and also in work from Sweden and from other countries, is to weave the pattern treadles in order: 1, 2, 3, 4 and repeat, without a tabby, producing pattern figures in pleasant variety simply by changes of color. This form of weaving has been described elsewhere in detail.

The above may be classed as standard methods of varying the overshot weave in treadling—each according to some special rule or technique. Patterns may also be varied as one may wish by weaving the pattern treadles in irregular order. This type of weaving is used largely for ornamental borders in pieces done in plain weave. A small, simple pattern is best for the purpose. Illustration (64) shows a student's sampler done in a number of variations on the "Honeysuckle" pattern. This little pattern seems to be easy for beginners and has been woven so much that most skilled weavers avoid it, but it has much charm and great adaptability. It is a good choice for first work in weaving.

The large, fairly intricate patterns do not lend themselves well to fancy treadlings, and perhaps for that reason there has been a recent fad for miniature patterns—such standard overshot patterns as "Lover's Knot," "Chariot Wheel" and "Queen's Delight" written as small as possible, and used for borders in variations of treadling or woven as all-over figures to give a texture effect. This is not an altogether desirable practise, as the proportions of the old patterns are necessarily distorted in writing them down to miniature size, and there are other weaves better adapted to texture effects than the overshot weave.

As the fancy treadlings follow no rule, they must be written down if one wishes to preserve a record, or kept in the form of a sample.

Perhaps this is as good a place as any to make some remarks about samples. A good collection of samples is invaluable to a weaver. When setting up the loom it is advisable to put on an extra yard for samples, and to *keep* the samples it is usually necessary to mount them. Otherwise they become bags or table mats and get away. Samples of what *not* to do are almost as useful as samples of successful projects and often save one from making the same costly error twice.

148 —

(64) Student's sampler showing a few of the many variations of the Honeysuckle pattern. Draft number 6.

V Notes on the Overshot Drafts

There appears to be no limit to the possible number of patterns—even for the simple overshot weave confined to its four blocks. The following collection of drafts makes no claim to completeness. It is no more than a selection of representative patterns. All the most famous of the old patterns—those woven many times and widely known—have been included, however. Sometimes many drafts of the same pattern have been compared in order to select the most pleasing and the most characteristic form. With these are many patterns that appear to have been known only in certain limited localities, and others that have survived only in the form of a single example.

The matter of names has proved extremely puzzling, because of the fact that the same pattern is sometimes known under many names, and also of the fact that a name was often used in different places for patterns not in the least similar. The names as given here are a compilation in which many weavers have coöperated, and are as nearly correct as it seems possible to be in the matter.

With two exceptions all the patterns of the following diagrams are "Old American." These two—"Monk's Belt" and "Honeysuckle"—have been included because they are so much used by modern American hand-weavers that it would appear foolish to omit them. "Monk's Belt" is distinctly a modern importation from Europe, and its introduction is no doubt due to the Scandinavian influence in modern American weaving. At the time when the old art was first revived no American teachers were available, most of the surviving weavers being illiterate mountain women or simple "ancients" without much ability for teaching. Weaver Rose was one of the few exceptions. When the demand for teachers became acute, what was more natural than to get them from Sweden, where hand-weaving was well known and widely practiced. So-called "embroidery weaving" and several other forms of the art sometimes seen in America are of Scandinavian origin. "Monk's Belt" is a very handsome pattern, but if one is interested in historical correctness it should not be used with typical colonial furnishings. Our art shows similar patterns, such as "Everlasting Beauty," but the effect of these is different.

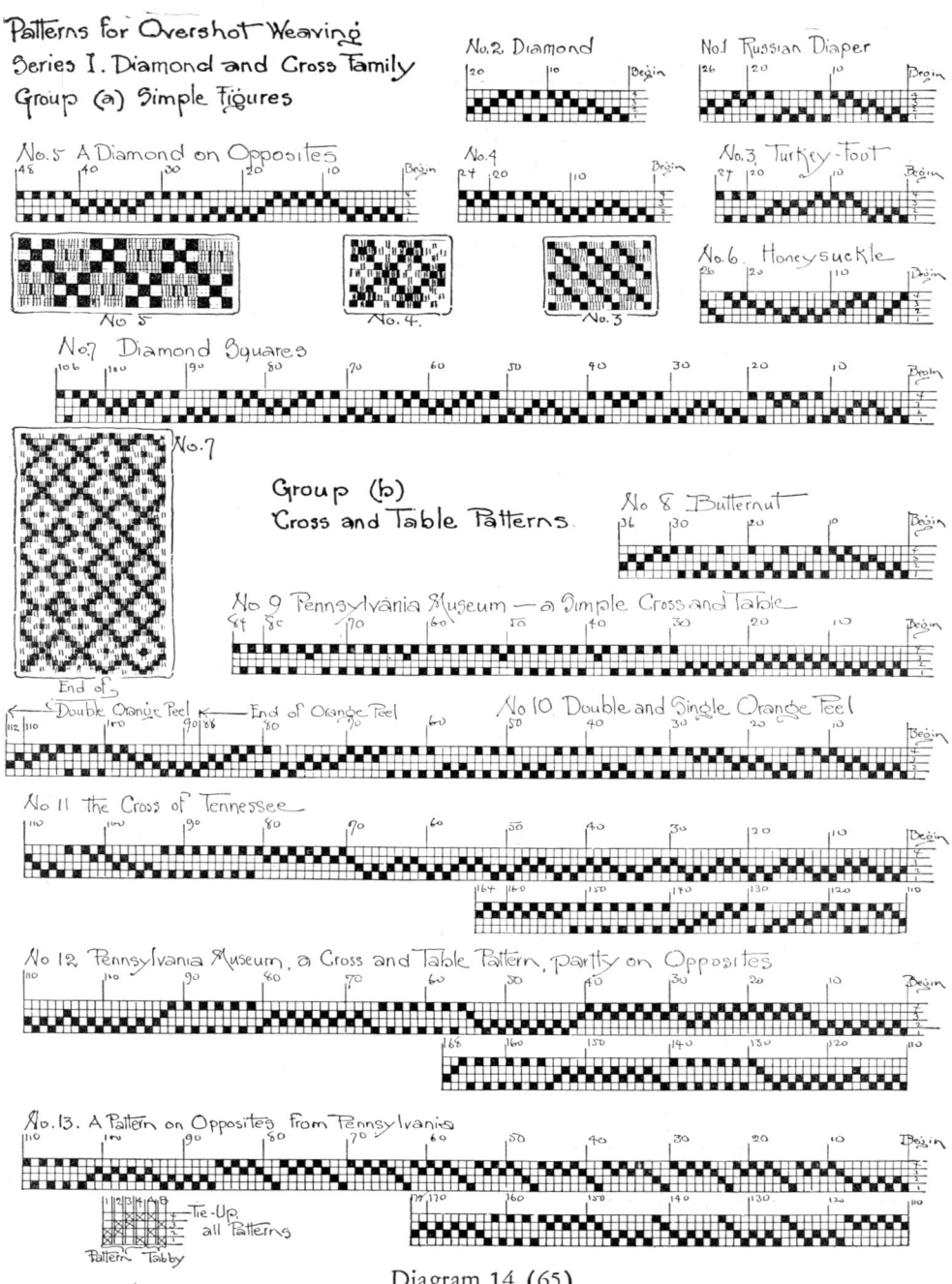

Diagram 14 (65)

— *151*

"Honeysuckle" came, who knows whence? It is a charming little pattern and resembles the flowery figure of "Pine Bloom," from which it was doubtless derived. Who began using it as a pattern by itself, separated from the characteristic "tables" of the old pattern,—and who named it,—no one seems to know, though the thing is so recent. There appear to be no ancient pieces in this pattern, but it has become so common of late that it is as hackneyed as a too-popular song. Unlike Monk's Belt it is distinctly in the American manner and goes well with colonial detail.

An attempt has been made in this book to classify the patterns so that anyone wishing to find the threading and the name of some particular pattern— of an ancient coverlet perhaps or a treasured heirloom—may at least have an idea in what part of the list to look for it. The classification has been made according to "weave"—that is, structure of the fabric—and also according to geometric similarity of the figures, after a plan somewhat like the classification of plants into families and genera.

Some patterns partake of the characteristics of more than one group, and might with propriety be classified otherwise than as has been done. The forms merge and blend and it is impossible to make entirely definite separation between groups. Our classification, however, is not a matter of exact science but is intended simply as a convenience to users of the drafts. The rule followed has been to classify a doubtful pattern with the group in which it is supposed a searcher would be most likely to look for it.

All treadlings given below are written for the six-treadle tie-up as shown at (b-5) and (b-8) Diagram No. 5, Illustration (45). For use on table looms or looms with a different tie-up they must be suitably transposed.

DIAGRAM 14 (65)

Patterns 1 and 2 are similar except that 1 has a block in the center of the diamond while 2 has not. These threadings are often used as borders. (See Diagram No. 13.)

Pattern 3 is on opposites and should be treadled as follows:

                Treadle 1, 6 times
                       3, 6 times
                       2, 6 times
                       4, 6 times

Series I Group (b)

No. 14 Perry's Victory (Rose)

No. 15 King's Delight

Group (c)
Diamond and Table Patterns

No. 16. Crown and Diamond, (Rose)

No. 17. John Walker

No. 18 Name Unknown

No. 19 White Mountain Coverlet

No. 20 Lily of the Valley, also Rose in the Wilderness and Bonaparte's March

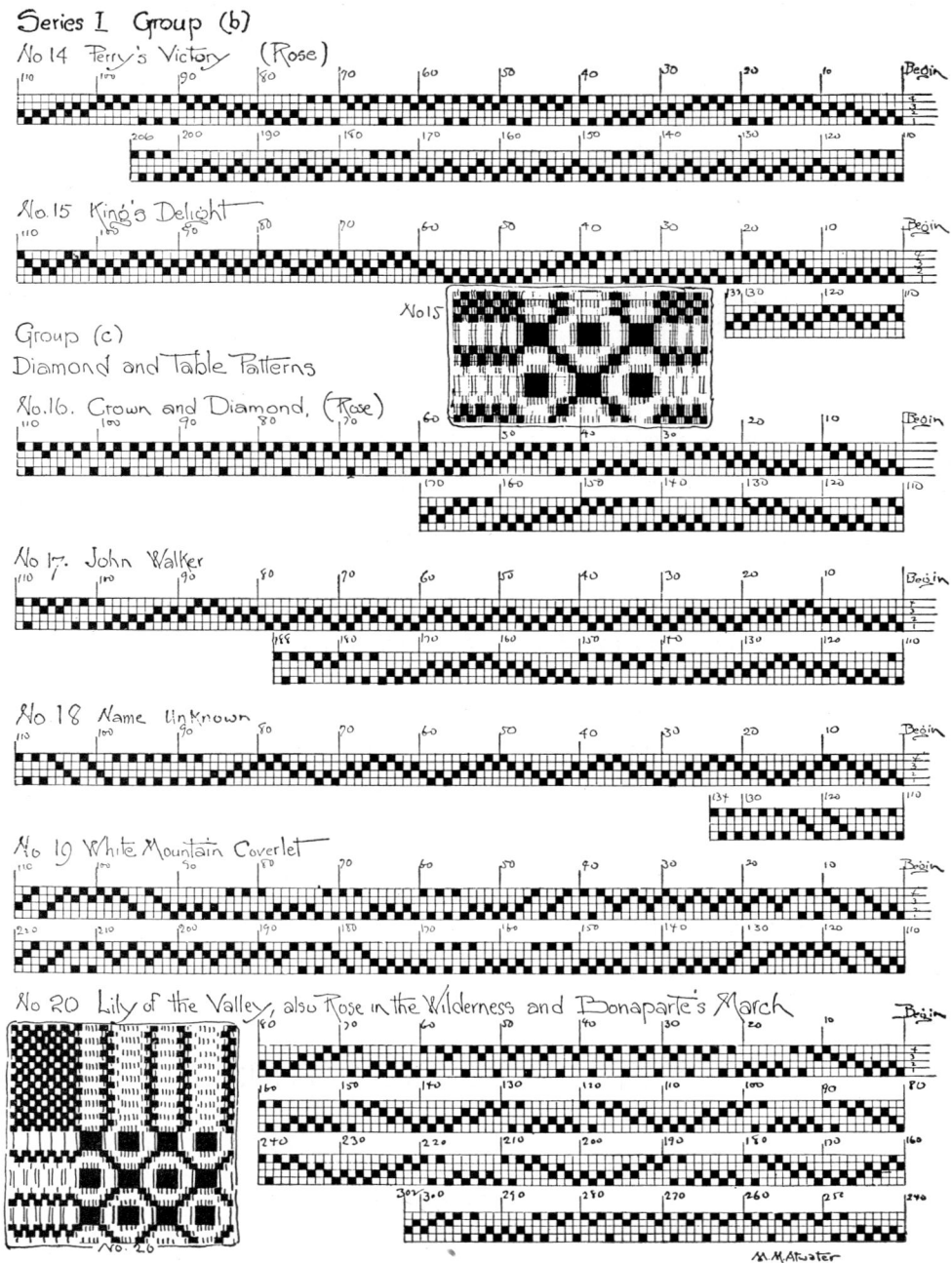

Diagram 15 (66)

(67) Indian War. A pattern partly on opposites. See draft number 22.

No. 4 is partly on opposites and should be treadled as follows:

> Treadle 1, 4 times
> 2, 4 times
> 1, 4 times
> 3, 4 times
> 4, 4 times
> 3, 4 times

No. 5 is a diamond figure on opposites and should be treadled as drawn in with the small accidental blocks omitted.

154 —

Series I., Group (c)
No. 21. Everybody's Beauty

No. 22. Rose of Sharon, or Indian War

No. 23. Governor's Garden, also Mountain Cucumber and St. Ann's Robe

No. 24. Miss Cobb Number One

No. 25. The Clifton Springs Coverlet

Diagram 16 (68)

No. 6 is the "Honeysuckle" pattern very widely used among modern weavers though apparently unknown in colonial days. It may be woven in a great many different ways and is useful for all small work. Illustrated (64).

No. 7 is a valuable small pattern, especially good for upholstery. It should be treadled "as drawn in."

No. 8 is an excellent pattern for small work.

No. 9 is a larger pattern similar to No. 8. Both of these are woven as drawn in. Illustrated (60).

No. 10 is a plain pattern used a good deal for coverlets. Illustrated (94).

No. 11 is shown at 5, Illustration (92).

No. 12 is an interesting pattern partly woven on opposites. It should be woven as drawn in with the small accidental blocks omitted.

No. 13 is illustrated (93).

DIAGRAM 15 (66)

No. 14 and No. 16 are both patterns from the collection of Weaver Rose. They are simple, rather plain patterns, but effective.

No. 17 and No. 18 are also plain patterns and suitable for couch covers or the coverlet for a man's room, rather than for more frivolous purposes.

No. 19 is similar to the patch patterns and though simple is very decorative. Illustrated (23).

No. 20 is a very plain pattern indeed, but many handsome old coverlets were woven on this treadling. Illustrated (41).

All these patterns are woven as drawn in.

DIAGRAM 16 (68)

Nos. 21 and 22 are similar patterns.

No. 22 is illustrated (6).

Nos. 23 and 24 should be woven as drawn in.

No. 25 is a pattern on opposites.

All these patterns are woven as drawn in, No. 25 being woven with the small 2-block accidental blocks omitted in the treadling.

156 —

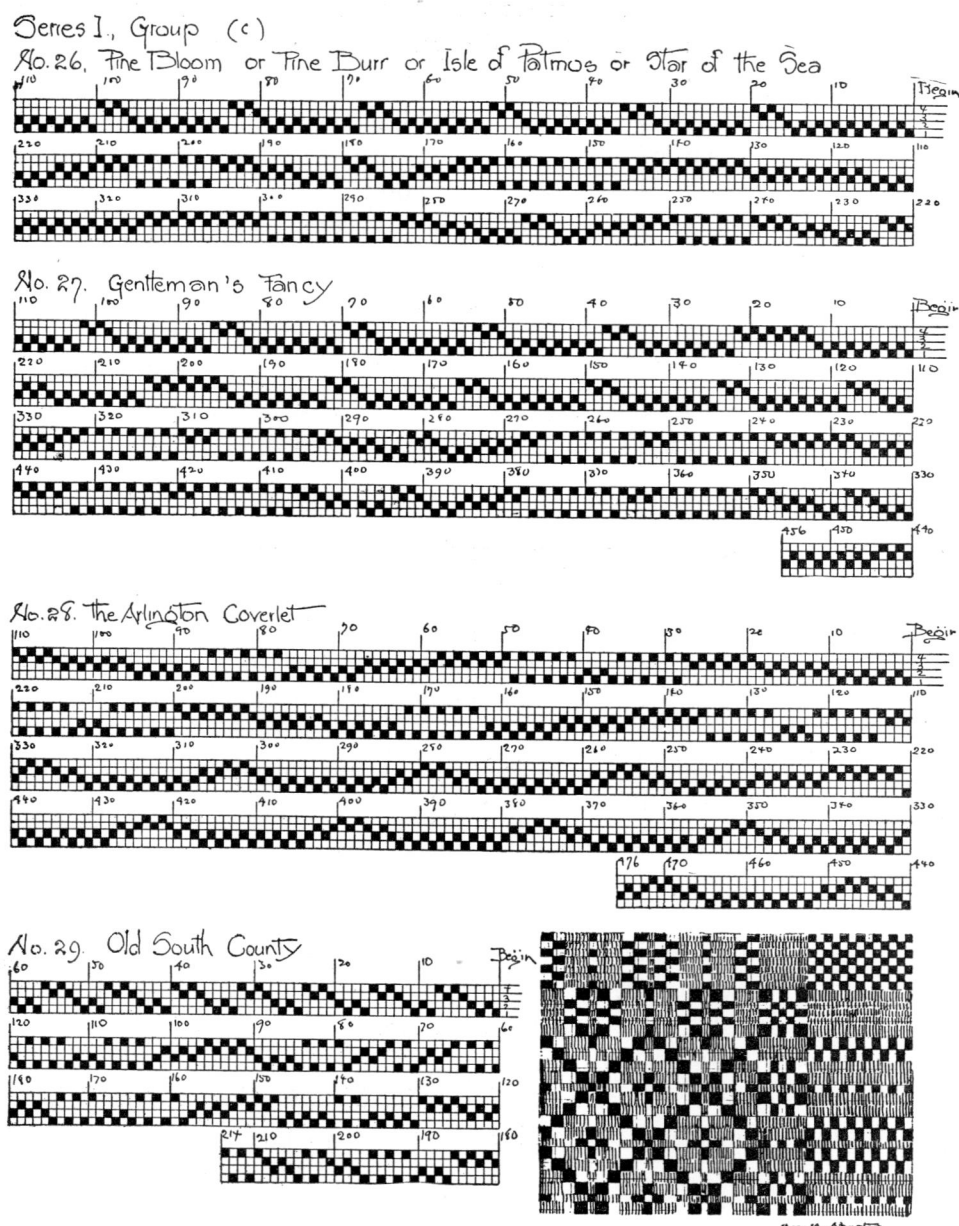

Diagram 17 (69)

Diagram 18 (70)

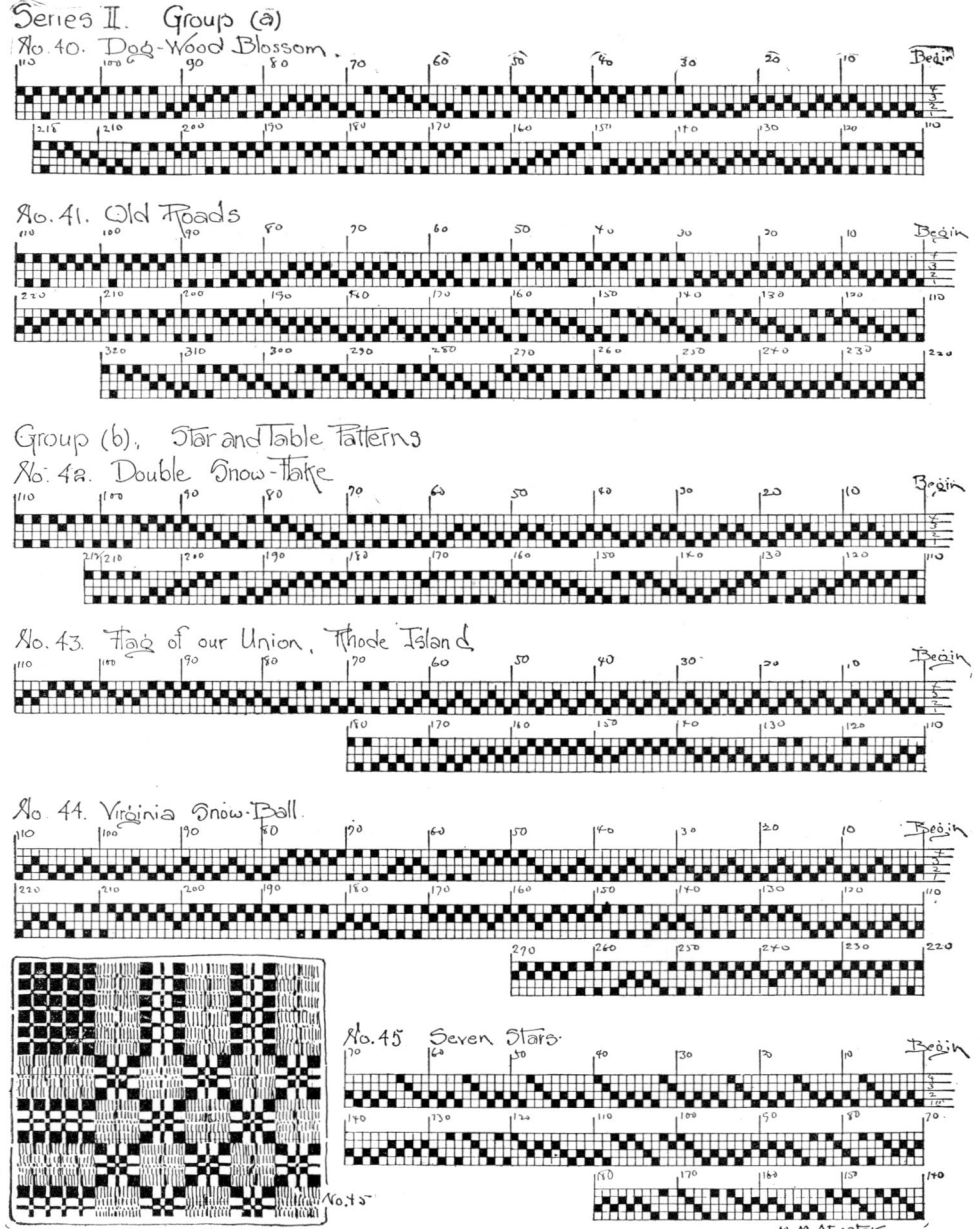

Diagram 19 (71)

DIAGRAM 17 (69).

No. 26 is one of the most famous and most admired of the ancient patterns. Especially in the South it appears in a great variety of slight variations woven in many different colors and different arrangements. The name in New England was "Isle of Patmos." The other names were used in different parts of the South. In weaving, the small two-thread accidentals should be omitted. The squares of the table and the blocks in the center of the Star figure are on opposites.

No. 27 is a pattern in some ways similar to "Pine Bloom," differing chiefly in the Star figure. It is a much heavier and more serious-looking pattern.

No. 28 is illustrated opposite page 20 of Eliza Calvert Hall's "Book of Handwoven Coverlets."

No. 29 owes its interesting character to the fact that it is written largely on opposites. In weaving, the small accidentals should be omitted.

All these patterns are woven as drawn in.

DIAGRAM 18 (70)

Patterns 30, 31, 32, 33, 34 and 35 are all good patterns for small work. No. 30, woven as drawn in, is illustrated at (a) and at (b) woven rose-fashion; 31, 32, 33 and 35, which are written partly on opposites, should be treadled as drawn in, with the small accidental blocks omitted. No. 34 is illustrated at (a) woven as drawn in and at (b) with a special treadling often used instead.

No. 36 should be woven as drawn in.

No. 37 is a simple figure rarely used alone. It is included here for the sake of continuity. Draft No. 108 gives this figure in combination with a "Sunrise" figure and an elaborate border. As illustrated at 37 the figure is treadled rose-fashion as follows:

First figure	Second figure
Treadle 2, 5 times	Treadle 3, 5 times
1, 6 times	4, 6 times
2, 6 times	3, 6 times
1, 6 times	4, 6 times
2, 5 times	3, 5 times

No. 38 and No. 39 are similar patterns, one somewhat plainer than the other. They are patterns of southern origin rarely if ever found in the North.

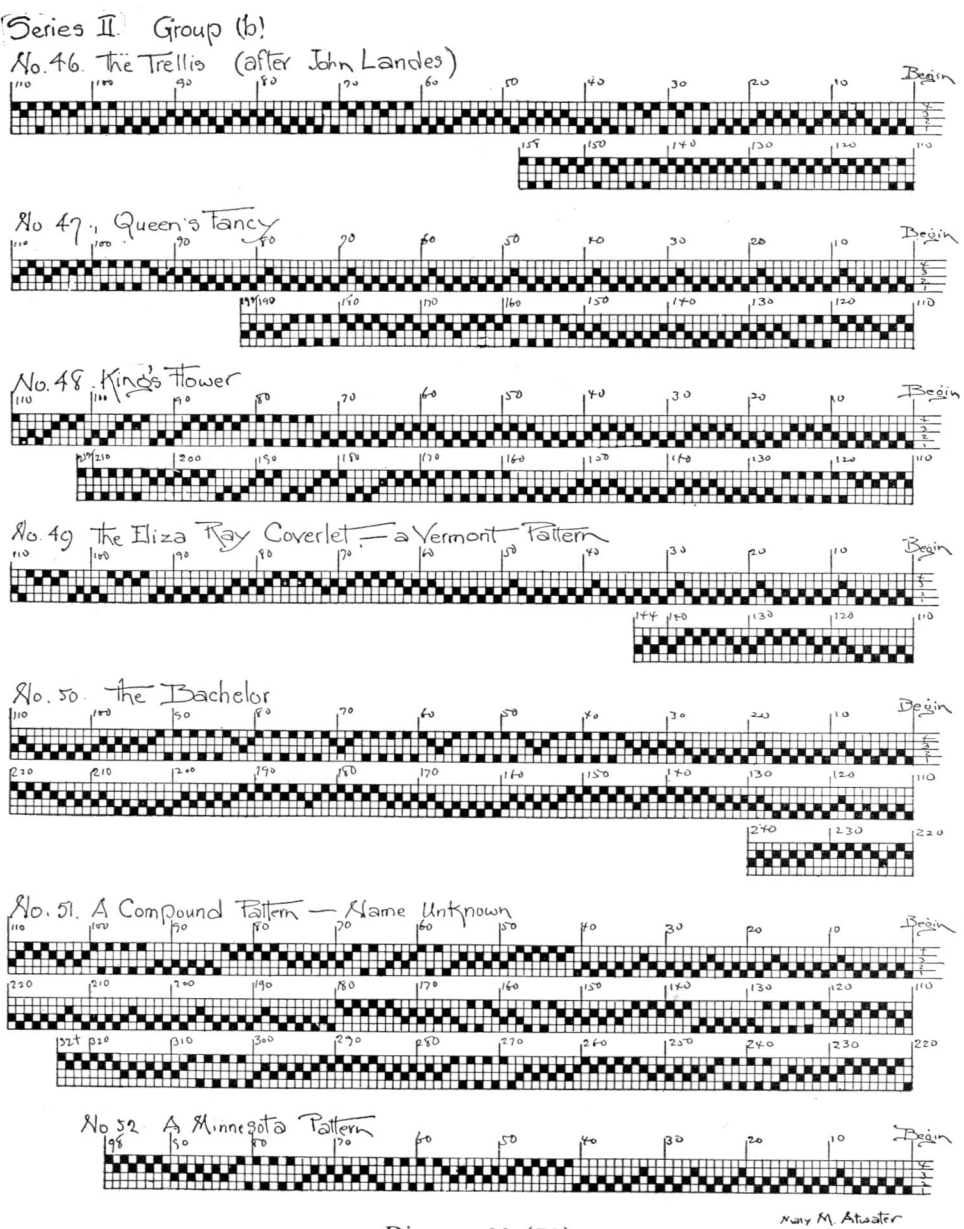

Diagram 20 (72)

They should be treadled as drawn in. The illustration opposite page 46 of Eliza Calvert Hall's book shows a similar pattern. (Illustrated (47).)

DIAGRAM 19 (71)

Patterns Nos. 40 and 41 are combinations of figures similar to Nos. 8 and 39. They should be woven as drawn in.

No. 42 is a very beautiful and much used ancient pattern. It should be treadled as drawn in, but may also be woven rose-fashion with pleasing results.

No. 43 is a plain pattern, interesting chiefly for its age and historic associations. Woven as drawn in.

No. 44 is a handsome pattern, written partly on opposites. Should be treadled as drawn in with the accidentals omitted.

No. 45 is a simple but effective pattern on opposites. Why it should be called "Seven Stars," it is difficult to say, as the number of stars appears to be thirteen.

DIAGRAM 20 (72)

No. 46 is a particularly charming pattern, adapted from one of the designs in the John Landes book. It should be treadled as drawn in. Nos. 47 and 48 are similar. No. 48 is by far the better known of the two, but No. 47 is in some ways better. Both are written partly on opposites and should be treadled as drawn in with the accidentals omitted. Illustrated at 3 (92).

No. 49 is an interesting little three-block pattern partly on opposites. In weaving omit treadle 4 entirely. Otherwise woven as drawn in.

No. 50 is a plain, serious-minded pattern.

No. 51 is a large and fanciful pattern,—illogical but charming. It consists of two small tables, an odd diamond figure and a figure of stars, partly on opposites. Should be treadled as drawn in with accidentals omitted.

No. 52 is a simple little pattern, partly on opposites, and may be treadled as drawn in, accidentals omitted, or rose-fashion as follows:

Treadle 3, 9 times
4, 9 times
2, 9 times
4, 9 times
2, 9 times
4, 9 times

Treadle 3, 9 times
1, 9 times
2, 2 times ⎫
1, 9 times ⎬ 4 times
2, 2 times ⎭
1, 4 times

— 162 —

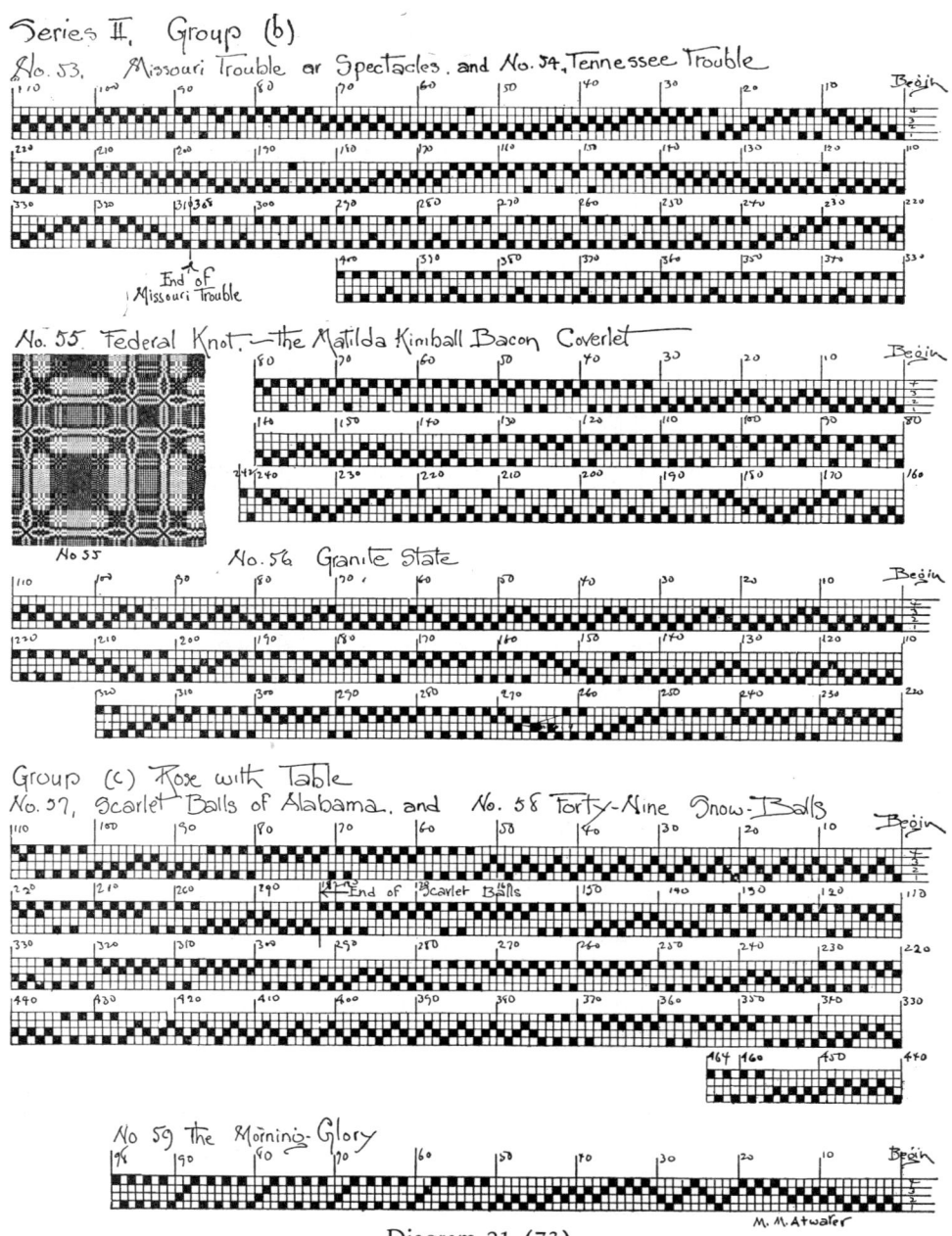

Diagram 21 (73)

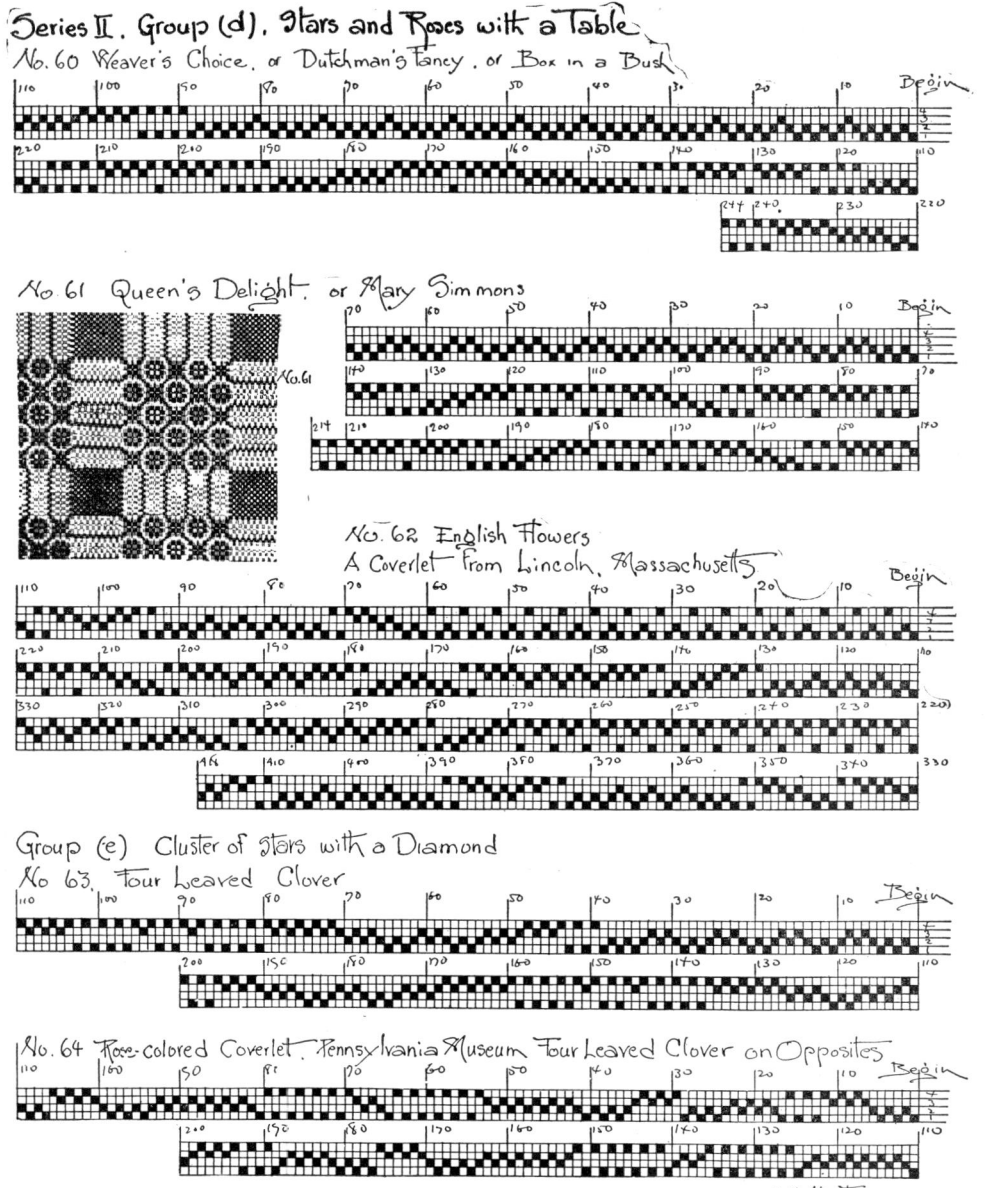

Diagram 22 (74)

DIAGRAM 21 (73)

No. 53 is a very famous old pattern—one of the finest.

No. 54 is similar but has a "window sash" figure instead of a single small table. The first 308 threads of the draft are the repeat from "Missouri Trouble." The entire 408 threads are the repeat of "Tennessee Trouble." Both patterns are woven as drawn in. Illustrated (9).

No. 55—the very handsome old coverlet from which this draft was made was woven in 1820 at Graystone, Albion, New York, by Matilda Kimball Bacon. It is an unusually fine example of the pattern usually known as "Federal Knot."

No. 56 is illustrated (27). It is a very simple and logical pattern.

Nos. 57, 58. "Scarlet Balls" and "Forty-nine Snowballs." The first 182 threads of the draft constitute the repeat of the pattern known as "Scarlet Balls" and sometimes as "Nine Snowballs." It is a very simple pattern, but charming. This is not woven as drawn in, but is treadled as follows:

```
Treadle 2, 2 times ⎫ Repeat          Rose—Continued
        1, 2 times ⎭ 13 times                ⎧ 1, 5 times
        2, 2 times                     Star  ⎨ 2, 4 times
      ⎧ 3, 7 times                           ⎩ 1, 5 times
      ⎪ 4, 7 times
 Rose ⎨ 3, 4 times                  Repeat Rose, repeat Star, repeat Rose.
      ⎪ 4, 7 times                  Repeat from beginning.
      ⎩ 3, 7 times
```

No. 58 treadle table as above. Then Rose, Star, Rose, Star, Rose, Star, Rose, Star, Rose, Star, Rose, Star, Rose, Table. Then:

```
Treadle 4, 8 times
        1, 7 times
        2, 8 times
        1, 7 times
        4, 8 times.  Repeat from the beginning.
```

No. 59 is an attractive small figure with a table on opposites and a three-block rose-shaped figure. Treadle as follows:

```
Rose—treadle 3, 7 times         Rose—treadle 3, 1 time
             2, 7 times                      2, 1 time
             1, 7 times                      1, 7 times
             2, 1 time                       2, 7 times
             3, 1 time                       3, 7 times
             2, 1 time         Table—treadle 4, 8 times ⎫
             1, 1 time                       2, 2 times ⎬ four times
             2, 1 time                       4, 7 times ⎭
```

DIAGRAM 22 (74)

No. 60 is an honest and straightforward pattern with little if any nonsense about it. Woven as drawn in.

No. 61 is a charming old pattern and appears among ancient "draughts" under the name of "Queen's Delight." Modern weavers know it as "Mary Simmons"—probably because it appears under that name in Eliza Calvert Hall's coverlet book. It is woven as drawn in.

No. 62 is an unusual arrangement with a good deal of charm. One complete repeat and a little over will make a pillow top. Put on a narrow border if desired. Begin threading the pattern at thread 409 of the draft; thread to the end; then one complete repeat of the draft as written; then from the beginning to thread 73. Repeat border, if any. This is woven as drawn in.

No. 63 is a pattern of four large star-figures inclosed in a frame. It should be woven as drawn in.

No. 64 is the same pattern as 63 but is written on opposites and the effect is very different. This draft was taken from a handsome old coverlet in the collection of the Pennsylvania Museum. Woven as drawn in.

DIAGRAM 23 (76)

No. 65 is a small wheel pattern used alone for small work and in combination with tables for coverlets. It should be woven as drawn in.

No. 66 is a very odd little pattern partly on opposites. The wheel effect hardly appears except when seen from a distance. There is an old coverlet in the Pennsylvania Museum woven on this pattern. The draft given here, however, is from the letter—quoted elsewhere—written by Weaver Rose of Rhode Island to one of his associates a number of years ago. The pattern should be treadled as follows:

Treadle 1, 2 times	Treadle 4, 4 times
2, 3 times	3, 4 times
3, 5 times	4, 4 times
4, 6 times	2, 4 times
2, 4 times	1, 4 times
1, 4 times	2, 4 times
2, 4 times	4, 6 times
4, 4 times	3, 5 times
3, 4 times	2, 3 times

(75) A Lover's Knot coverlet from the Newark Museum.

No. 67 is from a handsome old coverlet in blue and a brownish rose. The pattern, though extremely simple, is very effective when woven in two colors. For a coverlet it should be set off with a wide border. Woven as drawn in.

No. 68 is a very unusual and handsome arrangement of the Single Chariot-Wheel motif. An illustration will be found in Eliza Calvert Hall's "Book of Handwoven Coverlets," opposite page 106. As the treadling is somewhat obscure it is given below.

Treadle	1,	2 times
	2,	8 times
	1,	9 times
	3,	9 times
	2,	9 times
	1,	9 times
	3,	2 times
	1,	9 times
	2,	9 times
	3,	11 times
	4,	2 times
	3,	2 times
	4,	2 times
	3,	2 times

Treadle	4,	2 times
	3,	2 times
	4,	2 times
	3,	2 times
	4,	2 times
	3,	11 times
	2,	9 times
	1,	9 times
	3,	2 times
	1,	9 times
	2,	9 times
	3,	9 times
	1,	9 times
	2,	8 times

No. 69 should be woven as drawn in. Illustrated (26).

Series III. Wheel Patterns
Group (a) Star and Wheel Patterns, with a Cross or Diamond

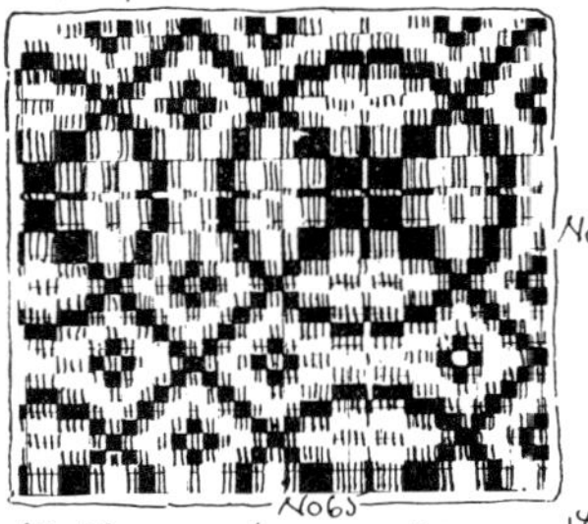

No 65 Single Chariot-Wheels, Small

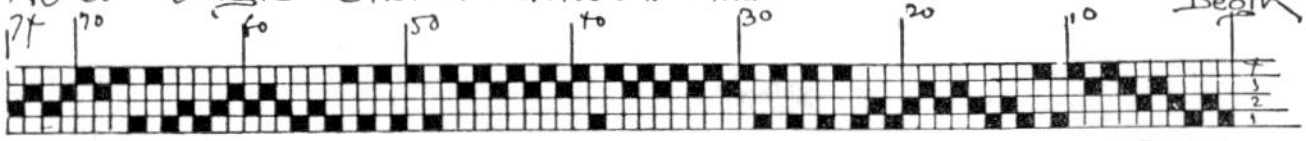

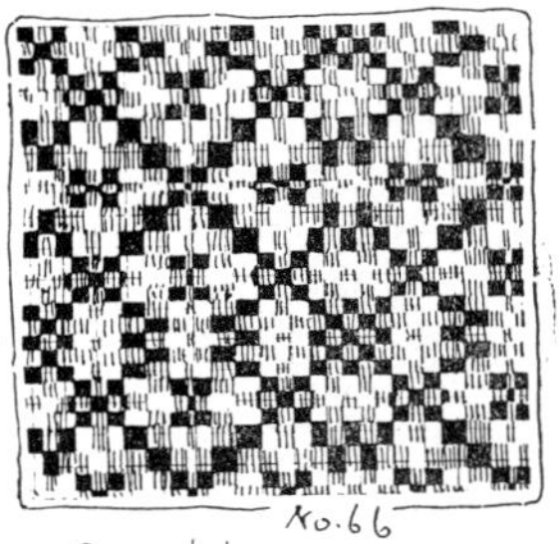

No. 66 "Guess Me" - Weaver Rose

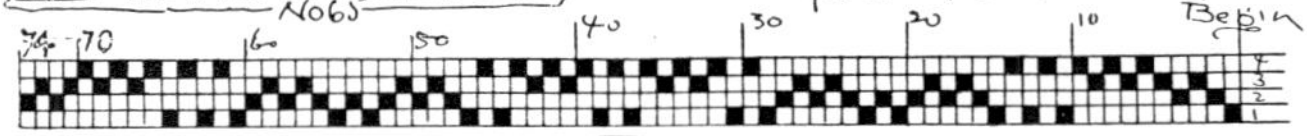

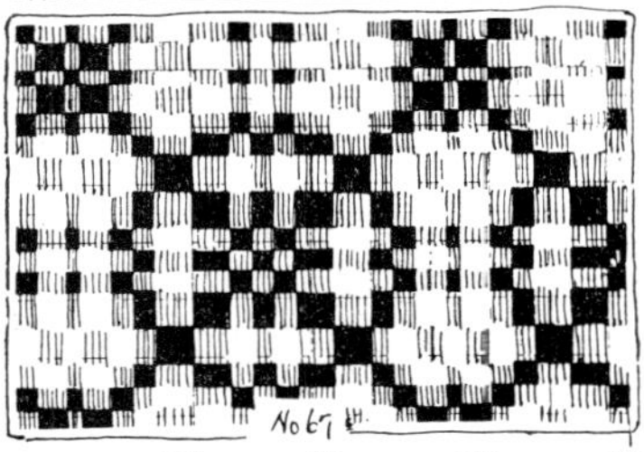

No. 67 World's Wonder, the Thayer Coverlet

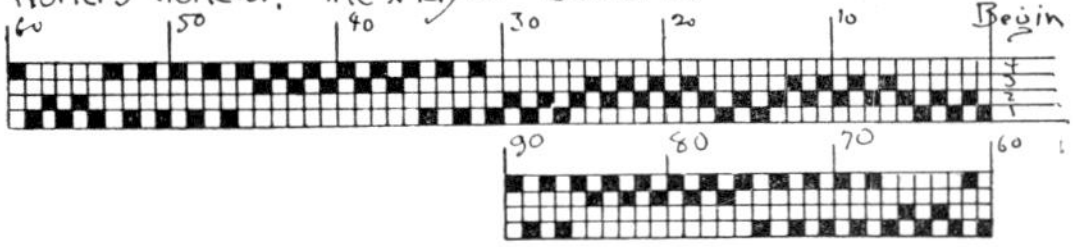

No. 68 Washington's Diamond Ring

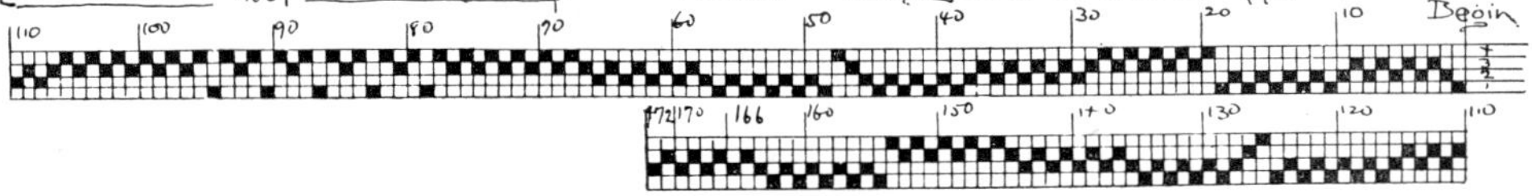

No. 69 The Rebecca Garrison Coverlet — a Simple Lover's Knot Design

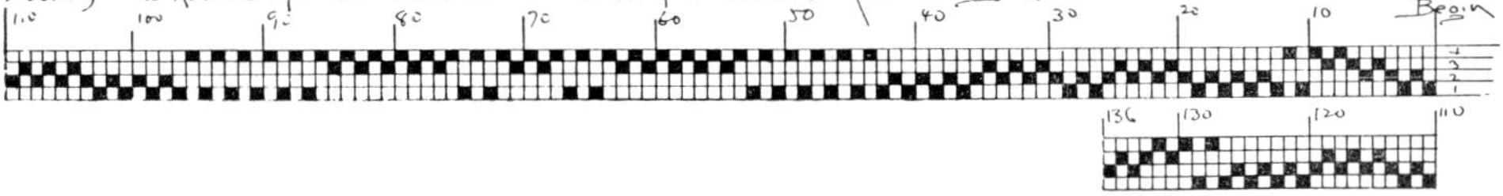

No. 70 From the Wade Collection, Pittsburgh Museum, a Simple Lover's Knot on Opposites

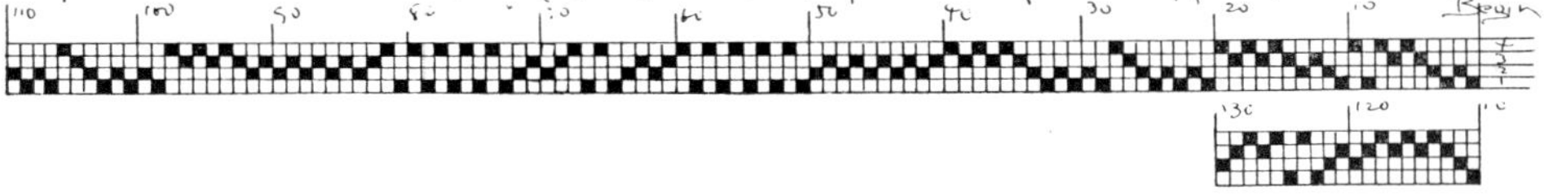

No. 71 The Cross Compass

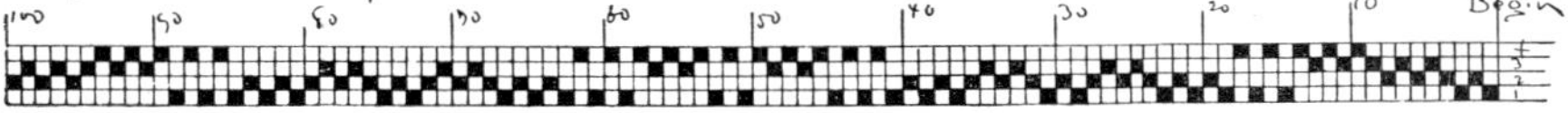

Diagram 23 (76)

(77) Ancient weaving pattern similar to draft 74, repeated twice with large table.

No. 70 is the same figure as No. 69—but what a difference in effect! As is true of all patterns on opposites, this is more subtle, more brilliant and at the same time less obvious than the pattern when drafted and woven in the usual way. A "Whig Rose" on opposites may be woven on the same draft by treadling the pattern rose-fashion. The pattern is woven as drawn in with the small accidental blocks omitted. Illustrated, 2 (59).

No. 71 is woven as drawn in.

DIAGRAM 24 (78)

No. 72 is a pattern on opposites. Very handsome indeed.

No. 73 is an extremely simple pattern taken from an old coverlet woven in two shades of brown on a linen base. The effect is charming.

No. 74 is one of the most famous of the old patterns appearing again and again in the old work in slightly modified forms. It is similar to "Lover's Knot." See Illustration (77).

No. 75 is a pattern similar to No. 73, only more elaborate.

No. 76 is illustrated (54), (55). This is a very interesting and unusual pattern.

No. 77 is one of the patterns written by the celebrated Weaver Rose.

Pattern No. 78 is illustrated (30).

All these patterns are woven as drawn in.

— 169

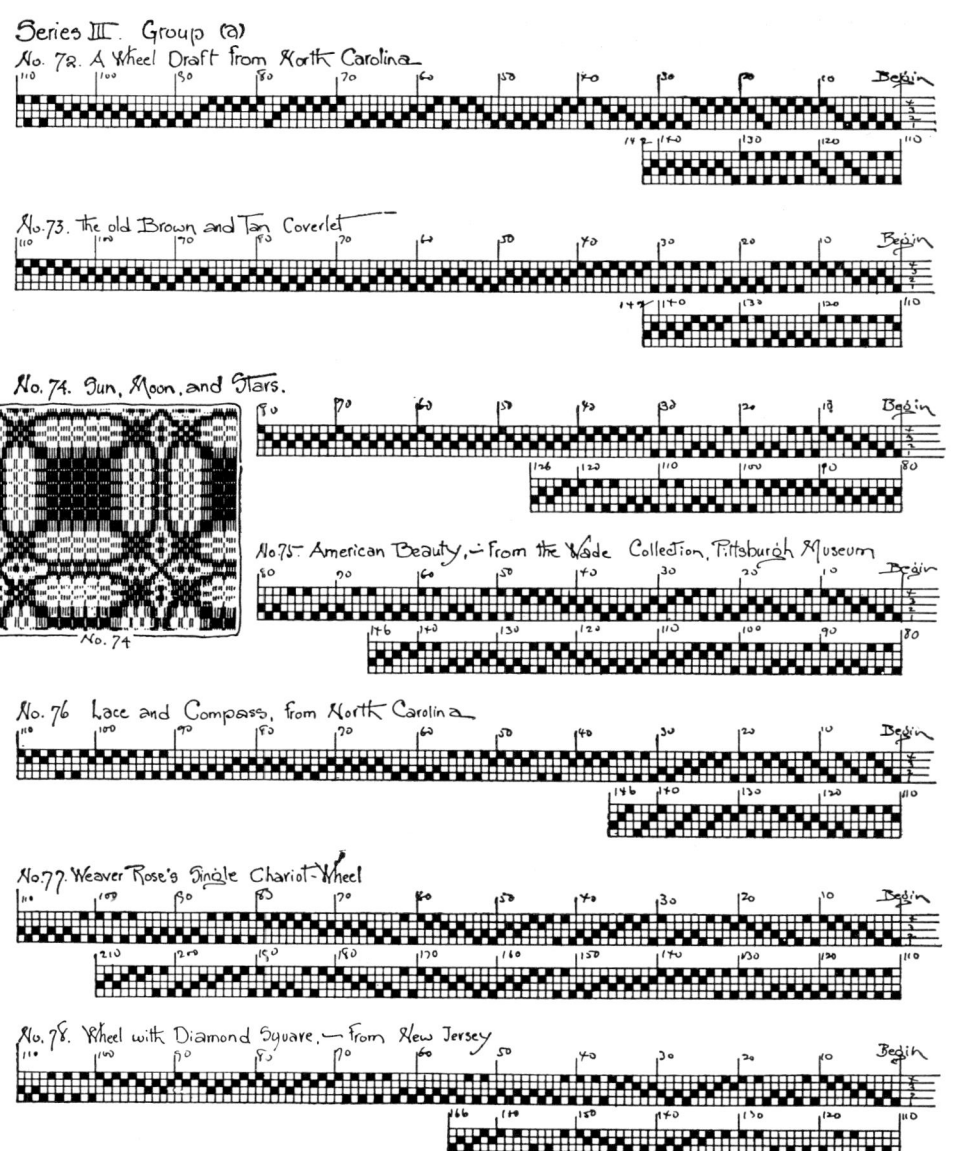

Diagram 24 (78)

170 —

Series III. Group (a)
No. 79. Lover's Knot, from a Pennsylvania Coverlet

Group (b) Single Wheels with Table
No. 80. Chariot-Wheel. Large,—three forms Sometimes called Christian Ring.

Table A ← End of Wheel
Table B Chariot-Wheel figure, as above
Table C Chariot-Wheel figure, as above

No. 81. On Opposites, from an old Massachusetts "Draught"

No. 82. The Arrow.

No. 83. Lover's Knot with Window-Sash. Rhode Island

M.M.Atwater

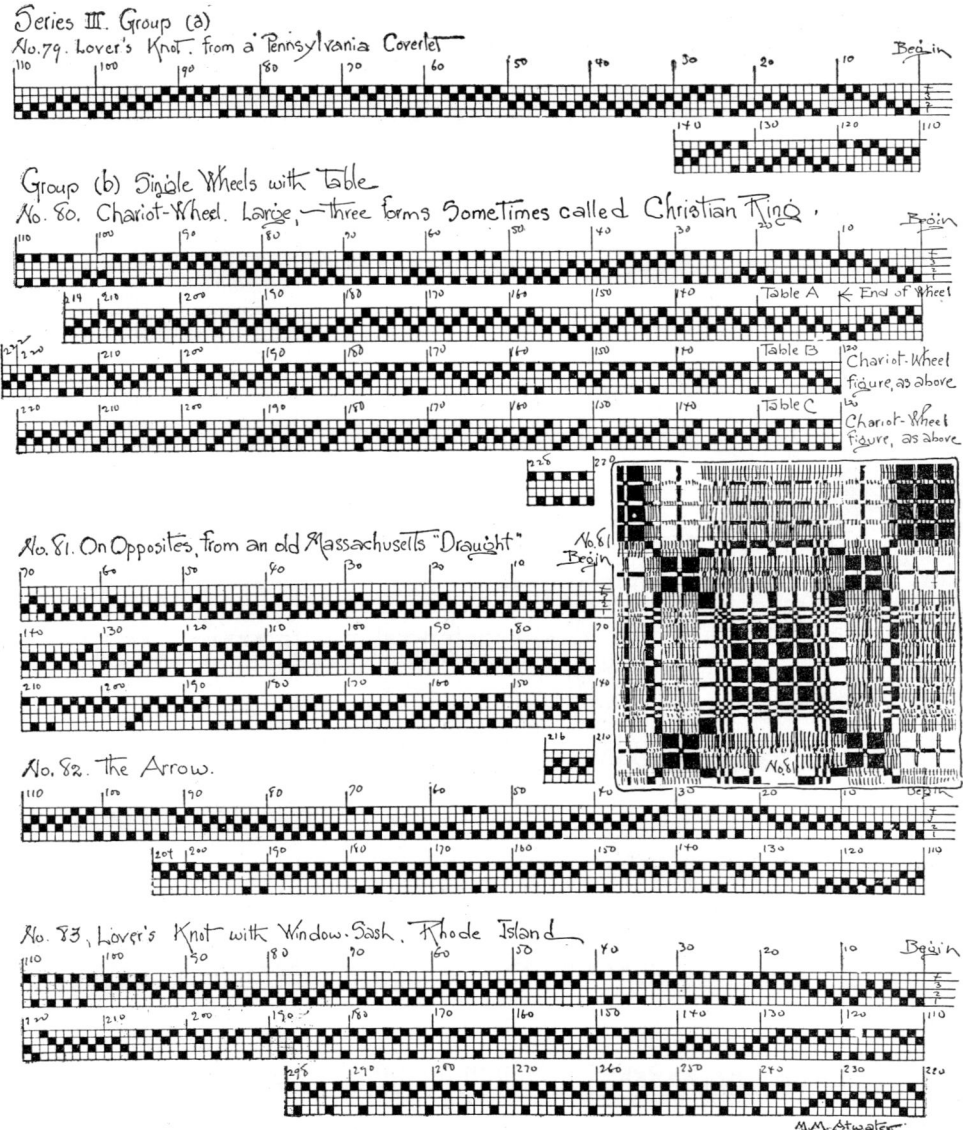

Diagram 25 (79)

DIAGRAM 25 (79)

No. 79 is an agreeable, simple pattern. Illustrated (32).

No. 80 is a famous pattern of wide distribution. It appears in three distinct forms, varied by the arrangement of the "table" or plain square. The pattern with Table A is illustrated (34). Table B is in a small diamond figure giving a lacelike quality to the pattern. Table C is on opposites and gives a bold and striking effect. Illustrated, 7 (92).

No. 81 is a wheel pattern, on opposites, very delightful. For a smaller figure with the same quality thread as follows: Begin with thread 31 of the draft and omit the 22 threads from 141 to 162, inclusive. This gives a repeat of 164 threads.

No. 82 is a simple wheel pattern, pleasing in effect. Why it is called "The Arrow" it is difficult to say.

No. 83 is a good large figure for coverlets or hangings.

All these patterns should be treadled as drawn in.

DIAGRAM 26 (80)

No. 84 is a very famous pattern. There are so many variations that it is hard to select the most characteristic forms.

No. 85 is a small simple pattern without very long overshot and is best for small work.

No. 86 is a very unusual "Chariot-Wheel," partly on opposites.

No. 87 is a pattern entirely on opposites, the effect being very different from the effect of No. 86.

No. 88 is a large and quite elaborate pattern.

These patterns are all woven as drawn in.

DIAGRAM 27 (81)

No. 89 is a pattern composed of nine small wheels and a "window-sash" figure. The 140 threads, beginning at 81 of the draft and ending on 220, make a double chariot wheel figure. The pattern should be woven as drawn in. Illustrated (40).

No. 90—this threading also weaves nine small wheels with a table, but the effect is different owing to the fact that part of the pattern is on opposites. It should be woven as drawn in, omitting the accidentals.

Series III Group (C). Clusters of Star-and-Wheel Figures with a Table
No. 84 Double Chariot-Wheels (A)
Church Windows

No. 85. Double Chariot-Wheels. (B) From an old "Coverlid"

No. 86 Double Chariot-Wheels. (C). Dillia Sharron's Draft. Warren County, North Carolina

No. 87 Double Chariot-Wheels. (D). — On Opposites

No. 88 Double Lover's Knot.

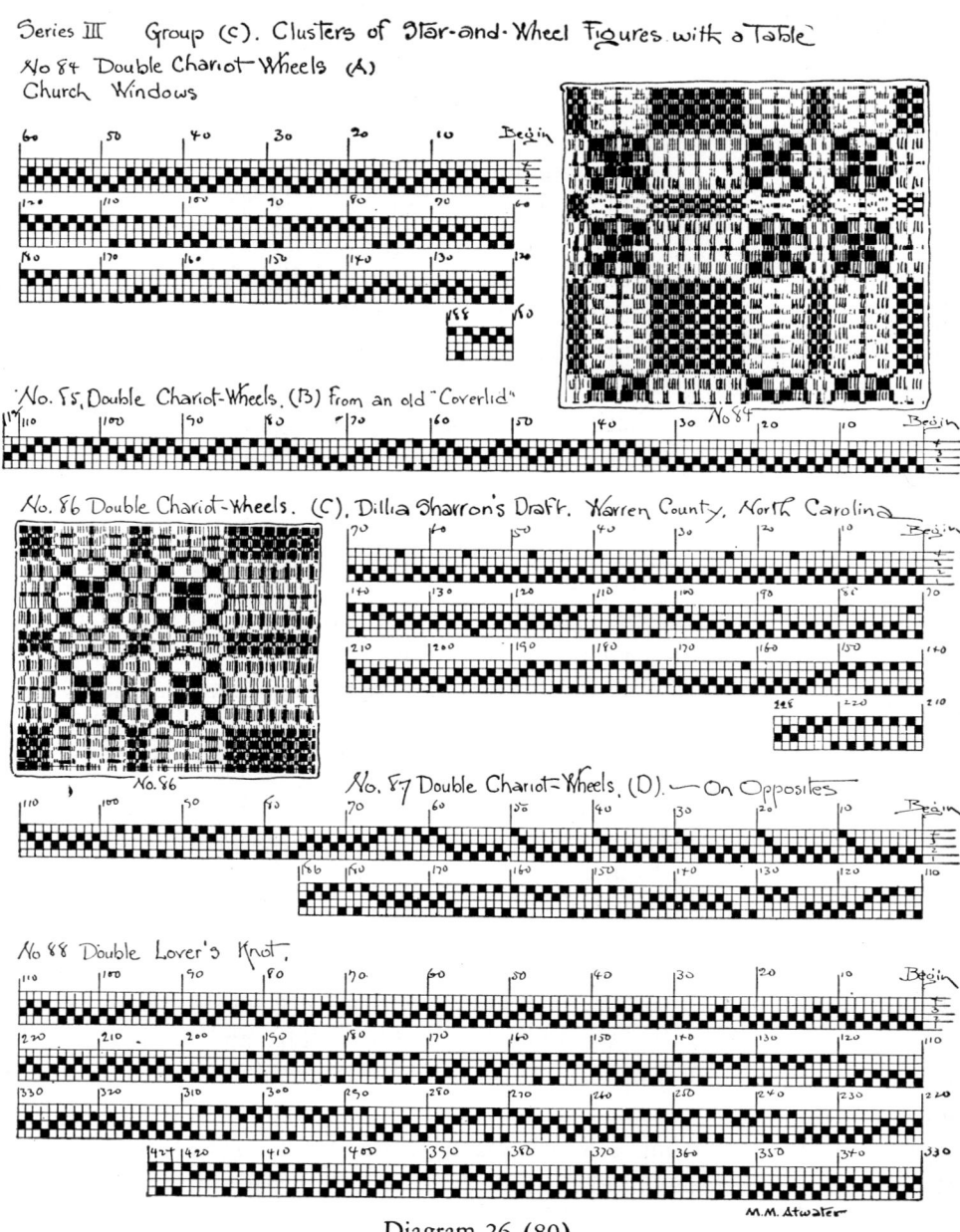

Diagram 26 (80)

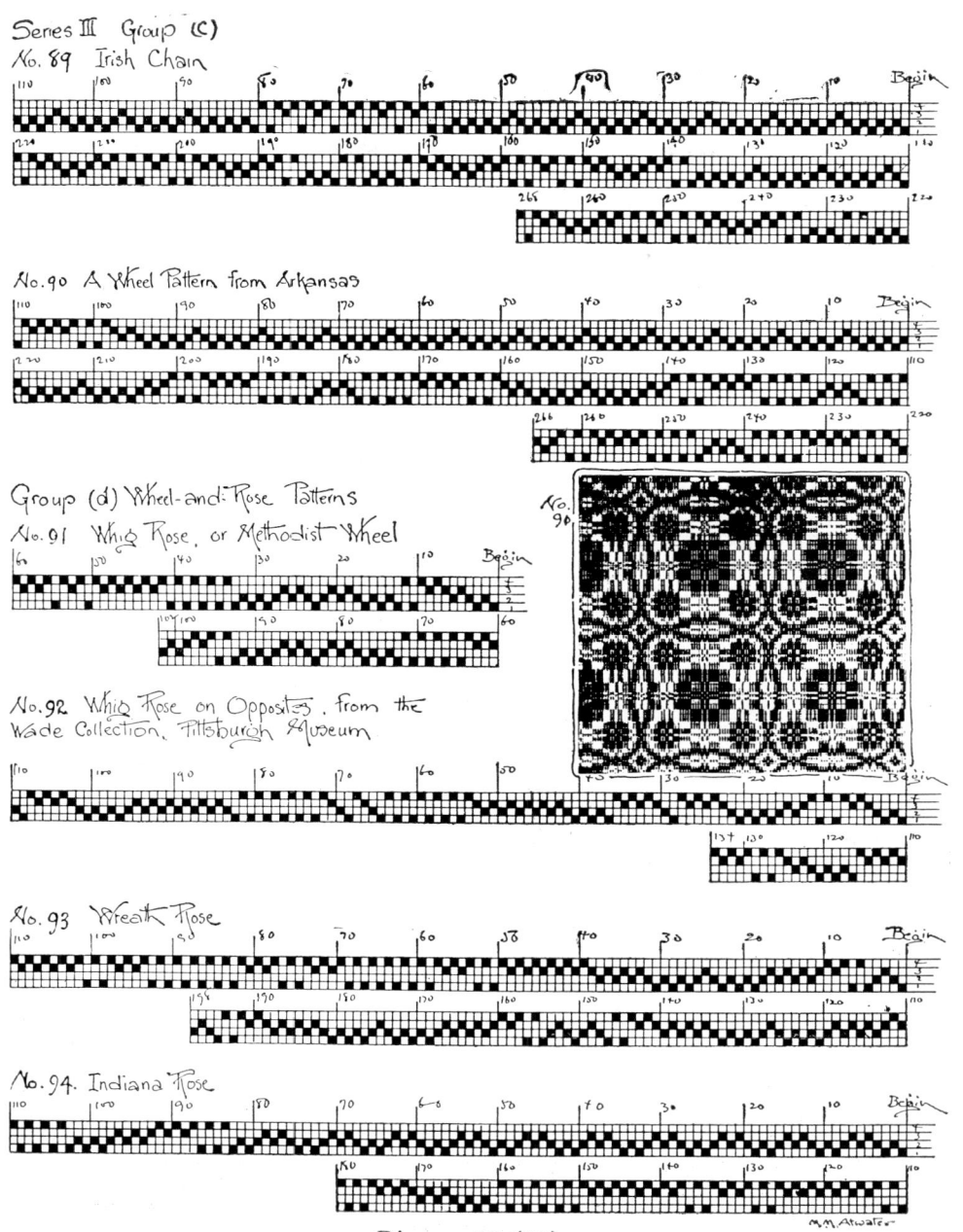

Diagram 27 (81)

174 —

Series III Group (d)
No. 95. Pond Lily

No. 96 Maltese Cross

No. 97 Large Maltese Cross from the old Daggett House Coverlet

Group (e) Wheel-Patterns with both Stars and Roses.
No. 98 Whig Rose and Lover's Knot

No. 99 A Small Pattern on Opposites

No. 100 Wheel of Fortune, or Cup and Saucer

No. 101 Wheels of Time, from North Carolina

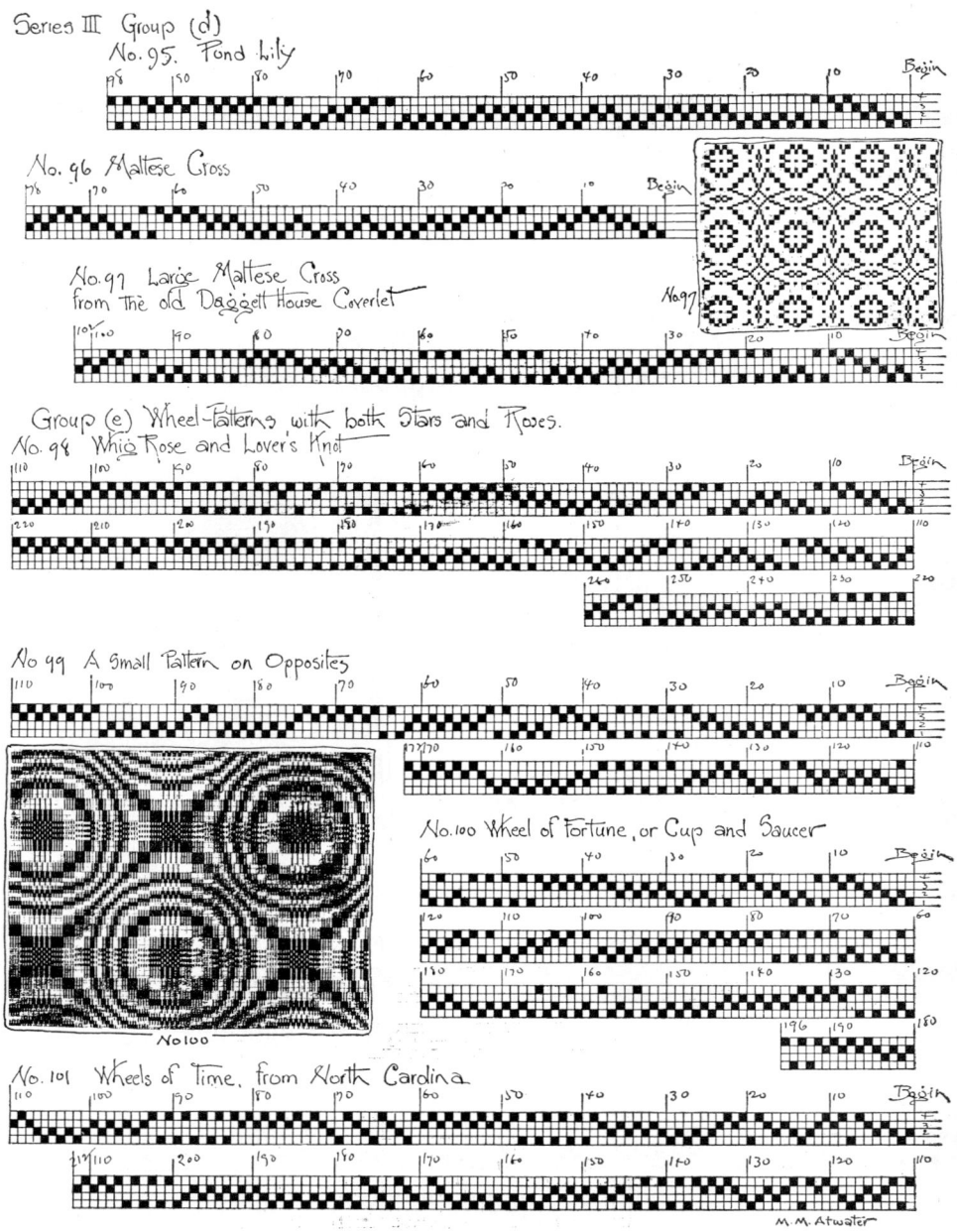

M. M. Atwater

Diagram 28 (82)

No. 91, illustration (7), is one of the oldest, best-known and best-loved of the old patterns. It appears in innumerable slight variations. A simple "Lover's Knot" pattern results from weaving this threading as drawn in. To weave as shown in the illustration treadle as follows:

Treadle 2, 3 times
        1, 3 times
        4, 3 times
        3, 3 times

Small Rose
Treadle 2, 5 times
        1, 5 times
        2, 2 times
        1, 5 times
        2, 5 times

Large Rose
Treadle 3, 9 times
        4, 9 times
        3, 2 times
        4, 2 times
        3, 2 times
        4, 9 times
        3, 9 times
Repeat Small Rose
Treadle 3, 3 times
        4, 3 times
        1, 3 times

Repeat

No. 92 "Whig Rose" on opposites. This is a similar figure to No. 91 but with a very different effect.

Treadle 3, 4 times
        1, 4 times
        2, 4 times
        4, 4 times

Small Rose
Treadle 3, 6 times
        1, 6 times
        3, 2 times
        1, 6 times
        3, 6 times

Large Rose
Treadle 4, 12 times
        2, 12 times
        4, 2 times
        2, 2 times
        4, 2 times
        2, 12 times
        4, 12 times
Repeat Small Rose
Treadle 4, 4 times
        2, 4 times
        1, 4 times

No. 93 "Wreath Rose." This pattern consists of one large rose and a group of small roses enclosed in rings.

Treadle 2, 2 times
        1, 2 times
        2, 2 times
        3, 2 times
        4, 2 times

Small Rose
Treadle 1, 7 times
        2, 7 times
        1, 2 times
        2, 7 times
        1, 7 times

Large Rose
  Treadle 4, 12 times
        3, 2 times
        4, 2 times
        3, 12 times
        4, 2 times
        3, 2 times
        4, 2 times
        3, 12 times
  Treadle 4, 2 times
        3, 2 times
        4, 12 times

Repeat Small Rose

Diamond Figure
  Treadle 4, 2 times
        3, 2 times
        2, 2 times
        1, 2 times
        2, 2 times
        1, 2 times
        2, 2 times
        3, 2 times
        4, 2 times

Repeat Small Rose
  Treadle 4, 2 times
        3, 2 times
        2, 2 times
        1, 2 times

This pattern may also be woven as drawn in, producing a "Lover's Knot" effect.

No. 94 treadle as follows:

Treadle 2, 4 times ⎫
        1, 4 times ⎬ 10 times
                  ⎭

Treadle 2, 4 times
        3, 5 times
        4, 5 times
        1, 5 times
        2, 5 times
        3, 12 times
        4, 12 times

Treadle—*Continued*
        3, 4 times
        4, 4 times
        3, 4 times
        4, 12 times
        3, 12 times
        2, 5 times
        1, 5 times
        4, 5 times
        3, 5 times

DIAGRAM 28 (82)

Pattern 95 treadle as follows:

Treadle 2, 3 times
        1, 3 times
        4, 3 times
        3, 3 times

Large Rose
  Treadle 2, 10 times
        1, 10 times
        2, 4 times
        1, 4 times
        2, 4 times
        1, 10 times
        2, 10 times

Large Rose—*Continued*
  Treadle 3, 3 times
        4, 3 times
        1, 3 times
        2, 3 times

Small Rose
  Treadle 3, 6 times
        4, 6 times
        3, 2 times
        4, 6 times
        3, 6 times

This pattern may also be woven as drawn in, producing stars instead of roses.

No. 96 treadle as follows:

Treadle 1, 4 times	Treadle 3, 6 times
2, 3 times	2, 6 times
3, 3 times	1, 6 times
4, 3 times	4, 3 times
1, 6 times	3, 3 times
2, 6 times	2, 3 times
3, 6 times	1, 4 times
2, 2 times	2, 3 times
3, 6 times	3, 4 times
2, 2 times	2, 3 times

This pattern is also excellent when woven as drawn in, but gives, of course, an entirely different effect.

No. 97 is an odd pattern. It should be treadled as follows:

Treadle 1, 4 times	Treadle 1, 4 times
4, 3 times	2, 7 times
3, 3 times	1, 7 times
2, 3 times	4, 7 times
1, 4 times	3, 7 times
2, 7 times	2, 7 times
3, 7 times	1, 4 times
4, 7 times	2, 3 times
1, 7 times	3, 3 times
2, 7 times	4, 3 times

No. 98 is a handsome pattern composed of alternating "Lover's Knot" and "Whig Rose" figures. It should be woven as drawn in.

No. 99 is a similar figure to the above, but much smaller and arranged on opposites. Woven as drawn in with the accidentals omitted.

No. 100 "Wheel of Fortune," etc. This is a very famous old pattern and a large number of drafts exist, differing slightly in detail. It is woven as drawn in. Illustrated (48).

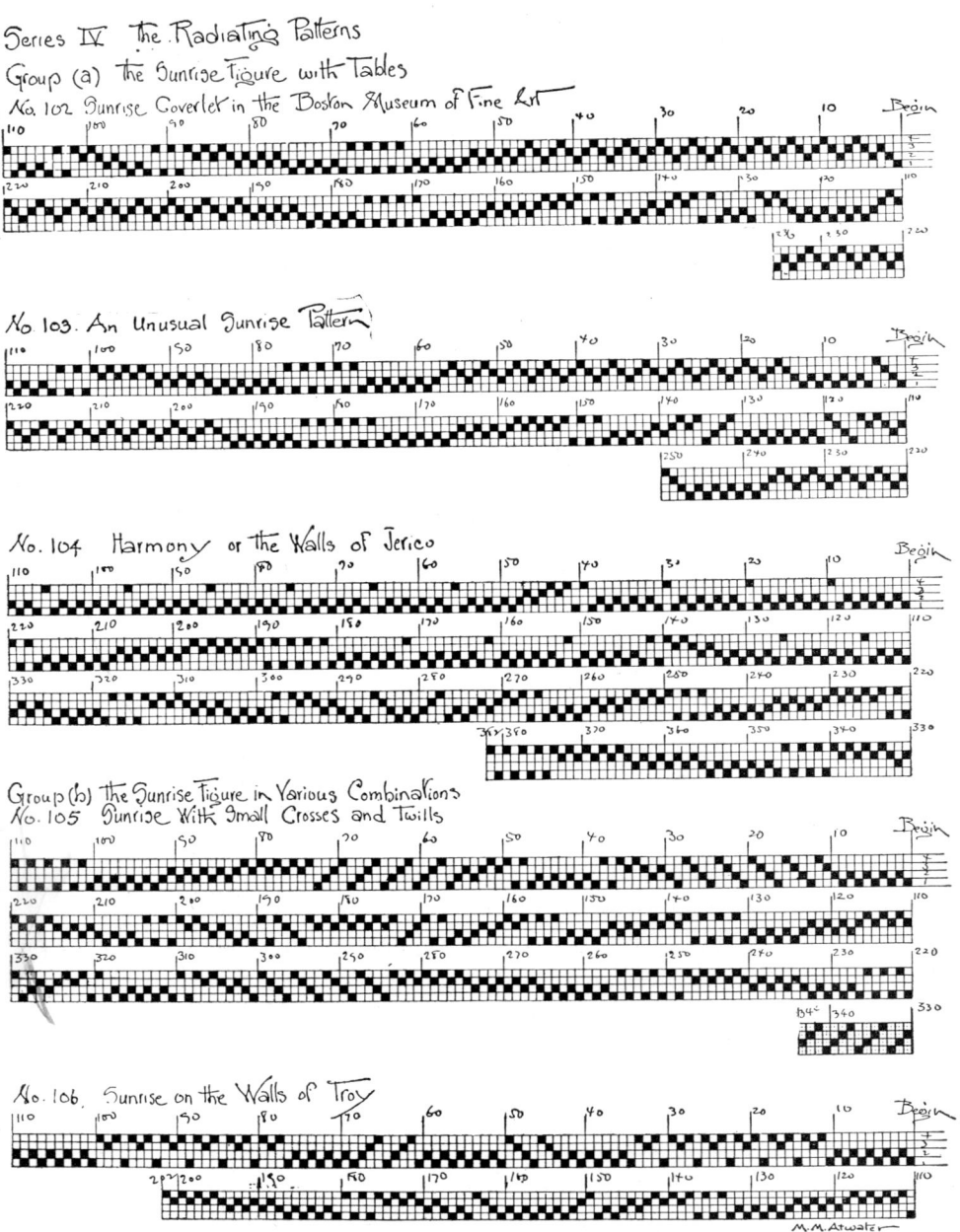

Diagram 29 (83)

No. 101 is a figure similar to No. 100 but arranged on opposites. As the treadling is a little obscure in places it is appended:

Treadle 1, 3 times	Treadle—*Continued* 3, 3 times
2, 3 times	4, 3 times
4, 3 times	2, 3 times
3, 3 times	1, 3 times
1, 3 times	3, 3 times
2, 3 times	4, 3 times
4, 3 times	2, 3 times
3, 3 times	1, 3 times
1, 6 times	3, 6 times
2, 7 times	4, 7 times
4, 10 times	2, 10 times
3, 12 times	1, 12 times
1, 2 times	3, 2 times
3, 2 times	1, 2 times
1, 2 times	3, 2 times
3, 2 times	1, 2 times
1, 2 times	3, 2 times
3, 12 times	1, 12 times
4, 10 times	2, 10 times
2, 7 times	4, 7 times
1, 6 times	3, 6 times
	Repeat

DIAGRAM 29 (83)

No. 102 is the Sunrise Coverlet in the Boston Museum. This is one of the handsomest of the "Sunrise" patterns. The ancient coverlet in question is badly woven in that there are numerous mistakes in both threading and treadling, but the effect is quite lovely. Two colors are used, a brown and a pinkish tan that may once have been rose. The colors are used in alternating blocks all through the work. The center of the Sunrise figure is the large 1-2 block, threads 114 to 124, the draft being written from center to center of the little cross between the two tables of a "window-sash" figure. The seam of a coverlet should fall where the draft begins. Should be woven as drawn in. Illustrated (3).

No. 103 is in structure a pattern similar to No. 102 but gives an entirely different effect.

No. 104 (illustrated (28)) is a very serious and balanced sort of pattern. "Harmony" seems, somehow, a better name for it than "Walls of Jericho."

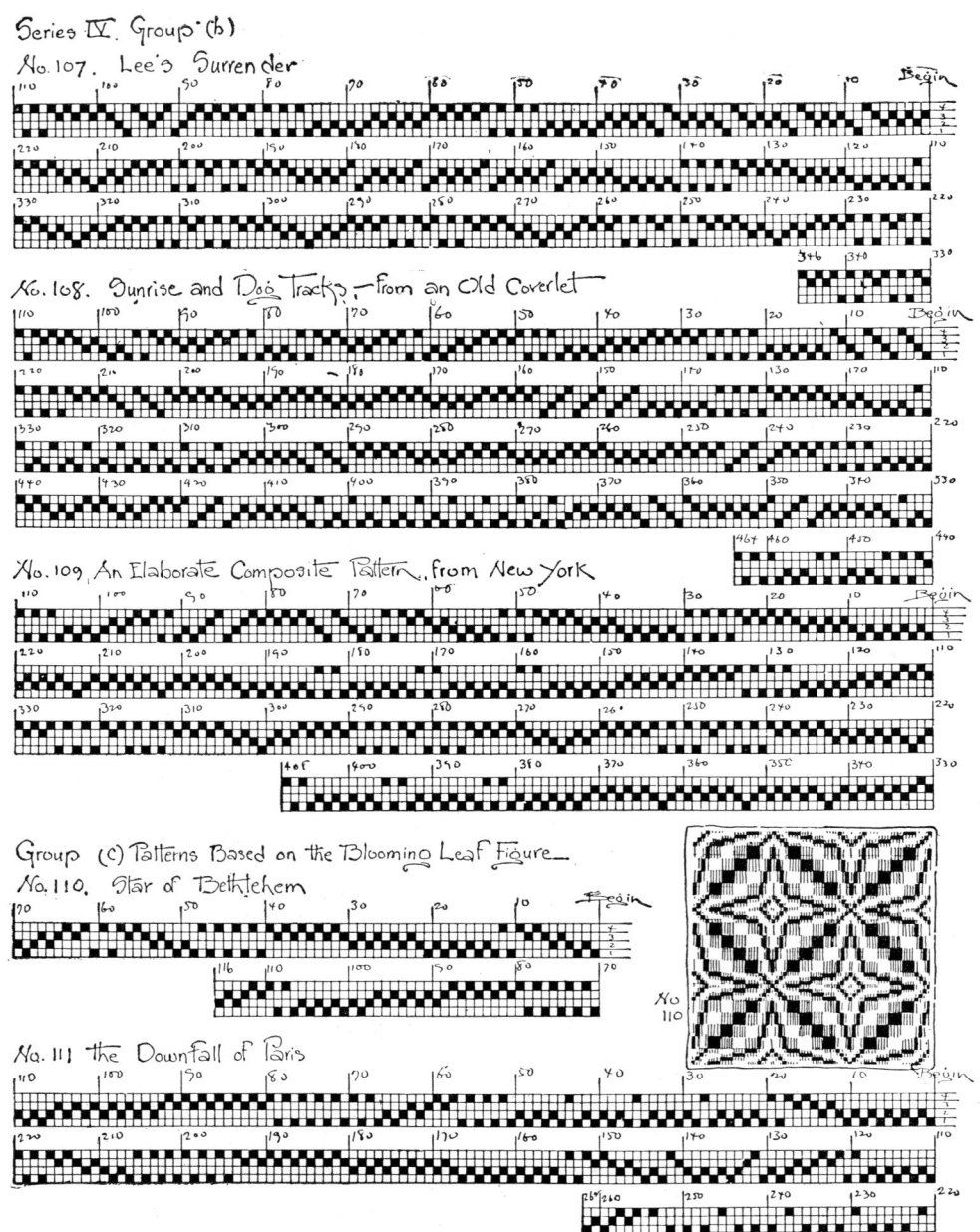

Diagram 30 (84)

However, both names are amusing. There is something very calm and dignified and purposeful about this pattern, though it is not really beautiful. It would not suit a frivolous occasion, but as a coverlet for a great four-poster in a serious and formal bed-chamber it would be perfect. Woven as drawn in.

No. 105 is the draft of a "Sunrise" pattern illustrated opposite page 32 of Eliza Calvert Hall's coverlet book. Woven as drawn in. Similiar to pattern illustrated (46).

No. 106 again is an interesting version of the "Sunrise" figure.

The pattern known as "Blazing Star" is woven on any "Sunrise" threading by treadling the blocks in succession as for twill:—treadles 1, 2, 3, 4, and repeat,—using the same number of shots each time. The pattern varies, of course, somewhat with the draft used. The "Blazing Star" illustrated in Eliza Calvert Hall's book opposite page 80 was woven on draft 104.

No ancient draft for "Sunrise" on opposites has reached me. There must have been one, and anyone wishing to produce such a pattern may do so by writing the blocks of the pattern in the succession shown on the little "Turkey-Foot" draft (3), Diagram 14.

DIAGRAM 30 (84)

No. 107, "Lee's Surrender," is a very famous and much admired pattern. It is illustrated (33). It will be noted it consists of a "Sunrise" figure between two tables written on opposites, with a large square composed of small stars. Woven as drawn in.

No. 108 is from an interesting old coverlet found in Cambridge, Mass., and apparently exactly the same as the coverlet in Eliza Calvert Hall's book opposite page 60. The coverlet in the illustration is so folded that the border does not show to advantage. The weaving was done in two colors. The effect of the extremely elaborate wide border and the plain central part is very good indeed. Border ends on thread 418. Repeat 419 to end for center.

No. 109 is a pattern composed of a "Sunrise" figure and a group of stars so arranged that a wheel-pattern is produced. Woven as drawn in.

No. 110 is a simple pattern, to be woven as drawn in.

No. 111 should likewise be woven as drawn in.

Series IV, Group (c)
No. 112. Blooming Leaf

No. 113. A Blooming Leaf from Arkansas

No. 114. North Carolina Beauty

Group (d) The Bow-Knot Figure
No. 115. Double Bow-Knot, or Maple Leaf, or Reed Leaf, or Double Muscadine Hulls.

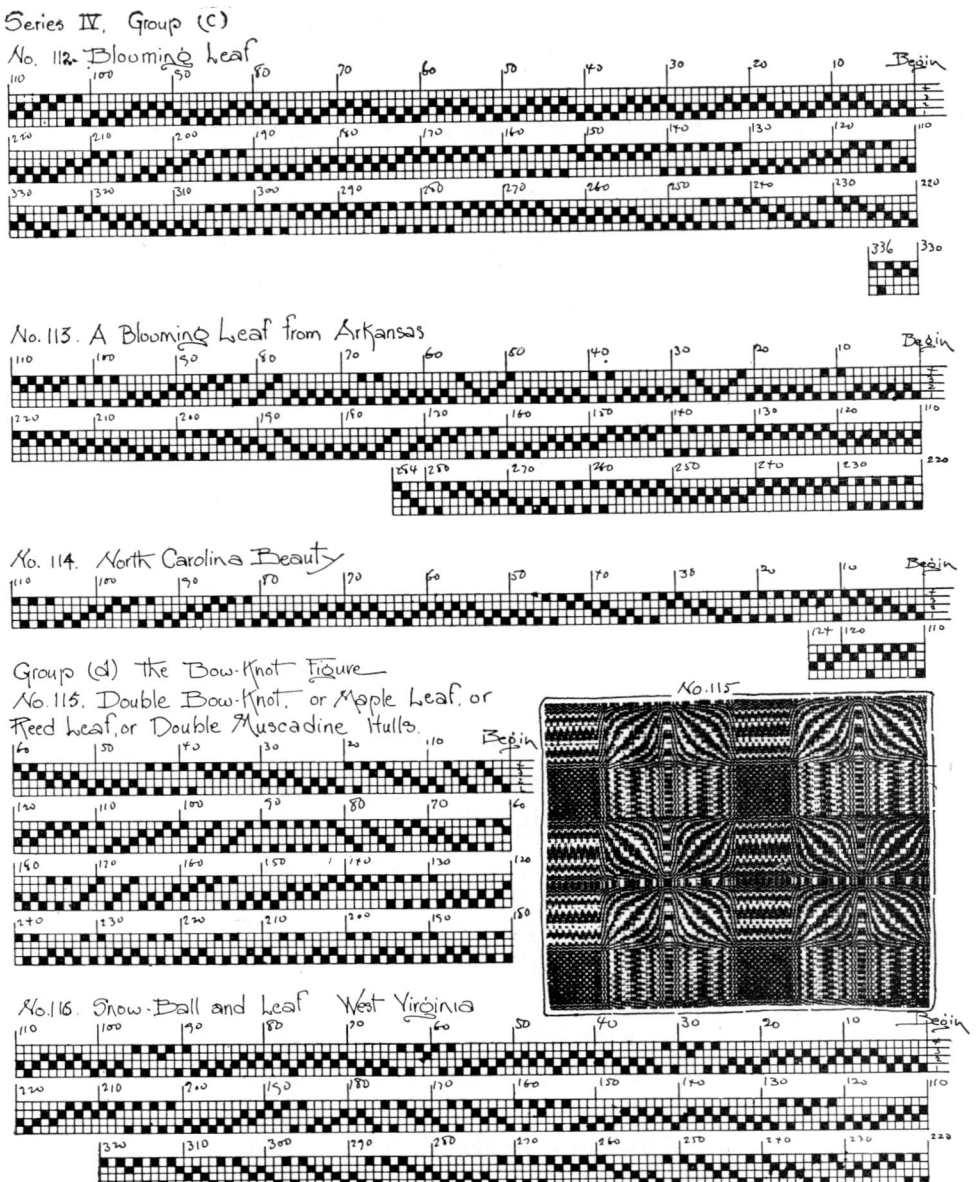

No. 116. Snow-Ball and Leaf   West Virginia

Diagram 31 (85)

— *183*

Series IV, Group (d)
No. 117. Fig Leaf or Wandering Star

No. 118. A Bow-Knot Draft from Kentucky.

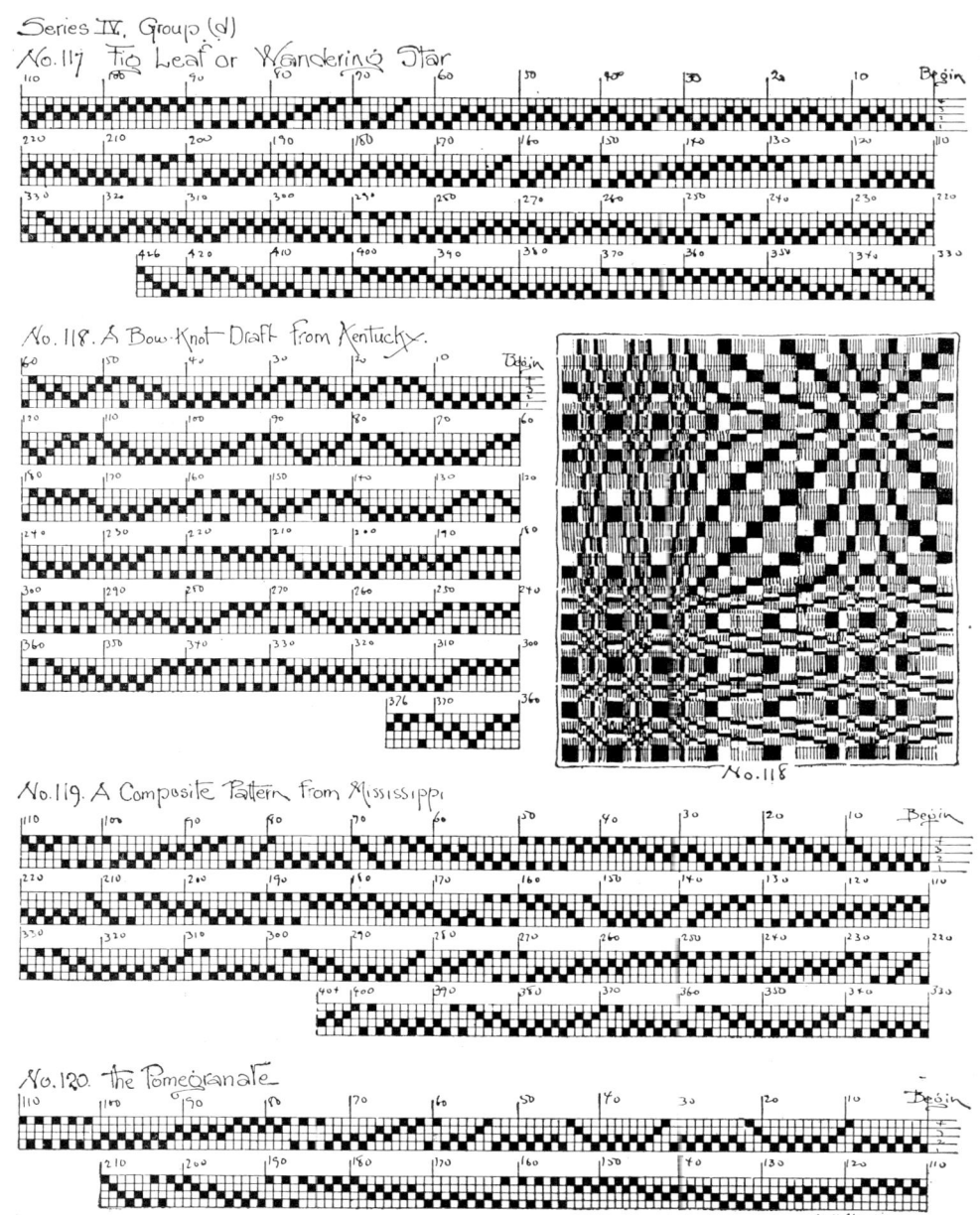

No. 118

No. 119. A Composite Pattern from Mississippi

No. 120. The Pomegranate

Diagram 32 (86)

DIAGRAM 31 (85)

No. 112 is a pattern composed of large flower-like figures separated by tables. It should be woven as drawn in.

No. 113 is a pattern similar to 112 but with more variety and rather more interesting in effect. Woven as drawn in.

No. 114 is a pattern composed of stars and leaf figures separated by curious oval forms. It is illustrated, 8 (92).

No. 115 is the typical form of a very famous pattern that occurs in a great number of variations, and like the "Sunrise" figure is found in many compound patterns. It may also be woven like "Blazing Star" and produces a palm-like figure. Illustrated (22). The pattern is ordinarily woven as drawn in.

No. 116 is an unusual pattern consisting of a bow-knot figure and a group of stars separated by small tables on opposites. As the blocks in this pattern are none of them very large, the pattern may be used for the weaving of upholstery as well as for coverlets, runners and the like.

DIAGRAM 32 (86)

No. 117 is a large and elaborate pattern consisting of a square in the "Sweetbriar Beauty" figure, surrounded by scallops and separated by large leaf-forms and small tables. It should be woven as drawn in.

No. 118 is a very unusual pattern on opposites. For lack of space only a part of the figure is illustrated, and as the treadling is somewhat obscure it is supplied below:

Blocks:
Treadle 1, 10 times ⎫
       3, 3 times |
       4, 3 times |
       2, 3 times |
       1, 3 times |
       3, 3 times |
       4, 3 times |
       2, 3 times ⎬ Repeat twice
       1, 10 times |
       2, 3 times |
       4, 3 times |
       3, 3 times |
       1, 3 times |
       2, 3 times |
       4, 3 times |
       3, 3 times ⎭

Treadle—*Continued* 1, 10 times
                      3, 3 times
                      4, 3 times
                      2, 3 times
                      1, 3 times
                      3, 3 times
                      4, 4 times
                      2, 5 times
                      1, 6 times
                      3, 8 times
                      4, 8 times
                      2, 9 times

(*Continued on next page*)

Treadle—*Continued* 1, 10 times
3, 9 times
4, 8 times
2, 8 times
1, 6 times
3, 5 times
4, 4 times
2, 3 times
1, 10 times
2, 3 times
4, 4 times
3, 5 times
1, 6 times
2, 8 times

Treadle—*Continued* 4, 8 times
3, 9 times
1, 10 times
2, 9 times
4, 8 times
3, 8 times
1, 6 times
2, 5 times
4, 4 times
3, 3 times
1, 3 times
2, 3 times
4, 3 times
3, 3 times

No. 119 is a pattern consisting of a group of leaf-forms and a square in a diamond figure. The first 142 threads of the draft may be used alone as a repeat if desired. This gives a pattern of leaf-forms that flow into one another.

No. 120 should be treadled rose-fashion as follows:

Treadle 1, 10 times
2, once
3, once
4, once
1, 10 times
4, once
3, once
2, once
1, 10 times
2, once
3, once
4, once
1, 10 times
4, once
3, once
2, once
1, 10 times
2, once
3, once
4, once
1, 3 times
2, 3 times
3, 3 times
4, 3 times

Treadle 1, 4 times
2, 4 times
3, 6 times
4, 6 times
1, 8 times
2, 8 times
3, 8 times
4, 8 times
1, 8 times
4, 8 times
3, 8 times
2, 8 times
1, 8 times
4, 6 times
3, 6 times
2, 4 times
1, 4 times
4, 3 times
3, 3 times
2, 3 times
1, 3 times
4, once
3, once
2, once

Series V. The Patch-Patterns
Group (a) Two-Block Patterns.

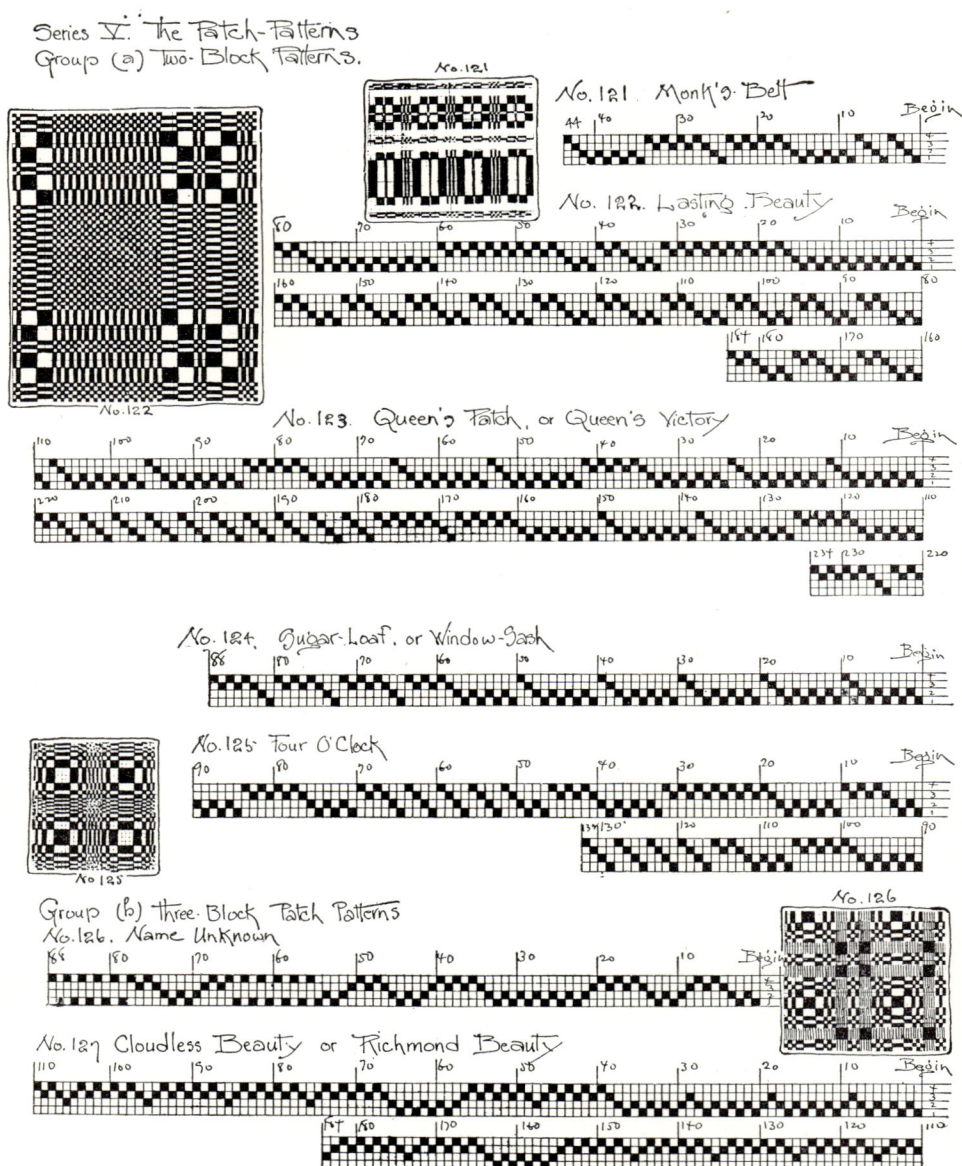

Diagram 33 (87)

DIAGRAM 33 (87)

No. 121—"Monk's Belt"—is not, strictly speaking, an American colonial pattern. It is a pattern of very general use all over the world, but especially in Russia, and in the Scandinavian and the Germanic countries. It is much used by modern American weavers and is included here for the sake of completeness. A number of the "Patch" patterns are similar in construction. There are in this pattern two pattern-sheds only, and a four-treadle tie-up can be used. In weaving on the ordinary six-treadle tie-up, treadles 2 and 4 are not used.

No. 122 is like a large "Monk's Belt" with the series of small blocks greatly increased. There are a large number of similar patterns used almost exclusively for the weaving of white counterpanes by the "Honeycomb" method, and these will be found in a later series of drafts.

This pattern may be made half the size shown here by making each block of half the number of threads indicated. A great many beautiful border designs may be woven on this threading.

No. 123, "Queen's Patch," is a simple pattern with a very handsome effect. It looks well when woven in two colors. Illustration 1 (92) shows a modification of this pattern as used at Berea, Kentucky, that differs slightly from our draft. Our draft is better for large pieces, and is very handsome for hangings or a couch-cover.

No. 124—"Sugar-Loaf," or "Window-Sash," is a pattern very attractive for small pieces and for weaving in a number of colors.

No. 125 is also a good small pattern. The first 64 threads of the draft may be used alone as a repeat if desired. This will make all the figures alike instead of alternating "open and shut" as in the diagram.

No. 126—small figure on opposites separated by blocks. This pattern is woven on three pattern sheds, using treadles 1, 3 and 4. Treadle 2 is to be omitted. Otherwise the pattern is woven as drawn in.

No. 127 is woven without use of the fourth treadle—the 1-4 shed. It is a plain pattern, but excellent for many purposes. It is similar in some ways to "Missouri Patch." This is the pattern called "Youth and Beauty" in Eliza Calvert Hall's coverlet book. The name "Youth and Beauty" appears, however, to belong properly to a different—though similar—pattern.

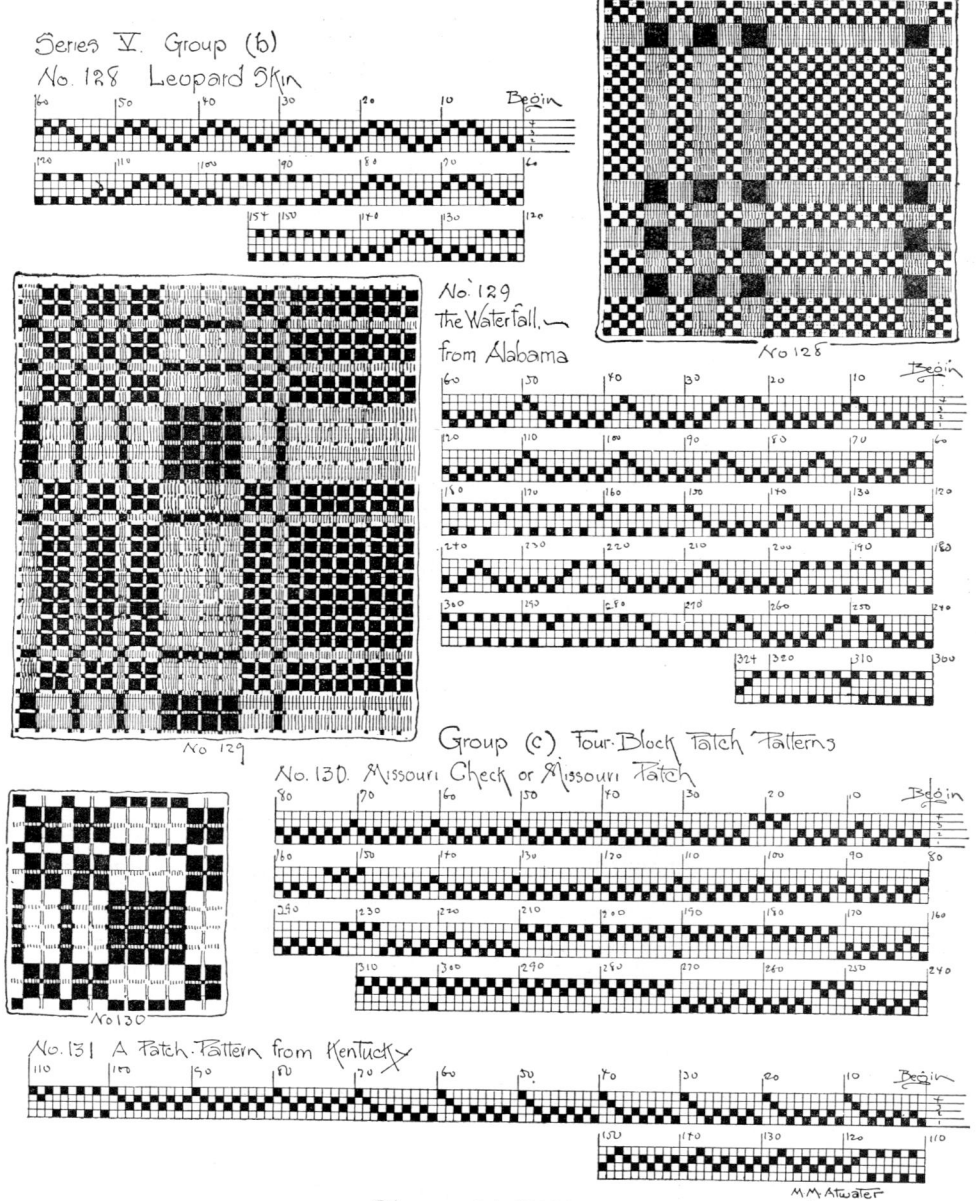

Diagram 34 (88)

— 189

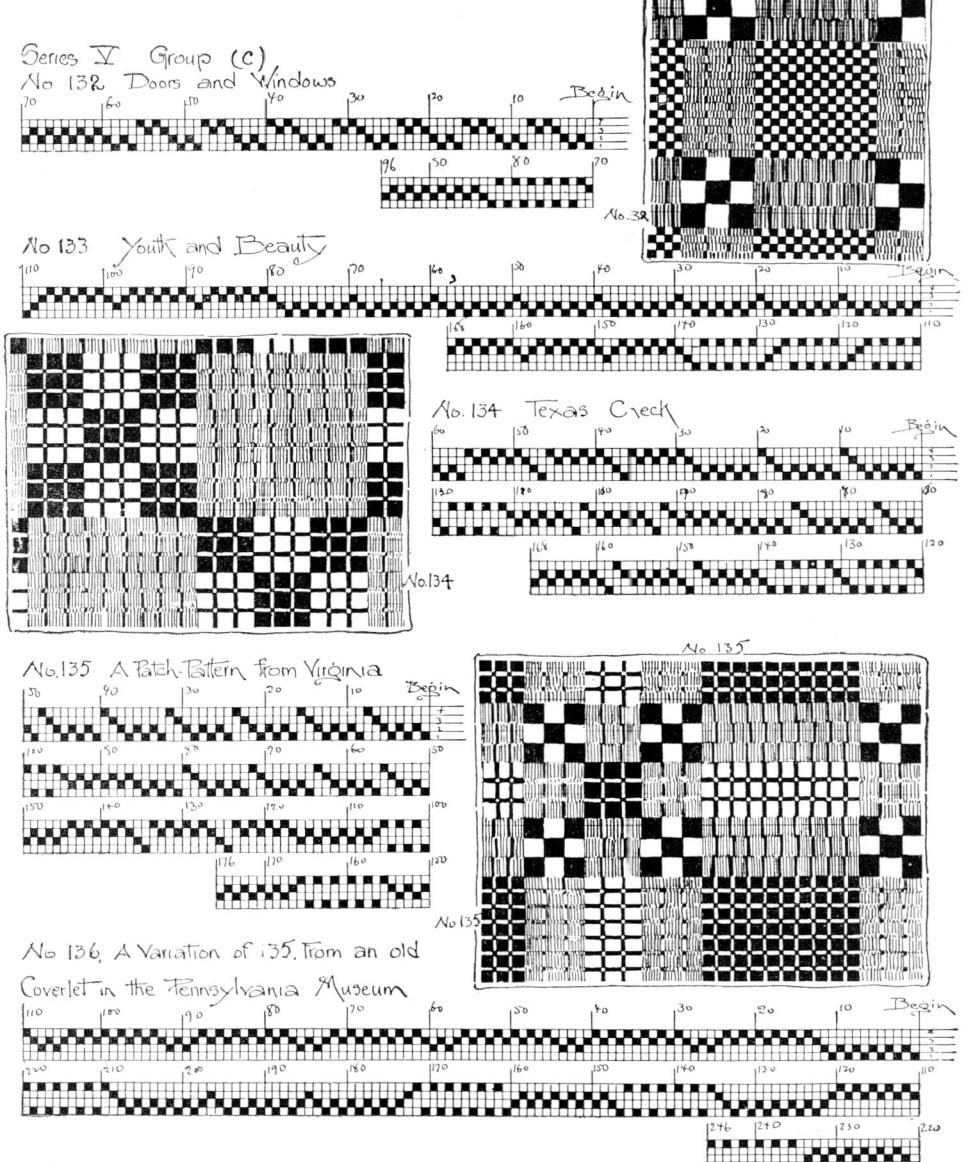

Diagram 35 (89)

190 —

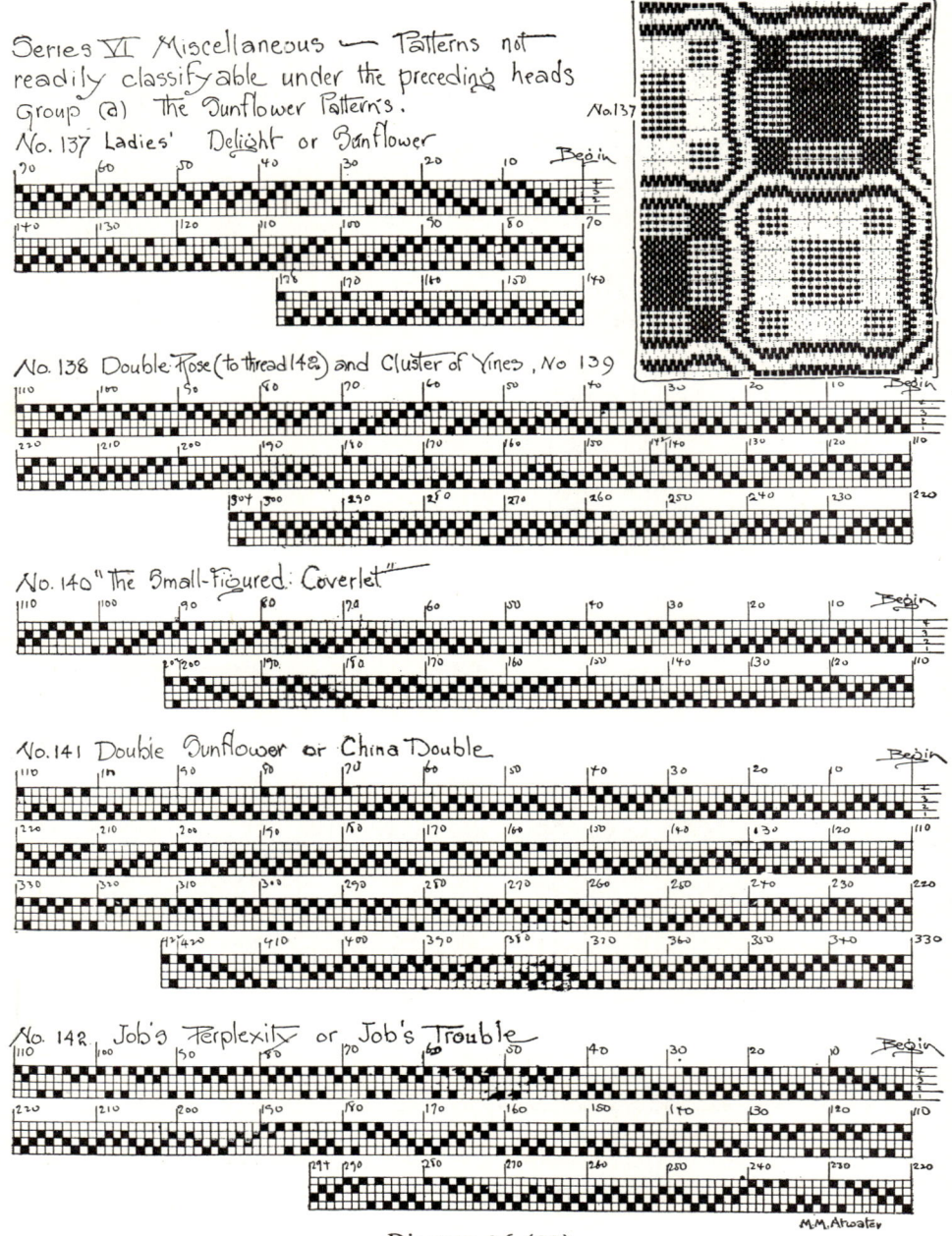

Series VI Miscellaneous — Patterns not readily classifyable under the preceding heads
Group (a) The Sunflower Patterns.
No. 137 Ladies' Delight or Sunflower

No. 138 Double Rose (to thread 142) and Cluster of Vines, No. 139

No. 140 "The Small-Figured Coverlet"

No. 141 Double Sunflower or China Double

No. 142 Job's Perplexity or Job's Trouble

Diagram 36 (90)

M.M.Atwater

Diagram 37 (91)

192 —

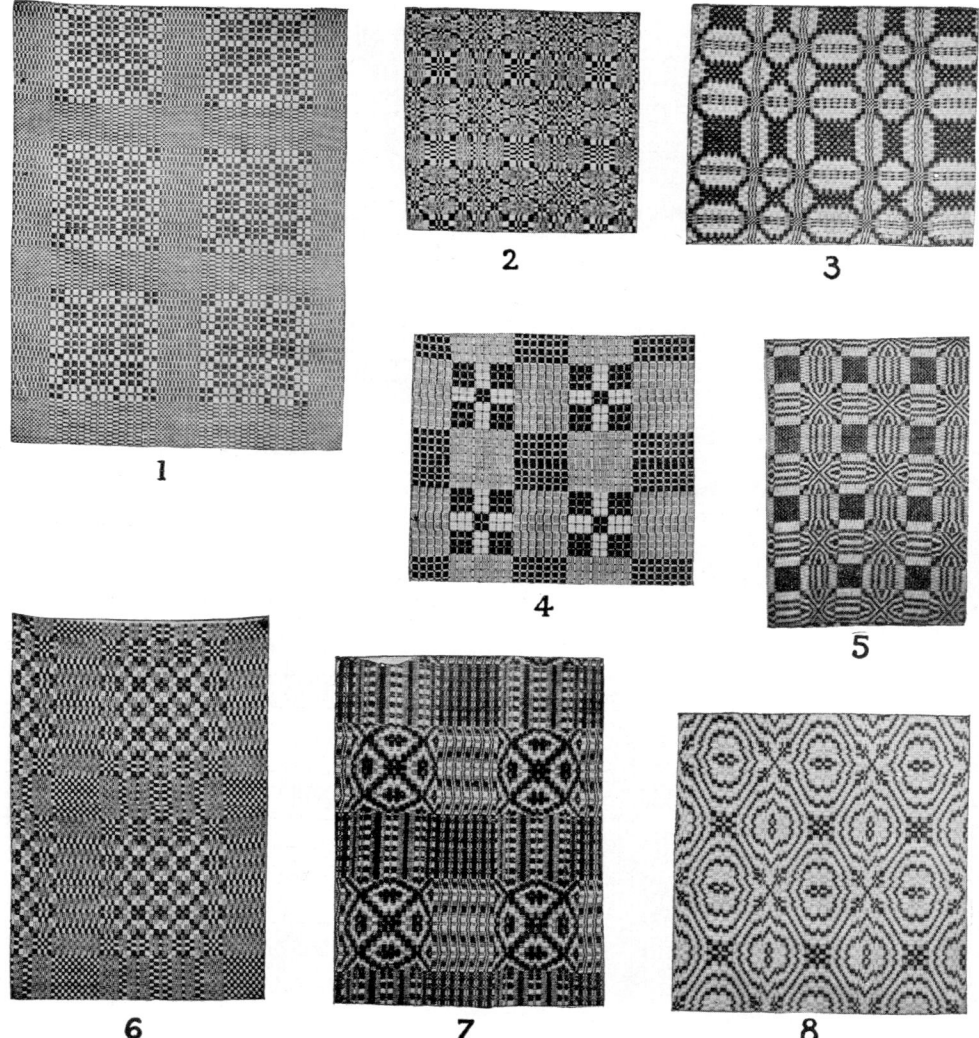

(92) 1. Queen's Patch. Draft number 123. 2. Lover's Knot on opposites, Wade collection. Draft similar to number 92, but woven as drawn in. 3. King's Flower. Draft number 48. 4. Patch-pattern from Kentucky. Draft number 131. 5. Cross of Tennessee. Draft number 11. 6. Old South County. Draft number 29. 7. Christian Ring. Draft number 80C. 8. North Carolina Beauty. Draft number 114.

— *193*

(93) A pattern on opposites. Draft number 13.

DIAGRAM 34 (88)

No. 128 is woven on treadles 1, 3 and 4. Woven as drawn in, omitting the small 2–3 blocks.

Nos. 129 and 130 are similar patterns in so far as the arrangement of blocks is concerned, but the effect is very different, as will be seen from the illustration. A small part only of the figure is illustrated at 130.

Pattern 129 is woven on three treadles, treadle 2 being omitted. Otherwise treadled as drawn in.

No. 130 is a four-block pattern. In treadling it is usual to omit the 1–4 accidentals between the 1–2 and 3–4 blocks. Treadled as drawn in.

No. 131 should be treadled:

Treadle 1, 8 times ⎱ 7 times
3, 2 times ⎰
2, 8 times ⎱ 3 times
3, 2 times ⎰
4, 8 times

Treadle 3, 2 times
4, 8 times
3, 2 times
2, 8 times ⎱ 3 times
3, 2 times ⎰

(94) Orange-Peel. Draft number 10.

DIAGRAM 35 (89)

No. 132 is similar to "Leopard Skin." Should be woven as drawn in, omitting accidentals.

Nos. 133, 134 and 135 are similarly woven—as drawn in, omitting accidentals.

No. 136, however, is woven exactly as drawn in, accidentals *not* omitted. The coverlet, of which this is the draft, is a very handsome one in black and red.

DIAGRAM 36 (90)

No. 137. This and the other patterns of the group are characterized by the fact that the figures interlock in an odd way, and are composed of small blocks of uniform size. No. 137 is written as small as possible, for use in upholstery. The pattern is excellent for coverlets, for rugs and other large work. For this use, the blocks should, however, be increased by two threads each, and the repeat will then cover 338 threads.

The draft may also be written with all 1–2 and 3–4 blocks increased by two threads and the 2–3 and 1–4 blocks left as they are. This makes a repeat of 258 threads. This and the other patterns in this group may be woven in two colors—1–2 and 3–4 blocks in the darker color, 2–3 and 1–4 blocks in the lighter.

Nos. 138 and 139 are similar patterns—the first 142 threads of the draft constitute the repeat for "Double Rose." The 304 threads of the complete repeat produce a pattern known as "Cluster of Vines."

No. 140 is a good small figure for upholstery.

No. 141 is a large and elaborate pattern, as is also No. 142. The size of the blocks in all these patterns is small, however, and therefore even when the figure is large, the fabric is exceptionally closely woven and solid. These patterns are useful for fabrics designed for hard wear,—rugs, upholstery and the like.

DIAGRAM 37 (91)

No. 143 and No. 144 are very much the same in construction but differ in proportion. The effect is quite different, No. 144 being a rather more dashing pattern than No. 143. Woven as drawn in.

("Federal Knot" and "Flag of Our Union," classified elsewhere, have some of the characteristics of these two patterns.)

No. 144 is called "The Hexagon" in North Carolina—it is somewhat difficult to see why.

The Group (c) patterns are particularly pleasing. The small pattern with no name, given at draft No. 146, is excellent for upholstery and all closely woven fabrics. The other two drafts are charming for large uses,—hangings, coverlets, pillow-tops, etc.,—but are inadvisable for rugs on account of the long overshot over some of the blocks.

No. 147 is probably the best known of the group and is a very striking and satisfactory pattern for coverlets. Modern weavers seem to know it by the name of "Miss Cobb No. 2" but the other two names are more ancient and rather more interesting. Illustrated (31).

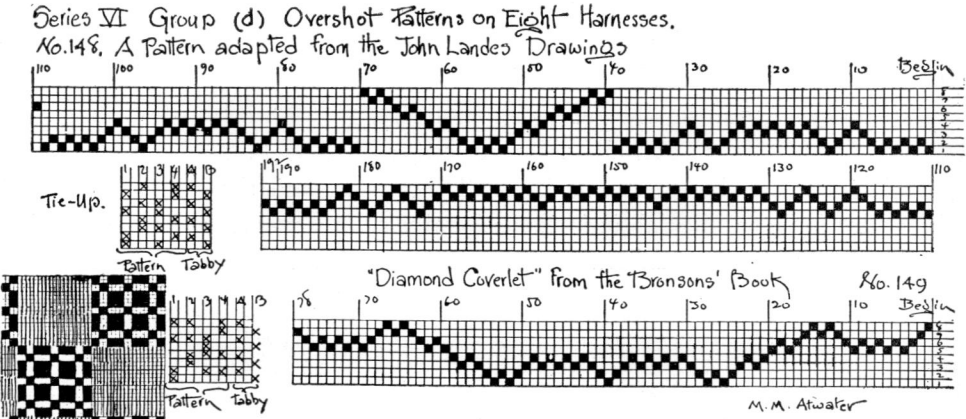

Diagram 38 (95)

DIAGRAM 38 (95)

No. 148 is the draft of a pattern in 8-harness overshot weaving. This is a very interesting weave but extremely rare. The pattern illustrated is from one of the John Landes drawings arranged for this type of weaving. The effect, as will be noted from the illustration, is of large half-tone areas with plain tabby squares behind the blocks of the pattern. The weave is given in the Bronson book, and draft No. 149 is taken from that book. Any four-block pattern can be drafted in this fashion for eight-harness weaving. Two methods of tie-up are given. Either tie-up can be used with either threading.

(96) Effect produced from arrangement of John Landes for 8-harness overshot weaving.

Chapter Twelve: Additional Four-Harness Weaves

There are, of course, many four-harness weaves besides the overshot weave. They cannot all be considered here, but there are several of special interest that should not be overlooked.

There are four-harness versions of the summer-and-winter weave and of the Bronson or spot weave, that will be considered in the chapters devoted to these techniques. There are the weaves used for the white cotton counterpanes made in the old day in the South; there are two very useful weaves for linens—"huck" and "Ms and Os"—much used in the old day as well as in our times; there is a weave of Scandinavian origin that has become so Americanized that it deserves mention as an American weave; and there are a large number of European weaves that will not be given here. Also there are many fascinating forms of pick-up weaving some of which will be described in the chapter on pick-up. The four-harness weaver does not lack for interesting adventure.

I Counterpanes

The white cotton counterpanes seem to have been a special product of the South, in the early day, though a few in tufted weaving were also made in the North. Woven tufting is very different from the tufting produced by hooking strands of candle-wicking through a woven fabric. It is more like the tufted borders seen in some pieces from central Europe.

Fine tufting is a business involving a great deal of time, and not many pieces are being made today. The technique, however, is simple. The warp may be a fine white cotton, say a 20/2 set at forty ends to the inch and threaded double, to a twill: 1, 1, 2, 2, 3, 3, 4, 4, and repeat. Or use a two-harness loom threaded: 1, 1, 2, 2, and repeat. Weave a tabby heading, ending with a shot of B tabby, thrown from right to left. With the shed still open, weave a strand of medium-coarse, soft white cotton, from right to left. Take up tufts on a fine wire, in alternate spaces between raised warp-ends. With the B shed still open, take the tufting material back through the shed from left to right. Beat well. Weave four shots in fine tabby, ending on B from right to left; weave the tufting material through the same shed and make the second row of tufts. It is a simple technique but must be carried out with precision. The tufts should not be too large and must all be exactly the same, the material taken over the wire in the same direction and the tufts not staggered but in the same spaces each time.

This method of tufting is sometimes used—in coarse material—for small rugs and bath-mats.

The old "dimity" counterpanes are quite plain, in a pattern of lengthwise raised stripes. Perhaps they look a little too much like the machine-made spreads one may buy at the store to be interesting to hand-weavers. But of course the hand-woven article always has a style and texture of its own and these bed-covers are useful and pleasant to make.

The material should be fine, unmercerized, white cotton both for warp and weft. An ordinary 20/2 cotton set at forty ends to the inch is suitable. Draft (a), Diagram 39 is from an old piece woven all the way in plain stripes. Draft (b), also from an old piece, is treadled differently, as indicated, and gives a honeycomb effect that is a good deal more decorative. This seems to me the handsomest of the old patterns presented here.

Draft (c) is the threading of an old piece in regular honeycomb weave, which requires further explanation. This weave, slightly different in effect due to a different balance of material, is to be found in the Scandinavian books and has a number of uses for things entirely different from the old white counterpanes.

For the weave as in the counterpane the warp and setting are the same as for the dimity patterns, but two kinds of weft are used—a fine weft like the warp and a strand of coarser, very soft cotton. Weave the first block—on the special tie-up—treadle 1, treadle 2 alternately for sixteen shots in fine weft. Weave tabby A, tabby B in coarse weft. Allow these tabby shots to lie very

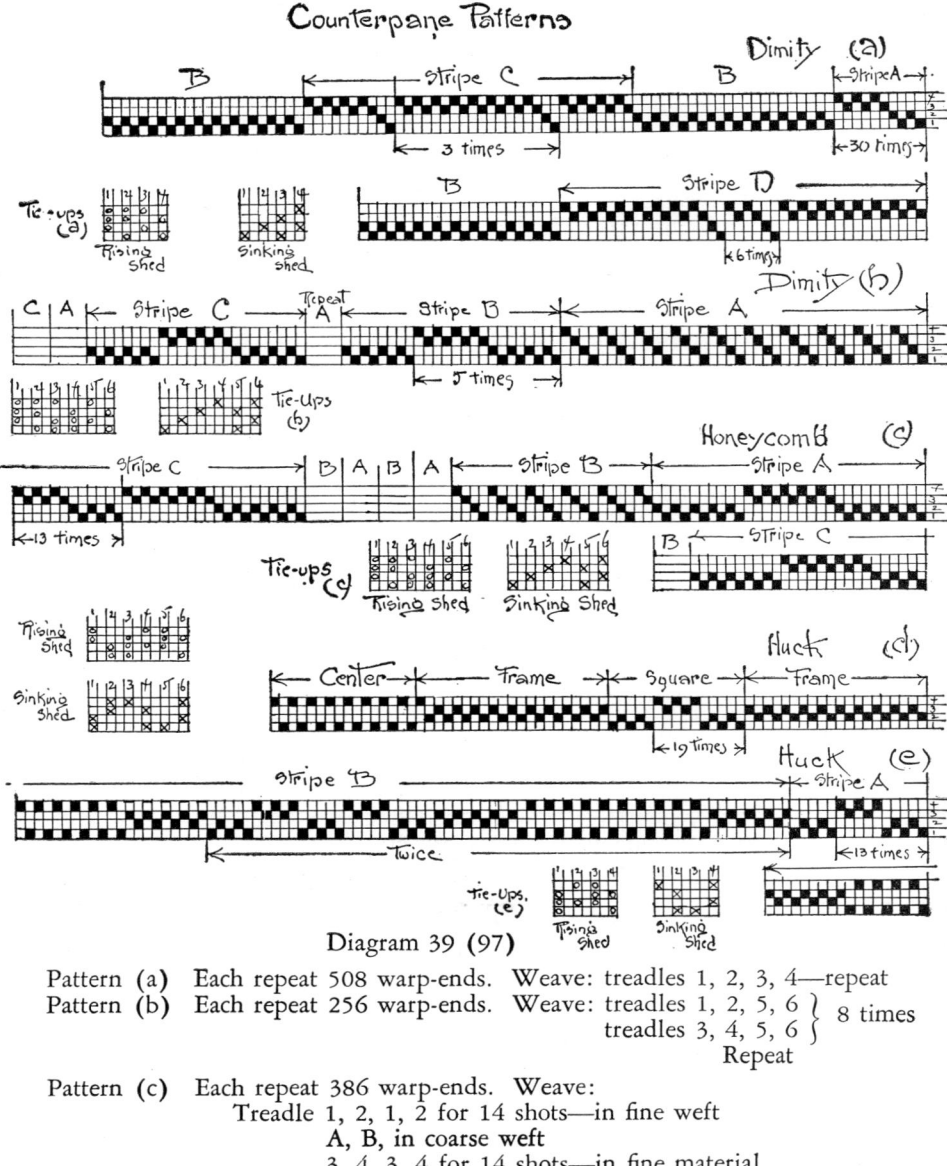

Diagram 39 (97)

Pattern (a) Each repeat 508 warp-ends. Weave: treadles 1, 2, 3, 4—repeat
Pattern (b) Each repeat 256 warp-ends. Weave: treadles 1, 2, 5, 6 ⎫
                                                     treadles 3, 4, 5, 6 ⎬ 8 times
                                                                         Repeat

Pattern (c) Each repeat 386 warp-ends. Weave:
                Treadle 1, 2, 1, 2 for 14 shots—in fine weft
                  A, B, in coarse weft
                3, 4, 3, 4 for 14 shots—in fine material
                  A, B, in coarse material
                        Repeat

loosely in the shed so that when beaten firmly they will take a curved line. Weave the second block: treadle 3, treadle 4 alternately for sixteen shots in fine material. Tabby A, tabby B in coarse material. Repeat.

The Scandinavian weave is exactly the same except that the warp is set farther apart and the fine weft covers it in the "dimples," while the coarse weft is heavier and is woven: tabby A, tabby B, after the first block and: tabby B, tabby A, after the second block.

Any overshot pattern may be woven in this manner if one chooses, though a pattern in which all blocks are fairly large should be chosen. Drafts 122 and 124, for instance, might be used. Four-block patterns may be woven in this manner also, though usually it is better to rewrite them with larger blocks. Draft No. 1, for instance, with twelve threads instead of four under each block. The 1-2 block should be woven on 1 and 2 alternately; the 2-3 block on 2 and 3 alternately, and so on, with the two tabby shots in coarse material between the pattern blocks.

When woven in the Scandinavian manner this weave is sometimes used for evening bags with the fine weft in a metallic thread and the coarse weft in a heavy silk or rayon. It should be noted that no matter what color or colors are used for the fine weft, the warp and the coarse weft must be of the same color. To make them of different colors ruins the effect. And no matter what material is used, this fabric should be very solidly beaten up.

Drafts (d) and (e) are also from ancient pieces and are similar in weave though treadled differently. Draft (d) was woven in lengthwise stripes all

---

Diagram 39 (97) (*Continued*)

Pattern (d) Each repeat 252 warp-ends. Weave:
Frame: Treadles 1, 2 alternately for 18 shots
4, 3, 4, 3, 4, 6, 5, 6, 5, 6—repeat 19 times
4, 3, 4, 3, 4
1, 2 alternately for 18 shots
4, 6 alternately for 50 shots
Repeat

Pattern (e) Each repeat 302 warp-ends. Weave:
Treadle 2, 1, 2, 1—fine material
2, coarse material
4, 3, 4, 3—fine material
4, coarse material
Repeat

(This pattern may be woven in squares in a manner similar to (d) if preferred.)

the way, and (e) was woven in squares. Of course draft (d) might also be woven in squares if one wished, and draft (e) in lengthwise stripes. The weave is a variation of the huck weave, otherwise used chiefly for linen towelling and linen table pieces.

As woven in the old pieces, draft (d) was woven in two kinds of weft, a fine and a coarse, treadled as follows—on the special tie-up as given: treadles 1, 2, 1, 2, in fine material; treadle 1 in coarse weft; treadles 3, 4, 3, 4 in fine weft; treadle 3 in coarse weft. Repeat.

Most of the old cotton counterpanes were finished with deep knotted fringes, sometimes quite elaborate in pattern. The material was not a hard-twisted cord such as is used in macramé, but a strand of soft-spun ends, all in white, of course. Notes on knotted and woven fringes will be found in the chapter on finishes.

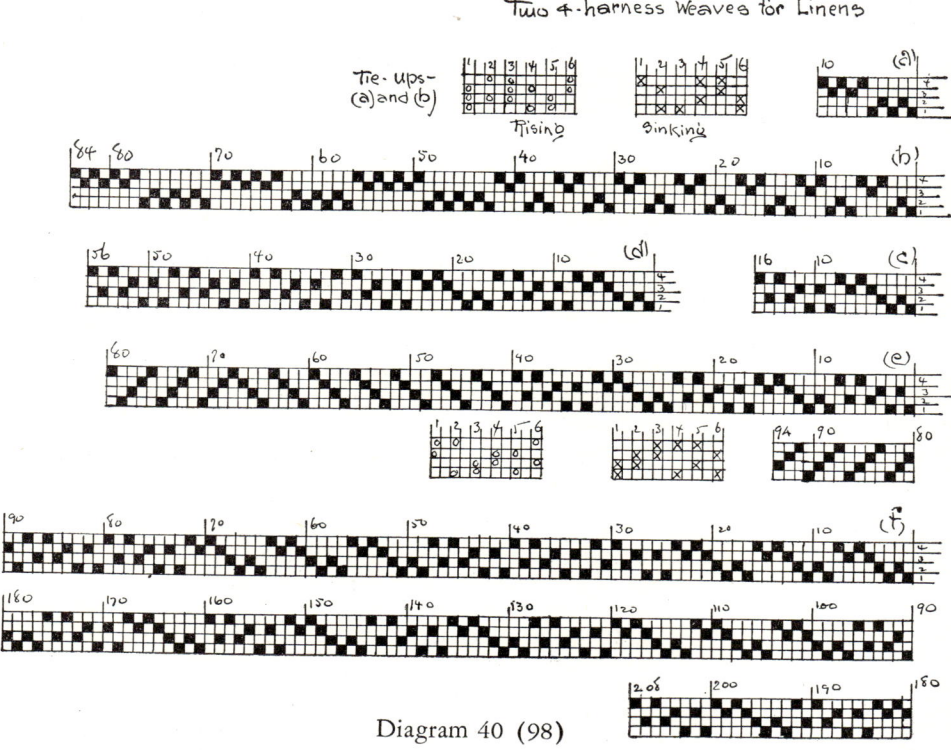

Diagram 40 (98)

Diagram 40 (98) (*Continued*)

(a) Plain Huck or Huckaback. Weave—special tie-up as given:
2, 1, 2, 1, 2, 4, 3, 4, 3, 4, and repeat
For tabby with this pattern weave treadles 2 and 4
Special treadling: 2, 4, alternately for 18 shots
Treadle 5, treadle 6 in double weft strands
Huck treadling, three times
Treadle 5, treadle 6 in double strands
Treadles 2 and 4 alternately for 18 shots
Treadle 5, treadle 6—double strands
    2, treadle 4
    5, treadle 6—double strands
    2, treadle 4
    5, treadle 6—double strands. Repeat

(b) Huck variation, "Raindrops." Weave:
First figure: 4, 3, 4, 2, 1, 2, repeated 7 times
Second figure: 4, 3, 4, 3, 4, 3, 4, 2, 1, 2, 1, 2, 1, 2—3 times

(c) Ms and Os. Standard tie-up. Weave:
Treadle 1, treadle 3, alternately for 8 shots
    5, treadle 6, alternately for 8 shots

(d) Ms and Os variation. Weave:
Treadle 5, treadle 6, alternately for 8 shots
    1, treadle 3, alternately for 8 shots
    5, treadle 6, alternately for 8 shots
    1, treadle 3, alternately for 34 shots

(Note: There is no true tabby in this weave but treadles 2 and 4 woven alternately will produce a small weave not far removed from the plain weave.)

(e) The Pennsylvania "E. F." towel—Ms and Os variation. Weave:
Treadle 5, treadle 6, alternately for 8 shots
    1, treadle 3, alternately for 8 shots
    5, treadle 6, alternately for 8 shots
    1, treadle 3, alternately for 8 shots
    5, treadle 6, alternately for 8 shots
Treadles 1, 2, 3, 4, repeated six times
    1, 2, 3, 2, 1
    4, 3, 2, 1, repeated six times

(f) From an old blue and white table cloth. Weave:
Treadle 1, treadle 3, alternately for 24 shots
    5, treadle 6, alternately for 24 shots
    1, treadle 3, alternately for 24 shots
    5, treadle 6, alternately for 24 shots
    1, treadle 3, alternately for 24 shots
    5, treadle 6, alternately for 8 shots ⎫
    1, treadle 3, alternately for 8 shots ⎬ 5 times
    5, treadle 6, alternately for 8 times ⎭

II Two Weaves for Linens

Two weaves much used for linens in the old day are huck or Huckabuck and "Ms and Os" and their numerous variations. These are both "fifty-fifty" weaves.

Two of the counterpane patterns—(d) and (e) Diagram 39—are partly in the huck weave, but as a rule this weave is reserved for linens. It is an excellent weave for plain towelling with hems and borders in tabby. The "raindrops" variation, draft (b) Diagram No. 40, is very attractive.

A treadling for the plain huck threading, adapted from a Scandinavian piece, is simple but excellent and may be used for table pieces. I have been told that a tablecloth woven in this fashion was part of the trousseau of a Swedish princess. Weave as follows:

tabby, 26 shots
treadle 5, treadle 6—in strands of three ends
regular huck treadling as on the draft, three repeats
treadle 5, treadle 6—in strands of three ends. Repeat, tabby, etc.

The huck patterns are handsomest when woven in all white, or in white for weft over a warp in natural linen. Or if a colored effect is desired use the same color and the same material for both warp and weft.

This weave is sometimes used—in all-wool—for baby-blankets and couch-blankets; it is, however, distinctively a weave for linens.

"Ms and Os" is a weave used chiefly for linens, though sometimes also for all-wool fabrics. It is handsomest when woven in all-white or in all one color.

The weave appears in a number of variations, a few of which—drafts (c), (d), (e) and (f)—are given on Diagram 40.

In this weave there is no true tabby, though a rather interesting plain fabric with double threads at intervals may be woven on treadles 5 and 6.

This is not a good weave for light, open fabrics; the warp should be set close and the beat should be firm.

III The Crackle Weave

The weave we know as the "crackle" weave does not, as far as I know, appear among the textiles of the American Colonial period, but it seems to deserve a place in a book on American weaving because of its current popularity.

The weave is of Swedish origin and in its home country goes under the name of "Jämtlandsvaev," but as this is to English speaking people something of a mouthful, and as we needed a handle for it, I coined the name "crackle" when I first published it in the "Shuttle-Craft Bulletin" in 1926—because of the background effect which somewhat resembles the crackle in pottery.

The weave is, in a way, a makeshift weave and includes some rather troublesome eccentricities, as makeshifts are apt to do, but for all that, it is a handsome and useful weave, giving four-harness weavers a method of producing a closely combined fabric similar in structure to summer-and-winter weave, in a wide variety of interesting patterns.

The summer-and-winter weave is a better and more logical weave, to be sure, but on four harnesses can be woven only in two-block patterns. The crackle weave is more versatile.

As the patterns we use in this weave, and some of the ways in which we weave it, are entirely different from the Swedish technique, this becomes an American weave though of recent adoption.

The weave consists of four pattern blocks each written on two sheds, as shown on Diagram 41 at (a). The "unit" of each block is four threads: 1, 2, 3, 2 for the first block; 2, 3, 4, 3 for the second block; 3, 4, 1, 4 for the third block and 4, 1, 2, 1 for the fourth block. However, when the blocks are written in sequence it is apparent that a "transition" thread must be added to each block to preserve the tabby alternation. Also, as each block overlaps the next by two threads, the smallest block when woven covers seven threads instead of four. This has to be taken into account when figuring the proportions of a pattern in writing a draft.

It is also apparent from a study of the draft that each shed weaves across two blocks. The 1-2 shed weaves over block one and also over block four; the 2-3 shed weaves across blocks one and two; the 3-4 shed weaves across

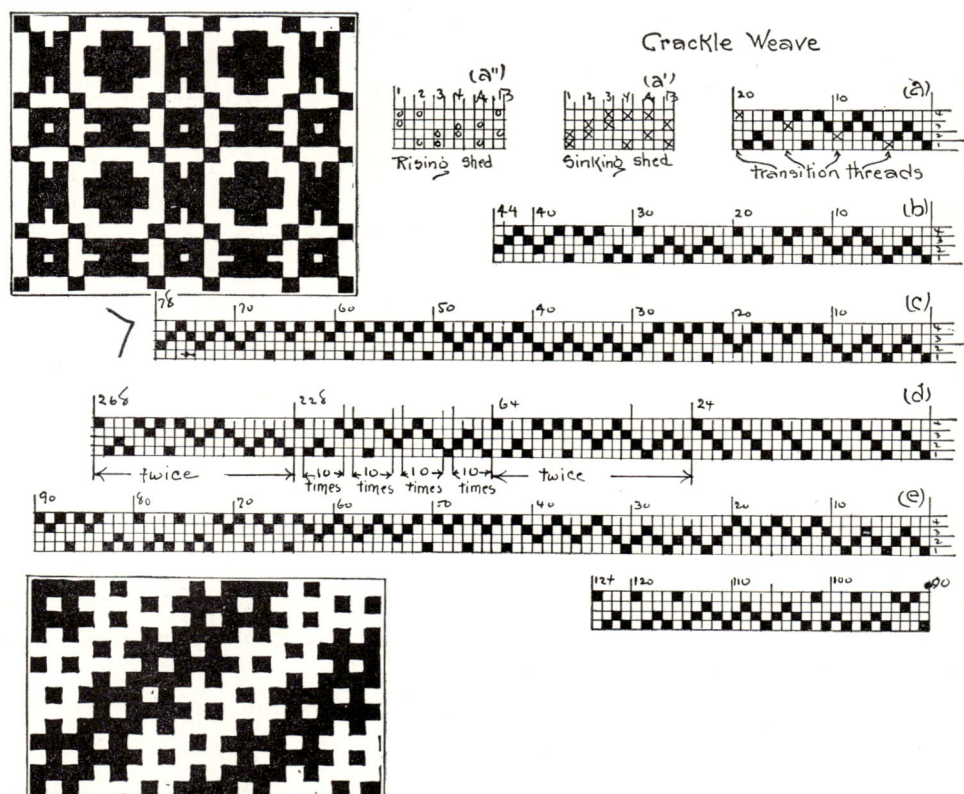

Diagram 41 (99)

(a) Twill succession of one-unit blocks—transition threads indicated by "X"
(b) Diamond Pattern. Weave:
Treadle 1, 5 or 7 times
2, 5 or 7 times
3, 5 or 7 times
4, 5 or 7 times
1, 5 or 7 times
2, 5 or 7 times
1, 5 or 7 times
4, 5 or 7 times
3, 5 or 7 times
2, 5 or 7 times
Repeat

(c) Colonial type pattern. Weave:
Treadle 1, 7 or 9 shots
3, 7 or 9 shots
4, 3 shots
3, 7 or 9 shots
1, 7 or 9 shots
4, 7 or 9 shots
3, 15 shots
4, 7 or 9 shots
Repeat

blocks two and three; and the 1–4 shed weaves across blocks three and four. The blocks overlap in the manner of a 2–2 twill.

Due to these peculiarities of structure it is difficult to write drafts for this weave. The things to avoid are skips of four threads—which spoil the effect of the weave—and the intrusion of an unwanted shed at some of the transitions, which show like the "accidentals" in patterns on opposites but are much more disfiguring.

The weave is useful for many purposes. As it is a closely combined fabric with no long skips, it is suitable for upholstery as well as for hangings, and it may be used with excellent effect for bags, table mats and other small pieces—even for rugs. It is not, however, a good weave for linens or for all-wool fabrics.

In this weave the material used for the tabby shots should be like the warp, and the pattern weft should be somewhat heavier and may be wool if desired, but if the pattern weft is quite coarse the warp should be set farther apart than for the overshot weave.

As ordinarily woven, one pattern shed is used for all the shots on any particular block; for instance block one is woven on the 1–2 shed, with alternating tabby, for the complete block. But one may also weave in the manner of the summer-and-winter weave, alternating two pattern shots for each block—the 1–2 shed and the 2–3 shed for block one, and so on. This gives an entirely

Diagram 41 (99) (*Continued*)

(d) Three Twills Pattern. Weave:
    Treadles 1, 2, 3, 4, one shot each
        —six times
    Treadle 1, 3 shots
        2, 3 shots
        3, 3 shots—twice
        4, 3 shots
        1, 30 to 36 shots
        2, 30 to 36 shots
        3, 30 to 36 shots
        4, 30 to 36 shots
        1, 3 shots
        2, 3 shots—twice
        3, 3 shots
        4, 3 shots
        Repeat

(e) Hesitation Twill Pattern.
    Treadle 1, 7 or 9 shots
        2, 7 or 9 shots
        1, 7 or 9 shots
        2, 7 or 9 shots
        3, 7 or 9 shots
        2, 7 or 9 shots
        3, 7 or 9 shots
        4, 7 or 9 shots
        3, 7 or 9 shots
        4, 7 or 9 shots
        1, 7 or 9 shots
        4, 7 or 9 shots
    Repeat

208 —

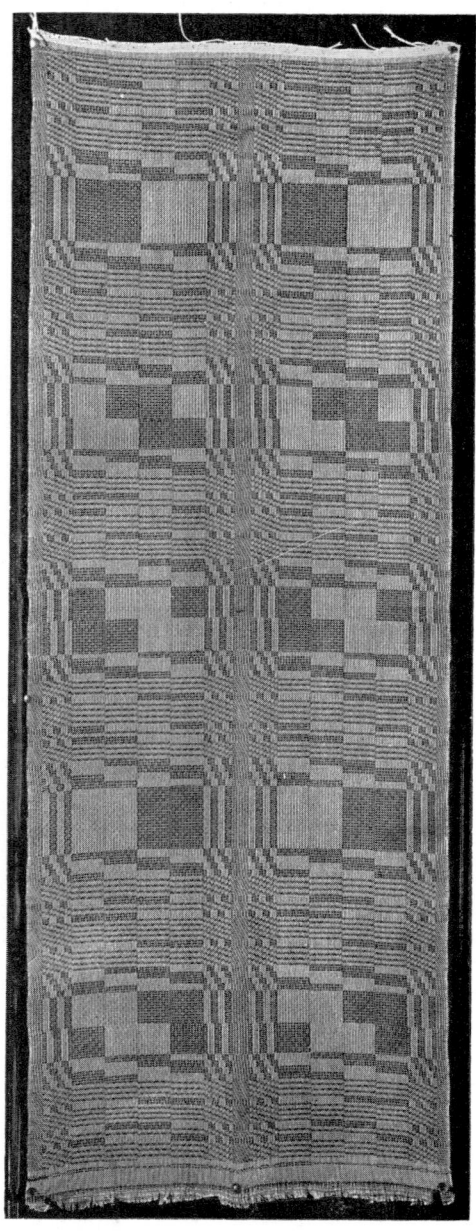

(100) Runner on two repeats of the "Three Twills" pattern. Draft (d). Diagram number 41.

(101) The "Three Twills" pattern in crackle weave. Draft (d). Diagram number 41.

different effect and texture from that produced by the conventional manner of weaving.

The Italian method of treadling described in Chapter Eleven, IV is very handsome in this weave, especially in a pattern made up of large blocks like the "Three Twills" pattern and the "Hesitation Twill" pattern given at draft (d) Diagram 41—especially when three colors are used. The colors interweave in an odd manner and rather unpredictable color effects may result; it is well to do some experimenting before embarking on an ambitious project.

As pattern blocks may be as large as one pleases in this weave, designs of the modern type may be produced.

Chapter Thirteen: The Summer-and-Winter Weave

The summer-and-winter weave is in many ways the most interesting and satisfactory of the American Colonial weaves. Where and when it originated I have been unable to discover. I have recently found some drafts in a similar technique in weaving books from Finland—but the weave does not appear in the Swedish books, the English books or the German books. One might, however, guess a Germanic origin as most of the old pieces in this weave appear to have been woven in Pennsylvania and there are a few drafts for it in a manuscript book in the library of the Pennsylvania Museum of Art in Philadelphia.

A good many old coverlets in the summer-and-winter weave have come down to us, but not nearly as many as those in the overshot weave, and not as many even as those in double weaving. One infers that the weave did not come into use till the end of the hand-woven era, not long before the introduction of machinery. Though most of the old pieces seem to have been made in Pennsylvania or New Jersey, I found one—the piece shown in illustration (111)—in Rhode Island. As far as I know, none were made in the South.

Other illustrations that show the weave are: illustrations (8), (105), (111), (113), (116), (120) and (135). The last is the same pattern as (111), with somewhat different proportions and photographed from the other side.

Which side of the fabric is to be considered the "right" side is a moot question, as the pattern is the same on both sides, with the light and dark transposed. I hold, however, that the side showing the figure in pattern weft against the light background—the "winter" side, I suppose—should be considered the right side.

Why "summer-and-winter"? I do not know unless for the reason that the weave is usually dark on one side and light on the other. I found the name attached to the two or three drafts in the old manuscript referred to above. Until that time we had been calling it the "one-three" weave, because of the structure of the fabric, but the old name is far more picturesque and fanciful so we adopted it.

When the revival took place this weave seems to have been completely lost—"mislaid" would perhaps be the better word. Weaver Rose did not know the way of it, nor did the surviving weavers in the South. The few old coverlets in the museums and private collections were all that was left.

I spent a great deal of time in research over this weave. I devised a special form of notation for it, copied after the notation used for double weaving and damask in some of the old books, and when I found those old drafts, written in the form I was using, I was very happy. As far as I know, the first printed information on this weave was contained in the chapter on the subject and the drafts as given in the first edition of this book. Since that time the weave has received wide acceptance.

I Structure

In the summer-and-winter weave the pattern weft passes over three warp-ends and under one across the blocks of the pattern, and under three over one across the background areas. It is woven over a tabby foundation, but the dots produced by the interweaving of the pattern weft gives the background a little "bird-eye" effect that is more interesting than plain tabby. The fabric produced is closely interwoven without long overshot "floats," which makes it far more durable than overshot and makes it suitable for many purposes for which the looser weave is impractical.

It is a delightfully logical wave, each unit being composed of four threads: one thread on harness 1, one thread on harness 2, and two threads on the pattern harness—whichever that may be. A unit of block one, for instance, is threaded: 1, 3, 2, 3, as shown on the diagram, and this unit may be repeated as many times as required for the size of the block. A unit of block two is threaded: 1, 4, 2, 4, and repeat for as many units as desired. These two blocks are the limit of the weave on four harnesses. Block three is threaded: 1, 5, 2, 5;

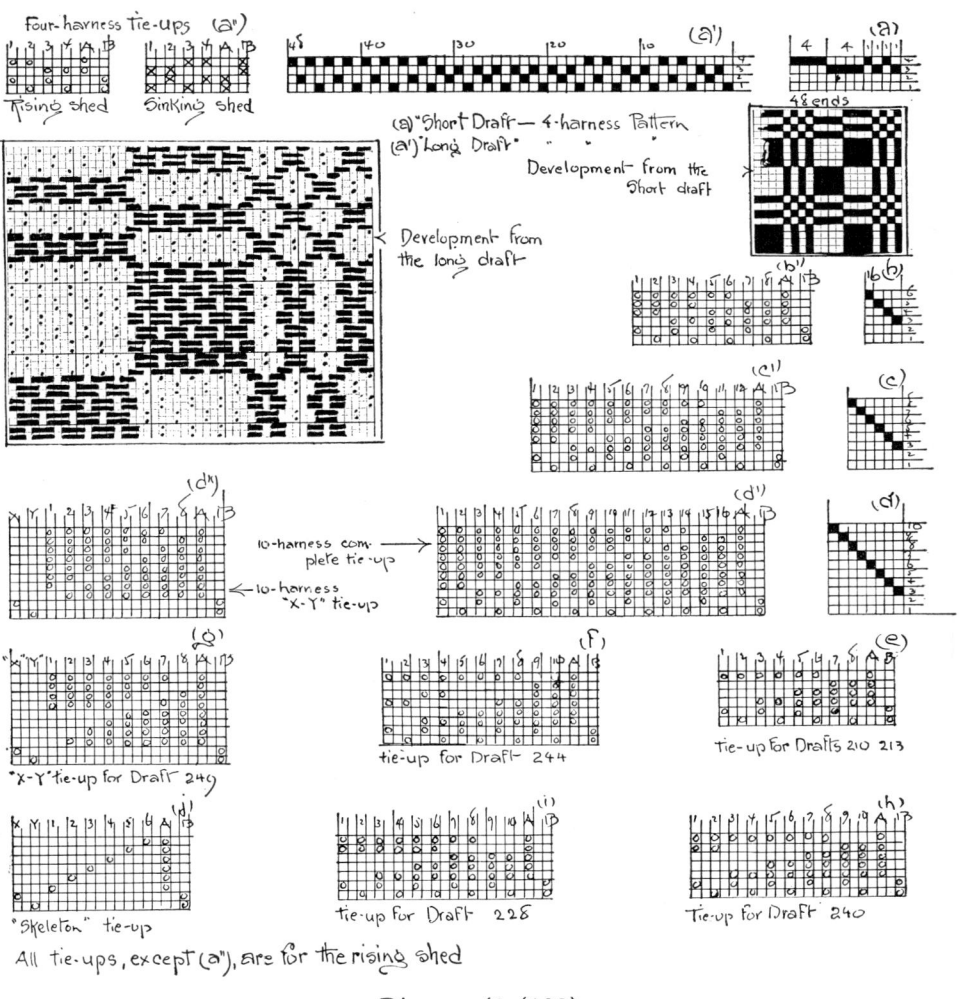

Diagram 42 (102)

block four: 1, 6, 2, 6, and so on. The two front harnesses carry the "ties" that tie down the pattern weft under every fourth thread, and one harness is required for each block of the pattern. A six-block pattern may be woven on an eight-harness loom and an eight-block pattern on ten harnesses.

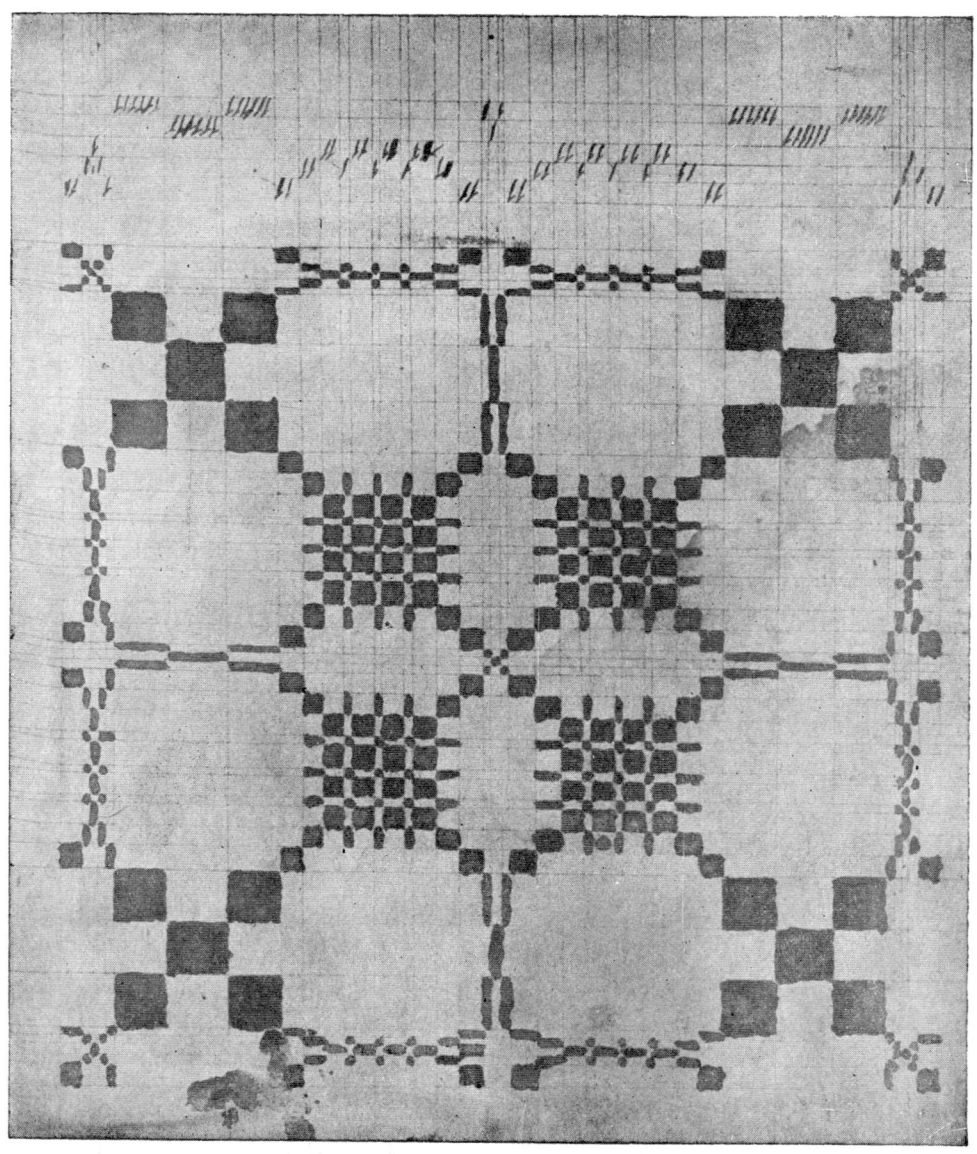

(103) Draft from an ancient notebook, Pennsylvania Museum. Written in units for summer-and-winter weave, double weave, or damask.

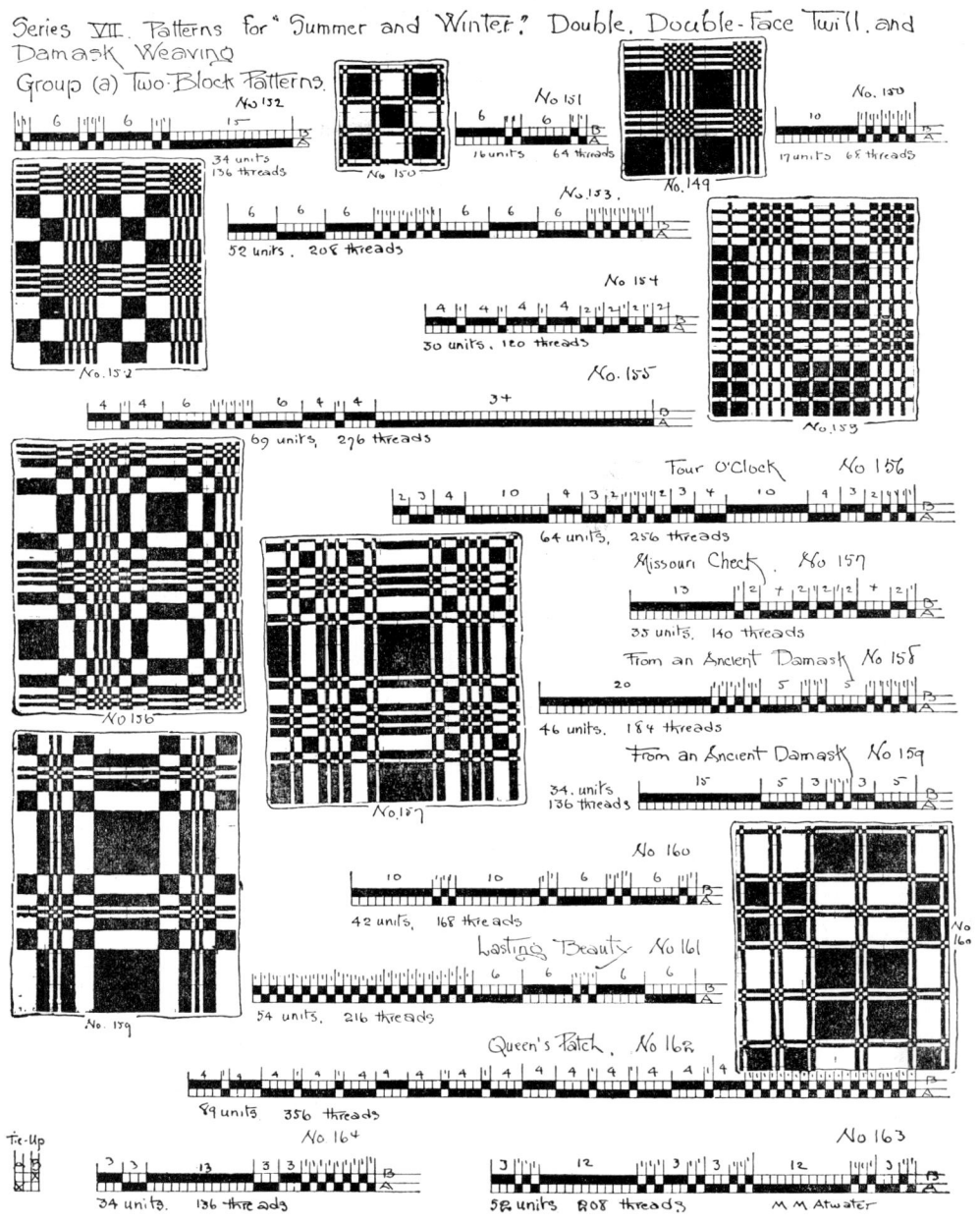

Diagram 43 (104)

As the weave is so regular in construction it is not necessary to write a thread-by-thread draft, and the drafts may be written by units, which makes them clear to the eye and easy to follow in threading and checking. Also, as the background is uniform, without half-tones or accidentals, a development made from the "short" draft, by blocking in the squares of the figure in solid black is entirely correct.

As the size of a pattern block in this weave is not limited by the practical length of an overshot skip, designing of patterns is much freer than for the overshot weave, and as blocks may be woven to overlap or to follow each other in any desired order, many interesting variations of figure are possible on the same threading. Patterns of the modernistic type may be produced in this weave.

(105) A two-block pattern in summer and winter weave on four harnesses. Similar to pattern for draft number 155, but simpler.

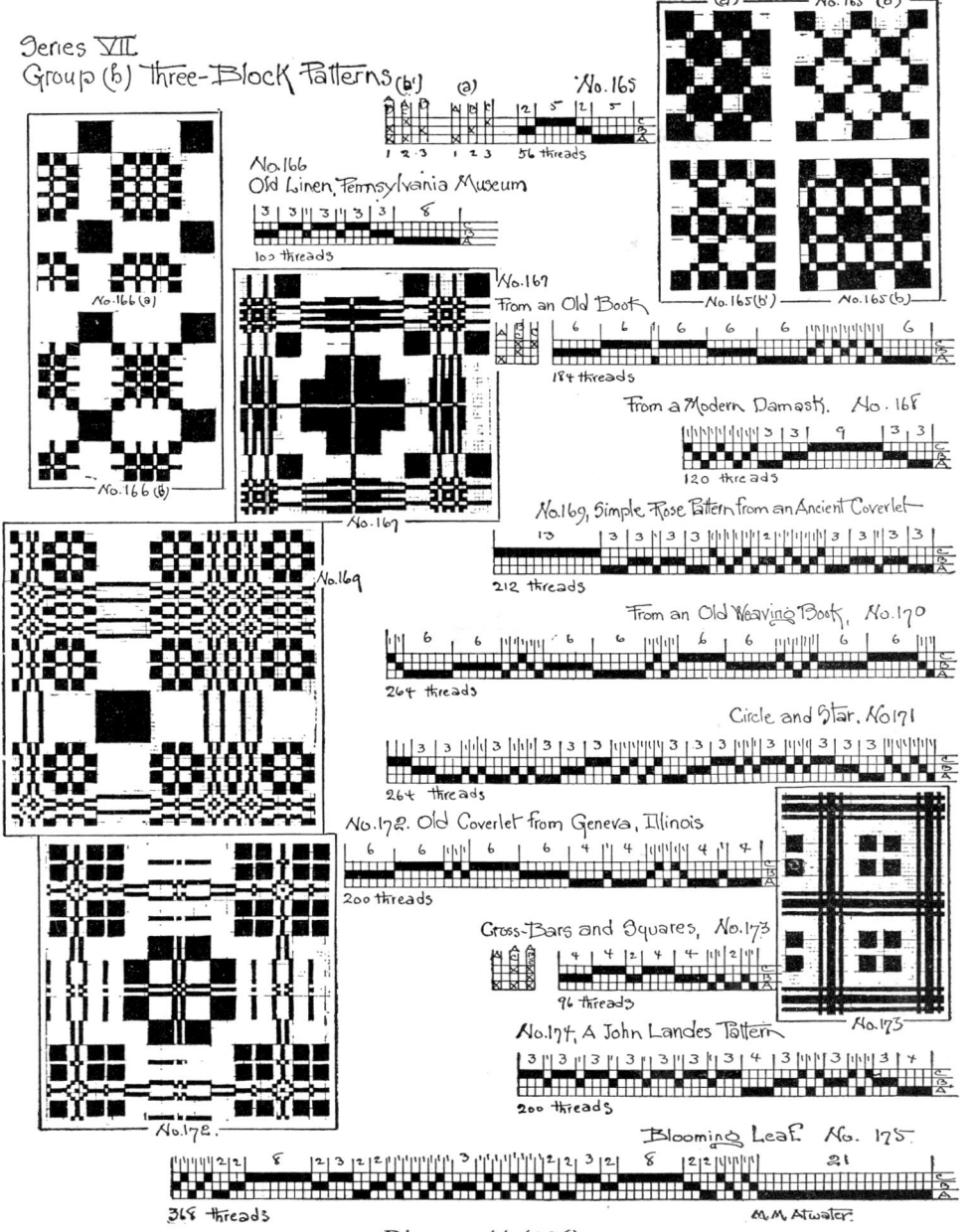

Diagram 44 (106)

This weave is handsomest in wool over a cotton foundation, though a pattern weft in a soft-twist cotton or a fine strand-cotton also makes a satisfactory fabric. This is not a good weave for linens as it gives the effect of a poor damask. Neither is it a good weave for all-wool fabrics.

The balance of material is important and does not permit of as much variation as in the overshot weave,—for the reason that exactly four pattern shots and four tabby shots must be woven for each unit of the threading, and if the material is too fine or too heavy to square the unit with that number of shots there will be serious distortion of the figure. It is impossible to give hard-and-fast rules in the matter as people beat differently, but a satisfactory combination for a light-weight but firm fabric—the handsomest combination in my opinion—is as follows: warp, 24/3 Egyptian cotton set at thirty ends to the inch; tabby weft, 20/2 cotton or #20 mercerized cotton; pattern weft, a good 15/2 worsted yarn such as "fabri," or a fine homespun. For a heavier fabric: warp, a 10/2 cotton set at twenty-four ends to the inch; tabby weft, the 24/3 cotton; pattern weft, ordinary homespun or a yarn of the "Shetland" weight. When correctly beaten these materials square very satisfactorily. Of course other materials may be used, but before embarking on an ambitious project it is advisable to weave a sample to make certain that the materials selected will give the desired result.

Coverlets in this weave are lighter in weight, with less wool in proportion to the cotton, than coverlets in overshot weaving. They are not, therefore, as warm when used as blankets. For modern use this is unimportant as we use other bed-coverings—electric blankets for instance—to produce warmth and the coverlet is used chiefly for decoration. But it is a point to be noted.

II Tie-Ups and Treadling

Each pattern block is woven on two sheds:—the pattern harness with harness 1 and the pattern harness with harness 2, exactly as it is threaded. For a two-block, four-harness pattern the same treadles are used as for the overshot weave, but the order is different because in this weave the tabby is on 1–2 and 3–4, and if one is accustomed to finding the two tabby treadles at the right, it is better to make the special tie-up as shown on diagram 42, (a^{II}).

The blocks may be woven in two different ways: with alternating tabby shots on A and B—One and one, as follows:

    Treadle 1, once   Treadle 3, once
        2, once   4, once
        1, once   3, once
        2, once   4, once
 Repeated for the number of units   Repeated for the number of units
    threaded under block one   threaded under block two

or in pairs:

    Treadle 1, once   Treadle 3, once
        2, twice   4, twice
        1, once   3, once
 Repeated for the number of units   Repeated for the number of units
    threaded under block one   threaded under block two

It will be noted that when the second treadling is repeated for a block of more than one unit, there are two pattern shots on each shed except the first and the last. A two-unit block on block one would be woven:

    Treadle 1, once   Treadle 2, twice
        2, twice   1, once
        1, twice

This follows the threading exactly, as will be apparent from a study of the development on the diagram, made from the thread-by-thread draft, diagram 42.

 Weaving in pairs is the preferred method of treadling and gives the handsomer effect. However, if the materials do not balance exactly and it is impossible to square the figures with four pattern shots to the unit, the one-and-one method may be used, permitting more or fewer shots to the unit.

 When weaving in pairs it is important to weave the B tabby shot between pairs and the A shot between unpairs. And note that the last shot of a block—a single shot—pairs with the first shot of the second block. When beginning, therefore, weave the B tabby and follow with the first pattern shot. The birdeye effect in the background does not result if the tabby shots are woven in the opposite order.

 Tie-ups for the more elaborate patterns are made in the same manner as for the four-harness weave: two treadles for each pattern block—pattern with 1 and pattern with 2—and two tabby treadles. The A tabby sinks the two front harnesses and the B tabby all the pattern harnesses, no matter how many there

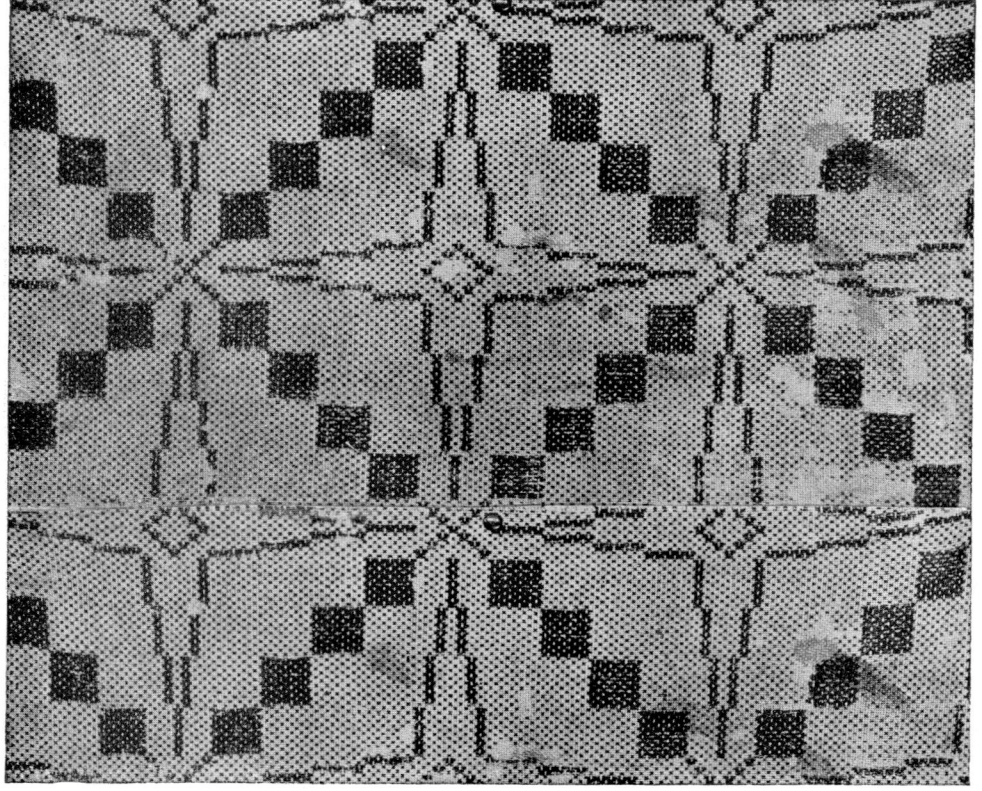

(107) From an ancient piece in summer-and-winter weave. Draft number 182.

may be. A six-block pattern on eight harnesses requires fourteen treadles for a complete tie-up and for this reason an eight-harness loom should always carry at least fourteen treadles.

The tie-ups as given with the patterns in this book show only the pattern blocks and not the complete tie-up for the loom. The reason for doing it in this manner is that these same pattern drafts may be used for double weaving, damask and double twill. For these weaves the units of threading are different and the tie-ups for treadling are different. Before making a tie-up for one of the more elaborate patterns in the summer-and-winter weave the tie-up should be written out in full. Diagram 42 gives tie-ups in this weave on six, eight and ten harnesses. (a), (b) and (c) are for patterns in which each block weaves separately, without overlapping, and should be used for such patterns as drafts 188, 202 and others. For patterns with overlapping blocks special tie-ups are required. For instance patterns 210 and 213 are woven on the tie-up shown in developed form at (e) on the diagram. The special tie-up for pattern 244 is given in developed form at (f), the special tie-up for pattern 240 at (h), and tie-up for 228 at (i). It is hoped that these tie-ups will sufficiently illustrate the manner of developing them. All have been written as for the rising shed, as looms with more than four harnesses are now all of this type and, of course, are exactly the reverse of a tie-up for the sinking shed. On a Swedish type loom with a double tie-up the raising ties should be made as shown and the sinking ties made to the blank spaces of the tie-up drafts.

Sometimes, especially for the modernistic effects in this weave, a good many more sheds are required than there are treadles on the loom. When this happens we resort to what we call the "X-Y" tie-up, as shown on the diagram. This method requires two treadles for the two tie harnesses, one treadle for each pattern shed, and two tabby treadles. If there are fourteen treadles there can be ten pattern sheds. In weaving it is necessary to use both feet for each shed—the pattern treadle first with treadle 1 and then with treadle 2.

(108) Ancient weaving in double-face twill. Draft number 178.

222 —

Series · VII. Group (c) Four-Block Patterns.
Figures of the Diamond Order

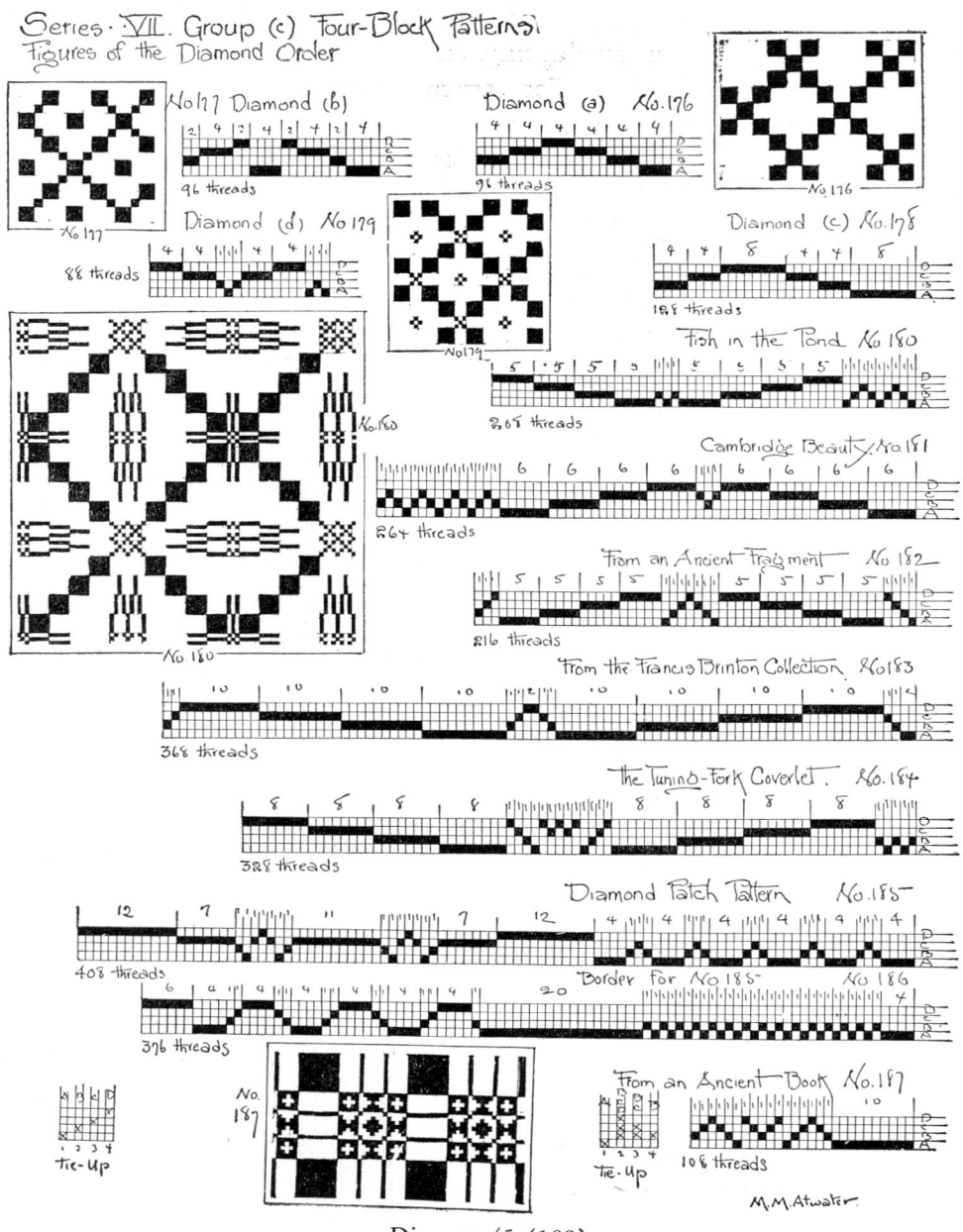

Diagram 45 (109)

(110) Mosaics. Draft number 196.

(111) An ancient piece of summer-and-winter weave from Rhode Island.
Pattern: Wheel of Fortune. Draft number 193.

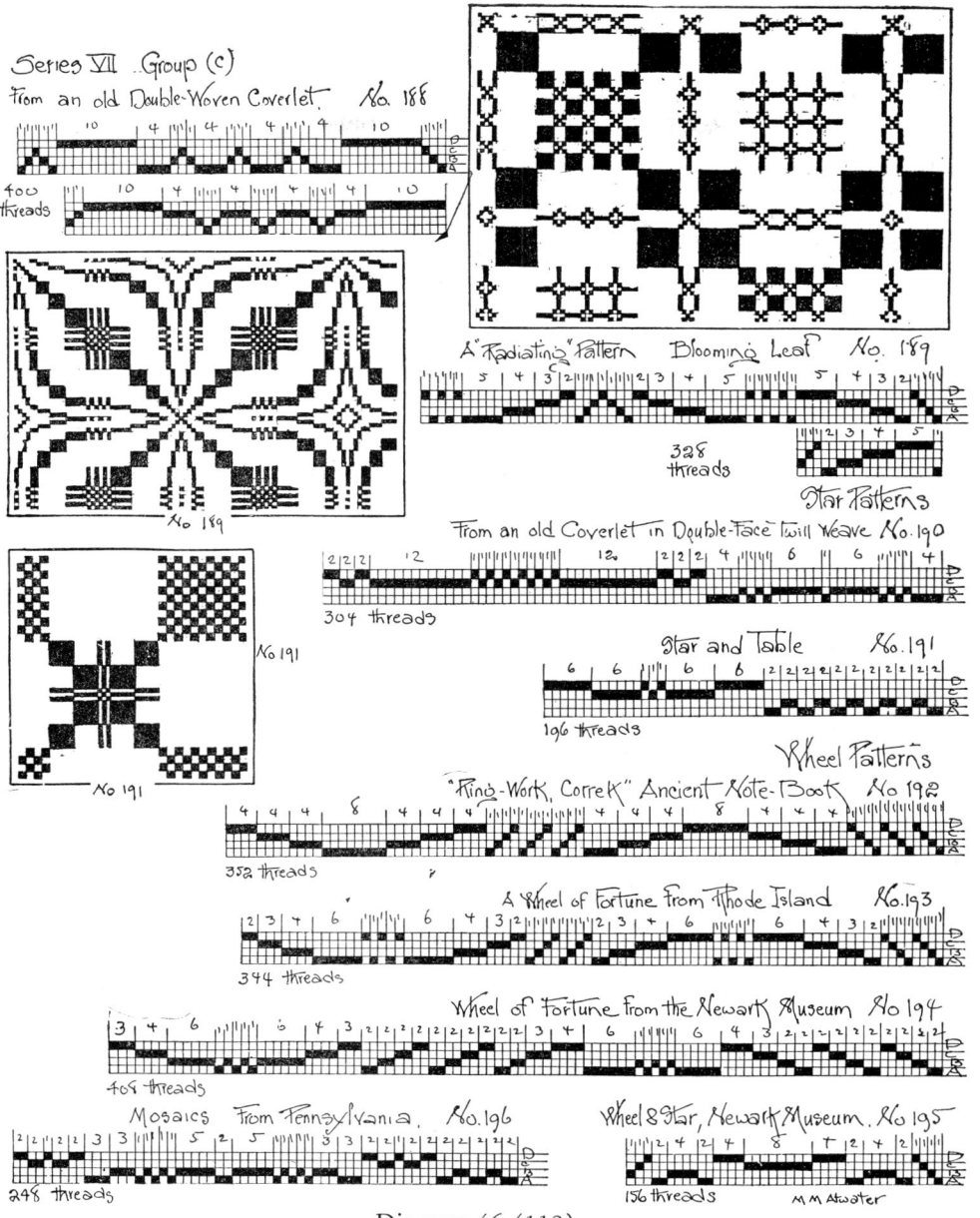

Diagram 46 (112)

(113) Lover's Knot, an ancient rose-colored coverlet in summer-and-winter weave, with a simple Diamond border. Draft number 198.

Diagram 47 (114)

228 —

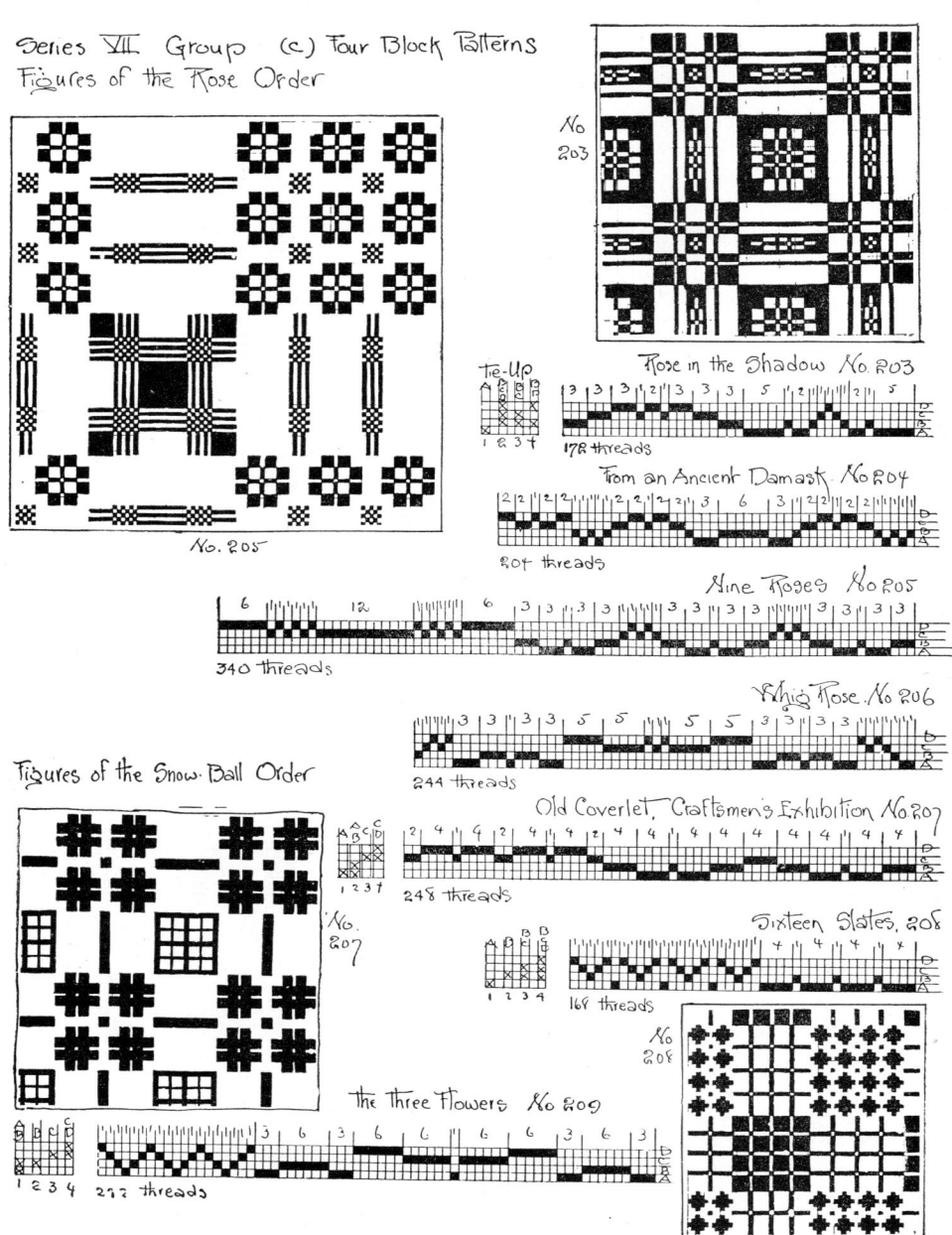

Diagram 48 (115)

— 229

(116) Single Snow-Ball pattern with Pine-Tree border, in summer-and-winter weave (modern).

230 —

Series VII. Group (c). — Four-Block Patterns — Figures of the Snow-Ball Order

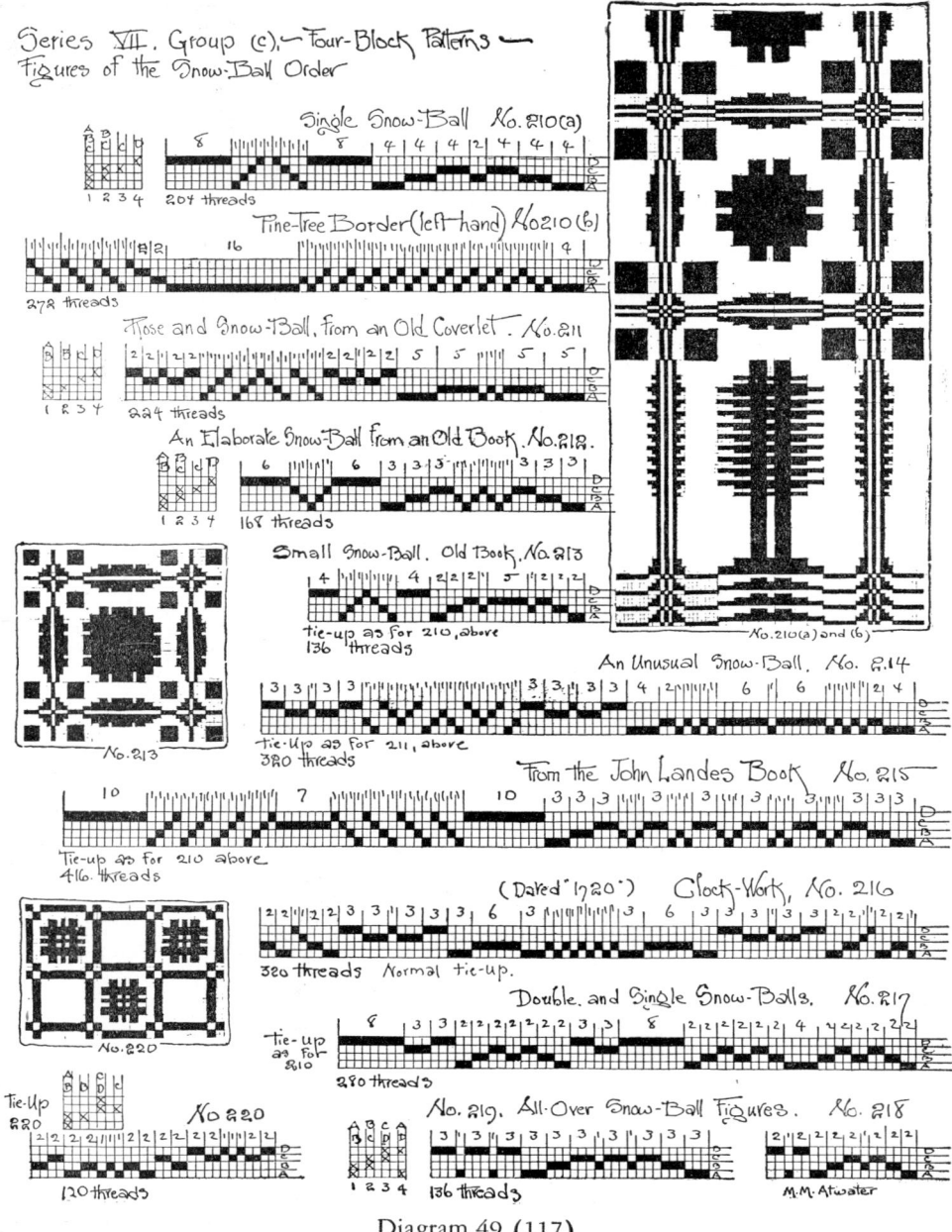

Diagram 49 (117)

— 231

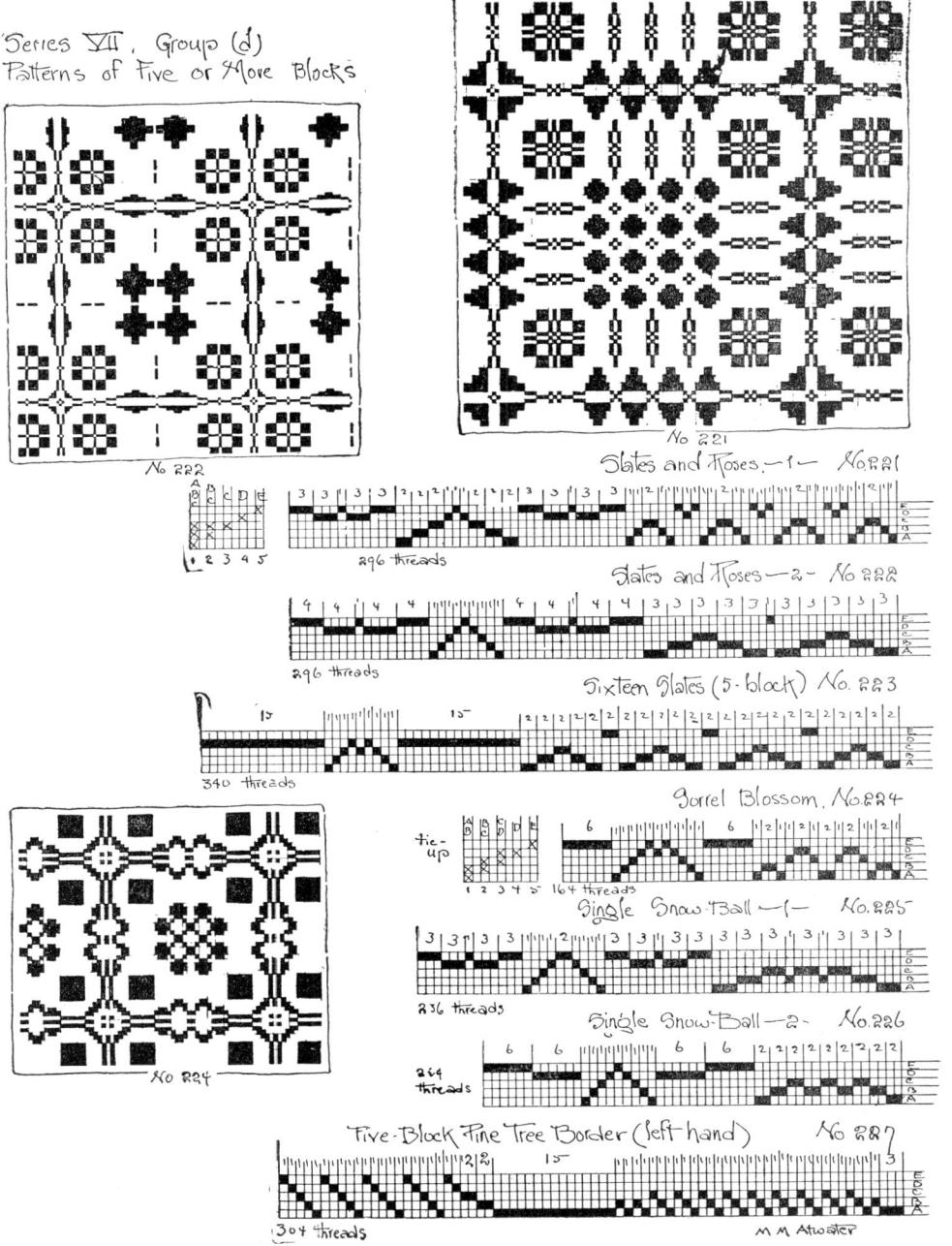

Diagram 50 (118)

— 232 —

Series VII, Group (d) —
Patterns of Five or More Blocks —
A Group of Snow-Ball Patterns

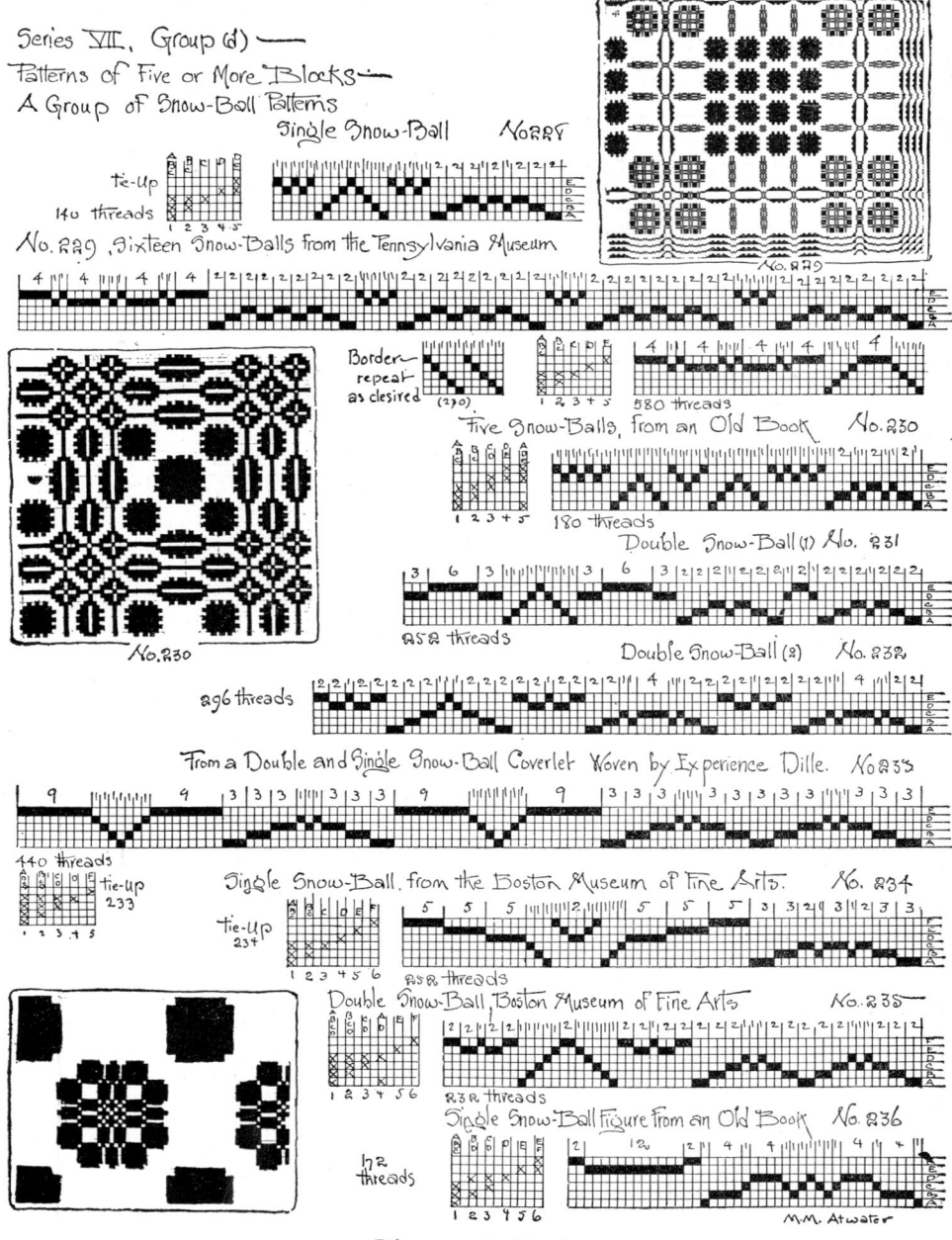

Diagram 51 (119)

(120) Summer-and-winter weave (modern), pattern Puritan Maiden or Lisbon Star, with Pine-Tree border. See draft number 238.

234 —

Series VII Group (d)
Patterns of the "Lisbon Star" Type —
on Five or More Blocks

Diagram 52 (121)

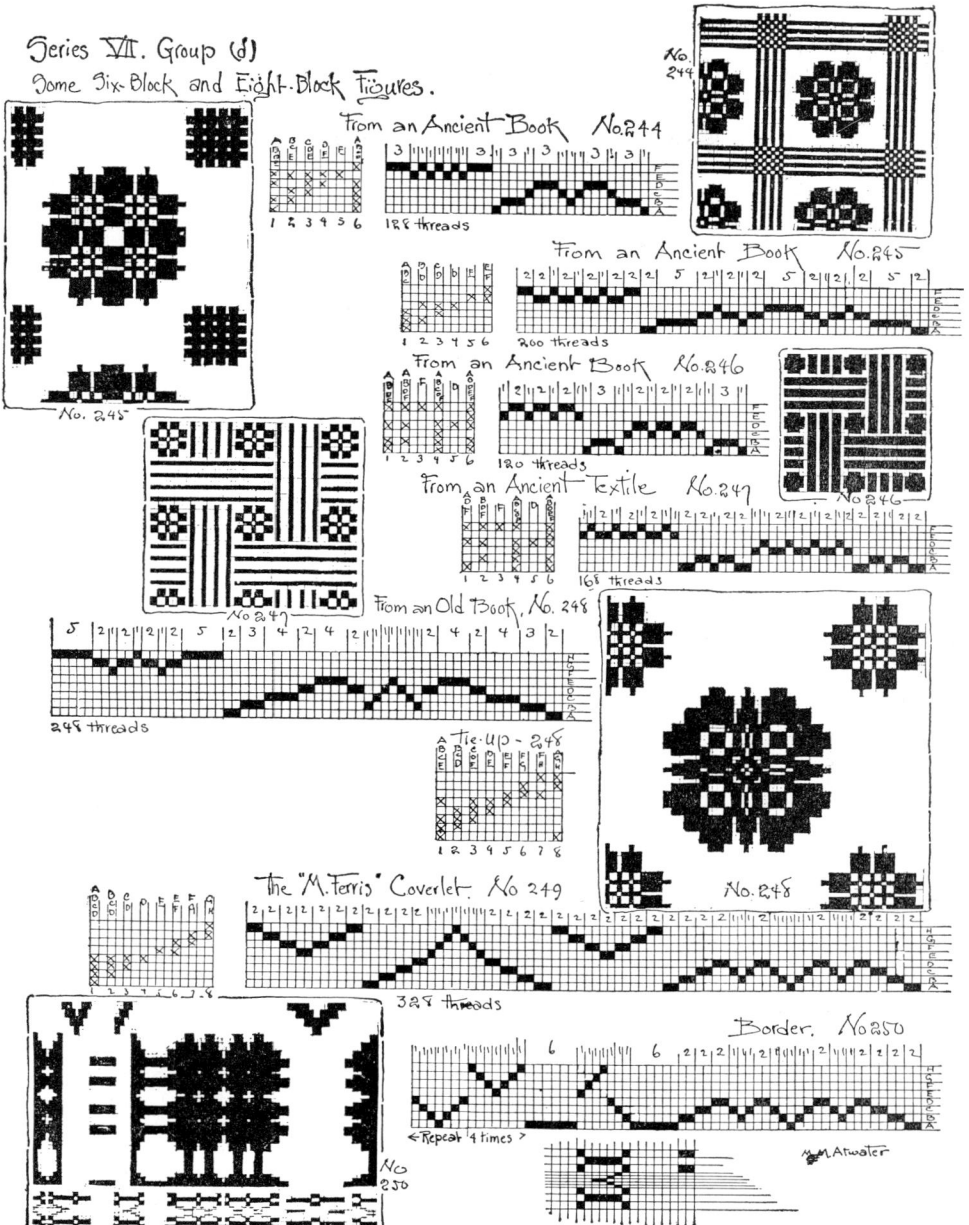

Diagram 53 (122)

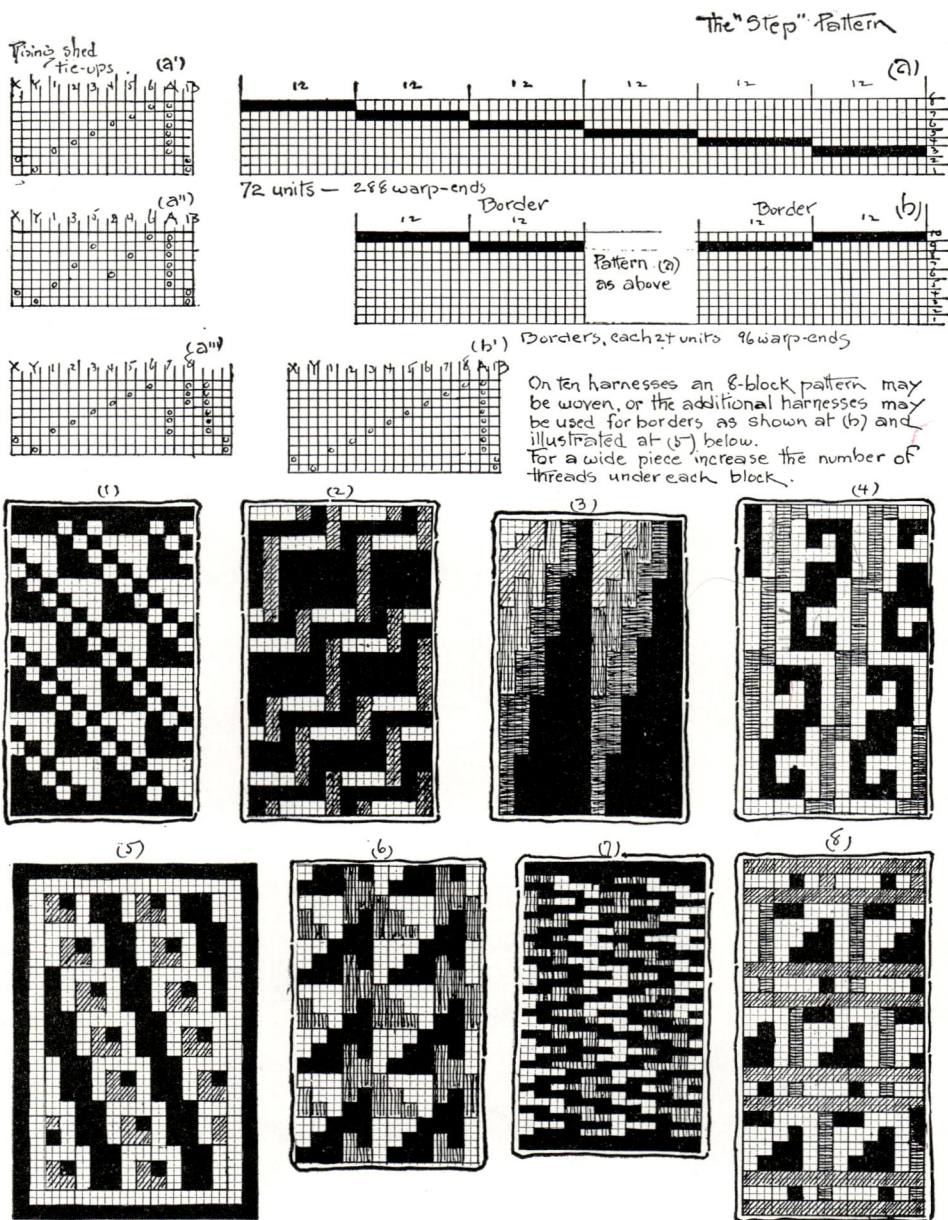

Diagram 54 (123)

Sometimes even this is not enough, and then we make what I call a "skeleton" tie-up, tying each treadle to raise a single harness, plus two tabby treadles. To weave on this type of tie-up involves some acrobatics at times as it is difficult to hold down five or six treadles at once with a single pair of feet. However, as the tie-up for eight harnesses takes only ten treadles, the additional treadles may be tied for any particularly difficult shed.

Another solution of the problem would be to install a set of draw-cords as on some Swedish looms. As there are over two hundred possible sheds in eight harnesses it is, of course, impossible to equip a loom with enough treadles for a complete tie-up.

To simplify the weaving of some of the complicated patterns, I make the tie-up with a tie to raise harness 1 on each pattern shed. The effect of weaving with a single tie-harness is to produce a fabric with lengthwise bars, similar to the effect of crackle weave. This, though not Colonial, is entirely suitable for the modern patterns and simplifies the treadling. Another method is to treadle X or Y as required and insert a light pick-up stick under the raised threads. Then both feet may be used to find the treadles required to make the figure.

The summer-and-winter weave lends itself agreeably to free design in a pick-up technique, as will be detailed in the chapter on pick-up weaving.

It is also possible to weave a summer-and-winter pattern in several colors. Pattern 247, for instance, may be woven with the horizontal lines in one color and the perpendicular lines in another, the little rose-figures in a third color, if desired, and the background in a fourth color. A set of treadles is required for each color, of course, and if the loom does not accommodate a sufficient number of treadles, these effects must be woven on a skeleton tie-up. In weaving in several colors, the same tie-harness should be used with each pattern shot of the series, followed by a tabby shot; then the second tie-harness with the pattern shots in the same order followed by the second tabby shot. Or both tabby shots may be woven each time.

It will be clear that patterns in summer-and-winter weave depend on tie-up and treadling fully as much as on threading, and a great variety of pattern effects may be produced on any threading in this weave. To be sure, a threading may be woven as-drawn-in, but this is likely to be the least interesting of the many ways in which it may be woven.

Many of the old pieces in this weave show four-block figures, clearly derived from the familiar overshot patterns. For instance the pattern shown in illustration (111) is the same figure as that in the overshot pattern in illustration (61), and draft 182 is exactly the same figure as that in draft 110. It does not appear to have been realized at first that the patterns used in double weaving may also be produced in the summer-and-winter weave. In the summer-and-winter weave patterns in which each block is woven by itself sometimes have a spidery effect, owing to the lack of the half-tone pattern; patterns in which two or more of the blocks overlap have a richer effect, as one may see by comparing patterns 167 and 172.

To weave patterns in this weave it is not enough to have the threading, except for weaving as-drawn-in, or even the threading draft and the tie-up—one needs either written treadling directions or a drawing of the proposed figure, the drawing being the easier to follow.

For the most varied effects a simple arrangement of blocks serves best, as for instance a twill arrangement of blocks of the same size as in the "Step" pattern, shown on Diagram 54. Such a threading might be on the loom for a long time, and one might weave on it a different pattern every day. A few possibilities are shown on the diagram to illustrate something of the range. On a loom with ten harnesses plain borders may be woven as shown on diagram 54 at (5), or a twill arrangement of eight blocks might be used.

For designs of this type one uses many more sheds than there are treadles on the loom, and unless the loom is equipped with a set of draw-cords one must resort to the skeleton tie-up. The pick-up stick is often useful in such a case even though the figure is woven on the threading and not by the pick-up method. Work as follows: Treadle for the pattern blocks to be woven and insert a light pick-up stick under the raised threads; treadle X and weave a pattern shot. Leaving the stick in place, treadle A and weave a tabby shot. Still without taking out the stick, treadle Y and weave a second pattern shot. Remove the stick and weave the B tabby. This is for weaving in a single pattern color.

When weaving in several colors, treadle X and insert the stick; treadle for the pattern blocks in the first color and weave; treadle for the second color and weave; for the third color—if a third color is used—and weave. Remove the stick and weave both tabby shots. Treadle Y and insert the stick; treadle for the pattern blocks as before and weave, using the colors in the same order as for the first series of pattern shots; take out the stick and weave the two tabby shots.

This is not as difficult in practise as it may sound in words. To weave in this manner takes somewhat more time, of course, than a straight-away treadling, but the effects are interesting and worth the trouble.

The above methods of using the summer-and-winter weave are definitely not Colonial practise, but lend themselves to modern design and modern color-effects.

III *Patterns*

The patterns given on Diagrams 43–53 are Colonial coverlet patterns, collected from museum pieces and pieces in private collections—many of them from pieces in double weave and some from ancient pieces in damask. Many of them are similar to well-known patterns in overshot weaving, but due to the fact that in these weaves the sizes of the blocks are not limited by the practical length of an overshot skip, the proportions of the figures are often quite different, with greater delicacy and distinction of design. Also as pattern blocks may be woven to overlap in any manner desired, greater richness of effect and greater variety is possible.

The freedom of design permitted by these weaves makes it possible to produce patterns of the modern type as shown on Diagram 54. For these effects some simple arrangement of blocks—a twill arrangement as in the "Step" patterns or a simple "point" arrangement—offers more varied effects than an elaborate threading.

Detailed treadlings are not given as most of the patterns are illustrated and it is far easier to weave from the illustration than from a long list of treadlings. Those that are not illustrated are similar to others shown in the drawings and can be treadled without difficulty, or developed on paper if that seems necessary.

Chapter Fourteen: The "Spot" or "Bronson" Weave

The spot weave, sometimes known as the Bronson weave, appears to be of British origin. At least I have never found it in Scandinavian books, or anywhere else except in an ancient English book on weaving and in the "Domestic Manufacturer's Assistant" by the Bronsons. Also, of course, it is among the weavings of the Colonial period.

I found the weave first in the Bronson book, given in a few drafts and without a name. When I prepared the material for the first edition of the "Shuttle-Craft Book" I wished to include this useful weave, and needing a handle for it I gave it the name of the authors of the "Assistant," for lack of another. Some years later I came on a few drafts in this weave in an ancient English book, under the name of "spot" weave. No doubt this is the correct name, but in the meantime the weave had become popular under the "Bronson" title, and as our current American variations of the weave differ greatly from the old English usage, it may as well continue under the "Bronson" name.

In England, according to the old book, the weave was used chiefly for woolen shawls, but American Colonial weavers appear to have used it almost exclusively for linens. In modern American practise it is used for such things as baby blankets, couch blankets or afghans, linens, in lace-effect for scarves and window drapery, and also for upholstery. It is a very versatile weave.

I Structure

The Bronson weave belongs to the group we know as the "fifty-fifty" weaves, in which warp and weft are the same or similar, and in which there are the same number of weft-shots to the inch as there are warp-ends to the inch in the set-

— 241

Bronson or Spot Weave — 4-harness and 5-harness drafts

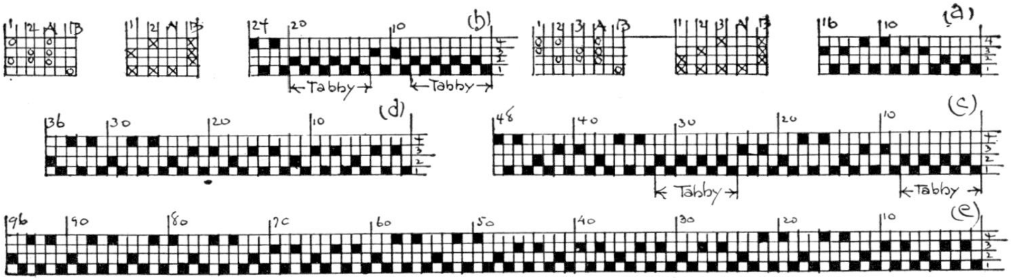

Rose and Diamond — Colonial — Bronson I

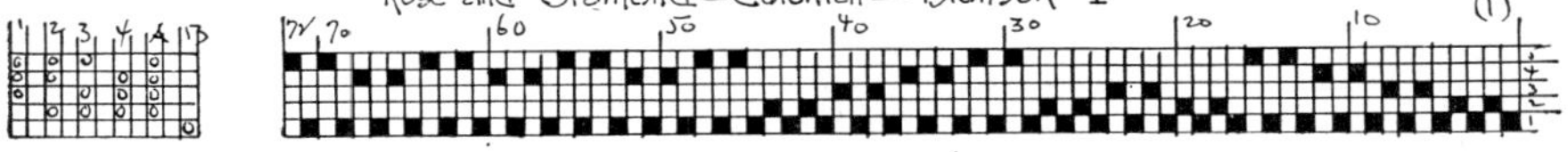

An old Tablecloth — Colonial — Bronson II

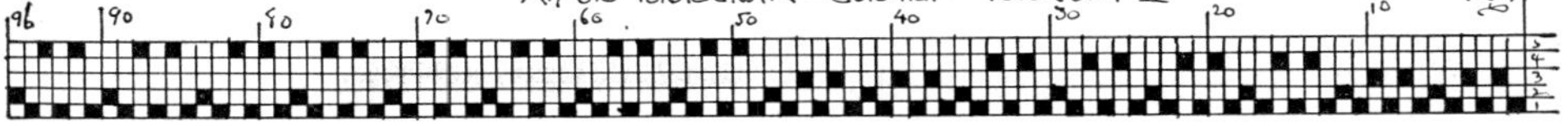

Pattern for a Lunch-Cloth, Bronson II

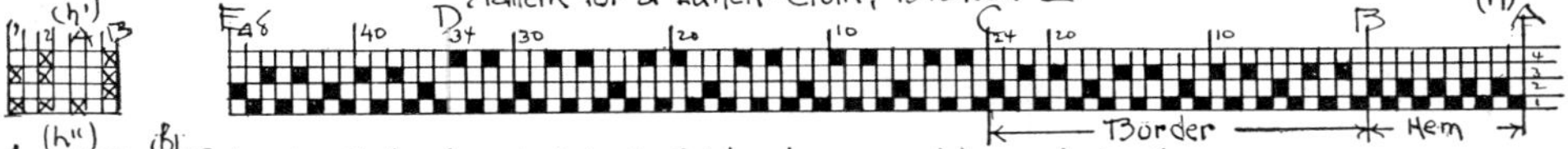

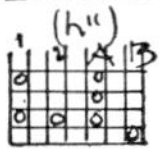

(h) For Lunch-Cloth thread: A-B for tabby hem, as wide as desired; Border, B-C; Body of piece: C-E as required; end C-D. Border, B-C. Tabby hem, A-B.

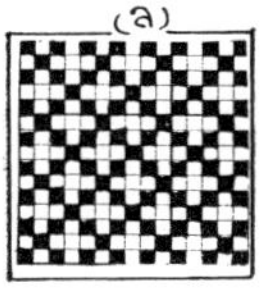

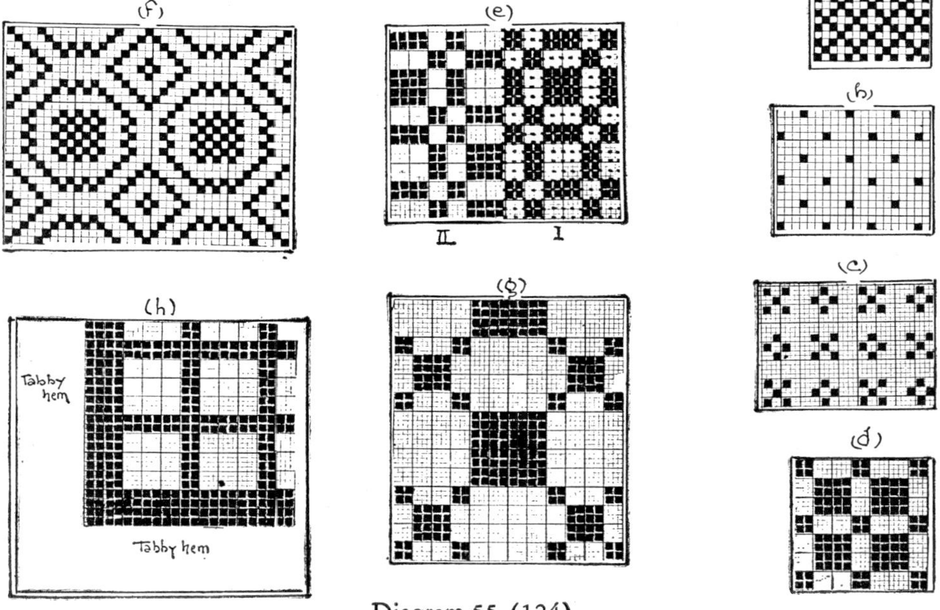

Diagram 55 (124)

ting. It is an unbalanced weave as half the warp-ends—for all patterns and on any number of harnesses—are threaded through the front harness. For this reason it is more conveniently woven on a loom of the "jack" type than on a counterbalanced loom. It may, however, be produced on the ordinary four-harness counterbalanced loom though it may be necessary to put in a corrective tie on the treadle that sinks the front harness alone and raises the other three.

Drafts for this weave are written in two different forms which I am calling "Bronson I" and "Bronson II." In the first form each unit of the weave consists of four threads, threaded alternately on the front harness and one or another of the pattern harnesses, as: 1, 2, 1, 2, 1, 3, 1, 3 and so on. In the second form the unit consists of six threads, the pattern block being threaded on four threads as above with two threads on the 1–2 shed between all pattern blocks, as: 1, 3, 1, 3, 1, 2, 1, 4, 1, 4, 1, 2, and so on. This may appear at first glance to be a minor difference, but in practise it is highly important. The Bronson II form permits much more variation of figure than Bronson I, and also makes it possible to weave a hem in plain tabby all around the piece, and to set off "spot" figures between tabby areas. Also the pattern blocks may be woven together in any desired arrangement, while in Bronson I adjoining blocks may not be woven at the same time due to the long skips that would result.

The pattern is produced in short skips of weft on one side of the fabric and of warp-skips on the reverse. As warp and weft do not interweave over the pattern blocks this structure definitely weakens the fabric. I have seen very old linen pieces in which the pattern blocks had worn away, leaving a design in holes, but as it would take a hundred years or so of hard usage to produce this effect it need not worry the weaver too much.

In the old day this weave was rarely attempted on four harnesses but oddly enough often on five harnesses, suggesting that weavers of that day may have rigged their four-harness looms with an extra harness to carry the "weave" threads. This is merely a guess, as I have never found notes or drawings to substantiate it in any of the old books or manuscripts I have examined. Two of these old five-harness patterns are given at (f) and (g) on Diagram 55.

Any number of harnesses may be used and on eight or ten harnesses many interesting and varied patterns may be produced.

II Warp-Setting and Treadling

The very different types of fabric that may be made in Bronson weave depend chiefly on the warp-setting and on the manner in which the tabby treadles are used.

For towelling and table linens the warp should be set as for a close, firm tabby—a 40/3 linen, for instance, at twenty-six or twenty-eight ends to the inch and a 40/2 or a #20 line linen at thirty-eight or forty ends to the inch. The weft should be of the same material, or material similar in grist, and the beat should be firm. The warp, of course, must be kept thoroughly damp or a firm beat will be impossible. If a "singles" warp is used, it should be thoroughly dressed with a warp-dressing of some kind and woven wet. In the old day linen weavers kept their wound bobbins in a bowl of water so that the weft was also dripping wet when woven, but as a rule modern weavers do not follow this practise.

Patterns of the Bronson I type are woven with the B tabby shot between all pattern shots, the A tabby being used only for headings. For instance draft (a), Diagram 55, is treadled:

>   A, B, A, B, repeated as desired for a heading or hem,
>   Pattern:
>   treadle 1, treadle B, treadle 1, treadle B
>   treadle 2, treadle B, treadle 2, treadle B
>   treadle 3, treadle B, treadle 3, treadle B
>   treadle 2, treadle B, treadle 2, treadle B
>   Repeat.

Pattern (f), Diagram 55, should be woven in the same manner, following the pattern "as-drawn-in" or "rose-fashion" as illustrated.

Patterns in Bronson II are treadled in a different manner. Draft (d), Diagram 55, for instance—using tie-up (b–1) or (b–2)—as follows:

> Treadle 1, treadle B, treadle 1, treadle B, treadle A, treadle B repeated four times
> Treadle 2, treadle B, treadle 2, treadle B, treadle A, treadle B repeated twice.
>   Repeat.

Every fifth shot, it will be noted, is woven on tabby A. Otherwise long warp-skips appear on the reverse side of the fabric. All patterns in this weave are

Bronson Weave — Eight-Harness "Point" Patterns

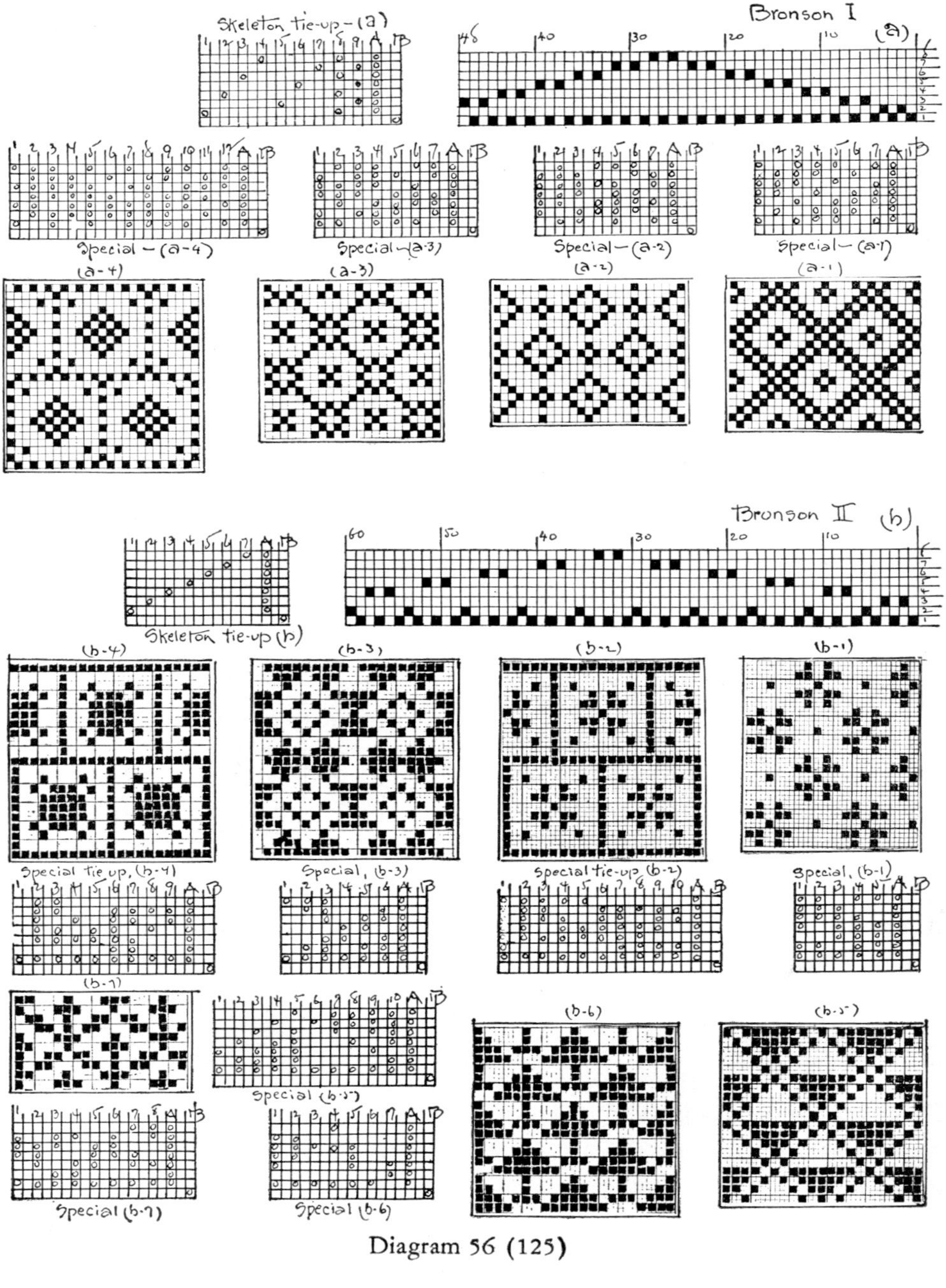

Diagram 56 (125)

treadled in the same manner, but may also be woven in the manner of Bronson I if one prefers. Pattern (d), Diagram 55 on tie-up (a–1) or (a–2) as follows:

> Treadle 2, treadle B, treadle 2, treadle B, treadle 1, treadle B, repeated four times
> Treadle 3, treadle B, treadle 3, treadle B, treadle 1, treadle B repeated twice.
> Repeat.

The effect of these two methods of weaving is indicated on the diagram. Any Bronson II threading may be woven in this manner, a shot on the 1–2 shed being woven for the fifth shot instead of the tabby A shot. However, if a tabby hem is desired, or tabby spaces between figures, this second method of weaving is of course impractical.

The simple "point" threadings shown on Diagram 56 will give an idea of the extremely varied pattern possibilities in a simple eight-harness threading in this weave. The designs illustrated are only a few of the hundreds that might be woven. Due to the fact that adjoining blocks may not be woven together in Bronson I, the figures in Bronson II are the more interesting. The "skeleton" tie-ups given for each draft may be used for free design with a large number of sheds, and special tie-ups are given for each of the figures illustrated. All these tie-ups are written for the rising shed as this weave would prove impractical on an eight-harness loom of the counterbalanced type.

It seems unnecessary to give detailed treadling directions for these figures as the treadles in the tie-up are arranged to be woven in succession: 1, B, 1, B. A. B; 2, B, 2, B, A, B, and so on. However, when a shed is repeated a second treadle has not been indicated, though it might be tied for convenience if desired. The illustrations make a sufficient guide. For instance in pattern (b–6) the pattern treadles should be woven in the following order: 1, 2, 3, 4, 1, 5, 6, 7 and repeat. The patterns that weave to a center and return should be woven in order to the center and then in reverse order back to the beginning.

As noted above, with the (b) threading, side-borders or hems in plain tabby may be made to any desired width by threading 1, 2, 1, 2, repeated as required.

III *Variations*

The Bronson weave is a very versatile weave and may be used for many purposes with slight changes of setting and treadling. As far as I know, these variations are modern adaptations of our own. I have never found them among the old pieces.

Variation One—Lace-Bronson

Any threading in Bronson II may be woven to produce an open, lacy fabric similar to the Swedish lace-weave but in much more varied designs. It is only necessary to set the warp as for an open tabby and to beat lightly. The manner of treadling is exactly the same as for towelling and table linens. However, in the pattern used there must be at least two repeats of the pattern unit. Patterns (d), (e), (g) and (h), Diagram 55, may be woven in the lace-effect as written, but for pattern (b), Diagram 56, the draft should be threaded: 1, 3, 1, 3, 1, 2, 1, 3, 1, 3, 1, 2, 1, 4, 1, 4, 1, 2, 1, 4, 1, 4, 1, 2 and so on. In weaving, each unit should also be treadled twice, of course. The lace-effect does not always appear prominently while the fabric is on the loom, but opens when the piece is washed.

The lace-weave is excellent for scarves, and light-weight, shawl-like baby-blankets when done in fine worsted, and for window-drapery done in a fine, rough linen. Mercerized cottons are unsuitable for this weave as are other smooth, slippery materials as the threads tend to run together in undesirable ways.

Variation Two—A Weave for Upholstery

As woven for linens and also as for the lace-weave, warp and weft are usually the same color as well as the same material, but as woven for upholstery colored weft materials may be used. The warp may be cotton or linen, set as for a normal tabby fabric, and the weft may be wool or worsted, rayon or other material as preferred. The weft may also be somewhat coarser than the warp for the pattern shots and in material like the warp for the foundation shots.

The method of treadling is similar to that used in the summer-and-winter weave and in overshot weaving: a shot of tabby, a shot of pattern, a shot of the reverse tabby, a shot of pattern, and so on. Either type of threading may be used, though the Bronson II patterns are the more interesting. An excellent, firm fabric results from this method of weaving. The wrong side is uninteresting, to be sure, but for upholstery, bags or pillow-tops this does not matter.

The Bronson weave, like the summer-and-winter weave, lends itself to some interesting effects in pick-up weaving, for which see the chapter on pick-up.

Chapter Fifteen: Double-Faced Twill and Damask

Though different in effect and in use, the double-faced twill and damask weaves are similar in structure. In fact they may be woven on the same threading and the same tie-up though the treadles must be used in a different order.

Double-faced twill is a handsome and substantial weave for coarse linens, for blankets and for upholstery. Damask is the most highly regarded for pattern weaving in fine linens, and is also woven in cottons. The same weave when made in silk is usually called satin.

For elaborate patterns in either of these weaves it is necessary to use a very elaborate loom, and most fabrics of this type are made on draw-looms or jacquard looms. No patterns in these weaves are possible on four harnesses, but some simple figures are within the capacity of eight-harness, ten-harness and twelve-harness looms.

I *Structure*

The simplest form of double-faced twill is based on the three-harness 2–1 or "jeans" twill. Each unit of the weave consists of three threads, threaded: 1, 2, 3 for block No. 1; 4, 5, 6 for a unit of block No. 2; 7, 8, 9 for a unit of block No. 3 and 10, 11, 12 for a unit of block No. 4, and so on. The figure is produced in weft-faced twill on one side of the fabric and warp-faced twill on the reverse. This is a "fifty-fifty" weave and warp and weft should be the same material or materials similar in grist, with the same number of weft-shots to the inch as there are warp-ends to the inch in the setting. Though usually woven in all-linen for table pieces and the like, or in all-wool for blankets, an excellent fabric for upholstery may be produced by weaving in hard-twisted wool over a warp of similar grist in either linen or cotton.

Damask cannot be woven on a threading for jeans twill, but may be woven on the same threading used for a 3–1 double-faced twill. For these weaves each unit is threaded on four harnesses: 1, 2, 3, 4 for block No. 1; 5, 6, 7, 8 for block No. 2; 9, 10, 11, 12 for block No. 3, and so on. The 3–1 double twill has a richer effect than the jeans twill. The damask woven on this threading is a "broken twill," showing no diagonal bars.

Illustration (127) shows a blanket in the jeans twill and illustration (108) a piece in the 3–1 twill.

A five-heddle damask, in which each unit of the weave is threaded on five harnesses, is richer in effect than the four-heddle damask described above. In this weave a unit of the first block is threaded: 1, 2, 3, 4, 5; and a unit of the second block: 6, 7, 8, 9, 10, and so on.

Diagram 57 shows at (a) a short draft for a simple two-block pattern and gives at (b), (c) and (d) the thread-by-thread drafts for this pattern in the various forms of the weave as described above, together with the tie-ups for double-faced twill and damask. Only the twill tie-up is given for (b) and only the damask tie-up for (d) as this threading is not used for double twill.

The double-faced twills are always woven strictly in the "fifty-fifty" manner, but damask is often woven with a weft a good deal finer than the warp and more weft-shots to the inch than there are warp-ends to the inch. Hand-weavers, however, usually prefer to weave it in the "fifty-fifty" manner.

There is nothing difficult about these weaves except that a fairly elaborate loom is required even for the simplest patterns. There is an English system of setting up the loom that permits a larger number of pattern changes than the system described above. By this method the front harnesses—three, four or five, according to the weave to be produced—are equipped with long-eyed heddles and produce the weave, a single harness only being required for each pattern block. By this method a four-block pattern in double twill or damask may be woven on eight harnesses. The adjustments, however, are difficult on looms of the type in use in this country and the method will not be described here in detail. It may be found in several of the technical English books on weaving.

Double-faced Twill and Damask

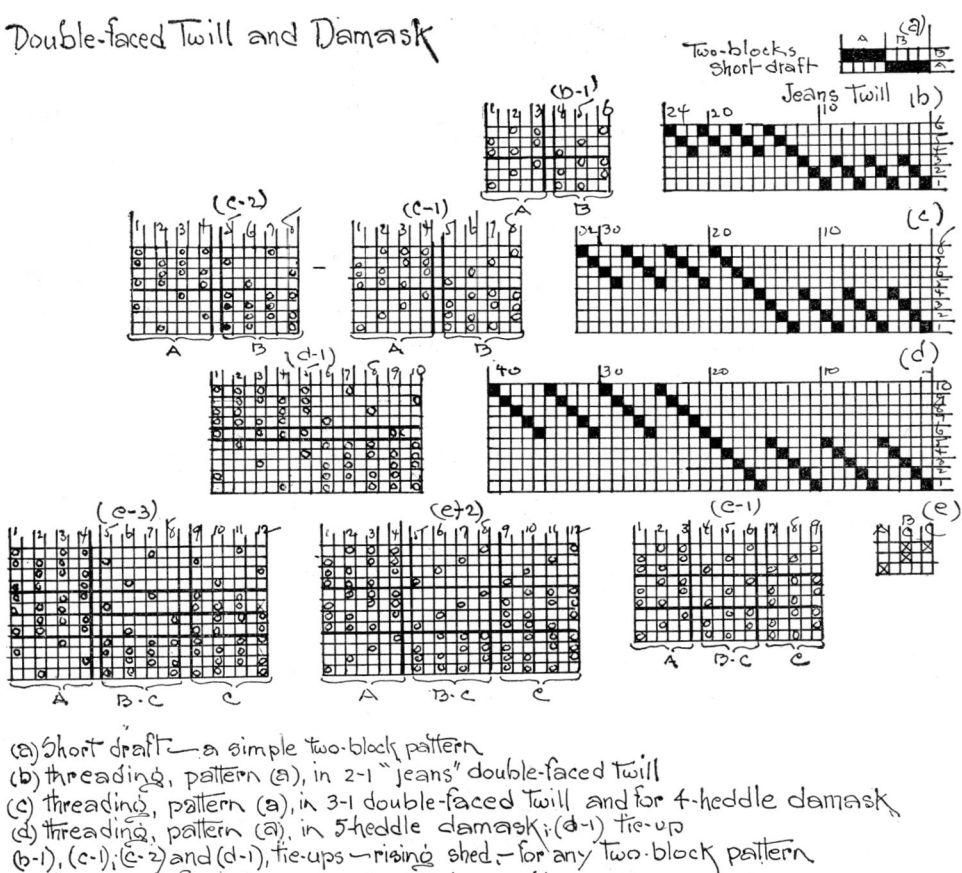

(a) Short draft — a simple two-block pattern
(b) threading, pattern (a), in 2-1 "jeans" double-faced twill
(c) threading, pattern (a), in 3-1 double-faced twill and for 4-heddle damask
(d) threading, pattern (a), in 5-heddle damask; (d-1) tie-up
(b-1), (c-1), (c-2) and (d-1), tie-ups — rising shed — for any two-block pattern
(e) tie-up plan for pattern No. 167, Diagram No.
(e-1) complete tie-up for pattern 167 in jeans twill on nine harnesses
(e-2) complete tie-up for pattern 167 in 3-1 twill on 12 harnesses
(e-3) complete tie-up for pattern 167 in 4-heddle damask on 12 harnesses

Diagram 57 (126)

(127) Ancient double-faced twill weaving, all wool, from a New Jersey blanket.

II Patterns, Tie-ups, and Treadling

Any of the patterns written in "short-draft" form, as given in the chapter on the summer-and-winter weave may be used for double-faced twill and damask, provided the loom to be used is equipped with a sufficient number of harnesses —three harnesses for each block in jeans twill, four harnesses for each block in 3–1 double-faced twill and four-heddle damask, five harnesses for each block in five-heddle damask. On a twelve-harness loom four-block patterns may be woven in jeans twill, and three-block patterns in 3–1 twill and four-heddle damask.

At (e) on Diagram 57 are given the tie-up plan for pattern No. 167 as given with the short-form draft on Diagram (44), and at (e–1), (e–2) and (e–3) the complete tie-up drafts for these weaves. It will be noted that in this pattern the second and third blocks weave together, and the first and third blocks weave alone. These tie-ups, therefore, apply only to patterns of this type and are not suitable for three-block patterns in which each block weaves alone.

The treadles for each block, on any of the tie-ups, should be woven in succession and repeated as may be required by the pattern. For pattern (a), for instance, in jeans twill weave on the (b–1) tie-up: 1, 2, 3, repeated four times; then 4, 5, 6, repeated four times. For the (c) threading and tie-ups repeat each set of four treadles four times. It will be noted that in tie-ups (c–1) and (c–2) the treadles are exactly the same, but arranged in a different order. Either weave might be woven on the same tie-up but the treadling would be confusing and it is better to make the special tie-ups as shown.

Either of these weaves may be produced in patterns as elaborate as one chooses by a simple pick-up technique that will be explained in detail in the chapter on pick-up.

Chapter Sixteen: The Double Weave

Double weaving—the making of two fabrics at the same time—has always been a thing of amazement. Joseph France in his "Weavers' Complete Guide" has this to say in a footnote: "The weaving of double cloth may be applied to many useful purposes as well as to articles of curiosity. It was on the principle of double cloth that David Anderson, Damask manufacturer of Glasgow, lately wove a shirt with a fine frill, double-stitched neck, shoulder straps and wrist bands; also gussets, buttons, button-holes, etc., with the Royal Arms emblazoned on the breast. The whole of this production was executed entirely in the loom, without the smallest aid of needle-work. The shirt was presented to His Majesty George IV, who was graciously pleased to express his high satisfaction with the ingenuity of the performance, and through the Right Hon. Lord Sidmouth, His Majesty's Secretary of State, remitted Mr. Anderson £50. Another specimen of Mr. Anderson's ingenuity in this line is deposited in the Hunterian Museum, Glasgow."

As far as I know, the American Colonial weavers never indulged in the making of "articles of curiosity" like George IV's remarkable shirt. But many handsome coverlets in double weaving have come down to us from the old day.

Probably most of these were the work of professional weavers, as the usual "domestic manufacturer" did not possess an elaborate loom carrying as many as twenty-four harnesses. Some of these professionals were undoubtedly the weavers who travelled the country with their equipment on ox-carts, stopping at a village or homestead to weave into fabric the yarns spun and dyed by the women of the community in preparation for their arrival. The "John Landes" book of drawings, and the "Speck" manuscript book now in the Pennsylvania Museum of Art may well have been prepared as pattern books to show prospec-

— 253

The Double Weave

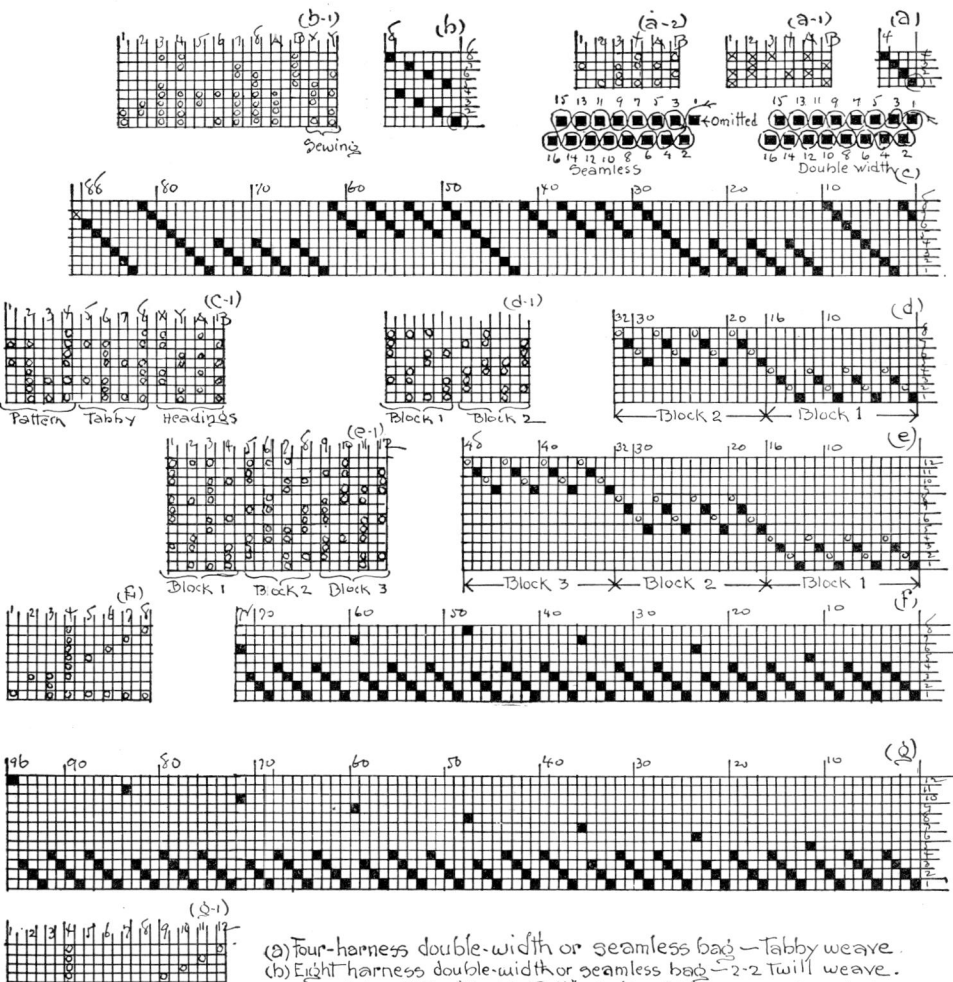

(a) Four-harness double-width or seamless bag — Tabby weave.
(b) Eight-harness double-width or seamless bag — 2-2 Twill weave.
(c) Overshot pattern — "Monk's Belt" — double width or seamless bag.
(d) Two-block pattern in double-plain weave.   ■ Dark, ▨ Light.
(e) Three-block pattern in double-plain weave.   "   "   "   "
(f) Quilted weave on eight harnesses.
(g) Quilted weave on twelve harnesses.

Note: For patterns (a) and (b), when woven for a seamless bag or tubing omit the first thread of the first repeat. For pattern (c), when woven for a seamless bag or tubing, add a thread on harness 7, after the last repeat, as indicated on the draft at "x".

Diagram 58 (128)

(129) Patterns for summer-and-winter or double weave. 1. Whig Rose. Draft number 206. 2. Single Snow-Ball. Draft number 226. 3. From an ancient damask. Draft number 204. 4. Two-block pattern, similar to draft number 163. 5. Philadelphia Pavement. Draft number 200.

tive customers. Though few drafts are given it is obvious from the drawings that these patterns were intended for double weaving. Many of them, to be sure, may be carried out in the overshot weave, the crackle weave and other weaves, and all may be woven in the summer-and-winter technique.

The John Landes drawings are of particular interest as this craftsman of the old day seems to have been an excellent designer as well as a master weaver, and his drawings have a charm of proportion not found in the stodgier "Speck" patterns. The collection of coverlets in the Pennsylvania Museum includes several exactly like drawings in this manuscript book and may well have been the work of John himself. Illustration (10) shows one of these coverlets.

A great deal of nonsense has been written about the double weave. In several books on American Colonial arts and crafts it is called a "lost art," with expressions of grief that such a beautiful thing should be lost forever to the world. This is unusually silly, even in the writings of people who know very little about their subject, as the Scandinavian books carry detailed directions for double weaving and it has never even been mislaid except temporarily in the United States. For that matter, nothing in weaving can ever be a "lost art" as long as a sample remains, for what one weaver has woven another can contrive to reproduce—perhaps on different equipment and by a different method but with the same end-result. So we need not feel too much sorrow over the dear, dead, double-woven coverlets of the Colonial period. We can make them ourselves quite easily provided we have looms equipped with from sixteen to twenty-four harnesses.

Most of the double weaving done today, however, is by the pick-up technique—either in the Finnish or the Mexican manner, which latter was probably also the method used in ancient Peru. More on this subject in a later chapter.

I *Structure*

Double weaving consists in making two separate fabrics, one above the other. This technique may be used in a number of ways: in the weaving of a double-width fabric, or a seamless bag or tubing; for interesting pattern effects, and for quilted fabrics.

Weaving double width and seamless tubing are entirely practical but not

(130) Double-woven coverlet in blue and white, rose pattern.

altogether satisfactory due to the fact that it is almost impossible to weave the edges so that no streak appears when the fabric is taken from the loom. There is no saving in weaving time, and whether a blanket or tweed yardage is handsomer with a streak through the center than when woven in two strips is open to question. However, as "articles of curiosity" these things have a certain value.

Two tabby fabrics may be woven at the same time on four harnesses, as illustrated at (a), Diagram 58. For a double-width piece, weave the treadles in 1, 2, 3, 4, order. For tubing, omit the first thread of the first repeat of the twill threading and treadle: 1, 3, 2, 4, and repeat. No pattern figures are possible in this weave except by the pick-up method to be described later, but if the warp is set fairly far apart and woven in stripes of color in a weft-faced rep the effect may be excellent.

For an "amazement" feature, useful for show-off occasions, treadle 5 and 6 alternately for a few shots to weave a single fabric. Then weave as tubing for a space; separate the two fabrics by treadling 3 and 4 together, tie-up (a–1), or treadles 1 and 2 together, tie-up (a–2), and insert a small pillow. Weave 5 and 6 alternately to weave the pillow in. This always causes much excitement. Patterns (b) and (c), Diagram 58, may be used for more elaborate effects in the same manner.

II Patterns in Double Weave

Pattern (b), Diagram 58, gives the threading and tie-up for weaving a double-width twill fabric. A twill tubing may also be woven on the same threading and tie-up, but for this the first thread of the first repeat should be omitted. Treadle: 1, 2, 3, 4, 5, 6, 7, 8 and repeat for a double-width fabric, and for tubing treadle: 1, 8, 2, 3, 5, 4, 6, 7, and repeat. It would, however, be better to retie the treadles so that they could be woven in regular order.

The most interesting use for this threading is in the making of blankets consisting of two wool fabrics "sewed" together at intervals to make a solid double-faced fabric. Blankets with a different tartan plaid pattern on either side may be woven in this manner. Thread as at (b), Diagram 58, one fabric on harnesses 1, 2, 3 and 4, and the other on harnesses 5, 6, 7 and 8. Weave with two shuttles, as follows: treadle 1, treadle 2, upper fabric; treadle 3,

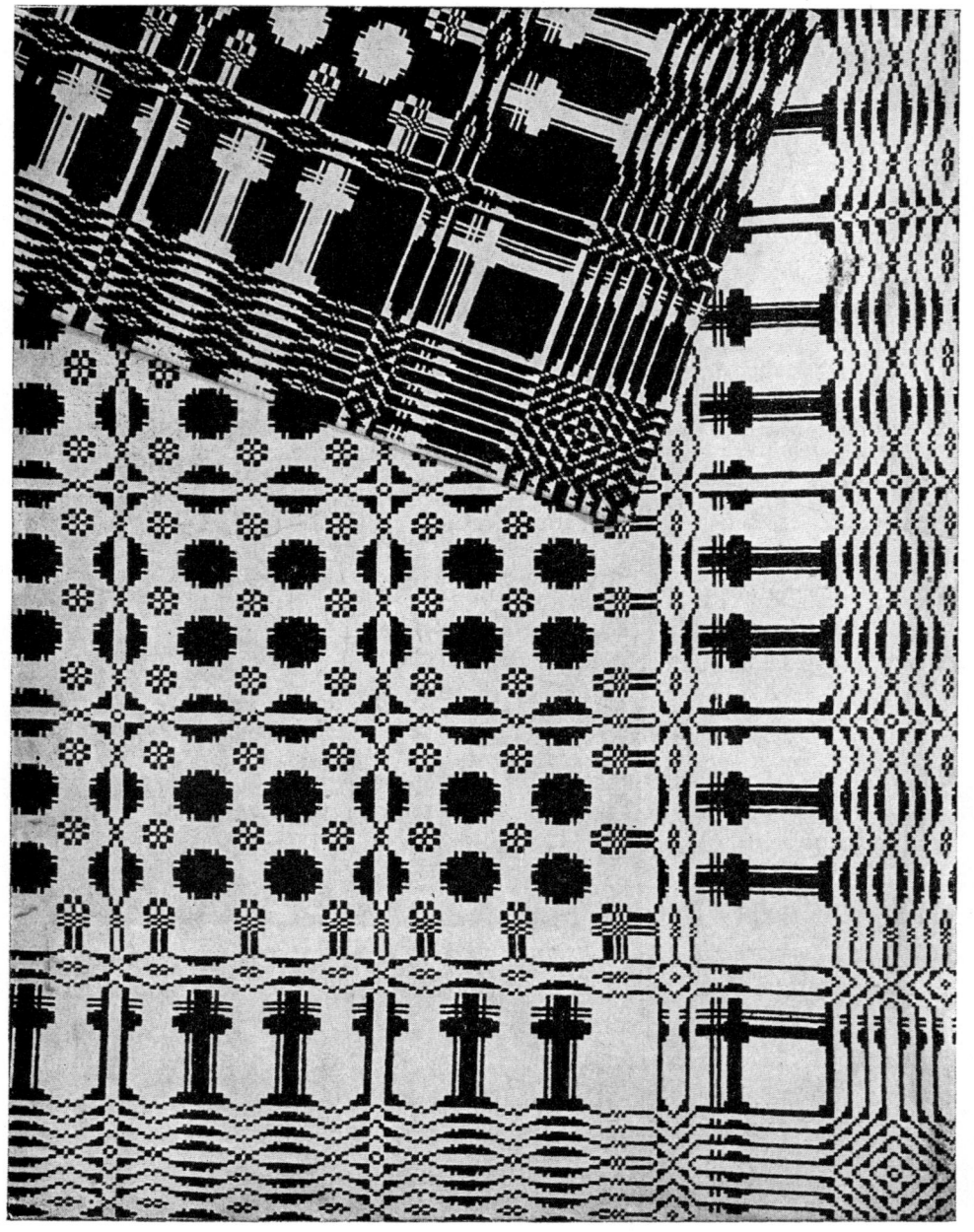

(131) An ancient double-woven coverlet from Pennsylvania, in a Double Snow-Ball pattern with a modified Pine-Tree border. Draft number 232.

treadle 4, lower fabric; treadle 5, treadle 6, upper fabric; treadle 7, treadle 8, lower fabric. Then treadle X and weave a "sewing" shot. This does not appear on either side of the fabric and may be a cotton thread finer than the yarns used for the twilled fabrics. After the next series of eight shots weave a sewing shot on treadle Y, and so continue. The sewing shots may be woven after every four shots of wool if one prefers.

A four-harness overshot pattern may be arranged to weave double width or as seamless tubing if one wishes. Such an arrangement of the "Monk's Belt" pattern is given at (c) on the diagram and should be woven with a tabby like the warp and a coarser pattern weft in the manner of the overshot weave. Treadle as follows:

>For tubing in plain weave, treadles 5, 6, 7, 8 and repeat.
>For double width in plain weave, 5, 7, 6, 8 and repeat.

Tubing in pattern, first block:

>treadle 5, tabby; treadle 1, pattern
>treadle 6, tabby; treadle 2, pattern
>treadle 7, tabby; treadle 1, pattern
>treadle 8, tabby; treadle 2, pattern
>Repeat for the size of block desired.

Pattern, second block:

>treadle 5, tabby; treadle 3, pattern
>treadle 6, tabby; treadle 4, pattern
>treadle 7, tabby; treadle 3, pattern
>treadle 8, tabby; treadle 4, pattern
>Repeat as required.

For double width in pattern, treadle:

>First block: 5, tabby, 1, pattern; 7, tabby, 1, pattern
>6, tabby, 2, pattern; 8, tabby, 2, pattern
>Second block: 5, tabby, 3, pattern; 7, tabby, 3, pattern
>6, tabby, 4, pattern; 8, tabby, 4, pattern

Any four-harness pattern may be arranged to weave in a similar manner—double width or tubing—on eight harnesses.

We think of double weaving, however, chiefly in terms of the old pieces in "double-plain" weave. In Colonial times the weave seems to have been used exclusively for coverlets. At least I have never come across any other old-time examples. The two fabrics woven for these pieces were a white cotton fabric and a wool fabric, usually in indigo blue though sometimes in a combination

(132) The Three Flowers taken from an ancient coverlet in white, red, and blue, double woven. Draft number 209.

(133) The "M. Ferris" coverlet—elaborate double weaving, from Pennsylvania. See draft numbers 249 and 250.

of indigo and madder. A fairly coarse cotton was used and a hard-spun wool of similar grist.

For such a fabric, with a warp of two different materials, it is desirable to use two warp-beams, as wool—being much more elastic than cotton—should be woven at a lighter tension than the cotton warp or the resulting fabric will pucker when taken off the loom. If the wool is very hard-twisted, however, the two materials may be warped together.

The setting in the reed should be designed to produce a firm tabby fabric in each material—twice as close as for a single fabric. If the material, for instance, requires a normal setting of twenty-four ends to the inch, the setting for double weave should be forty-eight ends to the inch.

The pattern is produced in figures of colored wool tabby against a background of white cotton tabby, with the reverse effect on the other side of the piece. Four harnesses are required for each pattern block, so that two-block patterns may be made on eight harnesses and three-block patterns on twelve harnesses. The English double-harness method referred to in the chapter on damask may also be used for the double weave, permitting four pattern blocks on eight harnesses, and so on.

(134) Cambridge Beauty. Draft number 181.

A simple two-block pattern for double weaving is given at (d), Diagram 58. The threading, it will be noted, is the same as for double twill or four-heddle damask in the same pattern, except that the warp is in two colors, alternately dark and light. The tie-up and treadling are entirely different, however. Weave the first block: 1, dark; 2, light; 3, dark; 4, light, and repeat four times—for the pattern as given. Weave the second block: 5, dark; 6, light; 7, dark; 8, light, and repeat as above. Any two-block pattern may be threaded and woven in this manner, a single unit of the weave being four warp-ends and four weft-shots—two dark and two light.

Draft (e) shows a simple three-block pattern on twelve harnesses, that may be woven in the same manner. The tie-up is arranged so that each block weaves separately, but may be modified as one pleases to weave two blocks at the same time as in pattern No. 167, cited in the notes on double twill and damask.

III Quilted Weaving

An interesting quilted fabric may be woven in the double-plain technique on eight or more harnesses. This weave is impossible on four harnesses without resort to the pick-up stick, as explained in the chapter on pick-up. On eight, ten or twelve harnesses, however, simple quilting may be woven as shown on Diagram 58 at (f) and (g). An upper and an under fabric are woven, with padding between, caught together at intervals.

The two fabrics may, if one chooses, be of different materials or may be different in color, the upper fabric being on harnesses 1 and 3 and the rest of the harnesses being threaded for the lower fabric. To weave: treadle 1, treadle 2, in weft like the warp for the top fabric; treadle 3, treadle 4 in weft like the warp of the under fabric. Repeat. Open the two fabrics by using treadles 1 and 2 together—a special treadle may be tied if one prefers—and insert the padding material. A wool unspun "roving," obtainable from woolen mills, is the best for the purpose, but a soft yarn may be used instead. Treadle: 5, 2, top fabric; 3, 4, bottom fabric; then 1, 2, 3, 4 and repeat as at first. Again separate the fabrics and weave the padding. Treadle: 6, 2, 3, 4; then 1, 2, 3, 4 and repeat, and again insert the padding. And so continue. Draft (f) shows a "point" arrangement of ties and may be woven to produce diamond figures or

(135) Ancient summer-and-winter weave from the Newark Museum. Pattern: Wheel of Fortune. Draft number 194.

other small figures. Draft (g) shows a twill arrangement of ties which may also be varied to produce a number of figures in quilting.

These quilted fabrics are useful for crib blankets, for baby hoods and jackets, for bed jackets and for tea-cosies; also for chair pads, table pads, holders for hot dishes, and so on.

A large book might be written on the possibilities of the double weave, and the above notes make no pretense of covering the subject completely. The attempt has been to provide some typical examples that will prove useful to weavers wishing to experiment along these lines.

— 265

(137) Bird's Nest with Pine-Tree border. Draft number 241.

(138) From an ancient coverlet in double weave. Draft number 214.

Chapter Seventeen: Leno

Something should be said about the cross weaves, gauze or "leno." A textile engineer once told me that the gauze mountings were the most difficult to make of all the Jacquard weaves. He also told me that the cross weaves were impossible for hand-weavers, which of course is not the fact. The gauze weaves go back for a thousand or more years, as witness the ancient weavings of Peru, and though many of the modern types of gauze weaving are impractical on ordinary hand-weaving equipment, some are not. And many of the gauze weaves may be produced quite simply on a two-harness loom by anyone with the desire and a pick-up stick.

The subject, however, is highly technical and no effort will be made here to cover it completely. Those who wish to make an exhaustive study of gauze weaving are referred to an excellent book, "Advanced Textile Design," by William Watson. The notes below are intended to supply practical directions for some of the simplest leno weaves that may be produced without great difficulty on any good hand-loom.

The leno weave is useful whenever a very open fabric is desired, as for transparent glass-curtains, light weight scarves and so on. A very open tabby fabric will not stand up under washing and use—the threads will draw together in places producing ugly streaks and spots. The twist in leno holds the weft securely, to make an open mesh that is entirely practical under use. The three-thread leno makes a firmer tie than the two-thread leno but the latter is entirely practical for most purposes.

The leno technique may also be used to produce zig-zag and diamond-shaped patterns in a close fabric, either in stripes or in an all-over effect.

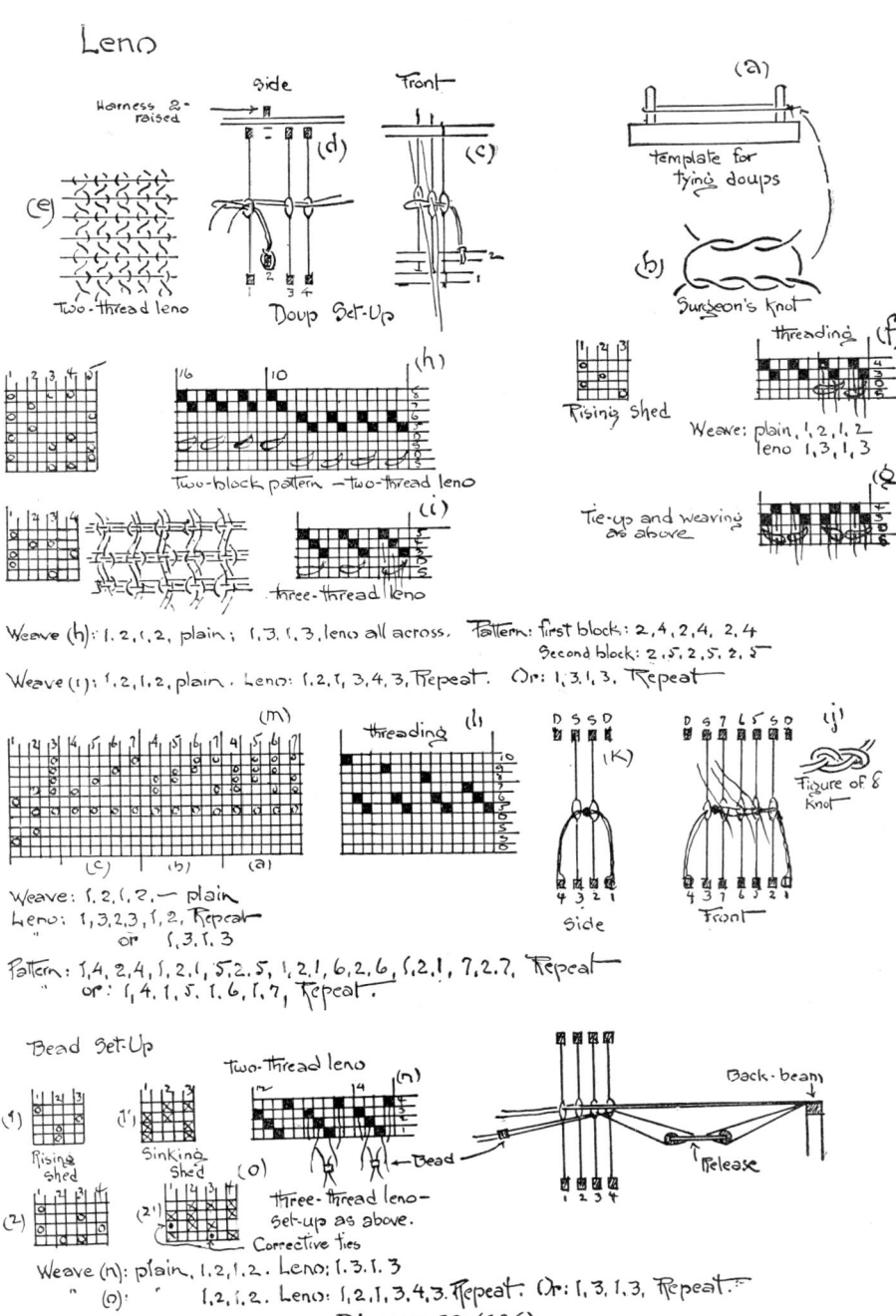

Diagram 59 (136)

1 The Set-Up

The weaving of a leno fabric is a very simple matter and goes very rapidly. The set-up, however, presents some difficulties. Some looms cannot be persuaded to leno well by the "doup" method shown on Diagram 59 at (a), but in such cases the ingenious "bead" method will give good results for the simple four-harness leno effects.

As a rule the "rising shed" or jack-type looms leno satisfactorily, and some of the counterbalanced looms can also be adjusted to do the same, but it is advisable to try a small sample set-up before embarking on a large project to make certain of the behavior of the loom. On a counterbalanced loom the bead method is advised.

The special doup heddles used in commercial gauze weaving will not fit on the harness frames of the ordinary hand-loom. Anyone planning to go in for gauze weaving on a commercial basis might find it desirable to have special harness frames installed for the use of these heddles, but most hand-weavers, who weave gauze occasionally only, can manage very satisfactorily with tied string doups in the pre-machine manner.

The "doup" is a half-heddle, usually attached to the bottom bar of harness 2 and brought through the eye of a heddle on harness 1—called the "standard." The doups may, if one prefers, be attached to the bottom bar of harness 1 with the standards on harness 2, but there seems no advantage in this and the tie-ups as given on the diagram are for the first described arrangement. For some weaves it is more convenient to attach the doups to the top bar instead of to the bottom bar if one wishes to weave the fabric right side up, but most looms operate best with the doups at the bottom.

A strong hard-twisted round linen is the best material of which to make the doups. Ordinary carpet warp or a mercerized cotton may be used too, but these materials tend to stretch and after long use may fray and break. It is important to make the doups exactly the correct length. If too short, they draw the warp into the eye of the standard which is apt to result in broken threads, and if too long, the shed is lost. The best procedure is to tie a sample doup on the loom: attach a double end of the material to be used to the bottom bar of harness 2 and bring one end in a loop through the eye of a heddle on harness 1; insert a pin through the loop to hold it in place and tie the two ends of the cord together, as tight as possible without raising harness 2 more than a trifle. Take this sample doup off the loom and use it as a guide. A template may be made by driving two large nails or pegs into a block of wood at the correct distance apart as at (a) on the diagram and the doups may be tied over this. Sometimes a book can be found of exactly the right size to serve as a template. For the simplest leno a doup will be required for each two warp-ends in the setting. The knot used in tying should be the "surgeon's knot," illustrated on the diagram at (b). This is simply a modified square-knot made with two turns instead of one in the first bend. Care must be taken to tie all the doups exactly alike.

(a) To make the set-up for 4-harness two-thread leno, first draw in the warp through the two back harnesses: 3, 4, 3, 4, as shown on the diagram. Next raise harness 2, so that the doups can be threaded easily through the eyes of the standards. Attach a doup to the bottom bar of harness 2 and take it from right to left through the eye of a heddle on harness 1. Take the first thread—threaded on harness 3—over the doup and draw the second thread—on harness 4—through the loop. Continue in this manner all across.

In sleying, each pair of threads connected by a doup must be taken through the same dent of the reed—no matter what the setting. For instance if the warp is a 24/3 cotton set at fifteen ends to the inch, use a 15-dent reed. Draw the first pair of threads through a dent, skip a dent and take the second pair through the third dent, skip a dent and so continue.

Only three treadles are required, as shown on the tie-up draft, and the tie-up is written as for the rising shed only. This form of set-up is not advised for a sinking-shed counterbalanced loom.

A variation is to thread the warp as shown at (g) on the diagram. For the first pair of threads take the doup through the eye of the standard from right to left, and for the second pair from left to right, and so alternately all across. This twists the threads in opposite directions.

(b) No pattern is possible on the four-harness plain leno except when supplemented by pick-up. However, on eight harnesses any two-block pattern may be woven as shown at (h) on the diagram. One block is threaded alternately on harnesses 5 and 6, to any desired width, and the second block on harnesses 7 and 8. The doups and standards for the first block are on harnesses 1 and 2 and the doups and standards for the second block on harnesses 3 and 4. The pattern, when treadled as given on the diagram, is in alternating squares of tabby and leno.

(c) The three-thread leno shown at (i) on the diagram, makes a stronger mesh than the two-thread leno. By the doup method this weave requires five harnesses. A three-thread leno may be woven on four harnesses by the bead method, as explained below.

(d) Those who have looms equipped with ten or twelve harnesses will find the set-up at (j), (k), (l) and (m) on the diagram useful. The doups and standards require four harnesses as shown, but a number of interesting patterns may be woven on the same set of doups, and there is the further advantage that the set-up may be made permanently on a set of four harnesses that may be taken out of the loom when not in use and replaced when desired. Doups tied in this fashion give the action of the slotted steel doups used in mechanical weaving.

For this set-up the doups should be tied on the loom. Attach a double end of the doup material to the bottom bar of harness 4; bring both ends through the eye of a heddle on harness 3, and tie a knot as close as possible to the eye of the heddle. A figure-of-eight knot is suggested. Then take the two ends through a heddle on harness 2 and bring them down and tie them to the bottom bar of harness 1.

The threading of the harnesses as shown at (l) on the diagram will give four blocks in three-thread leno, and may be woven to give a great variety of interesting patterns. If desired, each block may be threaded with several repeats to make any four-block figure.

The first three treadles, as shown on the tie-up at (m) weave tabby or leno all across. Three different tie-ups for the pattern are given at (m-a), (m-b) and (m-c). The (m-a) set will weave three blocks in leno and one block in tabby. This, of course, gives the most open effect. The set at (m-b) will weave two blocks in leno and two blocks plain, and the set at (m-c) will weave one

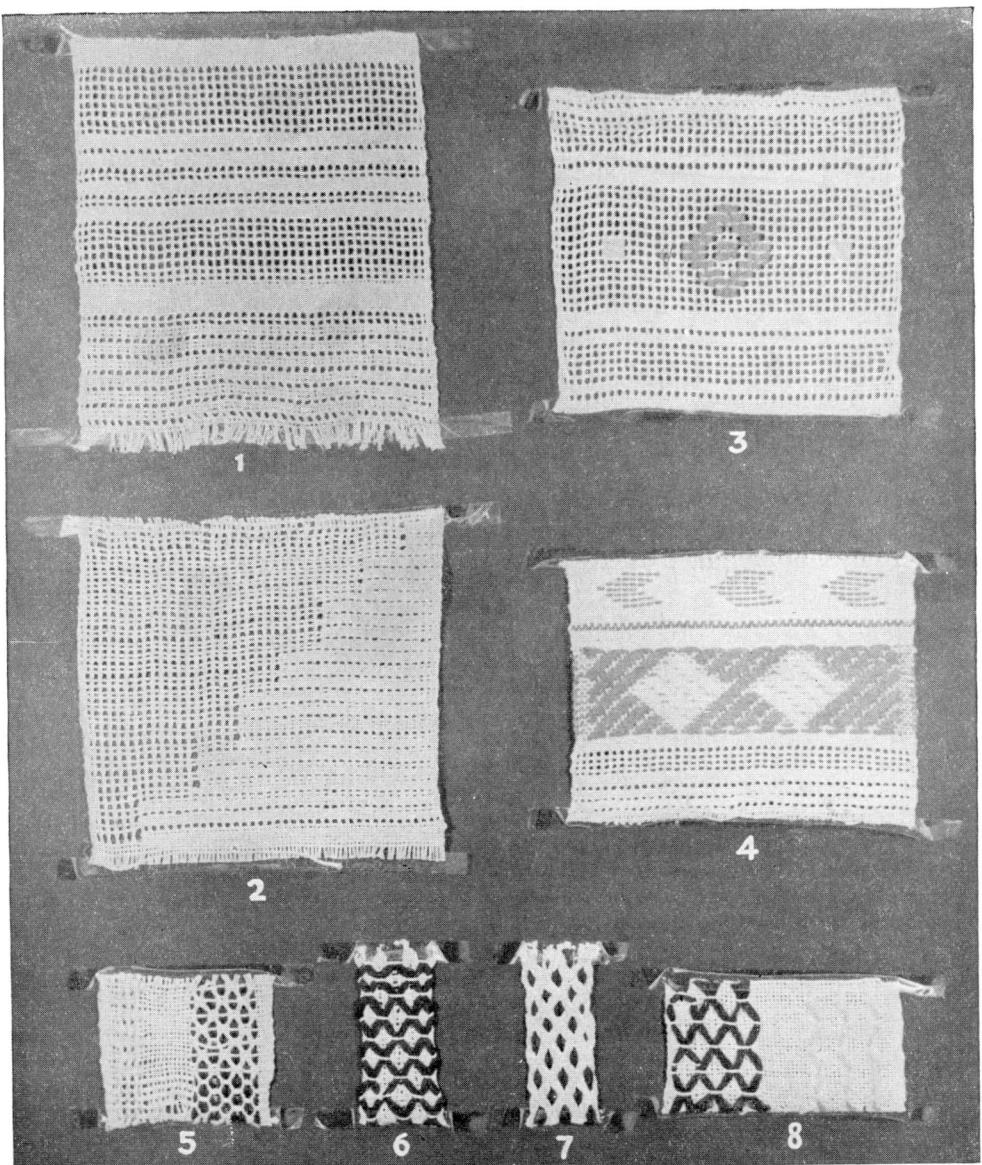

(139) 1. Coarse leno, with plain weave; 2. Coarse leno, with plain weave, in pattern; 3. Coarse leno with tapestry figure; 4. Coarse leno with ornaments in one-skip and tabby pick-up—Peruvian type; 5, 6, 7, 8 Leno pattern weaves.

block in leno and three blocks plain. Of course other arrangements of the pattern treadles might be made. The possibilities are varied and interesting and for those who have the necessary equipment this is probably the most useful form of leno set-up.

In taking the threads through the doups, have the standard on harness 2 to the right of the one on harness 3; take the two open threads of the threading—the threads on harnesses 5 and 6—over the doup and between the two standards; bring the pattern thread—on harness 7, 8, 9 or 10—through the doup. During this process harness 1 may be raised to make the doup easy to open.

It will be observed that no treadle ties at all are made to the two doup harnesses—1 and 4. The weight of the harness frames is usually sufficient to keep them down. If not, they must be weighted. The simplest method is to add sufficient heddles to give the necessary weight, or each harness may be tied directly to a treadle at the center of the loom—not to a lamm—and these treadles may be weighted as required. These treadles, of course, should not be used in weaving.

The leno sheds are often quite shallow and weaving must be done with a flat poke-shuttle. A better shed is obtained by providing a release for the twist threads. This is fairly simple for leno all across, or for two sets of twist threads as (h) on the diagram, and as explained below, but is somewhat complicated for four sets of twist threads as in the threading at (1), for which four releases would be necessary. However, if one is content to weave with a flat shuttle, or to use a shed-stick for the leno shots, the release is not strictly necessary.

(e) A double release is necessary for the bead-leno set-up, shown at (n) on the diagram. This is, however, not difficult to contrive as shown, and this method of making the simple two-thread and three-thread lenos on four harnesses will be found practical on looms that do not perform well with the doup set-up. For leno on more than four harnesses it is not recommended.

There is a drawback to the bead-leno—the twist thread is necessarily a double thread, and unless very fine material is used the effect is coarser than with the doup method. A double leno, though, is handsome and effective for many things so this is not a serious objection to the method.

(140) Fine leno with tabby and inlay figures. Part of a Guatemalan "Huipile."

As shown on the diagram each group of four threads is threaded: 4, 1, 2, 3. The threads on harnesses 3 and 4, which make the leno, are taken together through a bead, and the threads on harnesses 1 and 2 are taken over the bead. The beads used should be large enough to take the threads easily and without friction, but should not be larger than necessary. Beads of the long-shaped, tubular type should be used—not the round beads, which tend to catch in the sheds. Plastic "sippers" cut in ½" lengths make good "beads."

The mechanics of the thing is obvious: when harness 4 is raised and the threads on harness 3 are released, the two threads come up together on the right hand side of the free threads on harnesses 1 and 2. When harness 3 is raised and the threads on harness 4 are released the two threads come up together on the left hand side of the free threads. This makes the twist. A release, of course, is necessary, and might be contrived in various ways, depending on the type of loom used. If the loom carries more than four harnesses, for instance, the two back harness frames could be used for the release, each harness provided with heddles carrying an eye below the level of the regular heddle eyes, or with a bar set across the frame close to the bottom. The release

(141) A mountain woman at a colonial flax-wheel.
"Spinning is a delightful and gently soothing occupation."

harnesses should then be tied appropriately to the treadles. But as this form of set-up is used chiefly on four-harness looms this type of release is impractical.

I have found the affair illustrated on the diagram simple and effective: Two round bars, long enough to go across the loom and fastened together at the ends to form a light frame. The threads for harness 4 should be carried under the back bar of this frame and the threads for harness 3 under the front bar. This frame may simply hang on the threads. When harness 4 is raised the back bar will rise and when harness 3 is raised the front bar will rise. If the weight of the frame is adjusted to the warp, this automatic action will give all the release required.

II Leno Patterns

Diamond and zig-zag patterns in leno may be produced by making the twist threads in a coarser material than the rest of the warp, and in colors as desired. Four or six threads of free warp, on harnesses 1 and 2, should then be threaded between the leno threads, as—for zig-zag lines—(4) in pattern warp; 1, 2, 1, 2, 1, 2, in free warp; (3) in pattern warp, and repeat. For the diamond pattern: (4) in pattern warp; 1, 2, 1, 2, 1, 2, in free warp; (3) and (3) in pattern warp; 2, 1, 2, 1, 2, 1, in free warp; (4) and (4) in pattern warp, and so on. As the pattern warp has a greater take-up than the free warp it must be carried on a second warp-beam. In treadling, weave on tie-up (o) as follows: treadle 1 (leno); treadles 2 and 4 alternately for six shots; treadle 3 (leno); treadles 4 and 2 alternately for six shots. The pattern will be on the under side as woven.

Patterns of this type do not seem to me particularly handsome, but they may be found useful for some purposes. Fabrics showing patterns of this type may be found among ancient Peruvian textiles.

In sleying leno fabrics it must be repeated that all threads connected by a doup must be taken in a group, through the same dent of the reed and for such a fabric as the above a very coarse reed is required, as all eight threads in each group—two pattern threads and six plain threads—must be in the same dent of the reed.

The weavers of ancient Peru often used a leno foundation for patterns in a simple tapestry technique—very handsome for borders in curtains, for scattered detached motifs, for initials in the ends of scarves, and the like. This work may be done with small shuttles on the loom or darned in with tape-needles. On a loom with extra harnesses when used for a simple two-thread or three-thread leno all across, the threading may be made on the back harnesses, and two harnesses between the threading and the doups may be used to raise alternate groups of the leno to facilitate the tapestry process. These harnesses should be provided with tied heddles made with the bottom tie of the eye and no upper tie. Treadles raising these harnesses must, of course, also be tied to raise the doup harness to release the twist threads.

The leno weaves, though not the simplest weaves in the hand-weaver's repertory, present no great difficulties, as may be seen. For many useful purposes they are the best possible weaves and no one with a suitable loom need hesitate to try them.

Chapter Eighteen: Rug-Making

Rug-weaving is a special branch of the textile craft, and though many of the weaves and patterns used for other purposes may be adapted to the making of floor-coverings, most of our familiar weaves are poorly suited to the purpose. In a general way, hand-weavers—with the exception of course of those who specialize in rug-making—are less successful in this line than in any other.

And this is odd, because rug-weaving—of a very debased type, to be sure—was for a long time the only form of hand-weaving in general practise in the United States.

When, early in the eighteen hundreds, machinery took over the textile industry, a certain number of people continued to make rag rugs in plain weave on two-harness looms. This is still the only kind of hand-weaving widely known to the general public. If one sets up a hand-loom at a state fair, for instance—as I have done—ninety-nine out of a hundred of those who stop and gape will remark, "Oh, making rugs!" no matter how fine and delicate a web may be displayed on the loom.

In the old day, when all fabrics were hand-woven and were made to last a long time—when a suit of clothes might be passed by will from grandfather to grandson—every scrap of cloth was valuable, and even rags still had much solid substance. In those days the rag rug was a reasonable feature of domestic economy. But in our times most of the fabrics in general use are light and sleazy and when worn out have no value left in them. To cut such stuff into strips, sew them together and weave them into rugs is largely a waste of time. This is, to be sure, a suitable occupation for the inmates of state hospitals and other institutions where time has no value and is merely something to be got rid of as painlessly as possible, but an expert hand-weaver with a good loom should be able to find something better to do.

There are many excellent ways to make rugs—no need to resort to a poor technique even if the only available loom is equipped with only two harnesses.

What are the qualities that make a good rug? The thing should be firm and solid so that it will hold together under the beat of feet and the pull of the vacuum cleaner; it should be pleasant underfoot, and should be heavy enough to lie solidly on the floor. A heel-catcher is dangerous, and a rug that scuffs up with every passing breeze is untidy and unsightly. These are the most important considerations, though, of course, rugs should also be as handsome in color and design and texture as we can make them.

The most difficult part of the problem for most people appears to be the matter of getting sufficient weight and solidity. This cannot be accomplished simply by using extremely coarse materials. The most important factor is the structure of the web, as by using a suitable weave one may make heavy rugs of fine material. Another important factor is the beat. No one should attempt rug-making on a flimsy loom, and no one can make a good rug without putting into it a lot of heavy pounding with the batten.

I Rag Rugs in Plain Weave

Though the project is not a very interesting or profitable one, suppose a modern hand-weaver is seized by an overpowering impulse to weave rag rugs—just how should the distressing thing be done?

In the old day the rags for rugs were carefully cut and sorted according to kind and color, and in the weaving the colors were arranged to make a repeating pattern of stripes—the quite hideous "hit and miss" affair only too well known to most of us was not produced at all. Some of the old pieces that have come down to us are honest and not unsightly when used as floor-covering in an attic bedroom with an old spool bed and dormer windows. Not beautiful, but adequate and suitable. But for such a rug the material must be all of the same kind, and must be something with enough body to hold together under wear for at least a reasonable time. New material is best, of course, but a good wool rug-yarn costs no more and makes a better rug so there is no economy in this unless one is able to purchase suitable waste material—selvages, and so on.

If old material is used it must be properly prepared. It is entirely impossible to make a good rug from scraps of rag of different kinds and different widths, in short lengths—sometimes cut on the bias, sometimes cut in a spiral—sewed together crosswise of the strip. This is the way many people prepare carpet-rags and they should not be surprised if nothing results but lumps. Nobody should waste time and warp in weaving such stuff.

For a good rug the strips should be a yard or more long. If longer they need not be sewed but the ends may be beveled with the scissors and lapped under a few warp-ends and simply woven in. If, however, it is desired to sew the strips, lap the two ends for two inches or so, fold lengthwise and stitch lengthwise on the machine as close as possible to the fold. Then hollow out with the scissors where the ends are lapped, and no lump will appear in the weaving.

For ordinary rag rugs, carpet warp set at twelve ends to the inch may be used. A somewhat heavier rug results from setting the warp at fifteen to the inch and threading double: 1, 1, 2, 2, and so on. Rag rugs are sometimes woven in the twill weave, and are sometimes attempted in one or another of the pattern weaves, but the results are, as a rule, quite unsatisfactory.

One of the best weaves for rags is the Swedish "twice-woven" technique, but this is not popular among American weavers.

Rugs in plain weave are sometimes woven in a coarse, loosely spun cotton material known as cotton "roving." When first made these are sometimes quite attractive for use as bath-mats and bed-side rugs, when done in good colors and in a pleasing arrangement of stripes. Unfortunately they are apt to look quite forlorn after a few washings. Cotton chenille makes a much better rug, but should be woven in strands of several ends to give sufficient thickness. There are better ways to make chenille rugs, however.

II *The Pattern Weaves as Used for Rug-Making*

In the early days of the hand-weaving revival, rugs were often woven in the overshot weave and in the old Colonial coverlet patterns, the pattern weft being cotton roving, wool rug-yarn or chenille, and sometimes even rags. Some people

(142) Rug in crackle weave.

still weave rugs of this type, but we have come to realize that there are much better ways to make floor-coverings and the overshot rugs are disappearing. Though sometimes attractive in appearance, such rugs are lumpy underfoot, and when woven in patterns with long weft floats, may prove to be dangerous heel-catchers. The old-time weavers never used the overshot weave for rug-making.

However, anyone who feels the urge to make an overshot rug will have pleasant and fairly practical results if a suitable pattern and suitable materials are chosen.

Ordinary carpet warp for these rugs should be set at fifteen or sixteen to the inch. The pattern should be one with no long skips and also one with no two-thread skips as these cannot be woven square when a very coarse weft is used. Cotton chenille is the best weft-material—woven in a double strand for the pattern shots and single for tabby. The heavy cotton roving is too coarse and makes a clumsy effect. Draft No. 137, Diagram 36, gives good results. Other drafts of the same type that may be used in a similar manner are 138 and 142.

Crackle weave and the summer-and-winter weave are better than overshot for rug-making, though small rugs in these weaves are too light to lie well on the floor. For large rugs, made in strips and sewed together, they serve quite well. Medium-weight, wool rug-yarns are best for weft in such pieces, though cotton chenille is also satisfactory. Very coarse cotton roving will not do as it distorts the weave too much. The warp-setting should be fifteen to the inch as for overshot, and carpet warp may be used for the tabby shots. In the summer-and-winter weave two pattern shots instead of four should be woven to each pattern unit.

None of the "fifty-fifty" group of weaves is suitable for rug-making. Modified forms of both the weft-faced and the warp-faced rep weaves are, however, sometimes used for rugs. I once examined an ancient piece of carpeting made on two warps, one of coarse tow and the other of coarse, hard-twisted, wool yarn set in stripes of color, threaded on two harnesses—the wool on one harness and the tow on the other. The warp was set so close that the weft was completely covered. This weft was of two kinds: a tow like half the warp and a coarse strand made up of five or six narrow strips of rag. In weaving, the coarse strand was woven under the wool warp and the tow weft under the tow warp, producing a ridged fabric of the warp-faced rep order with a wool surface and a tow backing. This weave is practical for a hall-runner or for a stair-carpet. The technique is similar to the Swedish "matta" weave, which is explained in most of the Scandinavian books on weaving. It is not in general use among American hand-weavers.

Several forms of the tapestry weave are used for rug-making: Kilim, Soumak, the Navajo type of tapestry, and so on. These weaves will not be described here. There are many excellent books on the subject. As noted previously, tapestry weaving is a whole world in itself and cannot be included within the limits of this book.

III *The Special Weaves for Rug-Making*

(1) *Tufted or Pile Rugs*

From time immemorial tufted or "pile" fabrics have been highly regarded as floor-coverings, and have been made in many lands by a variety of textile techniques. The supreme in rug-making is, no doubt, the fine Oriental with its hundred knots to the square inch. American weavers, however, seem disinclined to spend the best part of a lifetime over one piece of weaving, and are willing to leave this sort of thing to the endless patience and the clever fingers of those who have grown up in the tradition.

The coarse variety of tied pile rug-making known in Sweden as "Flossa" or "Rya," is, however, fairly popular among us. Though much more rapid than the Oriental process, rugs made in the flossa technique take a great deal of time and a great deal of expensive material—and unless well designed may be quite hideous. As the process is described in the Scandinavian books it need not be detailed here.

Tufted rugs in cotton, made in a technique similar to that of the old tufted counterpanes, are attractive and useful as bath-mats and bed-side rugs.

(2) *The Navajo Saddle-Blanket Weaves, Diagram 60*

The tapestry rugs woven by the Indians of the Southwest are made chiefly **for sale,** and the technique is not very ancient as it appears to have been introduced **by the** Spaniards in the early days. The weaves used for the making of

(143) Small rug in Navajo saddle-blanket weave.

Indian Saddle-Blanket Weave

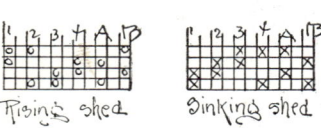
Rising shed.   Sinking shed.

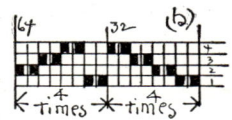

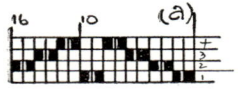

Diagram 60 (144)

saddle-blankets are—from the weavers' point of view—more interesting, as they are unique and appear to be far more ancient than the tapestry weaving. From the practical point of view, these weaves make excellent rugs and also, of course, very satisfactory saddle-blankets. There are still many parts of the country where the saddle-blanket is an article of daily use, and how to weave it is a question of special interest.

The Indians use for their weaving a type of loom that seems to us clumsy and inconvenient, but the saddle-blanket weaves can be produced without difficulty on any four-harness loom large enough and solid enough for rug-making.

For warp the Indians use a hand-spun, hard-twisted singles wool yarn, but ordinary cotton carpet-warp may be used instead. The fabric is a weft-faced fabric in which the warp does not show at all.

The threadings most used are twill and the two return twills we know as "bird-eye" and "goose-eye," and may be threaded single in a coarse warp set at six ends to the inch or in carpet warp set at twelve ends to the inch and threaded double, as shown on Diagram 59. No tabby is woven with the pattern but two tabby treadles are shown on the tie-ups for convenience in weaving headings.

The pattern effects are produced in an odd manner by weaving the four pattern sheds in regular order in a repeat of three colors, a single "unit" of the weave consisting of twelve weft-shots as follows:—in dark (d); medium (m); and light (l).

treadle 1, (d); treadle 2, (m); treadle 3, (l); treadle 4, (d)
treadle 1, (m); treadle 2, (l); treadle 3, (d); treadle 4, (m)
treadle 1, (l); treadle 2, (d); treadle 3, (m); treadle 4, (l)

This treadling repeated over and over produces a zig-zag figure. For diamonds, take the last shot of the treadling—4, (1)—as the center and repeat in reverse back to the beginning. Horizontal bands of color may be woven by weaving all four shots in the same color. Perpendicular stripes may be woven by omitting one of the sheds, weaving, for instance, the first three shots of the treadling, repeated over and over: 1, (d); 2, (m); 3, (1).

The best weft material for rugs or saddle-blankets in this weave is a coarse wool yarn, though if a very coarse rug-yarn is used it may not cover the warp properly, in which event the threading should be triple instead of double: 1, 1, 1, 2, 2, 2, 3, 3, 3 and so on. For bath-mats and bedroom rugs a light-weight cotton rug "filler" may be used as weft. Coarse cotton roving is too heavy for the purpose.

This weave tends to narrow in badly and a template may be found useful. However, if care is taken to keep out the edges this is not strictly necessary.

The edges sometimes give trouble. It is best to weave all three shots in the same direction, one after the other. The Indian pieces are finished with a twisted cord along the edges and this makes a very tidy finish and adds to the wear of the rug. It may be done on the loom though it takes a bit of time. Twist together—either on the spinning wheel or by hand—three firm, fairly coarse cords. Light-weight jute will serve. Wind the material into two balls. Attach the ends with the warp to the apron or bar and take the balls through the loom to the back-beam without taking them through the reed or through a heddle. The balls may be weighted and hung over the beam or may be tied to the beam itself—in which event, of course, they must be released and retied each time the warp is let out. When weaving, lift one of the three strands of the twist at either side of the loom and pass the weft shots through. On the return, lift the next strand of the twist, and so on. It facilitates matters to put a lease stick under the raised strands of the twist, when the three weft shots may be woven conveniently.

A similar finish might be made by setting up a leno twist on either side of the warp, but this would not give as firm an edge as the three-strand twisted cord.

The saddle-blanket technique, when correctly followed and with the weft solidly beaten together, makes a firm, thick rug that lies well on the floor.

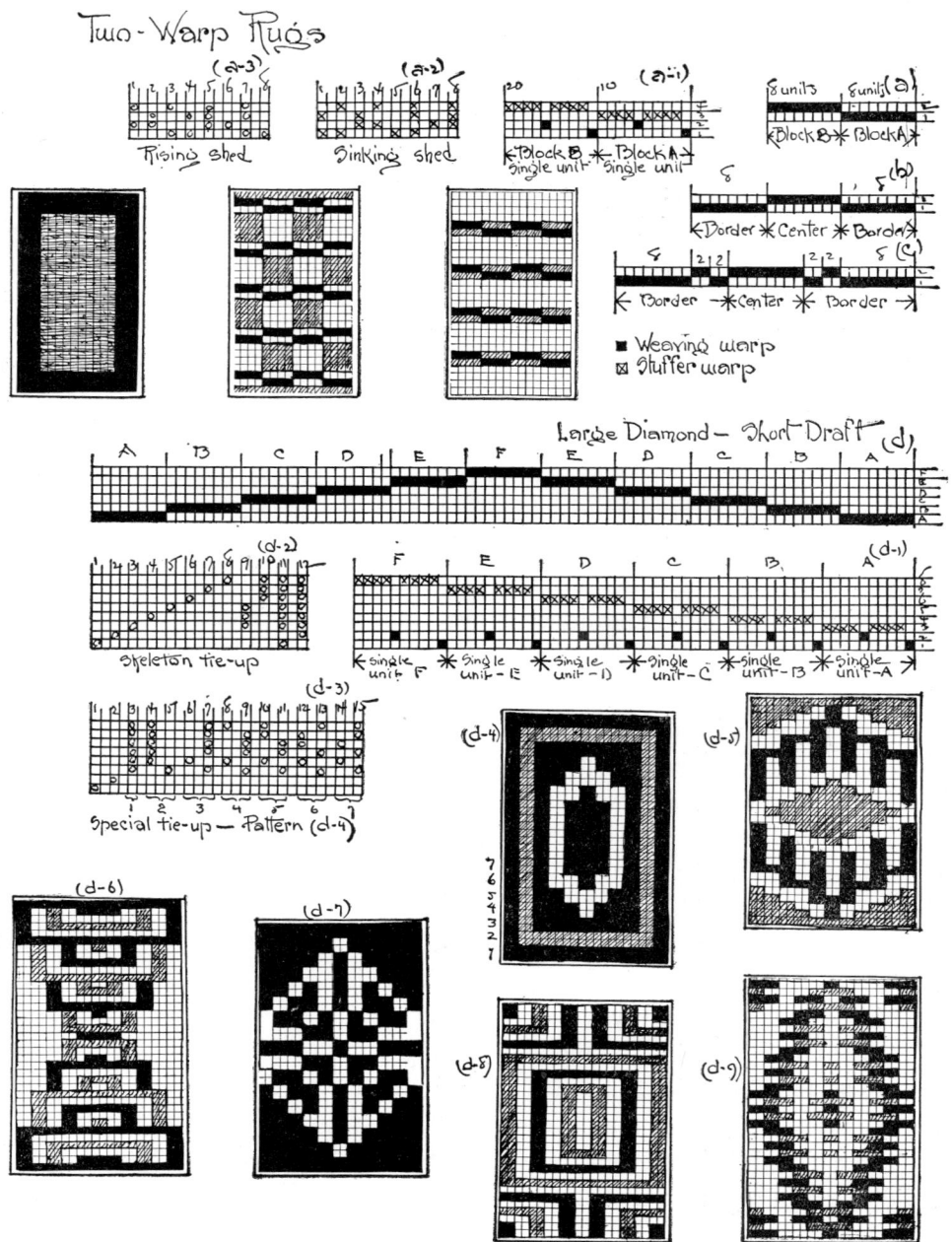

Diagram 61 (145)

(3) *The Two-Warp Rug Technique.*

The weave that in my opinion is the most practical and that offers the widest range of pattern possibilities for hand-woven rugs is what we know as the "two-warp" technique. This method of making rugs is fairly common in machine-weaving but has not been much used by hand-weavers till recently.

Handsome rugs in this technique may be woven on four harnesses though the more elaborate patterns require a more elaborate loom. The only special requirement is that the loom be equipped with two warp-beams. This is necessary as one warp is woven at a heavy tension and the other fairly slack, and one warp must be nearly twice as long as the other.

The advantages of the weave lie in the facts that rugs may be woven as heavy as one wishes, with the extra weight and thickness in relatively inexpensive material, that both sides of the piece are "right" sides—equally handsome —showing the same pattern though with colors reversed as in double weaving, that the surfaces of the rug are smooth and firm, and that the pattern possibilities are practically unlimited.

Any pattern for the summer-and-winter weave may be used for the two-warp rug weave—any two-block pattern on four harnesses, any four-block pattern on six harnesses, any six-block pattern on eight harnesses, and so on. The "unit" of the threading is similar, differing only in the fact that more threads are threaded on the pattern harnesses than in the summer-and-winter weave. This is shown on Diagram 61, at (a–1).

The "weaving warp" is carried on the two front harnesses and the "stuffer warp" is threaded on the pattern harnesses. It is the stuffer warp that gives the fabric weight and thickness and may be anything one chooses. The threading as given is for ordinary carpet warp which, in this arrangement, gives very satisfactory results when set at twenty-four ends to the inch for the stuffer warp and six ends to the inch for the weaving warp. Sley a 12-dent reed with one thread of weaving warp in the first dent, four threads of stuffer warp in the second dent, and so on.

It will be found a convenience to make the two warps of different colors. As the stuffer warp does not appear on the surface of the rug anywhere it may as well be in "natural" as this is the least expensive, with the weaving warp in tan or ecru or a shade to blend with the colors to be used in the rugs. The

(146) Two-warp rug in plum, red and gold. "Step" pattern, 10-harness.

weaving warp should be made at least one-and-three-quarters the length of the stuffer warp—slightly longer is a safer margin. If, for instance, the stuffer warp is made twelve yards long the weaving warp should be twenty or twenty-one yards long. If a heavier stuffer warp is used the weaving warp should be at least twice as long as the stuffer warp. It is difficult to be exact in the matter as the weight of the weft material enters into the problem—if a very coarse weft is used the relative length of the weaving warp should be greater.

The best weft material for rugs of this type is a medium weight wool rug-yarn, but light-weight cotton rug "filler" also makes excellent rugs, and properly prepared rags may even be used for simple patterns such as the one sketched at (b–1) on the diagram. For weaving in rags, only new material should be used, and the strips should be narrower than for the usual rag rug; the strips should be cut rather than torn to avoid linty fluff. A plain dark-colored fabric combined with a figured fabric gives a pleasant effect, as sketched.

Pattern arrangements for this weave are simple to make. The warp being set at thirty ends to the inch, and the unit of the threading covering ten threads, there will be three units to the inch. Suppose we wish to make a bath-mat 24 inches wide in pattern (a), using two repeats or four square figures as sketched: each square will be 6 inches wide and should be threaded with eighteen units of the weave, instead of eight as shown on the diagram. Suppose we wish to use pattern (b) for a 28-inch rug, with a border 5 inches wide: thread block A with fifteen units; block B with fifty-four units; block A with fifteen units. Pattern (d), as written, with eight repeats of the pattern unit under each block, will make a rug just under 28 inches wide; with nine units under each block it would be 33 inches wide.

An excellent pattern for rugs of this type is the "step" pattern given as for the summer-and-winter weave at (a), Diagram 54. In two repeats of this pattern there are twelve pattern blocks: if each block is threaded with eight repeats of the unit the rug will be 32 inches wide.

Small patterns may, of course, be woven in this technique, though a pattern made up entirely of one-unit blocks may prove somewhat difficult to beat together properly.

The weave lends itself easily to the weaving of free designs in the pick-up technique, as will be described in a later chapter.

In weaving, the stuffer warp should be kept at a strong tension and the weaving warp fairly slack. The treadling is very simple: for the first block on pattern (a) weave as follows: treadle 1, dark; treadle 2, light; treadle 3, dark; treadle 4, light. Repeat for the number of units threaded under the block. For the second block treadle in the same manner with the colors reversed: treadle 1, light; 2, dark; 3, light; 4, dark, and repeat. For solid color all across weave: 5, dark; 6, light; 7, dark; 8, light, or the reverse.

Four-harness looms are not always equipped with eight treadles; the solid effect may be produced by weaving treadles 1 and 2 together for treadle 6, and treadles 3 and 4 together for treadle 8 on tie-up (a–1)—treadles 6 and 8 may be eliminated. On tie-up (a–2) weave 1 and 2 together to eliminate 5, and 3 and 4 together to eliminate 7.

When the relative tensions of the two warps is correct the weft will beat together solidly. If the stuffer warp begins to show between the weft-shots, release the tension on the weaving warp. An automatic release on the beam is a convenience, as the weaving warp must be released frequently. A makeshift may be contrived by weighting the beam and leaving the ratchet free. By adjusting the weight to produce the desired tension much time may be saved.

Patterns may be woven in several colors if desired, as indicated on some of the sketches. When three colors are used in the design, however, the effect will be confused on the reverse of the fabric so that the rug will be definitely right- and wrong-sided. Also when three colors are used there will be more weft material on the wrong side than on the right side of the rug, which may exhibit a tendency to curl. An interesting way to restore the balance of material and to add to the effect of the rug is to weave a shot in a fourth color all across the upper side of the piece at intervals. This shot may be woven after each set of three pattern shots or farther apart. The color used for this fourth shot may be selected to harmonize or soften the other colors or to bring out one or another of the shades used.

The four-harness tie-up includes all the sheds available, but many of the desired effects on eight harnesses make use of many more sheds than there are treadles. For simple figures a special tie-up may be made, as given on the diagram for pattern (d–2). This tie-up, however, will weave the pattern in two colors only—not in three colors as sketched. For the solid dark border at the bottom, treadle: 1, dark; 1 and 3 together, light; 2, dark; 2 and 3 together, light. Repeat as required. For the second band weave 1–4, dark; 1–5, light; 2–4, dark; 2–5, light. Repeat as required. For the next block weave: 1–6, dark; 1–7, light; 2–6, dark; 2–7, light. And so on.

For the more elaborate effects it is necessary to use the skeleton tie-up, which may involve some rather complicated acrobatics. It is a help to treadle 1 and insert a pick-up stick under the raised threads. Then use the feet to find the pattern treadles required. Weave a shot of the first color. Leaving the stick in place, find the reverse pattern shot and weave with the second color. Treadle 2 and insert the stick and repeat the pattern shots.

Special threadings are not very important for this weave. As may be seen by the sketches it is possible to produce a great variety of patterns on a simple twill arrangement of blocks as in the "step" pattern or on a diamond arrangement as given on the diagram. One might weave for years on such a threading without finding it necessary to repeat oneself.

However, as noted above, any pattern suitable for the summer-and-winter weave may be used in the two-warp technique. Patterns 246 and 247, Diagram 53 for instance, would make handsome rugs—or 245 and 248, for that matter. Any of the patterns on Diagram 43 might be used for four-harness rugs in the two-warp weave—No. 161, for instance, with the large figure in the corners and the center in the alternating check, or No. 164 with the center threaded to the long block on B and the check repeated for the border. It might, however, be well to make the checks of two units each rather than of one unit each as shown on the drafts.

Rugs in this weave may be finished in the ordinary way with fringes. As the warp is heavy the fringe is handsomer than on ordinary rugs, and the Philippine tie, given at (f) Diagram No. 72, is suitable. The fabric is too heavy to be hemmed, and if a hemmed edge is desired, weave four inches using treadles 1 and 2 alternately. Insert a 2-inch shed-stick under this band of weaving and proceed with the rug. After a few inches have been woven the stick may be removed. Finish the other end of the rug in the same manner. When the rug is taken off the loom this single woven fabric at the ends may be turned under and hemmed.

I have no information on the origin of this weave. As far as I know, it was never practised in Colonial America and I have not found it in the Scandinavian books on weaving—or in any other hand-weaving literature, for that matter. It is, however, used in machine-weaving as noted above. Its introduction to hand-weavers is comparatively recent, but it has proved so eminently practical and it holds such interesting possibilities that it demands inclusion in any book on modern American hand-weaving. I may note that the pick-up technique in this weave and the multi-color practise are innovations of our own.

Chapter Nineteen: Pick-Up Weaving

The pick-up techniques come to many weavers as a revelation, as a door to a whole new world. On a simple four-harness loom—or on a two-harness loom for some of the handsomest pick-ups—the weaver equipped with a slender stick or two may produce practically any texture, in free design, as intricate as anything woven on a complicated draw-loom. Pick-up weaving, to be sure, takes more time than ordinary harness weaving, but many of the techniques are more rapid than might be imagined, and the results more than justify the time involved.

The prejudice many people seem to feel against pick-up weaving may be largely due to the fact that the only form of pick-up familiar to many weavers is the Swedish "dukagang" or "embroidery weave," which has a rather stiff, uncompromising effect of perpendicular lines in overshot, and which must be woven wrong side up in the loom with a mirror under the web if one wishes to see what one is doing. This form of pick-up will not be described here as it is set forth in detail in many Scandinavian books on weaving.

The current forms of pick-up weaving, which more and more people are enjoying, are based on the traditional weaves such as the summer-and-winter weave, the damask weave, and so on, or are adaptations of "native" American weaves—from ancient Peru, Guatemala, Mexico, and from our own Southwest.

These native weaves are of great antiquity. Some of the traditional patterns are so old that no one can say how old they are. The "Earth and Sky" pattern that appears in endless variations in all native American art from Alaska to the southern tip of South America has been found on carved stones said by archeologists to date from fifteen thousand B.C. No woven textiles of that period

(147) Two small rugs in two-warp pick-up. Upper, a "meander" in black and gold. Lower, a modernistic version of the "Earth and Sky" motif with a moon and a row of stars. (Rug-weave pick-up.)

remain, of course, though no doubt there was weaving—probably similar to the pre-Inca fragments that do remain. (See Diagram 66.)

The marvellous textiles of ancient Peru, like the native weavings of Guatemala and Mexico, were no doubt produced on the inconvenient body-loom, still in use in many parts of the world, but the same types of weaving may be accomplished far more easily and quickly on weaving equipment such as used by modern hand-weavers.

The chief charm of the pick-up weaves is in the matter of design. One may weave any figure that can be drawn on squared paper—not in one, but in most of the pick-up weaves. Birds and beasts, trees and flowers and even human figures, as well as bold modernistic geometric figures, may be produced in double weaving, in damask, in the summer-and-winter weave, in other textures. The pick-up weaves do not, to be sure, appeal to weavers who are "pattern blind," or to those who enjoy the orderly monotony of "yardage," but the great majority of those who have looms and enjoy design will find here the most fascinating ways of the craft.

The special tools of the pick-up weaver are extremely simple, consisting as they do of pick-up sticks of two kinds, in various lengths to go across wide or narrow warps. There should be thin, narrow sticks used on top of the shed simply to regulate the pattern, and wide sticks that when set on edge make a sufficient shed for the passage of the shuttle. Both should have rounded ends and beveled edges, and should be of hard wood and perfectly smooth. For some kinds of pick-up weaving the ordinary throw-shuttle, carrying a bobbin, may be used, but for most pick-up weaves the flat poke-shuttle is the better tool, so a stock of these—in different lengths—is also desirable.

I Pick-Up Forms of the Standard Weaves

Many of our familiar weaves lend themselves to the pick-up technique—even the plain weave as in the Mexican and Peruvian tabby pick-up. But the Colonial overshot weave does not give effects of much interest.

(a) The summer-and-winter weave, however, offers fascinating possibilities. Any threading for this weave that happens to be on the loom may be used as a basis for the pick-up technique, or the loom may be threaded as at (a) on

Tie-ups for Pick-Up Weaving

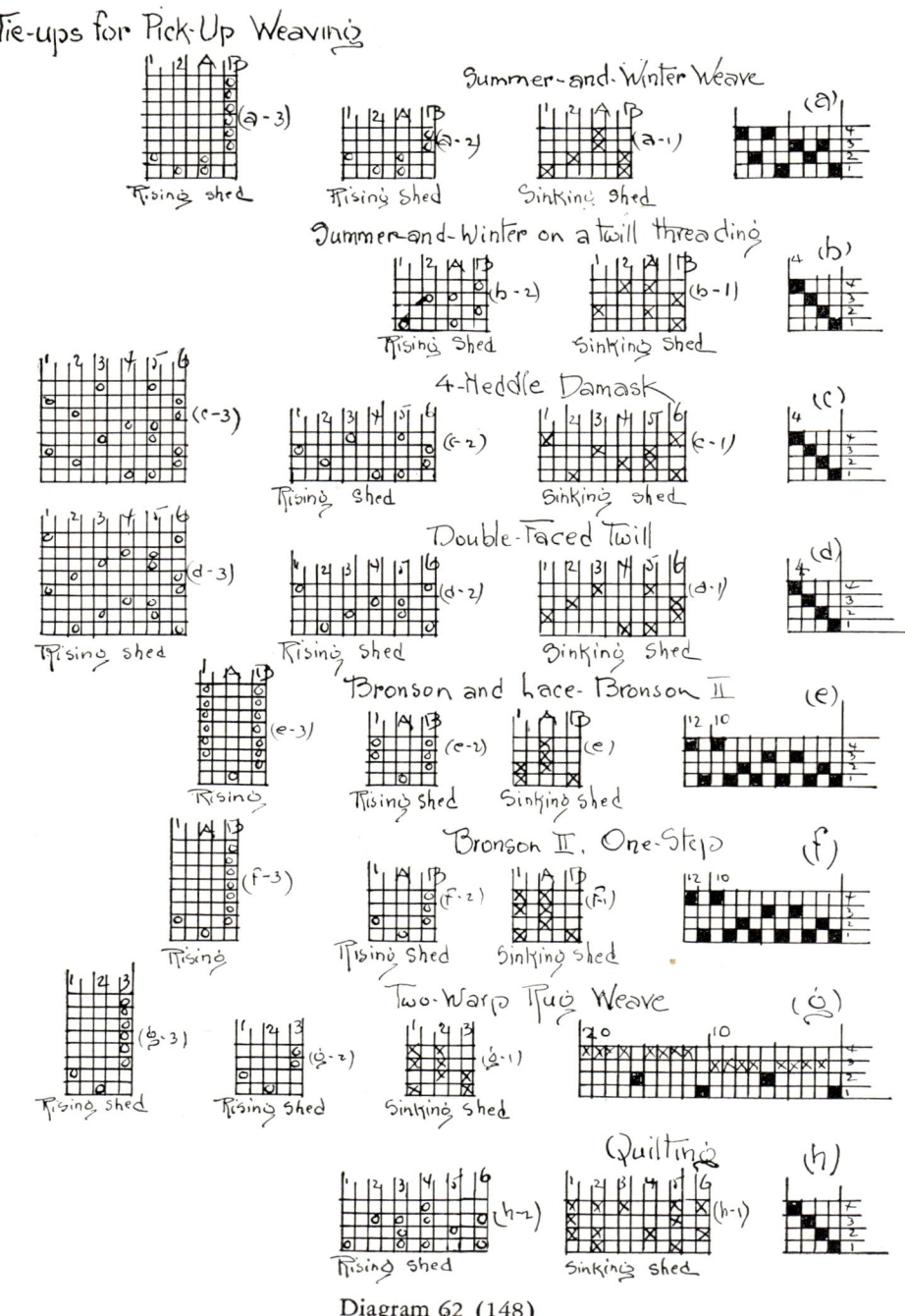

Diagram 62 (148)

Diagram 62, or in a four-harness twill as shown at (b). Only four treadles are required as shown in the tie-ups at (a–1), (a–2), (a–3), (b–1) and (b–2).

For the summer-and-winter weave type of threading as at (a), treadle tabby A, which raises all the pattern harnesses. Take up on the pick-up stick all the background spaces of the figure to be woven, allowing two of the raised threads to each unit of the design. The stick used should be one of the light, narrow sticks. With the stick in place, treadle on 1 and weave a shot of pattern weft. Do not remove the stick, but treadle on 2 and weave a second shot of pattern weft. Remove the stick and weave the two tabby shots. It is impossible to beat between the two pattern shots because of the stick. However, this causes no trouble. It is necessary to count the threads carefully for the first pick-up; the rest of the pattern usually follows without further counting.

Any pattern that may be drawn on squared paper may be produced in this manner.

(b) To produce the same weave on a twill threading as at (b), treadle in exactly the same way, using the tie-up as at (b–1) or (b–2).

The treadlings given above weave the figure in "one-and-one" style. If preferred the weaving may be done "in pairs" by treadling the pattern shots: 1, 2, for the first pair of each unit and 2, 1, for the second pair.

To be specific: for the "Earth and Sky" figure at (b), Diagram 64, proceed as follows: Weave tabby A, tabby B, ending on B. With the B shed still open take up on the pick-up stick the first sixteen threads; over the next sixteen, under the following sixteen, and so all across. With the stick in place treadle 1 and weave a pattern shot. Treadle 2 and weave a second pattern shot. Take out the stick and weave A, B in tabby. Repeat. For the next unit of the weave, with the B shed open take up the first sixteen threads, over two, under ten, over four, and repeat all across. Weave as before. For the next line of the pattern, take the stick under the first four threads, (*) over twelve, under two, over two, under six, over two, under eight; then repeat from (*) all across. Having got so far, the rest should be easy.

The pick-up must be made accurately, or the result will have a somewhat moth-eaten effect that is not very alluring. This is true for all work in pick-up, of course.

(c) For the pick-up in damask weave (c), Diagram 62, proceed as follows:

Treadle 5 and with the pick-up stick take up all the background of the figure, allowing two threads to each unit of the weave. With the stick in position, treadle 1 and weave; treadle 2 and weave. Take out the stick. Treadle 6 and make a pick-up over the same areas as the first pick-up. Treadle 3 and weave; treadle 4 and weave. Repeat for each unit of the pattern.

If the warp is sleyed as usual, two threads to the dent, draw a single thread through the first dent and then proceed at two to the dent. This will bring the 2 and 3 threads through the same dent and the 1 and 4 threads through the next, and when these sheds are opened the warp will come up in pairs, which will facilitate the pick-up.

This is a quick and easy pick-up, and though it would take a good deal of time to weave a wide tablecloth in this manner, it will prove an interesting way to weave borders for towels and table mats, lunch cloths and similar pieces.

(d) The double-faced twill may be woven in the same manner on the tie-ups as given at (d) Diagram 62.

(e) Bronson II and lace-Bronson may be woven as at (e). Treadle A and B, ending on B. Treadle 1 and make the pick-up. The warp will come up in pairs; take up the pattern allowing one pair to each unit of the weave—for lace-Bronson two pairs for each unit. Treadle A and weave; treadle B and weave; treadle A and weave. Take out the stick and weave B, A, B. Repeat. As it is impossible to beat in the ordinary manner with the stick in the shed, weave with a flat shuttle, and leaving the shuttle in the shed beat against the shuttle. For lace-Bronson, of course, the setting should be open and the beat light.

A Bronson threading may also be used for the Guatemalan one-skip pick-up, described later in this chapter, with tie-ups as at (f) on Diagram 62.

(g) An extremely interesting pick-up weave may be made on any threading for two-warp rugs, using three treadles only, as shown on the diagram at (g).

The weave is produced as follows: use treadle 3 which raises all the stuffer warp, and make the pick-up for either of the two colors to be used in the weft. Allow two groups of warp-ends—eight threads—to each unit of the weave. With the pick-up stick in position, treadle 1 and weave the first color. Take out the stick and pick up all the threads not taken up on the first pick-up. Treadle 1 again and weave the second color. Take out the stick; treadle 3 and make the same pick-up as for the first shot; treadle 2 and weave the first color.

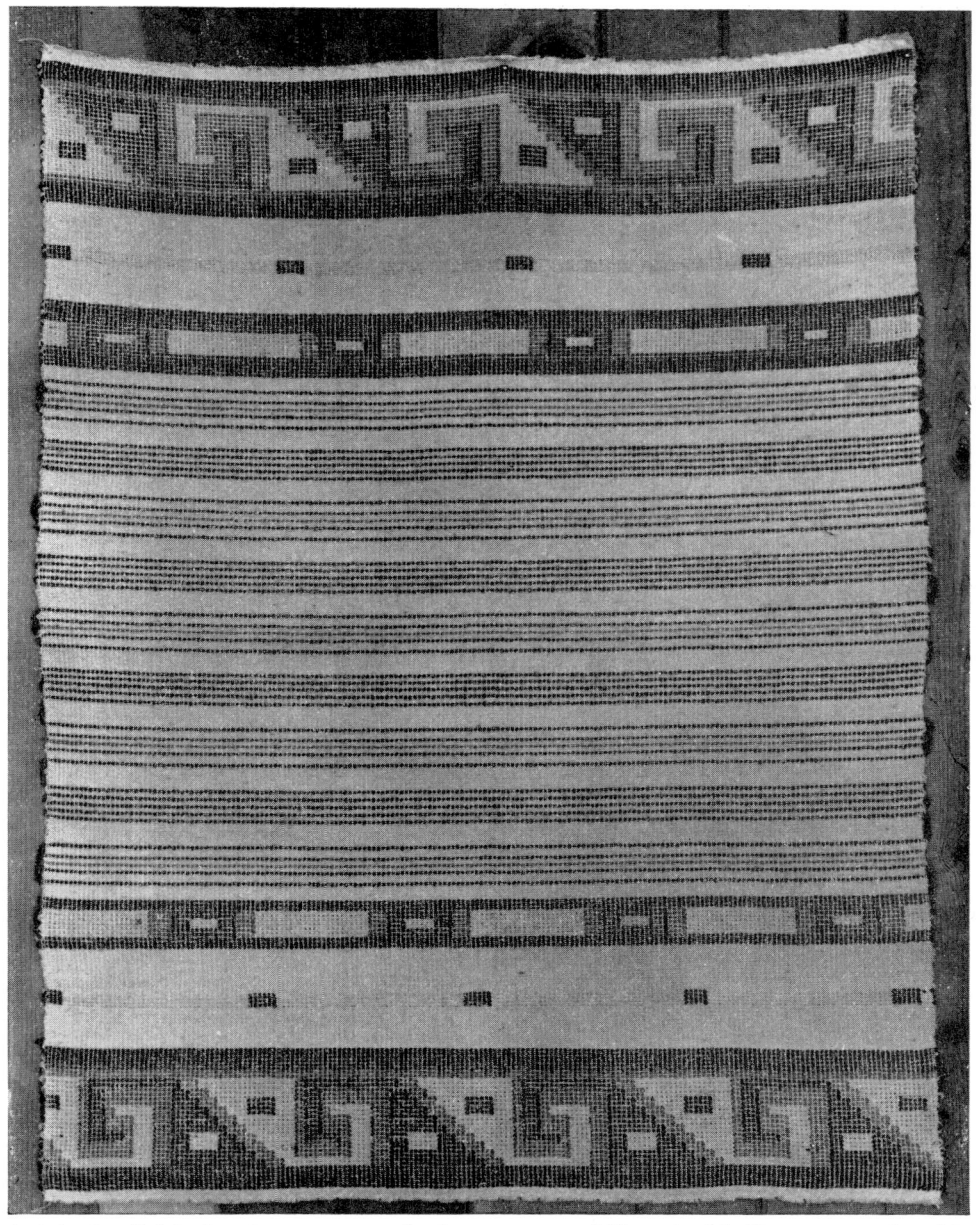

(149) Small blanket in summer-and-winter weave pick-up in black, cream and gold. The border pattern is based on the "Earth and Sky" motif.

Take out the stick; treadle 3 and make the opposite pick-up as for the second shot. Treadle 2 and weave the second color. This is the complete process. These four shots constitute a unit of the weave. Though a pick-up must be made for each weft-shot, it is a coarse and simple pick-up that may be made very rapidly and easily.

The only difficulty about this weave lies in the fact that the weaving warp is not at as heavy a tension as the stuffer warp, and the sheds may be rather shallow. If this proves troublesome a wide shed-stick may be put through the shed and set on edge to permit the passage of a large shuttle.

Any pattern for double weaving may be made into a rug by this technique, and in fact any pattern that may be drawn on squared paper.

Patterns may be woven in several colors: for the first color treadle 3 and take up on the stick all the stuffer warp except over the parts to be woven, and weave on treadle 1. Treadle 3 again and take up all the warp except over the parts to be woven in color 2. Treadle 1 and weave. Take out the stick and treadle 3 again, and take up all unwoven sections of stuffer warp and weave on 1 in color 3. Repeat these pick-ups in the same order and weave on treadle 2. This of course is slower than weaving in two colors, and gives a confused effect on the wrong side of the fabric, but some of the effects that may be produced are very interesting and as the material is coarse the work does not take an inordinate amount of time—far less time, for instance, than the making of a rug in the tied-pile "flossa" technique.

(h) The quilted weave may be carried out very simply and easily by the pick-up method, and the quilting may be done in a pattern as elaborate as one chooses. The plain twill threading is used, and woven to make two separate fabrics. The material and color of the two fabrics may be the same or different as one wishes. Thread: 1 for the upper fabric; 2 for the under fabric; 3 for the upper and 4 for the under fabrics. Treadles 1 and 2 weave the upper fabric and treadles 3 and 4 the under fabric. After weaving six shots on top and six shots below—either alternating the shots or weaving two shots on top and two shots below—treadle on 6, which separates the two fabrics, and weave a shot of quilting material, which may be a very soft yarn or an unspun wool roving. Treadle on 5, which raises half the threads of the under fabric, and make a pick-up, taking up the threads desired for the pattern. For instance, pick up one thread and skip seven, and so all across. With the pick-up stick in place, treadle 1 and weave a shot of the upper fabric. Take out the stick and weave treadle 2 for the second shot of the upper fabric. Treadle and weave 3 and 4 for the under fabric. Repeat treadles 1, 2, 3, 4 twice. Then treadle 6 and weave a second shot of quilting. Treadle 5 and make a second pick-up. For a diamond figure, for instance, take up a thread on either side of the first pick-up. Continue in this manner, picking up a "stitching" thread after each shot of padding.

The pick-up forms of the leno weave are found chiefly in the Mexican and Peruvian gauze weaves, and will be described in the following section.

For all the above weaves the pick-up stick used should be of the light, narrow type that rides the top of the shed.

II Nine Native American Pick-Up Weaves

The amazingly beautiful textiles of ancient Peru, of Guatemala and Mexico and of our own Indians of the Southwest show three principal techniques: tapestry, tied-dying or "jaspé," and pick-up, including the gauze or lace-weaves, which are a form of pick-up. There are also braiding, plaiting, knotting, and other minor forms of the textile craft. The following notes will deal only with a selection of the pick-up weaves. There are many others; these which I have chosen have, in my experience, proved best adapted to modern weaving equipment and most useful and interesting to modern hand-weavers.

(a) One of the most striking and interesting is a tabby pick-up that may be carried out on a two-harness loom if one wishes. This weave is found in Mexico and Peru, in somewhat different form, but seems unknown in Guatemala.

It is not a weave for fine materials. The warp should be coarse and set close, and the weft should be coarser than the warp. I have used carpet warp set at thirty ends to the inch and threaded double as shown on Diagram 63 at (a). Of course the same effect may be obtained by threading on four harnesses as at (b) with a 1–2, 3–4 tie-up to the treadles.

In the Mexican form of the weave, which is a good deal simpler than the Peruvian, the background fabric is a coarse tabby with the figures in overshot skips produced by the pick-up stick. The process is extremely simple: open a tabby shed and weave, in the color desired for the background. With the shed

302 —

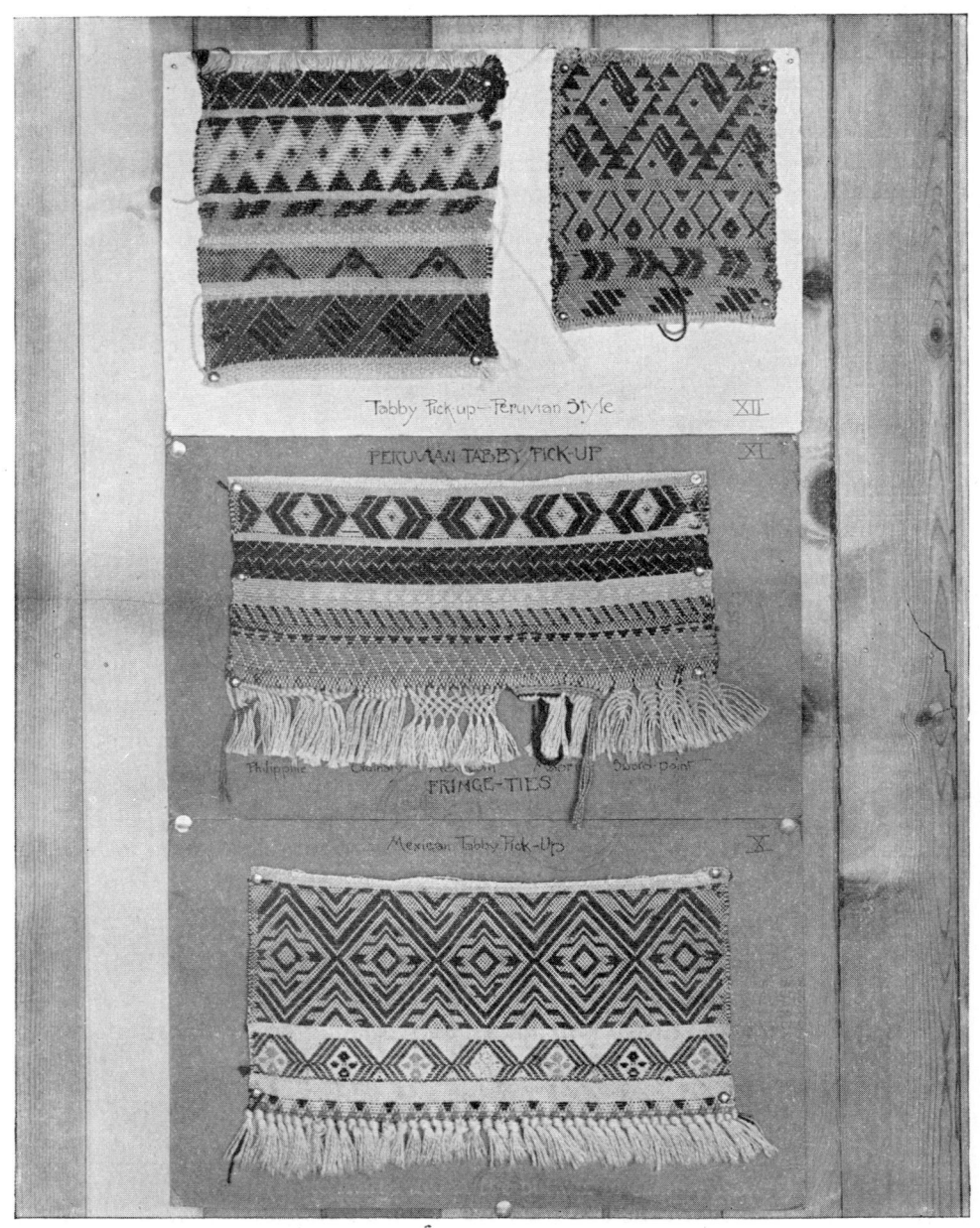

(150) Samples in tabby pick-up. 1, 2, and 3, Peruvian style; 4, Mexican style. (Note fringe ties at the bottom of sample No. 3.)

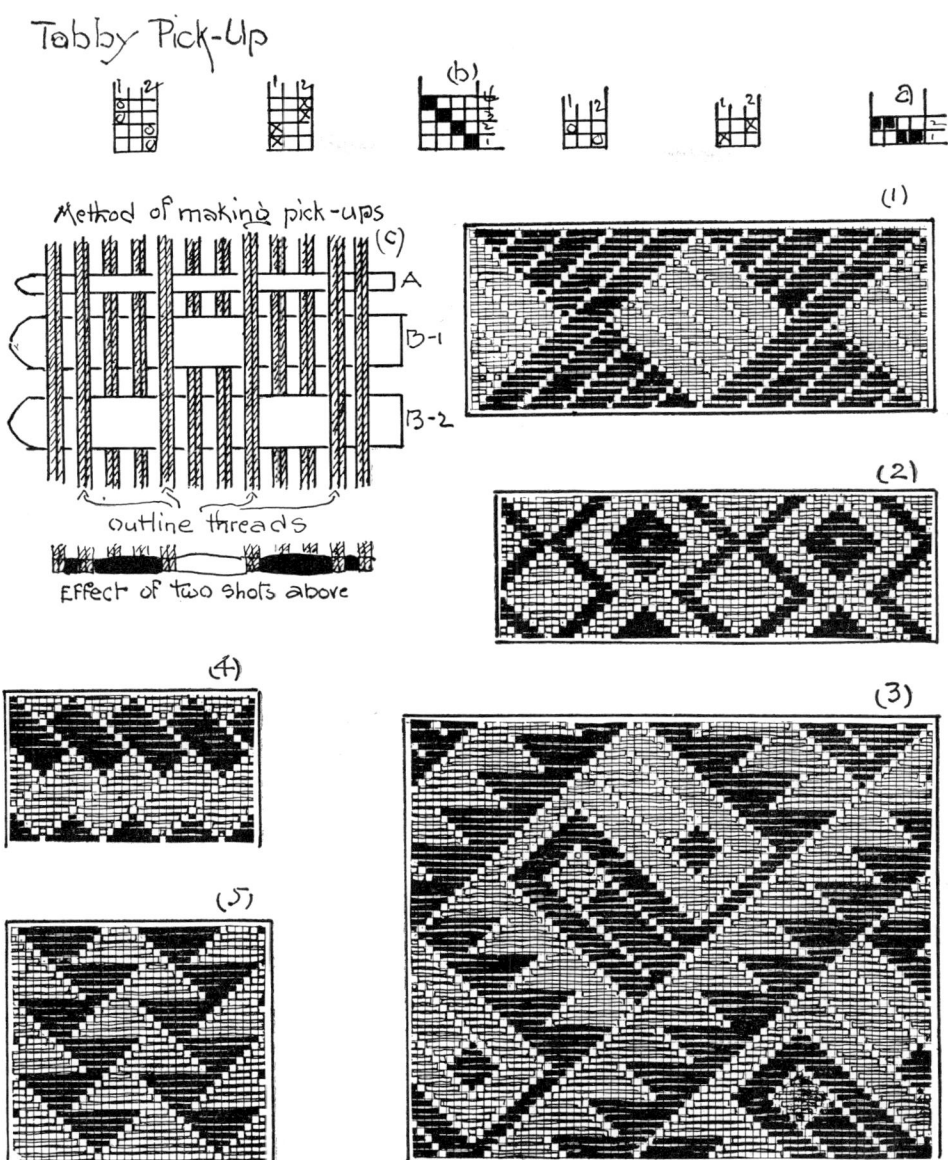

Diagram 63 (151)

still open make the pick-up, using a broad shed-stick and taking up all the background parts of the design. Set the stick on edge and weave a shot in pattern color. Change the shed and repeat: tabby shot, pick-up, pattern shot.

As both the tabby shot and the pattern shot are woven through the same shed, the pattern skip slides over the tabby when the weft is beaten together.

Owing to the structure of the weave, patterns built along diagonal and horizontal lines are desirable.

The Peruvian tabby pick-up is somewhat more intricate, and is also handsomer. In the Peruvian weave there is no tabby background but the entire surface of the fabric is covered by skips of pattern weft and the warp appears only as an outline to the figures. No tabby shot is woven. One color skips where the other color tabbies. The effect is very rich and striking.

The designs shown on Diagram 63 are all for the Peruvian weave. No. 3 is from an ancient Peruvian piece shown on Plate XX, 2 and 3, of "Les Textiles Anciens du Pérou" by Raoul d'Harcourt. Other interesting examples of the weave will be found in the same book.

How the Peruvian weavers produced the weave I do not know, but illustrated at (c) on the diagram will be found the method I find simplest and most rapid. Open a tabby shed and take up on a light pick-up stick all the outline threads of the design, always including the two or three threads nearest the edges to make a good margin. With the shed still open and the narrow stick in position, make a second pick-up using a broad shed-stick. Take the stick under all the outline threads raised by the first pick-up and under all the sections of the pattern that will be woven in the second color, leaving skips for the first color. Set the stick on edge and weave. Take out the broad stick, leaving the narrow stick in place, and make a similar pick-up for the second color. Weave. Change the shed and repeat.

For example, to weave pattern No. 1, as shown on the diagram, treadle on 1 and weave a tabby shot in the lighter of the two colors to be used—a tabby all across this time as this color does not make a skip in the first line of the pattern. With the shed still open make a pick-up for the second color: under the first two warp pairs then over two and under one all across. Set the stick on edge and weave a shot of the second color. Change the shed and weave a second tabby shot in the lighter color. With the shed still open make the pick-up for the darker color: the first thread to the left of the first outline thread; over one, under one; (*) over two, under one; over two, under one; over two, under one; over two; under two and repeat all across from (*). Set the stick on edge and weave a shot of the second color.

For the third line of the pattern use the light stick and make a pick-up of the outline threads as shown on the diagram. Then, with the broad stick, make a pick-up for the light color, going under all the raised threads except the single thread at the point of the reversed figure. Set the broad stick on edge and weave the light color. With the shed still open and the outline pick-up stick in place, slide the broad stick under all the outline threads as far as the point of the reversed figure. Pick up the thread over which the light weft made a skip. Set the stick on edge and weave.

Having got so far one should have no difficulty in continuing. The directions may sound complicated but in practise the thing is very simple and as the weft is coarse the work goes rapidly enough.

This weave is chiefly useful for bold effects in drapery and for borders. It is not a suitable weave for upholstery.

(b) Probably the best known of the pick-up weaves is the double-plain weave pick-up. This weave came to us first through the Scandinavian books, from Finland, and was known as the "Finnweave." But there are many ancient Peruvian pieces in this weave and it is extensively used in Mexico for bags and similar pieces. The Mexican method of producing the weave is far simpler and more rapid than the Finnish technique so it is now the Mexican method that is usually practised by American weavers and it is this method that will be described here. Anyone who wishes may find the Finnish technique in one or another of the Scandinavian books on weaving.

This weave is not suitable for linens or for rug-making. It is sometimes woven in all wool for blankets but is best in a cotton and wool combination as in the old coverlets, or in an all-cotton fabric. The material used may be as coarse or as fine as one chooses, but a fairly coarse cotton—a 10/3 for instance, at a setting of forty ends to the inch—seems to me to give the most satisfactory results. A mercerized cotton or a hard-twisted cotton of some kind should be used.

Patterns for Pick-Up Weaving

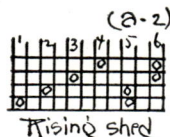
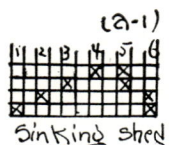

■ Dark colored warp
☒ Light colored warp

The "Earth and Sky" figure in it's fundamental form

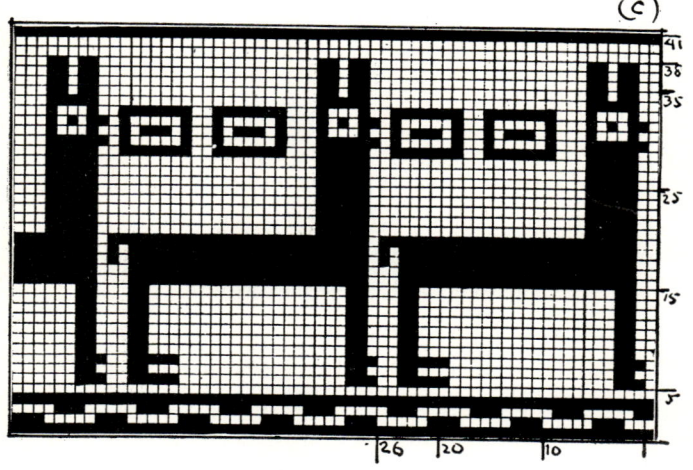

Llamas blowing bubbles— Peruvian. After d'Harcourt.

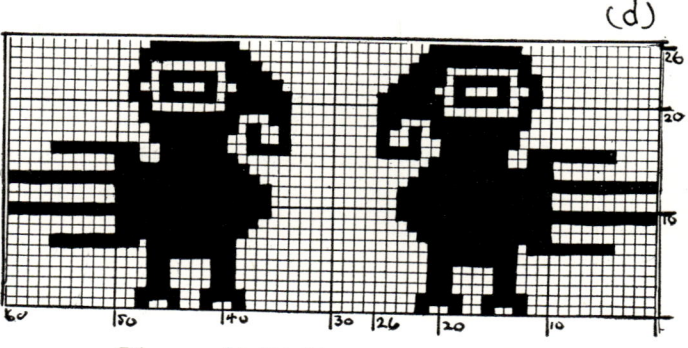

Pair of Parrots. Peruvian.

Diagram 64 (152)

The warp should be in two contrasting colors, threaded as shown on Diagram 64 at (a), and the weft should be the same material in the same two colors. A variation is to set the warp farther apart and to weave in a material coarser than the warp, beaten to give a weft-faced effect. In this case a number of colors may be combined in the figure; the pattern is, however, distorted on the wrong side of the fabric when the weaving is done in this manner. When woven in the traditional form of two "fifty-fifty" tabby fabrics, one side of the piece is as handsome as the other, the design appearing in dark on a light ground on one side and in light on a dark ground on the reverse.

On the set-up as shown on the diagram: to weave a dark fabric on top and a light-colored fabric below, treadle as follows when using tie-up (a–1) and a counterbalanced loom:

>   Treadles 5 and 1, together—weave dark
>   Treadles 5 and 2, together—weave dark
>   Treadle 3—weave light
>   Treadle 4—weave light
>   Repeat as required.

To weave the light-colored fabric above and the dark fabric below using tie-up (a–1) weave as follows:

>   Treadles 6 and 3 together—weave light
>   Treadles 6 and 4 together—weave light
>   Treadle 1—weave dark
>   Treadle 2—weave dark
>   Repeat.

On a rising shed loom and tie-up (a–2) weave as follows—for the dark fabric above and the light-colored fabric below:

>   Treadle 1—weave dark
>   Treadle 2—weave dark
>   Treadles 5 and 3 together—weave light
>   Treadles 5 and 4 together—weave light
>   Repeat.

For a light fabric above and a dark fabric below, weave:

>   Treadle 3, light
>   Treadle 4, light
>   Treadles 6 and 1 together—weave dark
>   Treadles 6 and 2 together—weave dark
>   Repeat.

Diagram 65 (153)

The figures of the pattern may be woven in the dark fabric against a light background, or in light against a dark background. Most people, however, find it easier to weave the figure as shown in the drawings—dark on light.

Extremely free design may be used in this weave, the only cautions being not to use a pattern made up entirely of very small blocks as these tend to have a "fussy" effect, and not to leave very large plain spaces as, unless tied together with reasonable frequency, the two fabrics—which are entirely separate throughout—will tend to bag under use.

It is usually desirable to begin with a heading in plain weaving with the dark fabric on top, followed by at least one repeat with the light fabric on top.

To weave a pattern begin by treadling on 5—either tie-up—which raises all the dark part of the warp, and take up the desired figure on a narrow pick-up stick. Allow two of the raised threads to each unit of the weave or each space of the squared paper. Treadle 3 and weave a shot of light weft. Treadle 4 and weave a second shot of light weft. These shots, of course, weave across the background. Take out the stick and treadle 6 which raises all the light part of the warp, and take up on the pick-up stick all the background areas, omitting, however, the first and last threads in each group. Treadle 1 and weave dark; treadle 2 and weave dark.

These four weft shots constitute a single unit of the weave.

It is impossible to beat in the ordinary manner between the two shots of each color, because of the pick-up stick in the warp. To get a good beat use a flat poke-shuttle and with the shuttle in the shed beat against it. This weave tends to narrow in, and ample allowance for take-up should be made when the weft shot is thrown. Some weavers use a template, but this is not necessary.

In Mexico the double-plain weave is used chiefly for bags, woven in cotton in white and black. Many of the ancient Peruvian pieces are long strips or runners, of unknown use.

Most of the patterns given with this section may also be produced in other pick-up weaves—the summer-and-winter pick-up for instance, and the damask and double twill pick-ups. The patterns have been selected to provide as much variety as possible, all drawn from native American sources. Scandinavian patterns may be found in the Swedish weaving books, and practically any figure

310 —

Variations of the "Earth and Sky" Motif from various sources — Peruvian, Mexican, Indian, etc. Also a Moon and Stars.

Pre-Inca sky figures — "Moon-House" above, Stars below. From Tiahuanaco, Bolivia

Patterns for Pick-Up Weaving

Diagram 66 (154)

one desires may be adapted to the purpose by drawing it on squared paper. Patterns in which horizontal and perpendicular lines predominate, and those with a diagonal effect are as a rule the most satisfactory. Circles and curved lines in general present some difficulties.

The "Earth and Sky" figure, shown on Diagram 66, in a few of its many forms, is probably one of the most ancient decorative motifs in the world. It appears in the carvings, the pottery and the textiles of all the Americas from prehistoric times down to the present. How far it goes back in time no one can say with certainty but, according to authorities, long before fifteen thousand B. C. And it is as new as the piece of work on my loom today. There is, I think, an extraordinary pleasure in using again a decoration and a symbol that has given beauty and meaning to the work of human hands down through the ages. It is a curiously satisfying design and lends distinction to almost anything one wishes to make. It answers, no doubt, to something fundamental in the human nervous system. The Greek fret and the Chinese fret are similar, but to me the American figure is handsomer, with its solid base of steps. To me it stands for America as a whole.

(c) A weave we know as the "One-Skip" pick-up may be woven on any Bronson II threading. It is given here rather than in the previous section because, as far as I know, it is found only in textiles from Guatemala. It is a very simple weave, but highly effective for borders in hangings, for table mats and bags, and similar things. It is not a weave for rugs.

The weave is used in two differnt ways: In the first manner the background is made up of short skips with the figure in plain tabby. It is used in the second manner for small detached figures, with somewhat the appearance of Swedish "dukagang," though usually woven right side up.

Nothing very elaborate in the way of pattern can be produced by the first method. Arrangements of diamond figures, diagonals and so on are best. Much more freedom of design is possible in the second method. Both methods are shown on Diagram 67.

The warp for this weave should be set as for tabby and two weft materials are required—a tabby weft like the warp and a pattern weft in color, in a coarser and softer material.

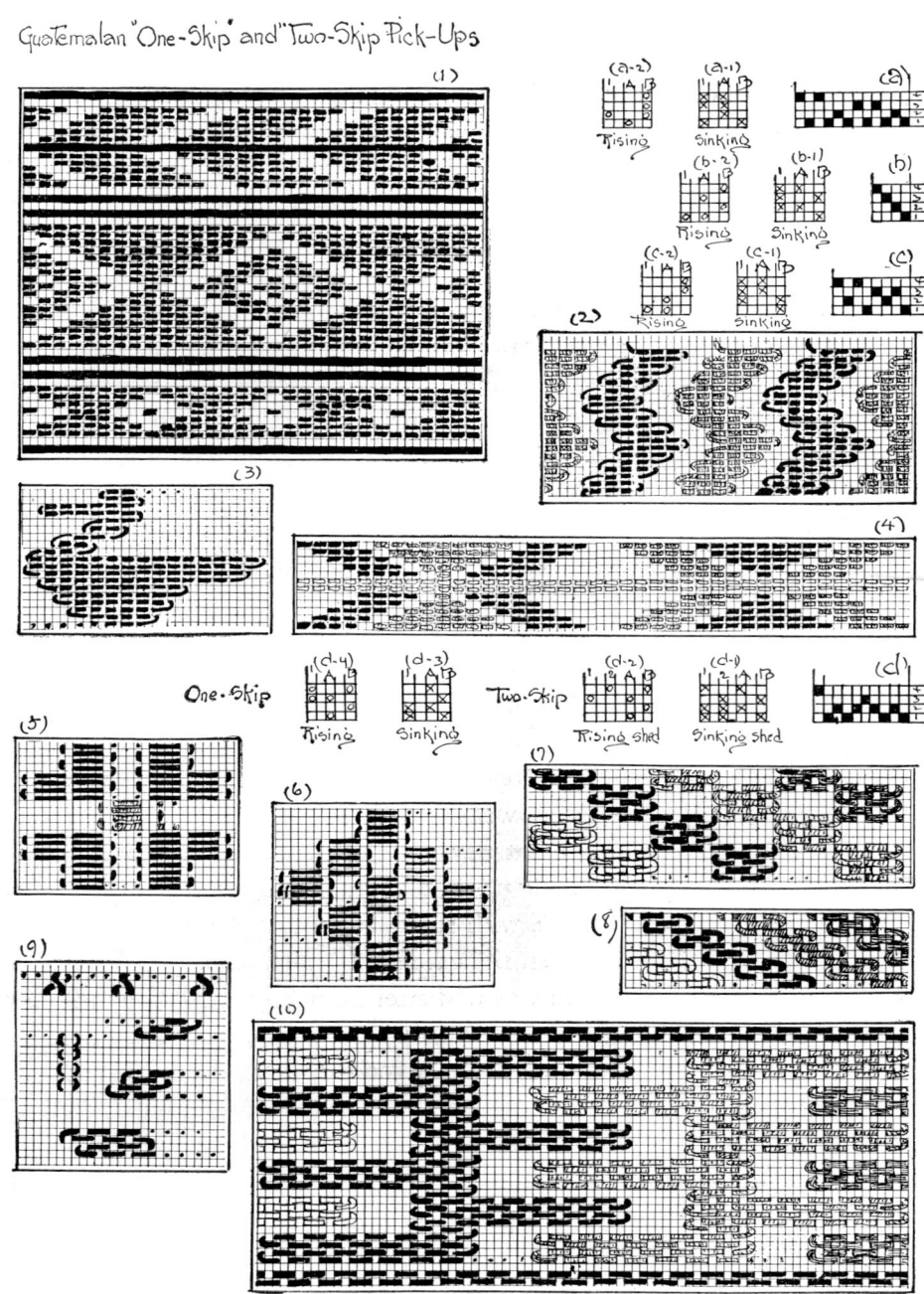

Diagram 67 (155)

To weave in the first manner, treadle on 1, which raises every sixth thread all across, leaving the rest of the warp in little groups of five threads. Slip one of the wide pick-up sticks under all the raised threads except where the figure is to appear. Here pick up the under part of the warp as required, never, however, picking up more than three adjoining groups, as to do so makes long skips on the under side and weakens the fabric unduly.

When the pick-up has been made, set the stick on edge to make a shed and weave a shot of pattern weft. Take out the stick and weave tabby A, tabby B. This is the complete process.

Note that at least two of the raised threads should be left at either edge and the pick-ups should not be carried beyond this point.

If a shorter skip and a finer effect is desired, either the twill threading or a summer-and-winter weave threading may be used for this weave, as shown at (b) and (c), Diagram 66. The threading at (d) used for the two-skip technique, may also be used for one-skip weaving if desired, as shown on the diagram.

Pattern No. (1) as shown on the diagram illustrates a few of the simple effects in one-skip weaving when woven all across in the first manner. The pattern at (4) shows detached figures in the second manner, the pattern weft being taken back and forth across a limited part of the warp, separate strands of weft being required for each part of the figure. The pattern weft is not carried on shuttles but is merely inserted with the fingers. In this pattern the ends are kept underneath the web and the effect is somewhat like Swedish "dukagang." In patterns (2) and (3) the pattern ends are kept on top, giving a less tidy but not unpleasing effect.

(d) The "Two-Skip" weave is similar to the weave above but usually woven in a more free-and-easy and dashing manner, with longer skips. It is a good weave for draperies, bags and so on. It should be carried out with a great deal of quite violent color—each feature of the design in a different shade.

In this weave the pattern weft is not carried on shuttles, as a different strand is required for each part of the pattern, and it is very easy to insert it where desired with the fingers. A single tabby shot is woven between pattern shots in this weave and the pattern weft is beaten close.

Of the figures shown under (d), Diagram 67, 5 and 6 are in a one-skip technique but require a fairly long skip to be effective. They may be woven on threading (d) with tie-up (d–1) or (d–2), using only treadle 1 for the pick-up; (7), and (8) are handsome when woven in many colors, as is also (10). When several successive borders of different types are woven in the same piece—a common practise in this weave—the same colors, arranged in the same order, should be used in each border. However, if the figures are approximately of the same width the same colors should not be put directly over each other but shifted slightly to the right or left, so that when seen from a distance the piece has the effect of diagonal bands of color. This is a prominent characteristic of Guatemalan weaving.

The small detached figures shown at (9) are used to enliven areas of plain weaving and are highly effective. They appear in many different forms, of which only a few can be shown here. The manner of producing them is clear enough on the diagram—except perhaps for the top row. These little remarks—I know no other name for them—are produced as follows: After weaving a tabby shot and with the shed still open, take a bit of pattern weft under one of the raised threads. Weave four or six shots of tabby. Cross the two ends of pattern material and turn each end back through a tabby shed. If made close together the ends of adjoining "remarks" may be permitted to meet, making a line of colored tabby all across. Or these little knots may be set farther apart, each on its own. The colors used should be the same as those in the main part of the weaving, arranged in the same order.

The Guatemalan method of anchoring the pattern weft at the beginning and end of a figure is worthy of note. Instead of turning the ends back into a pattern shed to conceal them they are simply taken under a few warp ends in a tabby shed as sketched on the diagram. This free and easy practise has the advantage of being rapid and practical, and the trails of little colored dots actually add interest to the effect.

(e) An interesting native weave—not a pick-up—may be produced on a simple four-harness threading in summer-and-winter weave. It is used in Totónicapán, Guatemala, for the aprons that are a part of the women's costume of that place—and as far as I know, nowhere else. The aprons are woven on a dark blue warp and tabby, with the figures in various bright colors, with white. Of course a different color may be used for the warp if preferred.

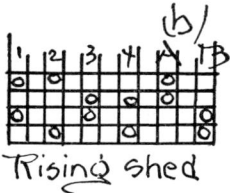
Rising shed

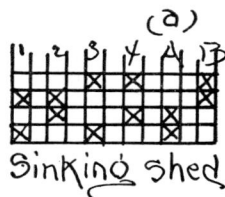
Sinking shed

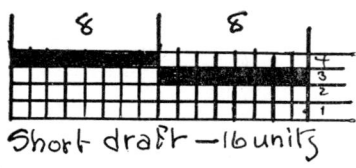
Short draft —16 units

Thread in summer-and-winter weave as above—eight **units** of 1, 3, 2, 3 and eight units of 1, 4, 2, 4, with the tie-up as given.

The main figure of the piece is woven as follows:

> 8 tabby shots in black and treadle A and B
> Treadle 1, white; 3, black; 2, white; 4, black—repeated 6 times
> Treadles 1, 2, 3, 4 in black
> Treadle 1, black; 3, white; 2, black; 4, white—repeated 6 times
> In tabby, on A and B, 4 shots in green; two shots in black—repeated 3 times;
>   4 shots in green
> Treadles 1, 2, 3, 4 in black
> Treadle 1, black; 3, white; 2, black; 4, white—6 times
> Treadles 1, 2, 3, 4 black
> Treadle 1, white; 3, black; 2, white; 4, black—6 times
> 8 tabby shots in black

A narrow band is woven:

> 2 shots of tabby in black
> Treadle 2, white; 4 shots of tabby in black
> Treadle 2, white; 2 shots of tabby in black
> Treadle 4, orange; 4 shots of tabby in black
> Treadle 4, orange; 2 shots of tabby in black

Another narrow stripe is woven:

> Treadles 1, 2, 3, 4—one shot each—four times in red; twice in orange; twice in red; twice in orange; four times in red.

These bands of pattern weaving, separated by tabby bands in several different colors, produce a very lively and interesting effect that is not in the least like our traditional summer-and-winter weave. When done in fine materials the effect is charming, and may be used for aprons, blouses, scarves in fine wool and for bags.

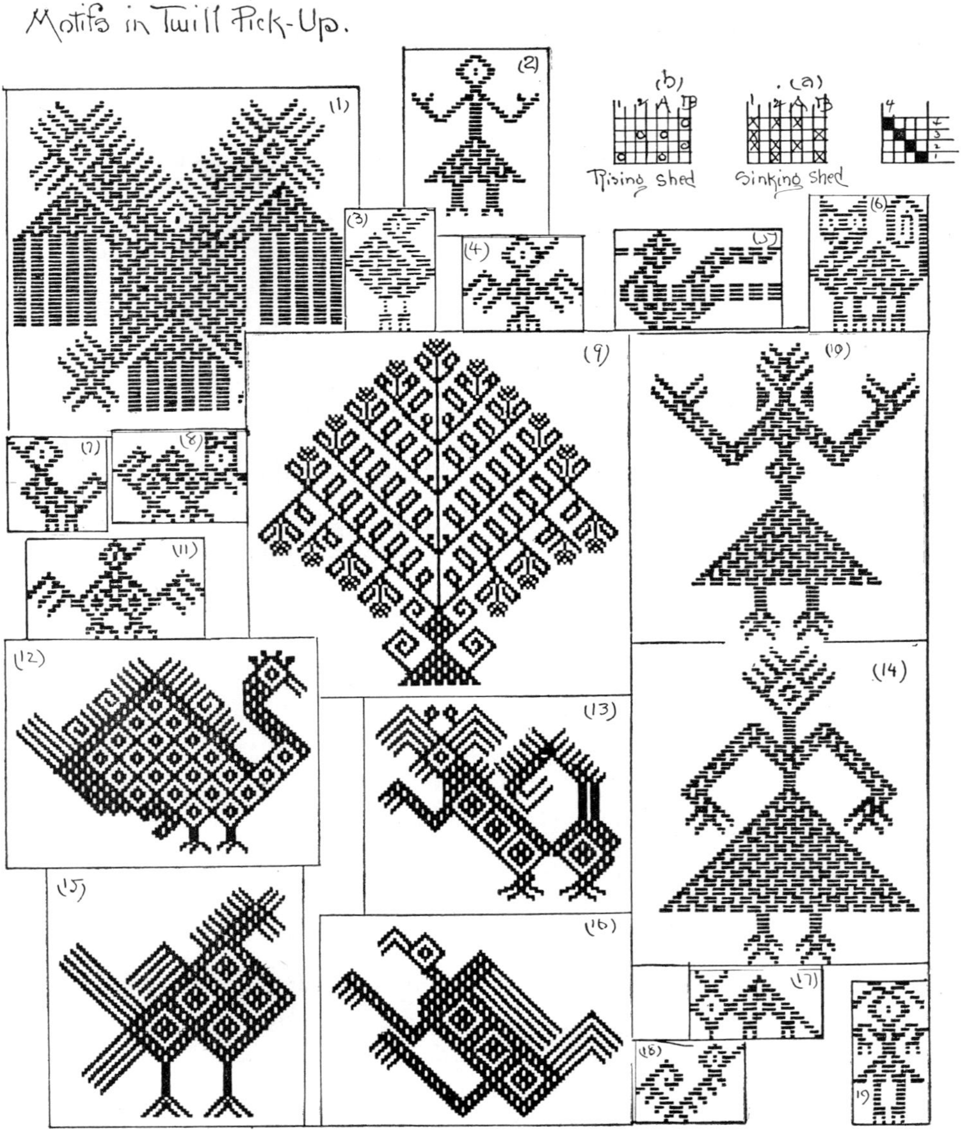

316 —

Motifs in Twill Pick-Up.

Diagram 68 (156)

(f) A weave much used in Guatemala for detached figures may be produced on a twill threading. In structure—oddly enough—it resembles a Russian weave used for linens, though of course in entirely different figures and with a different effect. The resemblance is no doubt purely accidental.

In the Guatemalan pieces the warp is usually of a very fine white or red cotton, or on a warp set in stripes of color, threaded double and set close. Threading and tie-up are as given on Diagram 68. The figures may be woven wrong side up but most people prefer weaving right side up in order to see what they are doing, and though it is somewhat of a nuisance to keep the ends of the pattern weft under the web, it is not too difficult. The pattern weft is carried back and forth over the figures only, and is not as a rule carried on a shuttle, though for large figures a small belt-shuttle is useful. The pick-up may be made with short sticks going across only the figures.

In one part of Guatemala these figures are often woven in a puffy effect that is rich and handsome. It may be produced as follows: allow the pattern weft to lie very loose in the shed. After a shot on treadle 1, treadle tabby B and insert a narrow pick-up stick and set it on edge close to the edge of the web. It will raise the pattern material in little loops. Take out the stick and weave the tabby shot. After the pick-up on treadle 2, treadle the A tabby and insert the stick, setting it on edge as before. Take out the stick and weave the tabby shot.

Figures woven in this manner make lively decorations for the corners of table mats, and may be used in many other ways.

(g) The techniques so far described have been of the "fifty-fifty" types of weaving or in weft-faced effects. A great deal of native weaving, however, is of the warp-faced type. No doubt the great difficulty in making the sheds on the prehistoric body-loom makes it easier to put the decoration into the warp rather than into the weft. With us the warping is the least interesting and often the most troublesome part of the textile process, so that we tend toward the weft-faced weaves. However, with a sectional warp-beam and an adequate creel, it is simple enough to warp as many ends to the inch as may be desired. Since in these weaves the warp is set close and the weft is comparatively coarse, with fewer weft-shots to the inch than in weft-faced weaving, the work goes

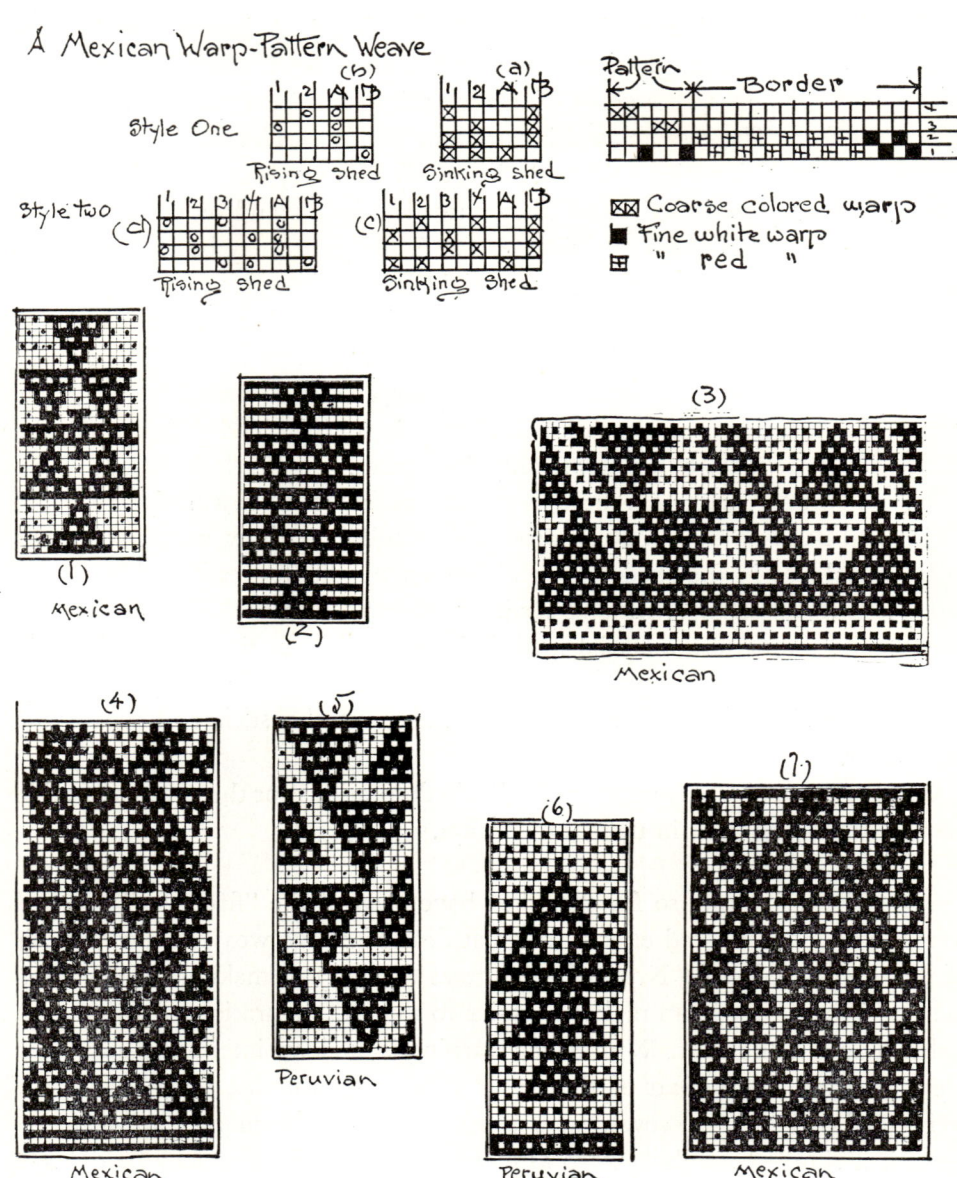

Diagram 69 (157)

rapidly. Many of the warp-faced weaves are very handsome and also practical for many purposes, and weavers who are unfamiliar with warp-faced weaving will find it interesting to adventure among them.

One of the best of the warp-faced weaves, in my opinion, is a Mexican technique often seen in belts and girdles but entirely practical in any width desired on an ordinary treadle loom. The effect is somewhat like summer-and-winter weave in warp-face except that the background has a different texture. This weave is useful for upholstery, for bags, mats, pillow-tops and many other things. The Mexican pieces are usually woven in a coarse dark blue cotton for pattern over a fine white foundation, and usually with a close-set border in red. But of course any colors may be used. Bold geometric designs in which horizontal and diagonal lines predominate are usually the most successful, but designs of birds, beasts, flowers and human figures are also possible, as shown in illustration (158).

Thread as shown on Diagram 69. Without the border the weave may, if desired, be put on three harnesses, but on a counterbalanced loom it is better to include all four harnesses in the tie-up to preserve the balance. As both the background and the pattern warp interweave with the weft, both materials may be warped at the same time. However, if a very long warp is planned it might be advisable to warp them to separate beams.

The warp for this weave should not be set as close as for most warp-faced weaves. If a 10/2 cotton is used for the fine part of the warp and double ends of soft-twist six-strand 20/6 cotton for the pattern, a 15-dent reed sleyed with one white thread and two colored threads to the dent will give a satisfactory effect. The weft should be the same color as the fine warp—usually white—but in a somewhat coarser thread.

The weave may be produced in two different ways as illustrated by figures (1) and (2) on the diagram. The Mexican weave, in figure (1) and in all the other figures illustrated except (2), is the handsomer, due to the interesting texture of the background. Unfortunately this cannot be clearly shown on the drawing. The weave as shown in figure (2) is found in Peruvian, Bolivian and Guatemalan textiles. These weaves are often used in belt-making, and sometimes for bands of pattern weaving set between bands of close-set fine warp in stripes of color, threaded as for the border. Bolivian and Peruvian bags are

(158) Mexican warp pick-up weave.

frequently made in this manner. The pattern weaving may, however, be full width of the piece. These are excellent fabrics for upholstery.

The tie-ups at (a) and (b) are for the Bolivian weave. To weave pattern (2), weave as follows:

Treadle and weave A

Treadle 1, and with a narrow pick-up stick take up four double threads where the figures are to be. Treadle B and weave. Take out the stick. Treadle and weave A. Treadle 2 and make the second pick-up, taking up three threads above the first pick-up. Treadle B and weave. And so continue.

The Mexican technique is similar though a little more complicated. For the plain background effect as at the bottom of figure (3) treadle and weave: B, 1, B, 2 and repeat—using tie-up (c) or (d). For the solid effect all across treadle and weave: A, 3, A, 4 and repeat.

For the figure as at (1) after weaving treadle B, treadle on 1 and pick up four pairs of colored threads where the figure is to appear. Treadle 2 and weave. Treadle B and weave. Take out the stick; treadle 2 and make the second pick-up—of three pairs of pattern threads above the first pick-up. Treadle 1 and weave; treadle B and weave. Continue in this manner as far as the center. All pyramidal figures such as (5) and (6) should be woven in the same manner. For V-shaped figures, such as the upper part of pattern (1), reverse the process: after weaving A all across, weave treadle 1. With the shed still open pick up a single thread as required by the figure. Treadle B and weave. Treadle 2 and weave. With the shed still open make the second pick-up. Treadle B and weave. Treadle 1 and weave. And so continue.

It will be noted that when weaving slanted lines as patterns (3) and (7) the edges are clear on one side and feathered on the other. This may or may not add to the effect but it is a part of the structure of the weave. In pattern (3), when woven in the first treadling the pyramids will have clear edges and the inverted figures will be feathered.

(h) An interesting warp pick-up weave—Mexican—is shown on illustration (159) and on Diagram 70. A similar weave, used for belt-making only, as far as I know, is also found among Peruvian textiles. The foundation warp for

(159) Mexican runner in two-warp pick-up—blue and white.

this weave is ordinarily a fine white cotton, threaded double or triple and set close, with a pattern warp in coarse colored cotton or wool.

The pattern warp and the foundation warp do not interweave, the pattern ends making skips over or under the foundation fabric. For this reason there is less take-up in the pattern warp than in the foundation warp, and if the loom used is equipped with two warp-beams it is advisable to warp the two materials separately. However, unless a very long warp is planned, the two materials may be warped together to the same beam, and the slack in the pattern warp—when it develops and becomes troublesome—may be controlled in the following manner: use treadle 1, which raises all the pattern warp, and insert a stout stick under the raised ends, behind the heddles. Take this stick back over the slab-stock and down to a point under the warp-beam. Attach it to the bottom member of the loom frame by cords and snitch-knots. By drawing up the knots from time to time the slack may be taken out of the pattern warp. This is a makeshift but an entirely practical one. The method cannot be used for the making of two-warp rugs because the wastage would be too great and also because the tension on the stuffer warp is too heavy.

In the piece shown in the illustration the foundation warp is a very fine cotton set at seventy-four ends to the inch and threaded triple: 1, 1, 1, 2, 2, 2 and so on. A 20/2 cotton threaded double at a setting of forty-eight ends to the inch would give a similar effect.

In the piece shown in the illustration the pattern warp is in an extremely coarse, hard-twisted cotton in blue. The pattern shown on the diagram is from a piece in which the pattern warp is in coarse wool in the colors indicated. Of course any other colors might be used.

All the pattern ends might be threaded on harness 3 if preferred, but the threading as given is advisable. Some of the figures may be woven on this threading using treadles 2 and 3, though most of the pattern must be picked up on treadle 1—which raises all the pattern warp.

Weft for this weave should be in the color of the foundation warp—usually white—but a good deal coarser. How much coarser is a matter of taste.

The method of weaving is extremely simple: alternate treadles A and B as desired for a plain-weave heading. Then treadle on 1 and insert a narrow pick-up stick under the raised pattern warp. Weave A, B, A, B, under the

324—

A Mexican two-Warp Pick-Up.

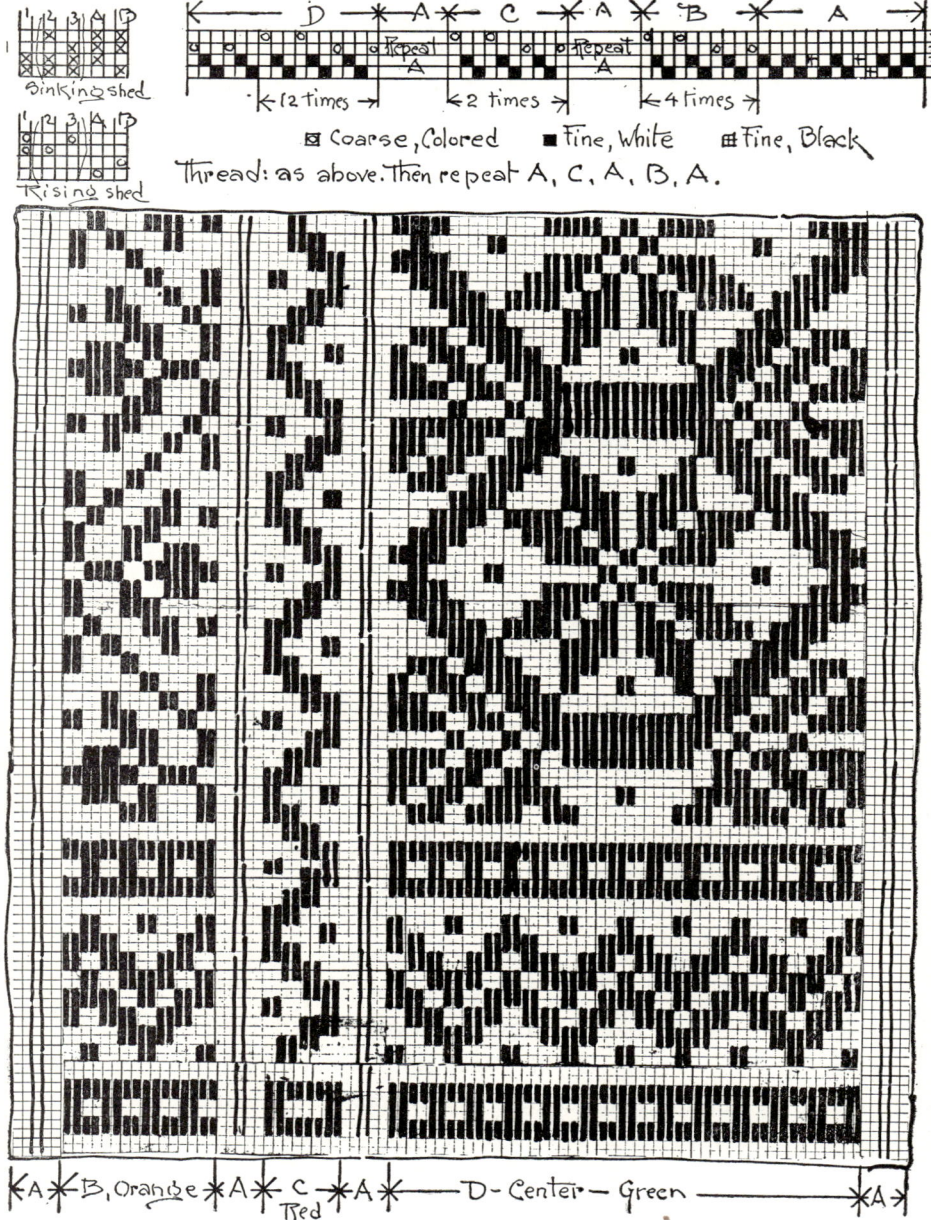

Diagram 70 (160)

stick. As it is impossible to beat in the ordinary manner with the pick-up stick in place, weave with a flat "poke-shuttle" and, leaving the shuttle in the shed before taking it through, beat against the shuttle.

For the second row of the border, as shown on the diagram, treadle on 2 and insert the pick-up stick. Or treadle on 1 and take up on the stick alternate pairs of pattern warp. Weave A, B, A, B, under the stick as before.

If the pattern threads tend to cling together, giving unwanted dots of color in the background, proceed as follows: after making the pick-up raise all the foundation threads. This may be done on tie-up (b) by treadling A and B together. On tie-up (a) another treadle must be added, tied to sink harnesses 3 and 4. Insert a second pick-up stick under the foundation threads and the pick-up and over the pattern threads not taken up on the stick. However, if the tension of the pattern warp is preserved this is usually unnecessary.

Very free design is possible in this weave, but no very large areas of plain background should be included in the pattern as the long skips of pattern warp left on the under side of the foundation weaken the fabric unduly.

This is a bold and effective weave, handsome for runners such as the Mexican piece illustrated, for wall-hangings and draperies—if only one side is to be in evidence—for pillow-tops and similar projects. It is, of course, not a weave for rugs, upholstery or linens.

(i) The Mexican and Peruvian gauze weaves are the pick-up version of the cross weave. They are simple and quite easy and can be used in a variety of ways. Most of them are made on a tabby set-up though for one of the Peruvian weaves described below a four-harness leno set-up is more convenient.

A narrow pick-up stick may be used for the pick-up, though a large, blunt crochet hook with a long handle is a more convenient tool. The shank must be long enough to go all across the warp.

The various forms of the weave are based on two simple pick-ups as shown on Diagram 71—a one-and-one pick-up and a two-and-two pick-up. For the one-and-one effect, open the A tabby shed, which raises the outside thread on the right. Take the hook or stick under the first two bottom threads and draw them toward the right; then take the hook over the first of the threads in the

Picked-Up Leno Lace-Weaves

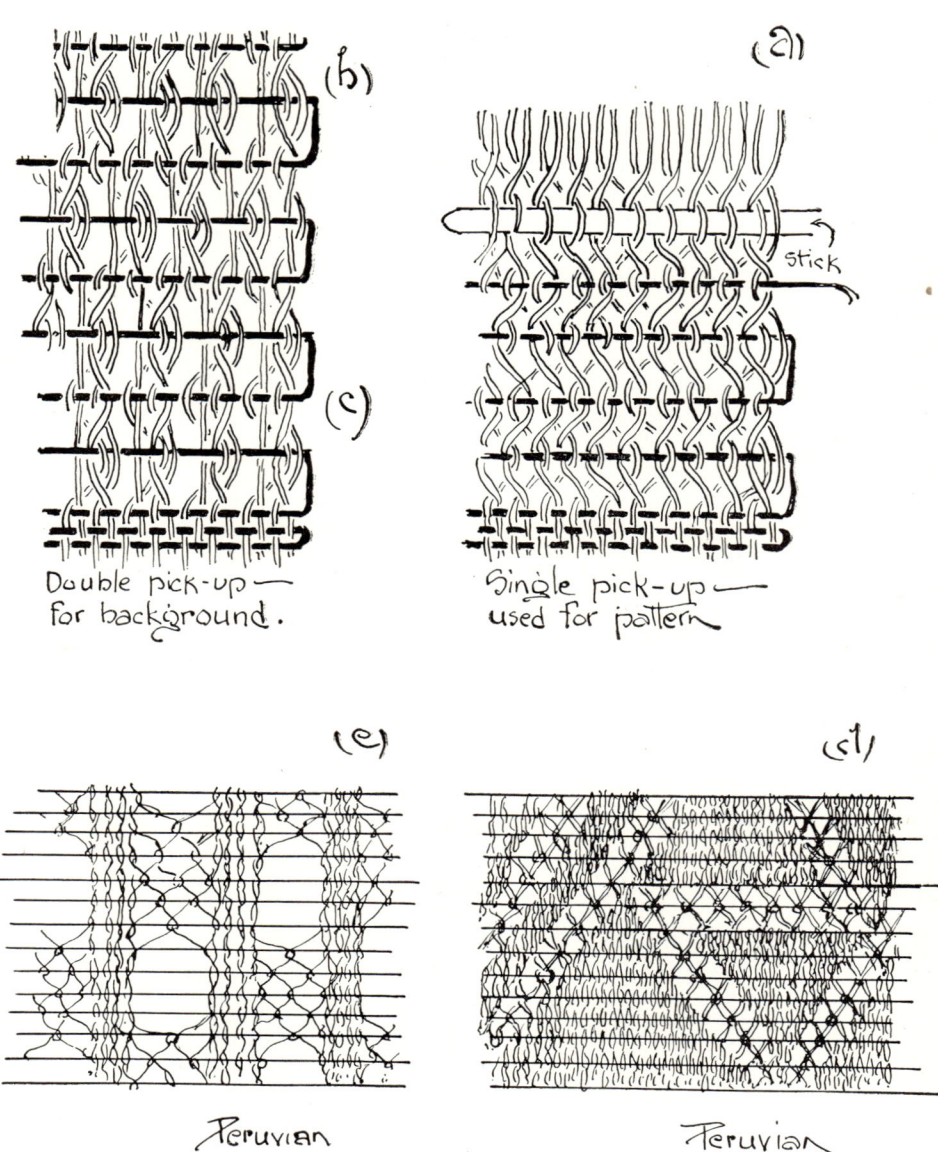

Diagram 71 (161)

top shed. After this take up one from the bottom and go over one of the top threads all across.

When the pick-up has been made insert a narrow shed-stick through the shed made by the hook; set the shed-stick on edge and weave a shot of weft—usually in material like the warp. Take out the stick; treadle B and weave. Treadle A and make a second pick-up like the first. Simply continue in this manner as desired: treadle A and make the pick-up; weave; treadle B and weave; repeat.

For the two-and-two effect treadle A as before; take the stick under the first two threads of the bottom of the shed and draw them to the right as before, but take the hook over the two upper threads. Continue by picking up two from the lower part of the shed and going over two of the upper part of the shed, all across. Weave. Treadle B and weave. Repeat as desired. This produces a square mesh. For a handsome diamond-shaped mesh, pick up and weave as above for the first row of crosses. For the next row, pick up one and go over one; then continue two and two all across. Weave the two rows alternately.

Most of the patterns are produced by using the two-two pick-up as the background, with figures in the one-and-one effect. However, in the figure sketched at (d) on the diagram the main part of the weave is in the one-and-one pick-up with diagonal lines in the two-and-two effect.

For a Peruvian form of the weave that has the effect of eyelets in a solid fabric, weave B, A, B. Then with the A shed open, take a pick-up stick through the shed taking up a two-two cross where an eyelet is desired. Set the stick on edge and weave. Weave B, A, B and on A make a pick-up for the second row of eyelets, and so continue. This weave is effective for table pieces and for scarves in fine wool.

Patterns in these weaves may be anything one chooses. It is suggested, however, that simple figures are more effective than those with much fine detail, and patterns built on diagonal and horizontal lines are particularly handsome.

The lace-weaves tend to narrow in a great deal and when areas of lace-weaving are introduced as decoration or as borders for a plain-weave fabric it may be necessary to use a template. This may be made of a narrow, flat strip of wood with a pair of small brads at either end, projecting just enough to catch the edges of the web. One may use the template on top of the web—

where it is somewhat awkward to weave over—or under the web if preferred. Either way, a template is something of a nuisance and is rarely necessary, but required at times. If the whole piece is in lace-weave the narrowing in makes no great difference if due allowance has been made for it in setting up the warp.

For some patterns, as for instance for the Peruvian effect sketched at (e) on the diagram, a plain leno set-up may be used. Weave the cross-shed with the treadles, and where the pattern is desired make the appropriate pick-up on the return B shed.

The above are merely a selection from the many fascinating weaves that may be produced with the pick-up stick. They will, however, give an idea of the diversity and practically unlimited possibilities of these forms of weaving.

Chapter Twenty: Finishes

The proper finishing of a hand-woven fabric or piece of weaving is of prime importance, and is sometimes neglected—with unhappy results. The finish of certain fabrics—linens, all-wool fabrics and so on—has already been discussed in previous chapters. Overshot pieces with a cotton base and a pattern in wool usually require no finish other than the clipping of loose ends, the mending of broken warp-ends and so on. The finish of a fabric made up of several kinds of yarn in both warp and weft is apt to present a special problem that can be solved only by experiment and experience.

Hand-woven fabrics for clothing require special tailoring. If such fabrics are made up at home it is well to draw the pattern on the cloth with chalk or crayon and to stitch on the machine on either side of the lines before cutting. The stitching holds the fabric in shape and prevents ravelling. Unless properly made up, a hand-woven dress or suit may prove a disappointment.

Hand-woven bags require expert mounting. No matter how handsome the piece of weaving, if the thing is made up in a clumsy "home-made" manner it will be a failure. Elaborate commercial bag-mountings, however, are inappropriate. The shape and style of a bag is a matter of the fashion of the moment, and nothing very useful can be said here on the subject. But a bag should never be dowdy or clumsy. It must be smart and handsome or there is little sense in making it at all.

The question of fringes is also largely a matter of fashion. There are years when everything drips with fringes and there are years when everything is severely hemmed or bound and fringes are taboo. But of course those who weave for their own satisfaction may fringe or hem as taste suggests.

Many of the old coverlets were fringed, as for instance the one shown in illustration (17) where the fringes serve as a border. And almost all the old white cotton counterpanes were finished with knotted fringes—sometimes quite elaborate.

Many native pieces are woven with a selvage on all four sides. This is something that may be done on a prehistoric loom but not on a modern hand-loom. Pieces from Peru and Bolivia are almost always finished with a narrow braid on all four sides. This braid has a leno structure and is almost always made with a little diamond pattern. It may be woven on some sort of loom, but more likely the sheds are picked up by the fingers. The oddest thing about this finish is that the weft thread that weaves the braid also goes through the fabric and must be carried on a needle instead of a shuttle. This braid makes a tidy and practical finish and could be simulated by narrow tapes in card weaving or woven on the "inkle" loom.

Many Mexican bags are finished at the top with elaborate double braiding, as are also many Peruvian bags. Many Indian pieces—girdles and runners and so on—are finished with very long braided fringes.

Many of the ancient Peruvian pieces are finished with an odd fringe composed of woven tabs an inch or so wide. As this finish is not very handsome and is troublesome to make, specific directions will not be given.

I Woven Finishes

Fringes woven across the ends of coverlets are fairly common and quite easy to make. The one shown in illustration (17) is typical: following a woven pattern block of the main pattern there is a row of leno, probably picked up with the fingers or with a coarse crochet hook, as described in chapter nineteen.

In this particular piece eight shots of pattern weft are then woven, one shot on each of the pattern sheds in twill succession, followed by a few shots of tabby and a second leno band followed by another narrow stripe in pattern weaving. The fringes do not appear to be tied but were probably finished with needlework in hem-stitch.

To carry this fringe along the sides it would be necessary to weave a number of similar bands with headings in tabby, that would then be hemmed to the fabric and pieced together as required.

Fringes may be woven lengthwise on the loom as shown at (a) on diagram 72. Two narrow warps for the headings should be set at a distance apart equal to twice the desired length of fringes. Weave each heading with a separate shuttle carrying tabby thread, and weave the fringe material all across on a third shuttle. When woven, cut through the center as indicated.

At one time tea-napkins, table mats and similar pieces were made with fringes on all four sides. This rather unpleasant fashion may return. To produce the effect, set the warp for the mat in the center of a wide loom, and on either side at a suitable distance set four threads to hold the fringe. Weave all across. After weaving, the extra warp threads must, of course, be drawn out, and the edges of the piece should be finished with needlework.

A fringed edge across the top and bottom of a piece will hold fairly well without knotting or needlework if woven in the Spanish stitch as follows: open a tabby shed and—beginning at the right hand side—take the shuttle under four threads. Change the shed and weave back to the edge. Change the shed and weave toward the left under eight threads. Change the shed and weave back under four threads. Continue in this manner all across—forward under eight, back under four. This is a good way to make the edge of a fine wool scarf, when a fringe is desired.

II Knotted and Braided Fringes

For some pieces long braided fringes done in the Indian manner are very handsome. The braid oftenest used is illustrated on the diagram at (c). It is a four-strand braid and is most effective when made in two colors—two strands of each color. To make it, hold the two strands of one color in the right hand and the two strands of the second color in the left. Take the upper strand on the right under the braid, up between the two strands on the left and back to the right. Take the upper strand on the left behind, up between the two strands on the right and back to the left. This braid may be made as rapidly as an ordinary three-strand braid and is handsomer. Note that the two strands of the first color remain throughout in the right hand and the other two strands in the left. The colors never change sides.

Most of the old counterpanes, as noted above, are finished with knotted

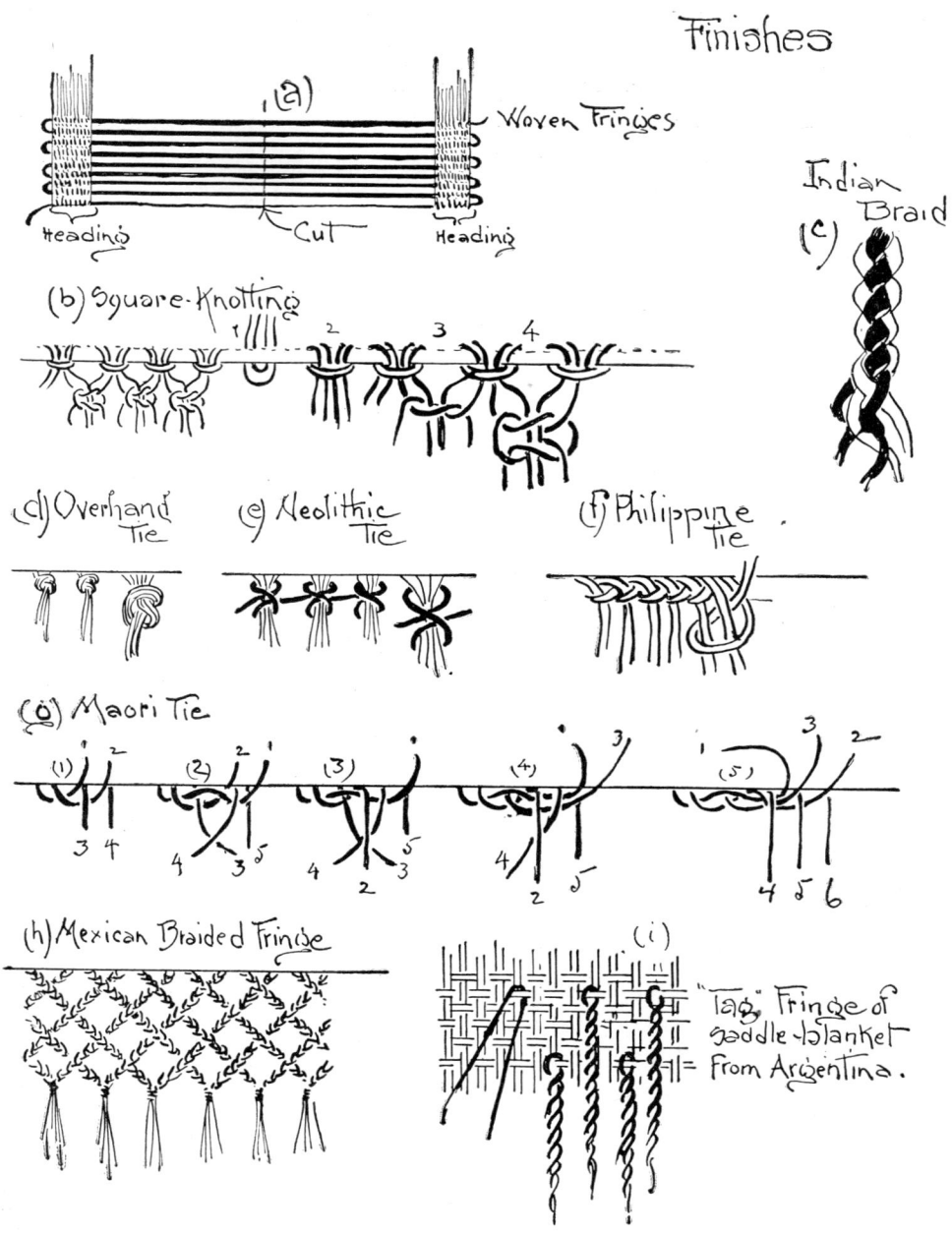

Diagram 72 (162)

fringes. The warp in such a piece is too fine to be used in knotting so these pieces are hemmed across the top and bottom and strands of material are drawn through the fabric above the hem, as shown at (1) on the drawing at (b) on the diagram. The knot ordinarily used is the "Solomon Knot," sometimes called the "Sword-hilt Knot," and used in most macramé work. Sailors call this "square-knotting." Many of these fringes are tied in elaborate macramé patterns, for which see any good book on knotting. The material used, however, is not a cord as in ordinary macramé but a strand of many ends of fine cotton. The knot may be tied in one movement but is then difficult to draw up evenly and—especially in soft material—it is advisable to make it in two ties as indicated on the sketch.

The knot oftenest used in tying the fringes of rugs is the single overhand tie shown at (d) on the diagram. This is perhaps the poorest of the possible finishes as it is lumpy and it is somewhat difficult to tie it evenly and close enough to the edge of the web. The ties at (e) and (f) will be found more satisfactory.

If the warp is rather sparse, as in a rug over a warp set at twelve ends to the inch, the Neolithic tie is best. This, as shown on the diagram, consists of two half hitches tied with a separate strand, over a group of warp-ends. This tying strand should consist of about three ends of carpet warp and should be as long as four times the width of the rug. Begin at the left hand side of the piece and make the ties as shown. This tie may be made on the loom. If the piece is off the loom, instead of making the tie with the long strand and pulling it through, make a turn around the thumb of the left hand with the tying strand and draw the fringe ends through. Care must be taken not to draw up the edge of the rug, but to pull the knots tight.

This is a useful tie for many things other than rugs. It makes a neat and practical finish and is not lumpy.

If the warp is close-set, as in two-warp rugs and warp-faced fabrics, a better tie is the Philippine tie shown at (f) on the diagram. The tie may be made with strands of two warp-ends, or three if preferred. For the tie as shown, beginning at the left, make the tie with the fifth and sixth ends over the first four. The tie is a simple half-hitch taken upward. Bring the fifth and sixth ends down; discard the first two ends, and tie over the remaining four ends with the seventh and eighth ends, and so continue. This tie makes a tidy little braid along the edge of the web. If desired it may be tied across both sides of the piece, using half the warp for the ties on one side and the other ends for the tie on the reverse.

If no hem is desired, and the material is so heavy and stiff that a hem is impractical—as in rugs made of jute—the Maori tie shown at (g) is the one to use. This tie should be made on the wrong side of the piece. The turned back warp-ends should be clipped, but not clipped too short, and a facing strip sewed over them.

The Mexican braided fringe shown at (h) is attractive but takes some time in the making. The warp-ends should be braided separately in small three-strand braids and these braids should then be interlaced as shown and each two fastened together with a knot or a lashing.

The odd fringe at (i) is useful for some pieces. It consists of separate strands of material taken around a weft-shot as shown on the diagram, and then twisted. Hard-twisted material should be used and to make the twist, untwist the ends and then allow them to twist together. This type of fringe, which should perhaps be considered a tag decoration rather than a fringe, may be carried around all four sides of a piece. It has an unusual and interesting effect.

There are, of course, many other ways to make fringes and to finish hand-woven pieces. Those described above are merely a selection, chosen because they are simple and practical. They add to the appearance of a woven article and so deserve a place in the hand-weaver's "bag of tricks."

Postscript

In reviewing what I have written it suddenly comes over me that this is a story of adventure. Each detail of procedure, each bit of ancient lore, each pattern, each special weave has behind it—for me—its own little history of difficulties and disappointments leading at last to the heart-warming thrill of achievement. Of those adventures that ended differently nothing need be said. If there were no failures the achievements would not be so precious.

There has been much burning of the midnight kilowatts and acres of cross-section paper have been blackened, and here—set down in what I have tried to make an orderly and useful form—is the result. It is little, I know, compared to the "unknown vast," but there is the challenge: so much lies ahead for the adventurer into this, one of the most ancient and still one of the newest arts of man.

With thanks to all the good weavers who have helped me along the way and with greetings to the latest new weaver, shuttle in hand, just opening the shed for the first weft-shot of a fine new fabric, here is THE END.

Index

	Page
Adjustments	95, 97
Allowance for wastage	54
American weaving, origins	2
Appreciation of pattern	72, 73, 78
Arranging, borders	136, 137
pattern for coverlet	137, 138, 139
"As drawn in," treadling	141, 142, 143
Battern	37
Bead Leno	274
Beaming, chained warp	86, 87
Beat	58, 105, 106
Blanket, double twill weave	257, 259
Blanket, Thomas	4
Bobbins, how to wind	105
Borders	44
Borders, arranging	136, 137
Bout	83
Braided finishes	331, 333, 334
Breast beam	32
Bronson or Spot weave, history	240
Lace weave	246
for linens	243
pick-up	298
one-skip pick-up	298
structure of weave	240, 241, 242
treadling	243
for upholstery	246
warp-setting	243
Calculations	52, 54
Capes of the loom	35
Cartwright, Dr.	10, 12, 13
Chained warp	85, 86
Choice of color	79, 81
material	47
pattern	78
weave	45, 46

	Page
Classification of patterns	151
Cloth beam	32
Cole, Thomas, of Reading	2
Colonial color schemes	81
patterns	74, 76
Weavers' Association	16
Color combinations	80
diagonal, Guatemalan	314
effects in the twill weave	117
Combinations of material	58
Corkscrew twills	117
Correcting bad color	81
faulty warp	87
errors in set-up	102, 103
Cotton, counts, calculations	52, 54
chenille	50
in Colonial times	47
qualities of	47, 48, 49, 50
roving, "rug filler"	50, 52
tabby	50
warp	6, 50
weft	52
Counterpanes	
dimity	199
finishes	202
honeycomb	199
huck	201, 202, 204
tufted	198, 199
Coverlet patterns	2
pattern names	149
Crackle weave	45, 205
Italian no-tabby	210
patterns	208, 210
structure	206
weaving	207, 210
Creel	39
Crepe	58
Cultural value of weaving	19

[337]

	Page
Damask	63, 248
English method	248
patterns	257
pick-up	297, 298
Decline of hand weaving	14, 15
Dampening warp	58, 63
Definitions	22
Design, books	72
modern	74
suggestions	78
traditional	76
Dornik	122
English	122
Doornock	6
Double plain weave	252
history	252, 255
"lost art"	255
materials	262
patterns	257, 258, 262
pick-up	305, 307, 309, 311
quilting	263, 264
tubing	256, 257
width	256, 257, 259
Double twill	247
pick-up	298
Doups	267
Drafts	87
Draft-writing	128, 129
Drawing-in	87, 88
hook	89
Draw loom	4
"Earth and Sky" motif	311
Eight-harness twills	119
overshot weave	95
Elaborate borders	140
English dornik	122
English Weavers' Guild	2
Factories, textile, first in England	2
first in U. S.	6
second in U. S.	6
William Penn's	6
Fifty-fifty weaves	46, 58
Finish	329
for linens	66
for wool fabrics	61
Finishes, braided and knotted	331, 333, 334
woven	330, 331
Folding frame loom	35
Frame of loom	35
Fringes	330, 331, 333

	Page
Fulling mill	6
Fustian	6
Gauze, see Leno	
Mexican	325
Peruvian	327
Granny knot	91
Guatemalan color diagonal	314
jaspé	111
method of anchoring ends	314
one-skip pick-up	311, 313
"remarks"	314
Totonicapan apron	315
two-harness rep pattern	111, 112
two-skip pick-up	313, 314
Guide, warping	83
Guilds	2
Habblethorne, Morgan	4
Half tone	126
Handle	22
Hand loomed	23
Hand woven	22
Hargreave's spinning Jenny	10
Harness	35
Harris yarn	55
Heddle frames	35
Heddles	35
Hemp	67
Homespun	54
Honeycomb weave	199, 201
Hook	89
Hound's Tooth	119
Huck, huckaback	202, 203, 204
Instruction	26
Interim weaving	15
Italian no-tabby, overshot weave	145
crackle weave	210
Jack loom	35
Jacquard	13
weaving	13, 14
Jaspé	30
Guatemalan	111
Jean	6
Jeans twill	115
Jute	67
Kay's patent	8
Knife, in sleying	89

	Page
Knots, granny	91
loop	94
snitch	94
square	91
tying-in knot	94
weavers'	92, 94
Lace-Bronson	246
Lamms	37
Lease	85
Leno weave	265
bead set-up	272, 274, 275
doup set-up	268, 269, 270
patterns	270, 272
release	272, 275
sleying	276
tapestry motifs	275
Lie of the weft	105
Linen, affinity with water	63
counts	65
finishing	66, 67
refractory quality	62
suitable weaves	45, 63, 67
types of	61
warp-dressing for	63
Linsey-Woolsey	56
Loom, counterbalanced	35
folding	35
frame	32
functions	32
jack	35
primitive	30
table	35
two-harness	32
Loop knot	94
Loose ends	107
Materials, choice of	47
for first weaving	42
Metallics	68
Mexican gauze weave	325, 326, 328
tabby pick-up	301, 304
warp pick-up I	317, 319, 321
warp pick-up II	321, 323
Miniature patterns	147
Modern weaving	18, 19
Ms and Os weave	204
Narrowing in	105
"Native" weaving	18
nine weaves	301–338
Navajo saddle blanket	282, 283, 284, 285

— *339*

	Page
Newbury, Jack of	2
No-tabby weave, Italian-Swedish	147
Italian	145
Notation	129
Occupational Therapy	19
One-skip pick-up	311
Opposites	127
Originality	27, 29, 30
Overshot weave	123
arranging—borders	135, 136
arranging coverlet	137, 138, 139, 140
draft from sample	134, 135
draft writing	128, 129
half-tone	126
notation	128, 129
rugs	11, 280, 281
structure	125, 126
uses	45
woven as drawn in	141, 142
woven rose-fashion	144
Pattern appreciation	72
blindness	72
choice of	72
misuse of	73, 74
Patterns, Colonial coverlet	74
modern	74
Penn, William, factory	6
Peruvian gauze	325, 327
tabby pick-up	304
Pick-up weaves, Bolivian	321, 322
Bronson lace	298
damask	297, 298
double plain	305, 307, 308, 309
gauze	325, 326, 328
Mexican warp-face I	317, 319, 321
Mexican warp-face II	321, 323
one-skip	311, 313
quilting	300
Summer-and-winter	295, 296
tabby	301, 303, 304
twill	317
two-skip	313, 314
two-warp	298, 300
Pierson, John	6
Pile weaves	282
Plain weave	109
Plastics	68
Queen's delight, coverlet	104
Quilted weave	300

	Page
Raddle	39, 86
Rag rugs	67, 278, 279
Ramie	67
Ratchets	32
Rayon	67
Reeds	37, 42
Release, leno	272
Releasing tension	58
"Remarks," Guatemalan	314
Rep, warp-faced	111, 112
weft-faced	113
Return twills	122
Revival of weaving	17, 18
Rising shed	95, 99
Rose-fashion	142, 144
Rose, "weaver"	15, 16, 17
Rug weaving	45, 277, 278
Rug techniques, Colonial	281
Navajo saddle-blanket	282, 284, 285
overshot	280, 281
pile	282
rag	278, 279
two-warp	289–298
Samples, importance of	147
Setting, warp	8, 69, 70, 71
Shedding mechanism	35
Shepherd's check	119
Shoes for weaving	103
Shuttles	39
Shuttle-race	37
Sinking shed	98, 99
Slab-stock	32
Sleying	8
Snitch knot	94
Soft-twist cotton	50
Spinning Jenny	10
Spools	39
Spot weave, see Bronson	
Spun glass	68
Square knot	91
Standard tie-up	99, 100
String heddles	35
S-twist yarns	58
Summer-and-winter weave, uses for	45
history	211, 212
materials	218
patterns	238, 239
pick-up	293, 295
structure	212, 216
tie-ups	219, 220, 221
treadling	219

	Page
Swift	39
Synthetic yarns	67, 68
Tabby	110, 114, 117
cotton	50
linen	65
pick-up	301, 304
wool	58
Technical terms	23
Template	327
Tension	109
Tensioner	39
Test for wool	55
Texture	6
Texture weaving	27
Thick-sett	6
Throw-shuttle	39
Throwing the shuttle	104, 105
Tied dying	50, 30
Tice, John	4
Tie-up, four-harness	99, 100
damask	251
double-faced twill	251
Bronson weave	241
summer-and-winter	220, 237
Totonicapan apron	314, 315
Tweed	110, 119
Tweeling	6
Twill, color effects in	119
corkscrew	117
Dornik	122
double	247
edges	119
eight-harness	119
jeans	115
pick-up	293, 295
variations	117
Two-harness weaves tabby	114
warp-faced rep	111, 112
weft-faced rep	113, 114
Two-skip pick-up	313
Two-warp weave	287–295
Tying-in	89, 90
knot	94
Upholstery weaving	46
Bronson weave	246
Warp	22
beam, sectional	32
calculations	52, 54
dressing	63

	Page
Warp (*cont'd*)	
setting	69, 132
tension	107
Warp-faced rep	111, 112
Warp-faced weaves	45
Warping, board	85
chained	65, 86
correcting faulty	87
sectional	83, 84, 85
Washing, linen	61
wool	66
Wastage	54
Watching the feet	104
Weaving as a business	19
as drawn in	141, 142, 143
definition	21, 23
instruction	26, 27
no-tabby, Italian	145, 210

	Page
Weaving as a business (*cont'd*)	
on opposites	144
on paper	130, 131, 133
rose-fashion	142, 144
technique	105
Weaver Rose	15, 16, 17
Weavers' knot	92, 94
Weft-faced rep	114
Weft-faced weaves	45
Weft knots	107
Weighting harnesses	107
Winding bobbins	105
Woof	22
Wool warp	54
Wool, worsted	54, 55, 56
Writing drafts	134, 135
Z-twist yarn	58